JULIAN SYMONS
A Bibliography

Julian Symons, publicity photograph used by Viking *for* Death's Darkest Face, *published October 16, 1990. Photo by Jerry Bauer.*

JULIAN SYMONS
A Bibliography

WITH COMMENTARIES & A PERSONAL MEMOIR
BY JULIAN SYMONS & A PREFACE BY H.R.F. KEATING

BY JOHN J. WALSDORF
WITH THE ASSISTANCE OF BONNIE J. ALLEN

OAK KNOLL PRESS, NEW CASTLE, DELAWARE
AND
ST PAUL'S BIBLIOGRAPHIES, WINCHESTER
1996

For
Quinn Joanna Walsdorf
and
John J. Walsdorf II

First published in 1996 by OAK KNOLL PRESS, 414 Delaware Street,
New Castle, DE 19720, USA
and ST PAUL'S BIBLIOGRAPHIES, West End House, 1 Step Terrace,
Winchester, UK
as part of the *Winchester Bibliographies of 20th Century Writers*

ISBN 1-884718-22-1 (USA)
ISBN 1-873040-31-8 (UK)

Library of Congress Cataloging-in-Publication Data

Walsdorf, John J.
    Julian Symons: a bibliography with commentaries & a personal
memoir by Julian Symons & a preface by H.R.F. Keating / by John J.
Walsdorf with the assistance of Bonnie J. Allen.
        p.   cm. — (Winchester bibliographies of 20th century writers)
    Includes bibliographical references and index.
    ISBN 1-884718-22-1 (alk. paper)
    1. Symons, Julian, 1912- — Bibliography.   I. Allen, Bonnie J.
II. Title.   III. Series.
Z8857.7.W35   1996
[PR6037.Y5]
016.828'91209–dc   96-12092
                                                                    CIP
A CIP catalogue record for this book is available from the British Library.

Printed in the United States of America

Contents

List of Illustrations

Preface

Julian Symons, the Writer
by H.R.F. Keating

A thread running through a great deal of Julian Symons's fiction is the image of the mask, whether in the form of a disguise or as a metaphor for the elegantly exposed hypocrisies of everyday life. It is, therefore, somewhat ironic that so much of his writing has been to a certain degree masked by the success and popularity of his crime fiction, considered by many to be a frivolous genre. His writings as a poet (described by a fellow poet as being "sharply rational"), as a biographer, as a charming and acutely self-analytical autobiographer, and especially as a literary and social critic deserve more public acknowledgment than they have received.

Symons's choice of biographical subjects ranges in time from Carlyle to Dashiell Hammett, enabling him to analyze with keen intelligence the spirit of other ages and to exercise his gift for perceptive literary criticism. His memoir of his elder brother, A.J.A. Symons, reveals autobiographical glimpses of a warm self inclined to be hidden under a carapace of coolness. That warmth is a quality that emerges in his slim autobiography, *Notes from Another Country*, and in the intriguing, half-disguised accounts of friends and acquaintances in *Portraits of the Missing*.

Symons's literary criticism, only some of which has been snatched from the pages of newspapers and culled from reviews to be collected in two volumes—*Critical Occasions* and *Critical Observations*—is marked always by rapier stabs of insight, an ever-modest reluctance to claim any sort of infallibility (would that all critics shared this trait), a meticulousness in reading and research, and touches of teasing humor. In a swift aside on a moralizing detective story that was said to be the favorite of Stanley Baldwin, Symons flicked out that this claim tended "to confirm one's gloomy views of politicians' literary taste." Yet it is his habit not to indulge in the smart crack at the expense of any author. In place of the firework insult, Symons puts considered, well-expressed dissent.

It is when he has turned to social criticism, often melded with the literary, that Symons's importance as a writer is perhaps most evident. *The Thirties: A Dream Revolved* has been called the definitive history of that time and merited a new edition fifteen years after its first appearance. *Makers of the New: The Revolution in Literature 1912-1939* is rather more than a simple assessment of the writers of the period; an implied criticism of society runs like counterpoint through it. It is sad that a study like this should have paled beside the body of the crime novels.

Makers of the New displays to the fullest Julian Symons's talent (perhaps too weak a word) for lucidity. Sentence after sentence is written with a clarity that is as engaging as it is illuminating, but truth is never sacrificed to elegance. Everywhere there are qualifying phrases: "it seems to me" is a characteristic, recurring refrain. Judgments are based on rocksolid fact that is supported by enormously wide reading. Nowhere is Symons bamboozled by any current cants, nor is the lucidity only a matter of style. The book places in context the slew of writers that emerged with new ideas just before World War I—Joyce, Eliot, Pound, the neglected Wyndham Lewis, the even more neglected Robert McAlmon—with well-organized illumination that is wonderfully exhilarating to experience.

Opposite the title page of *Portraits of the Missing* is a long list of nonfiction titles followed by the words, in modest lowercase, "and many crime novels." Perhaps Symons would like the whole corpus of his writings to be regarded in this light. But the voice of the people is loud, and aside from a few conventional experiments in his early days, his crime novels do carry forward the social and even philosophical ideas and insights he has expressed more formally elsewhere.

The first work of crime fiction to show clearly an individual voice was *The Thiryfirst of February*, which was also Symons's first crime novel, as distinct from fairly frivolous if unconventional detective stories. In this novel he daringly put no actual crime other than the supposed murder that the implacably vindictive detective inspector believes, quite falsely, has been committed by the disillusioned advertising executive hero, Andy Anderson. And there is no last minute, with-one-mighty-bound ending. No matter what writer one chooses as having first discovered the sub-genre of the crime novel, Julian Symons here laid trenchant claim to being the guiding star.

This claim is confirmed in Symons's next novel, *The Narrowing Circle*. Its setting is a pulp fiction publishing firm, as powerfully illuminating in regard to the society of the time as Andy Anderson's cynically seen advertising agency. The plot is driven by the rivalry, both professional and romantic (or perhaps merely sexual), between the murder victim and the prime suspect, David Nelson. Although the police detective accepts the evidence that frees the suspect, Nelson is ultimately hanged by society's subtle noose, the narrowing circle of human possibilities. Symons has taken us far from the happy simplicities of Agatha Christie.

And yet as a crime novelist, Julian Symons proves to be not only the excoriator but also the jester. He plainly delights in stories that are as complicated and comprehensively teasing as Dame Agatha's, as evidenced by *The Plot Against Roger Rider*, *The Man Who Killed Himself* (in spite of the somber ending), and *Something Like a Love Affair*. He brings to these works a gift for comedy that is so effective, the reader will involuntarily and invariably laugh out loud in invigorating response. In reviewing *The Man Who Lost His Wife*, I compared Symons to Waugh, and I stand by that comparison to this day.

Interspersed with these works are the darker, more satirical examinations of our humanity and the society we have constructed. In *The Color of Murder*, a book that earned him the Gold Dagger award from the Crime Writers Association (he was later awarded the Association's Diamond Dagger for lifetime achievement and made a Grand Master by the Mystery Writers of America), the protagonist, John Wilkins, is a man under immense pressure from society. Wilkins is no more than an assistant manager of the complaints department of an Oxford Street store, yet the madness that afflicts him and has made him withdraw into a fantasy life is handled with tremendous authorial ingenuity, and he represents all of us in a fate that few have completely escaped.

Equally ingenious is the development of Magnus Newton, the Q.C. who defends Wilkins on the charge of murder. Newton is a recurring figure if not a running hero in Symons's books (he appears in *The Progress of a Crime*, *The End of Solomon Grundy*, and *The Man Whose Dreams Came True*). He is the flip side of the thoroughly deranged Wilkins, though for all his barrister's cool, he, too, is from time to time in the grip of fantasy, risking the loss of a case by "occasionally ignoring an obvious line of questioning while pursing some fanciful idea of his own." Here we have under the mask of everyday intelligence the dangerous welter of the loosed imagination. Similar figures pepper the Symons tally of titles.

Masks, hypocrisies, and pretense provide a theme that is particularly evident in *The End of Solomon Grundy*, with its hero, again an advertising man, living in an ultra-typical middle-class outer suburbia estate known as The Dell. Alongside the excoriation such a setting rightly gives rise to, the playful Symons is at work. The story is linked to the children's chant "Solomon Grundy born on a Monday...", but the story told is scarcely innocent. Grundy commits murder, is found Not Guilty thanks to dubious evidence and, once freed, commits another murder.

It is the same sort of setting, the suburbia of the hypocrisies, that Julian Symons uses in "The Tigers of Subtopia," perhaps the most successful of the many short stories he has written, a remorseless study of collective pomposities masking an unpleasant sexual undertow. Most of his stories, however, are plot driven, which is the nature of crime fiction. The sheer cleverness of plot dazzles, revealing a slightly different aspect of Symons the jester.

The lighter side of Symons was perhaps the motivating force for his excursions into the classic crime territory of Victorian and Edwardian England, land of ironclad hypocrisies. These are scathingly enough shown up, flicks of the excoriator's whip, in *The Belting Inheritance, The Blackheath Poisonings, The Detling Murders,* and *Sweet Adelaide. Sweet Adelaide* also reflects his interest in real-life crimes, further demonstrated by *A Reasonable Doubt,* which suggests what actually happened in the famous Bartlett case ("Now she's acquitted she should tell us, in the interests of science, how she did it.").

In *The Players and the Game,* Symons plunges into a world yet more horrible than that of Solomon Grundy. The plot is based on the real-life *folie a deux* Moors murderers, the couple who tortured and killed children, burying them in remote parts of Yorkshire. Once again, two sides of Symons are at work. One presents a convincing recreation of what may have gone through the minds of the killers, remote from our humanity but still human. The other, concealing identities with tremendously adroit skill, presents a pure, properly clued puzzle that will defy almost every reader.

The playful Symons is in some ways more prominent in two books that pay explicit tribute to the founding fathers of the art he has practiced with such success himself. *A Three-Pipe Problem* ingeniously takes an actor famed for his TV impersonations of Sherlock Holmes and plunges him, half-convinced that he is Holmes and hiding behind that mask, into a delightfully comical adventure. Yet this, too, sends darts rather than shafts of light into the dark places of society. *The Name of Annabel Lee* pays tribute to Edgar Allan Poe, partly in its use of the name that beats rhythmically through one of Poe's poems and partly by immersing the professor-hero into a disorienting, deadly, Poe-like love affair. The story may be seen as a struggle between the logical Poe and the visionary Poe that Symons examined in his biography *The Tell-Tale Heart.* In the same way, two figures "as nearly as possible identical" have twined their way through Symons's fiction: the jester Symons and the excoriator Symons.

Introduction

"Why do you collect Julian Symons?" The question was put to me by a visitor viewing my more than 1000 books of all varieties—first editions, U.K. editions, book club editions, paperbacks, another 100 or so magazines with articles by and about Julian Symons, plus more than 100 letters between Julian and myself— what I call my Julian Symons collection. Before any thought of this book, before any thought of collecting Julian Symons, there was one book that caught my attention. The book, *Bland Beginning*, was in its own way responsible for my interest in collecting the works of this man, who was presented with the 1990 Cartier Diamond Dagger Award for his lifetime achievement in the world of crime fiction.

Bland Beginning was Julian's third mystery. Published some forty years ago, it is still very readable and enjoyable, and it is still in print. In my first letter to Julian, written to him at his London address at Albert Bridge Road on April 13, 1975, I mentioned that I had been asked by a friend if I had ever read "that story about Wise called *Bland Beginning*." I had not, so my friend gave me a paperback copy. I, in turn, loaned it to someone else and never got it back! My letter continued:

> Thus began my own quest for Symons. Each catalogue I got, each bookstore I went into, brought forth the inquiry for *Bland Beginning*....Then a week ago...I saw that Gollancz was to reprint this work. I sent off an order only to find three days later that a local secondhand bookstore had the first U.S. edition for sale. I bought it at once, and my quest can end.

Before the ink had dried on the main body of my letter, I added a postscript: "Lest you think I can now rest easy with my copy of *Bland Beginning* in hand, I will tell you that I have just finished reading *The Quest for Corvo*, which I enjoyed greatly. Now I will have to find your biography of your brother!"

In the intervening years, my quest for Symons has taken me to bookshops all over the U.S. and U.K., including shops specializing in mysteries as well as those featuring general titles; the wide range of Julian's interests and talents—poetry, social history, literary biography, and mystery—has involved looking in many corners and searching many subjects.

It has also involved the collector's greatest pleasure: meeting an author on his home ground or in one's own home. Over the years I have had brief encounters with Julian and his charming wife, Kathleen, in London restaurants, at their home in the south of England in the seaside town of Walmer, Kent, and best of all, for one delightful week in 1976, Kathleen and Julian were guests in my home in Portland, Oregon.

What did these encounters reveal of Julian Symons, the man? First and foremost, on reflection, one remembers the humor. I once reported to Julian that while reading his autobiographical stories and sketches in *Notes from Another Country*, my laughter disturbed my wife, who had been sound asleep at the time.

His humor, quintessentially British, is dry, sometimes self-effacing. I, touched perhaps with a slight bit of hero worship, once remarked on how wondrous I found it that Julian can average about a book a year, and he replied: "There really isn't that much to it. If you wanted to write a mystery novel, you could. It is mostly a matter of just doing it. Plodding away. The thing will come out."

In comments Julian prepared for me on *Notes from Another Country*, he says: "...the Julian Symons known to one person—friendly, helpful, easy-going—is not the truculent, awkward, and intellectually snobbish person known to another." I have never known or seen that latter side of Julian Symons, and I truly doubt that he can actually produce witnesses to swear to his being "truculent, awkward, and intellectually snobbish." In person, one finds him warm, intelligent, kind, and rather patient with collector-bibliographers who ask endless questions and are always on the lookout for just one more rarity.

But, besides his character traits, why have I chosen to spend 15 years of my collecting life and countless dollars in this seemingly endless pursuit? Part of the answer may be buried in the man I find in Julian, but another part is in his writing. In Dilys Winn's book *Murder Ink*, editor and critic Clifford A. Ridley comments that "there are but a handful of true stylists among us: Julian Symons, Peter Dickinson, Ken and Margaret Miller, Ngaio Marsh, P.D. James." The reviewers have been equally kind, heaping praise on Symons's work and peppering their reviews with comments such as "deft story telling," "literary wit," "intelligent whodunit," "first-class biography," "a superior book," "brilliance in prose and insight," "master of his craft," "a touch of style," "one of the most brilliant crime writers" "one of the most talented living writers of crime stories."

Perhaps the single greatest reason why Julian Symons has remained, from a collector's viewpoint, such an interesting subject to pursue is the variety of his work. Not only are there the traditional books to look for, such as the first English and American trade editions, but there are also the many off-prints, reprints, and finely printed editions that make the quest all the more enjoyable and challenging.

Finally, some reflections about working with Julian Symons. In *Certain Small Works*, Robert H. Taylor tells of the troubles Julian's brother A.J.A. had while trying to do a bibliography of Max Beerbohm. Beerbohm wrote to A.J.A. Symons:

> I mean don't make any reference of any sort to me in your table of thanks....For if mankind knew I had helped you, mankind would think me a vain and fussy person, in love with homage and advertisement....And really and truly I am not that sort of person—am I?

Later in the essay Taylor tells of Beerbohm's refusal to help A.J.A. find a copy of a pamphlet published under a pseudonym, remarking "...alas, I can't find a copy. Please therefore abstain from any mention of this work." Taylor appends the remark: "What a devilish thing to do to a bibliographer!"

For my part, working with Julian on this bibliography has been a labor of joy. Letters asking for help, clarification, or general information often brought replies by return post. Phone calls were taken (sometimes, I fear, at some inconvenience because of the eight-hour time difference between Portland, Oregon, and Walmer, Kent) with a pleasantness of voice and a warmth of friendship. No bibliographer could rightfully expect any more help than I was given, and for this help and kindness I extend my deepest thanks to both Julian and Kathleen.

A note on what you can expect to find in this book and what is missing: First and foremost, the information is, for the vast majority of the entries, taken from the book in hand. Failing that, known items that are still missing from my collection are marked "not seen." I have tried to cover all U.S. and U.K. editions of the fiction and nonfiction works by Julian Symons in both the hardback and paperback forms. (A very few Canadian editions have found their way onto the list, too.) I have tried to list all of the books that Julian edited, contributed to, or was anthologized in, again including U.S. and U.K. editions in hardback and paperback. And I have included a selected list of more than five hundred contributions to U.S. and U.K. magazines from 1937 to 1994.

I have not tried to cover foreign language publications, nor have I tried to include the hundreds of newspaper articles and letters written during the past fifty-seven years.

In many cases, the first listing of a major title is followed by a comment under the heading "Symons's Note." Julian wrote these notes especially for this book, and they will greatly enhance the reader's understanding of the thought behind the works.

A note on "Size" in Sections A through C. All sizes for hardbound books are taken from the title page. All paperback sizes are taken from the front cover, giving height before width in all cases.

The Appendix lists the most useful and most readily available biographical and critical writings relating to Julian Symons. I have not attempted to make this list exhaustive, nor have I tried to include the many author profiles and book reviews that been printed over the past fifty years.

My thanks go out to unnamed booksellers and librarians who have helped in my quest for information relating to various editions of Symons's work. Also, thanks to Kim Anderson, Christine Bunch, Bob Carlin, Marylou Colver, Kathy Cronin, Bill Gosling, Preston McMann, Bill Peterson, Chris Pym, Charles Seluzicki, Lona Stamper, Chris Tyzack, John Walsdorf II, and Paul Woods, all of whom helped with this book. Last, but most important, is my special thanks to my Portland-based editor, Suzy Blackaby. Without her help and encouragement, this book would never have been completed.

Julian Symons: Autobiographical Notes [1]

One should begin at the beginning, but in terms of personal memory what is that? I have always wondered at those who remember incidents of very early childhood in exact detail, things seen in the pram, conversations heard in the high chair. Do they remember or invent? Of my own life up to the age of six I recall almost nothing: being wrapped up and carried down to the cellar during a zeppelin raid, playing in a tent put up by my sister Edith under the dining room table, being taken by my parents to see the Armistice parade and wondering at the different uniforms. That is all, or almost all. And by then it was the end of 1918, and I was six-and-a-half years old.

Start again then, start with facts. I was the last child in a family of seven, two of whom died in infancy. Four boys and a girl survived, and I was separated by a gap of eight years from Maurice, the nearest to me in age. We lived in Lavender Hill, a busy road which was the dividing line between working class Battersea and middle class Clapham, and in 1919 we crossed the line, moving to a big house in Cedars Road, Clapham. For me this square gray Victorian edifice was not merely a big house, but The Big House. I was taken to see it several times before we moved in and, wandering about its twenty rooms, running around in the large back garden, counting the stairs on the four separate flights (I can still remember the number on each flight), I wondered at the size of it all. Our Lavender Hill house was cramped for the size of the family and had only a small yard. Cedars Road was another world.

The change came about during a brief period of family prosperity. I know nothing of my father's background, nor even his name except that it was not originally Morris Albert Symons. He must have been one of the mass of Jewish immigrants who came to Britain in the last years of the nineteenth century, but I do not know when, or whether he came from Russia or Germany. One of my brothers said that he came from Bialystok, now in Poland but then in Russia. On the other hand he was said to have attended Heidelberg University and I had two uncles, known to us as Uncle H and Uncle G, whose names were Herman and Gustave (my own second name is Gustave). So did my father have German and/or French antecedents? I have never been able to find out. Research at Somerset House proved fruitless, since to trace details of British naturalization one

[1] Reprinted from *Contemporary Authors Autobiography Series* published by Gale Research Co., Book Tower, Detroit, Michigan, 1986. Reproduced by kind permission of the author.

must know the original name. It is also possible that my father was an illegal immigrant who never applied for naturalization.

He was a shopkeeper who sold secondhand goods of all kinds, without much success until World War I. During this war he made money, enough to buy auction rooms in central London, where he blossomed as an excellent auctioneer, and to acquire the Big House. He also bought an Overland car and hired a chauffeur to drive it. And he fulfilled a lifelong ambition by becoming a racehorse owner. He bought four horses, which ran with very little success and were ruinously expensive. Within three or four years, the family prosperity faded under the stress of such extravagances, never to revive. The horses went, so did the car and its chauffeur, so did the auction rooms. We moved briefly to Brighton where my parents ran a small hotel, then back again to Clapham when the venture failed. Part of the Big House was let, some of the garden sold for building. My father still set out for central London every day, looking for his lost fortune, but he never found it. When he died in 1929 his estate was valued at four pounds.

In those difficult years we were saved from real hardship by my mother, Minnie Louise Symons. In manner soberly English as my father was exuberantly Jewish (yet with something exotic in her background, for although her family name was Bull, Frenchmen and Spaniards lurked somewhere in her ancestry), prudent as he was extravagant, she saved and scrimped and provided, and we survived.

Our family life was strange. My father was not a practicing Jew, none of his children ever attended a synagogue or (at least in my case) went to church. Yet we lived, more or less voluntarily, in a state of isolation. My father and mother had no family friends, no near or distant relatives came to see us or we them, and the children received no encouragement to bring friends home, at least in my father's lifetime. Some mysterious quarrels, perhaps to do with money lent and not repaid, alienated us from Uncle H and Uncle G. My father was a gregarious hail-fellow-well-met man outside the house, but within it he behaved with Victorian severity. One friend of my eldest brother, AJ, was ordered out of the house because he sat with one leg over a chair arm. I never heard a swear word used by my father, nor did any of us use one in his presence. I never heard anything approaching a dirty or even risqué joke. My eldest brother, AJ, who adopted those initials in his teens in place of his given name of Alphonse (another hint of French connection), put it clearly in an essay written near the end of his short life:

> Differences, dating back to days before my own, never reconciled and never explained, cut my father off even from correspondence with the majority of his blood relations; and my mother, an only

child, seemed to have no kith or kin even to quarrel with. Confined as I was within a narrow enclave with three brothers and a sister as fellow prisoners, the world seemed to have begun at the point when my consciousness entered it. Lacking cousins to provide easy cuts to acquaintance outside our own fireside, we developed without realizing it a cult of isolation, and, in place of friendships beyond ourselves, accepted and enjoyed an intense, introverted domesticity, made up of games which we had ourselves invented, and customs incomprehensible (by) those not in the know.

Since I have mentioned AJ, this may be the place to tell more of the family story. AJ became a dandy, a wit, book collector, connoisseur of wine and food. He founded the First Edition Club for collectors of fine editions and, in partnership with the great French gourmet André Simon, founded also the Wine and Food Society. He wrote a classic of modern biography, *The Quest for Corvo*, and projected what would have been without question the definitive biography of Oscar Wilde, but had completed only a few chapters of this last book when he died at the age of forty-one. Of my other brothers and sister, only one survives as I write. My mother outlived her much-loved husband by more than thirty years, dying at the age of ninety-two. She successfully defied the local Council's compulsory purchase order on the Big House, living there until the end of her days. It has gone now, however, turned into part of a council housing estate.

This was the world in which I grew up, a shy awkward child, "imprisoned in the tower of a stammer," as Auden puts it, a stammer that made it difficult for me to utter an unflawed sentence, a stammer that vanished only when I recited poems or took part in school plays. The confines of my world were narrower even than those of my brothers and sister, since I was so much younger than the rest that I took almost no part in the War Game, the Race Game, or most of the other games invented by AJ. In our Brighton days I was sent to a school for backward children. I remained bottom of the class at another fee-paying school, but flourished in the hurly-burly of the local state school.

It would have been wrong to call me unhappy. I invented games of my own and played them by myself. I had friends and went to their houses, although they never came back to mine. And as I moved into the middle teens and began to know girls, my stammer faded, although it has never completely disappeared. If the years from nought to six are an almost complete blank in my mind, those from twelve to eighteen are etched there with extraordinary vividness. I lived within two hundred yards of Clapham Common, about which music hall comics used to tell jokes, like the one about the young boy who started to walk across the Common one night and came out at the other side a married man with three children. The summer evenings of those years stretch endlessly in my remembrance, playing cricket, sitting in deck chairs on the Common talking to friends, strolling around the bandstand, picking up girls, taking them onto the grass. The novelist Pamela Hansford Johnson, a contemporary of mine in Clapham, wrote years later in an essay of walking over the Common with Dylan Thomas, holding hands and avoiding the twined bodies on the grass. She was not amused when I said that one of those she nearly stepped on could have been mine. In recent years I lived again for a while near the Common and found the experience affecting, troubling. I had written in a poem of the 1930s of "Feeling odd when I walk over it / If I let myself remember I can remember," but those ghosts that never return are just the things it is useless to remember.

Like AJ and Edith, I left school when I was fourteen (my other brothers won scholarships and so had two more years of education). My parents despaired of my getting a job because of the stammer, but I had taken a course in shorthand and typing, managed to get through an interview without a single hesitation, and was employed first as shorthand-typist, then as secretary, in a small engineering company. I stayed in the job for eleven years, until the war forcibly removed me from it.

As I look back on my childhood and adolescence I see that they were ordered largely by my relationship with my father, or the lack of it. Short, ruddy, fair, neatly bearded, thin in youth but potbellied in middle age (he was nearly fifty when I was born), my father seemed to his acquaintances an outgoing, generous man. He was such a man: but he was also short-tempered, given to shouting, quickly angry and just as quickly cheerful. As I remember it, I was always frightened of him. If he saw me playing solitary games with soldiers in my bedroom, he would tell me to get them cleared up and make the place tidy; when he found me reading an article on Marshal Lannes in the *Encyclopaedia Britannica*, he took the volume from me, turned the pages until he found the name of Linnaeus and, frantic with irritation, said: "Read *that*, sir, read something useful." No doubt he would have welcomed some retort, for he throve on rows, the passionate expression of feeling, easy anger followed by expansive gestures of reconciliation, but there was no retort from me. I am sure he meant no harm to me, but I think he wrought it.

He died when I was seventeen, and by that time I had largely escaped from the enclosure of the Big House: escaped in the summer to the Common, in the winter to the local Temperance Billiards Hall where I played snooker. I came home one evening in December 1929 and found him reading.

He had had two heart attacks in the past few months and was reluctant to go to bed. That night he had a third attack and died. Following the coffin to Wandsworth Cemetery, I was not conscious of deep sorrow nor of any emotion except ignoble relief and a hope that life might be easier now.

The important thing about a writer is his books, the important thing about a writer's life the way in which it has affected his work. My life has been no more eventful than most, perhaps less, and to describe its course in detail would be pointless as well as dull. But what happens to us in childhood and youth leaves a permanent imprint on the psyche: my father's personality, our family isolation, my stammer, these played important parts in making the kind of person I became. (There is a fuller account of those years in a collection of autobiographical stories, *Notes from Another Country*.)

Along with my emotional development, or lack of it, went a burgeoning, an opening out, of the intellect. Like AJ, I educated myself, and the process was extraordinarily exciting. People sometimes ask whether I regret being cut off from schooling so early and not going to university. The answer must be *yes*, at least in the sense that through a university education I would have learned techniques of research invaluable to the biographer and historian I became, instead of having to work a method out for myself. Yet there are rewards in ignorance. To encounter the glories of English literature head on, without preparation, without being told which books one should admire and the proper reasons for admiring them, all that can be marvelous for an enquiring mind.

From the age of sixteen or seventeen I lived for years in a state of permanent intellectual intoxication. One blessing of my tedious job was that it gave me plenty of time for reading, even in office hours. I read voraciously, erratically, making exciting discoveries every month. I read AJ's collection of nineties writers so thoroughly that I could have passed an examination on the work of Ernest Dowson, Lionel Johnson, and even such almost unknown figures as John Barlas and Eugene Lee-Hamilton. I romped and roamed through English poetry, with a tendency to reject what was popular and easy and concentrate instead on the awkward, crabbed, difficult. Palgrave's *Golden Treasury* passed me by, I gave no more than cursory attention to the Lake Poets, and Shelley and Keats, but by the time I was twenty-one I knew a great deal about Pope, Dryden, "Hudibras" by Samuel Butler, the Elizabethans and Jacobeans. I read all the minor Elizabethan dramatists in the Mermaid Library editions, from Webster and Tourneur to Marston and Heywood. I read much more verse than prose and ignored altogether the great English nineteenth-century novelists, from Jane Austen to Trollope, reading instead Tolstoy, Turgenev, and, in particular, Dostoevsky. I made some attempts on philosophy but found Plato uncongenial and gave him up, could not understand Kant, but settled down with Schopenhauer and Nietzsche. I became much absorbed, and am still, with problems of free will and determinism.

This curious course of reading was no doubt prompted in part, if I am to be ruthless with my youthful self, by a sort of culture snobbery. Some of my friends among the Clapham Common intelligentsia had been to grammar schools, were well acquainted with the *Golden Treasury*, had read the romantic poets, but were bowled over by quotations from *Hudibras* or *The Duchess of Malfi*. But with allowance made for such snobbery, most of my reading did reflect a preference for the harsh over the bland, for satire and realism over romance. As the years passed, some of these gaps in my reading were remedied. I discovered Dickens with astonishment and even wrote a short book about him; became immersed in Trollope during World War II, in part no doubt because the world he described was so unlike the one I saw around me; tried but rejected Thackeray. In general, though, my reading was preparation—not, of course, a conscious preparation—for immersion in modern literature, especially modern poetry, and even more particularly into the work of Wyndham Lewis.

I first heard of Lewis when, at the age of eighteen, I bought in Charing Cross Road a copy of his book-magazine *The Enemy* and read in it his attack on Gertrude Stein and the *transition* editors, "The Diabolical Principle," understanding little of the argument but impressed by the writer's fine rhetorical scorn. I went on to read Lewis's fiction, *Tarr* and *The Apes of God*, and the two great socio-philosophical books he had recently published, *The Art of Being Ruled* and *Time and Western Man*. Lewis's ideas about the nature of society made a deep impression on me, in particular his views about the cult of youth and the widening intellectual and artistic influence of homosexuality. Provocative aphorisms marked every few pages of his critical writing, like his remark that "to attach, as the humanitarian does, a mystical value to *life* itself, for its own sake, is as much a treachery to spiritual truth as it is a gesture of 'humanity,'" and his suggestion that men and women only *think* they wish they were free, while in fact "they depend for their stimulus on people, not things." Lewis's writing, as distinct from his paintings and drawings, has been misleadingly attacked in some places, ignored in many others. For me he remains the most original thinker about art and society and the most remarkable English stylist of the twentieth century.

When I first met and talked to Lewis, it was with trepidation. He was notoriously suspicious, even paranoid, said to keep a spy-hole in his studio through which visitors could be examined. I found that, at least so far as a young admirer was concerned, Lewis much more nearly resembled the view of him taken by his friend T.S. Eliot: "A mild, detached man, who could never be the dupe of an idea, but who would be rather inefficient in private affairs, the prey of pickpockets, and the recipient of many a leaden half-crown." In the late thirties I published a special number of my little magazine, *Twentieth Century Verse*, in his honour. It was a pleasure to do so at a time when he was most fiercely under attack. At this time he produced three ink drawings of me and, a few years later, a portrait in oils. Lewis was poor at the time (as indeed he was through most of his life) but knew me to be poorer. I paid him £5 for the three drawings and £10 for the oil, so that in effect he gave me these pictures.

I have mentioned *Twentieth Century Verse* and should say something about the magazine, which I founded and ran single-handedly from 1937 until the war. I had been writing poems since my late teens, but it was difficult, not only for me but for other young poets, to publish them. Nowadays magazines proliferate in Britain and America: in the thirties there was only one intellectually and poetically respectable verse magazine in Britain, Geoffrey Grigson's *New Verse*. The reason for the existence of *New Verse*, Grigson said later, was W. H. Auden's poetry. My admiration for Auden was and remains great, but there were good poets outside the Auden circle, and *Twentieth Century Verse* gave a platform to them. They included Dylan Thomas, Roy Fuller who later became Oxford Professor of Poetry, George Woodcock who left England for Canada in 1949 and has been in recent years a guru for a generation of Canadian writers, and Gavin Ewart. There were other names, known at the time, that have disappeared from the record books. And—perhaps the magazine's most interesting achievement—I did something to bridge the gulf that yawned at the time between American and British poetry by printing the first work of Wallace Stevens to appear in Britain and running a special American number that included poems by Delmore Schwartz, Yvor Winters, John Berryman, Allen Tate, John Peale Bishop, Conrad Aiken. Mine was a very little "little magazine," most issues no more than thirty-two pages, but to have run it for three years with no more backing than that provided by my weekly wage packet was something that, looking back, I'm pleased about. When I gave up it was not through lack of money but because I thought the kind of poetry I admired would not survive in wartime.

And what of my own poems? They are embalmed in two books, *Confusions about X* (1938) and *The Second Man* (1943), plus a couple of privately printed booklets of the last decade. I cannot pretend—I wish I could believe otherwise—that I was more than a minor poet of the thirties and forties. A couple of poems, "Pub" and "Hart Crane," have survived into recent anthologies, but the impulse that moved me to write poetry has not survived. It is one of the sorrows of my last decade that when I sit down to write a poem the result is a fragment, a few unsatisfactory lines.

One writes about things separately, but they go on together. My boring but undemanding job was a kind of backcloth against which what I thought of as my "real" life went on, running *Twentieth Century Verse*, engaging in occasional desultory love affairs, becoming involved in left-wing politics. A reviewer of my collection of essays, *Critical Observations*, writing in 1982 in *The Times Literary Supplement*, said: "What Symons himself did most of in the thirties. . . was to run his little magazine and run about with a bunch of anarcholeftists such as George Woodcock, Roy Fuller and Ruthven Todd. These were chaps, like Symons himself, who weren't in any of the Oxford and Cambridge sets, who were marginals of the literary world. . . . In that world of factions and the house organs of factions it didn't count, say, simply to sing the 'Internationale'—even to sing it on a tube-train, as Symons reports that he and Woodcock once did. It mattered more in whose name you sang it." The remarks are fair enough comment on my adherence to theoretical Trotskyism for several years from 1938 onwards. I was a member of the Fourth International for only a few months, but my view of Trotskyist theory was "right," the belief that it made sense of the behavior of the most powerful nations, lasted much longer. But belief in any kind of Marxism involves an optimism about the nature of human beings that, for me, did not survive the revelations of the concentration camps. It is not the nuclear bomb that seems to me the crucial reality of the twentieth century, but the concentration camps. As what happened in them was understood, they provided for rulers in many countries a kind of textbook for the unacknowledged exercise of power, so that later developments of organised torture and deprivation, tacitly or openly endorsed by "civilised" governments, whether they called themselves authoritarian or democratic, came as no surprise. After Belsen, Dachau, Auschwitz, it was no longer possible to be optimistic about the fate of humanity.

This memoir is designed to stress what seems to me important in my life at the expense of the inessential. In that light my war service seems to call for no more than a paragraph. (Again, anybody curious to know more is referred to *Notes from Another Country*.) It will come as no surprise after what I have said about my politics at this time that I refused conscription on the ground that this was a capitalist war, had my plea rejected by a tribunal, and eventually accepted induction into the armed forces. I spent nearly two years in the army, nine months of them in hospital.

This was not the result of a war wound, for I never saw action. A benevolent neurofibroma in my left arm was taken out by an army surgeon, the job botched so that the radial nerve was severed, my wrist fixed by a now-outdated operation called a tendon transplant. There was a brouhaha about the botched operation, and in January 1944 I was returned to civilian life.

So much for army service, which in an emotional sense affected me very little. Still, in that emotional sense, the most important event of my life took place in October 1941, when I married Kathleen Clark, whom I had first met two years earlier at Roy Fuller's flat. We have been together for more than forty years, and I cannot imagine what my life would have been without her. In temperament she is outgoing, warm, impulsive, emotionally generous, and I have often wondered why she put up with somebody who in a basic sense is none of those things. As Roy Fuller wrote in dedicating a novel to her:

> Fiction must almost be in vain
> For whom the real can entertain

That capacity to be entertained by the colour and comedy of life's everyday roundabout was instantly attractive to one not always observant of such things. My deeper feelings, then and now, are expressed in a poem I wrote to her during the war, from which I quote some verses:

> I think of these last two years
> Stamped permanently upon our wavering lives.
> I think of you. The very face of love
> Speaks, and tells me what love gives:
> This power to see and move
> Outside ourselves, these trees and this green view:
> As I, alone and idle here, see you,
>
> So easily laughing and so quickly happy
> Or quickly sad, for whom the natural
> Events of life are tidal like the sea:
> For whom the world is all
> Simple, made up exclusively of people:
> Now, although each church steeple
>
> Reveals the power of idols, every action
> Involves its opposite and must disclose

A painful birth of bureaucratic faction,
Today when every rose
Shows up its worm, I more than ever preserve
This radical and single love we serve.

I should not find it easy to say more and, since she is about some things more reticent than I, she would not wish me to do so.

When I came out of the army it proved less easy than I had expected to find a job, but eventually I got one as copywriter in an advertising agency. Kathleen was working at the BBC. I stayed in the job for nearly four years, liking advertising people but disliking the work. I left it and became a free-lance writer, with the help of George Orwell.

I should say a little about my relationship with Orwell and my friendships with him and others. The T.L.S. reviewer already mentioned comments on this: "Like most of the authors he chooses to celebrate, the friends he writes about in these essays are not the mightiest of literary names. But whoever you are, as Symons's friend you have bestowed on you an extraordinarily endearing love...as one-time editor of *Twentieth Century Verse* Symons still grants the pull of the old obligations and associations." I tend to shy away from such large words, but it is true that my attachments are mostly immediate and firm and that many have lasted a long time. The list of old poetic friends, some known and others forgotten, includes Roy Fuller and Robert Conquest, George Woodcock, Ruthven Todd, H.B. Mallalieu, but there are more recent ones like Bill Pritchard of Amherst College, the American crime writer Ross Macdonald, the Danish critic Harald Mogensen and his wife Kirsten, the Swedish writers Per Wahlöö and Maj Sjöwall. I did not see Macdonald often, yet regarded him—and the feeling was reciprocated—as a close friend. I met Wahlöö and Sjöwall only twice, but the rapport between us was instant. I know myself to be insensitive in some ways, and indeed such insensitiveness may be a necessary armour for a writer, but I hope such failure of feeling does not extend to friendship.

And so to Orwell. We met first in 1943 and remained friends until his death in 1950. What did I like about him? We were linked by being both in the terminology of the time premature anti-Stalinists, deprecating the myth of the virtuous Soviet Union long before it was fashionable to do so, but it was Orwell's general heterodoxy that drew me to him, as it drew me to Wyndham Lewis. Their politics were very different, but both were sceptical about many things that people take for granted, both were freewheeling radicals. I regard myself as a freewheeling radical too—that is, as somebody on the Left but having no party adherence—although the result of this is that sometimes friends find me voicing what they think of as distinctly right-wing opinions.

Why did Orwell like me? Primarily, I think, because of my lack of curiosity about the background and habits of other people (a trait that has sometimes maddened Kathleen). I am not sure that I knew Orwell's name was really Eric Blair, but if I had known, it would not have interested me much. Orwell detested people asking questions about his background, and I am sure my incuriosity was a mark of virtue in his eyes. I should add perhaps that Orwell had no influence on me of the kind that Lewis had. A lunchtime session with him meant a few drinks in the pub with George and a gossip about current politics, nothing more. If in the late forties anybody had told me that TV and radio interviewers and writers of theses would be asking what Orwell had said to me about America and Zionism and the Labour Party in Britain, I should have laughed at them. So, I daresay, would he.

Orwell wrote a weekly column called "Life, People—and Books" in the *Manchester Evening News*, evening paper of the *Manchester Guardian*. With the success of *Animal Farm* he determined to give it up, and he persuaded them to give me a trial. His advocacy must have been forceful because they had never heard of me and were not at all keen to employ me. The engagement went from month to month, and I could have been sacked at any time. The money was not really enough to live on, but I immediately said to Kathleen that I would like to give up my advertising job, and she replied casually that if I felt like that, no doubt I should. A few months later she became pregnant and left her work at the BBC. In 1948 our daughter, Sarah, was born, in 1951 our son, Marcus. By then I was fully and finally a free-lance writer.

Astonishing, or at least surprising, to have got so far without mentioning the work for which I am best known, the writing of crime stories. I became a crime writer as it seems by chance, although those who believe as I do that the general course of our lives is determined by the middle teens will feel that some such apparent "chance" was inevitable.

I have already mentioned Ruthven Todd. In the late thirties he and I lived opposite each other in a Pimlico square. Ruthven had acted as some kind of functionary at the Surrealist Exhibition held in London in 1936, and we planned a murder mystery which should be set at a similar exhibition. Some of our friends would be introduced, and either killed off or appear as particularly nasty suspects. Ruthven overflowed with bizarrely ingenious ideas but did no actual writing, and in the end I wrote the book myself. I regarded it as a joke, no more, and did not send it to a publisher.

This typescript, done on green paper turned yellow at the edges, was found by Kathleen six years later. I had just emerged from the army and was looking for the job I eventually found in advertising. She read it and said it was quite funny in parts. Perhaps I might send it to a publisher, perhaps it might make a little badly needed money.

The Immaterial Murder Case was a very dotty crime story, with discussions of an art movement called Immaterialism (you painted only what was not there), some poems meant to parody current fashions, and a critic found murdered inside a hinged egg-like sculpture. The hero drifts through the book looking for a new kind of electric razor. In terms of plot the book is ludicrously bad—at one point I included a four-page chart showing the characters' movements, as much for my benefit as for that of readers. I sent the typescript to Victor Gollancz, probably the only English publisher who would have been ready to consider such a zany detective story. He accepted it, and it was published in October 1945, although I had to wait a dozen years for American publication. I had made Ruthven the murderer, and he was much upset by the caricature of him when he read the published book. Partly because of this, partly because it seems to me so bad, I have not allowed the book to be reprinted in the past thirty years.

Since then I have published twenty-three crime stories, along with some twenty biographies, social, literary, and military histories, and collections of essays. During this whole period I have also written reviews, for ten years as a columnist in the job Orwell got me, then as reviewer for the *Sunday Times*, at first of crime stories and later of all kinds of books, and also as reviewer for many papers in Britain and America. This is what my life has been about—it seems to me that, for any writer, his life must in any serious sense have been "about" his work, rather than his relationships with other human beings. Now that I have reached my seventies it seems natural to cast back and ask what I think of it, what it has been worth. I am conscious—how could I not be?—that this very thought of weighing life in the belief that it is "about" anything at all rather than just to be lived, says something about my character.

My first three crime stories, including the unfortunate *Immaterial*, I look back on without pleasure. They were set in one orthodox pattern of the British crime story at that time, consciously light, bright, and determinedly "civilized." The fourth, *The Thirty-First of February* (1950), is another matter. I must at this time have had some nascent ideas about doing all the things in the form of the crime story that one can do in a "straight" novel, in the way of character development and saying something about the form and shape of society. The book is set in an advertising agency and based on my own experience of advertising. There is a puzzle to be solved—did copywriter Anderson kill his wife or did she just fall down the cellar stairs?—but this goes along with a vision of the nightmare world Anderson inhabits and the mechanical nature of his reactions to the events that eventually overwhelm him. I had been rereading Dostoevsky, and my police inspector carries echoes of the Grand Inquisitor. The book was admired rather more than it was liked, and although it sold better than any of my earlier stories, did not move me anywhere near the best-seller class, from which I have always been precluded, in part because most crime readers have a preference for blandness, so that characters meant to be realistic seem to them just dislikeable. I was naturally pleased when a few years ago the super crime buff Dilys Winn picked out the book as one of the five best crimes stories ever written, less happy that it was dismissed by the equally expert buffs Messrs, Jacques Barzun and Wendell Hertig Taylor as a book "swamped in personal problems and unpleasant physical characteristics."

Really, however, I am little moved by the opinions of critics or the views of editors in publishing houses. I have been lucky in finding editors in England and America who have become personal friends, George Hardinge of Collins and then Macmillan in one country, Joan Kahn of Harper and St. Martin's Press in the other, but although I listened to their views with respect I am never finally swayed by them. It is not that I think I know better: rather that when a book of mine is finished, I may be aware that it is not my best work, may even be disappointed in it, but I know also that no changes I can make will substantially improve it. George always, Joan eventually, respected this feeling, even though they may not have shared it.

The Thirty-First of February showed me the way I wanted to go in writing crime stories. Since its publication, the best of my books in this field have all been based on the view that a crime story can have the depth and subtlety of characterization, the moral and social point, of what is generally called a "straight" novel. Of course crime stories of this kind are a small minority of the vast total output, but they exist, and both as practitioner and critic I have worked over the past thirty years to see this acknowledged and to ask that such crime stories should receive serious criticism. That is the burden of my history of the genre, *Bloody Murder* (1972). In the U.S. the book was called *Mortal Consequences*, but the revised and up-dated edition published in 1985 has the title *Bloody Murder* in both countries. This was a campaign against the odds, since many critics and readers regarded the crime story as a literary form stamped "For Entertainment Only," but the battle has been won in the sense that Hammett and Chandler, Ross Macdonald, Highsmith, le Carré, and Sjöwall-Wahlöö, along with some other writers are now treated as serious novelists. It would be wrong to pretend that the success is, or will be, total. I was giving some lectures on the art of biography in Canada a few years ago when an amiable academic said: "Why do they take anything you say seriously? After all, you're a crime writer." He meant no offense; his bafflement was genuine, and his assumption that crime writers are by definition an inferior breed is still widely shared.

"If you want to show the violence that lives behind the bland faces most of us present to the world, what better vehicle can you have than the crime novel?" That question rhetorically asked in the preface to an omnibus edition of mine published in 1966 still represents my view. I would accept what George Woodcock has said about my crime stories in general, that they deal with a world "where the murderer and the victim seem to attract each other...where the hunted man may be objectively innocent but subjectively culpable, and where the forces of law are unpredictable as the defenders of true order. In the end it is not for the way he solves the details of crimes that Symons's novels are interesting, but rather for the way he finds their causes in the minds of men and the shapes of societies." I should accept also some of the limitations that Woodcock and others have pointed out. My strengths as a novelist are in writing dialogue, the creation and analysis of character, the depiction of middle-class or slightly seedy society; my limitations a failure in describing action (the effects of violence concern me, not the violence itself), lack of interest in creating a tight and watertight plot, a tendency to remain detached from the characters so that some readers find it hard to become involved in the story. This last is perhaps not a deficiency so much as the expression of a temperament always looking for human ironies.

The crime stories I regard as my best work in this field are not always the ones most liked by readers. *The Thirty-First of February* would certainly be one of them. Two more are *The Colour of Murder* (1957) and *The Progress of a Crime* (1960), which won the British Crime Writers Association and the Mystery Writers of America awards respectively, as the best books of their year. Three others that seem to me good are *The End of Solomon Grundy* (1964), *The Man Who Killed Himself* (1967), and *The Man Whose Dreams Came True* (1968). It is always difficult to judge one's recent work, but I should be inclined to put with them *The Criminal Comedy of the Contented Couple* (1985). In several books I have tried to extend the crime story's boundaries in one way or another, sometimes in relation to subject, sometimes by offering ambiguous or deliberately anticlimactic denouements. In the late seventies, I set out to write a crime story with a period setting, chiefly to see if I could do it. I was pleased with *The Blackheath Poisonings* (1978) without thinking, as some critics seemed to do, that it was my best work. The two Victorian stories that succeeded it seemed to me less good, and having proved my ability to write such a story—at least to my own satisfaction—I have returned to modern reality. The strategies for doing so aren't always easy. As Ross Macdonald once said, we write on the backs of torn-off calendar sheets, so that "a writer in his fifties will not recapture the blaze of youth, or the steadier passion that comes like a second and saner youth of his forties." The observation is more poignantly true in one's sixties and seventies. Feelings have dulled, sympathies have changed, but still one hopes that there are new tricks to be turned, and some original observations to be made in the form of the crime story, about "the minds of men and the shapes of societies."

Somebody said recently that I am perhaps the most honoured of modern crime writers. It rarely feels like that, but when the various awards are added up, perhaps it is true. I don't propose to list them here, but I have valued particularly the Presidency of the Detection Club in which I succeeded Agatha Christie, and the Grand Master Award from the Mystery Writers of America in 1982.

But I have not answered directly my own question: was the time and energy spent in writing crime stories worthwhile from any point of view other than that of earning a living? In principle I have no doubt that it was. The crime story is a wonderfully flexible literary form. In the hands of a good writer it can be used for anything from Kafkan ambiguity to raw slices of Zolaesque realism. A criminal theme is the sturdiest of backbones for a plot, and there is nothing intrinsically sensational or trivial about it— the sensationalism and triviality come, if they do, in the treatment.

There is nothing demeaning, then, in the *form* of the crime story, but what about my own books? Were they worth doing, can they stand the test of rereading when the answers to the problems set in the stories are known? In relation to my best half-dozen novels, yes, I think and hope so. When I think of some of the others the answer would have to be a reluctant or penitent no. But the best of the books seem to me not only ingenious crime stories but also good novels, and if I am right, that is their justification. There have been times during the writing of them when, at the end of a day's work I have put down my pen, reread what I have written and found it good, or at least known it was the best I could do. That feeling, far from self-justification or self-aggrandisement, is the purest pleasure experienced by a writer.

My crime stories, along with some other books related to the genre like the large factual *Crime and Detection*, a history of real life crime from the early nineteenth century up to the year of its publication, 1966, have been used to finance the writing of other books. Some of these have been biographies, of characters as diverse as my brother AJ, Dickens, Carlyle, Poe, Dashiell Hammett, and the remarkable swindler Horatio Bottomley; some, like a history of Britain's 1926 General Strike, are social history; two books about Victorian military campaigns are military history; *The Thirties*, a short personal book about British literature and society during that decade, might be called literary criticism flavoured with autobiography; *Notes from Another Country*, autobiography shaped into the form of stories. Almost all of these books were widely and warmly reviewed. None of them could I have afforded to write, if I had not been financially bolstered by the crime stories.

As I have said, it was in relation to the research and writing of some of these books that I felt my lack of education. If I had been to a university I should have known where and how to look for information about my subjects, would have organized it more quickly and methodically, would not have wasted time in looking up secondary authorities when primary ones remained unexamined. Yet I don't seriously regret any of this, for the process of scholarly discovery, and of learning how to organize and shape a work of nonfiction, has been as splendidly enjoyable and revelatory in its very different way as my ignorant early burrowing into English literature.

The belief that the writing of biography is an art as well as a craft, and that any biographer approaches his subject from a personal point of view whether he admits it or not, has grown in me over the years. No biography can ever be objectively true: that is what makes it more than, and different from, a record of social or historical fact. Nor is any biography ever complete. No matter how many its page, something will have been omitted, and for those omissions the biographer is responsible. Every biography involves acts of choice and is thus, at least potentially, a work of art. It also involves responsibilities, much greater than those understood by biographers in the past. They assumed that there was some final "truth" to be told, and that this truth might justify ignoring embarrassing or discreditable passages in their subject's life. For us no such truth exists, and along with that awareness goes the obligation neither to invent facts nor to delete them, the duty neither to twist nor embroider reality.

That, very briefly, is the credo to which I have tried to adhere in treating my various subjects. It is right to say *my* subjects, for Carlyle, Bottomley, and Poe were subjects pressed by me on publishers never more than tepidly agreeable. In the case of the General Strike the publisher was positively discouraging, saying that he could not imagine who would want to read such a book, although if I really wanted to write it he would be prepared to offer a small advance. My short studies of Dickens, Conan Doyle, and

Hammett, were commissioned, but I would not have undertaken them unless I had felt some personal involvement with the subjects.

My first biography, that of my brother AJ, is a special case, but the later choice of particular subjects reflects my changing concerns over the years. In 1950 I had an overwhelming desire to write about Carlyle, although my knowledge of his works was then far from complete, and later I had similar feelings about Bottomley and Poe. What joined these three and made them interesting to me, what driving impulse made me in the early sixties spend weeks in the libraries of the War Office and the Royal United Services Institution buried in Blue Books, White Papers, and the letters and memoirs of Victorian Generals, research which I could not now contemplate without a shudder? The answer, as near as I can see one, is my interest in the blending of failure and success, and my feeling for what are from my point of view good men gone wrong, radicals who have lost or denied their early beliefs. Such was Carlyle, a radical of deepest dye in his own phrase, who turned to belief in savagely autocratic rule; such, I thought when I began research into his life, was Bottomley, although he proved to have been only an engaging scoundrel using radical phrases; such were the trade union leaders who half-heartedly backed the General Strike. The Victorian military campaigns I wrote about were both failures, their leaders the acclaimed commanders of their time. Poe's life is a story of immense ambition, great talent, and in practical terms, almost total failure. Perhaps this choice of subjects reflects my own gradual disillusionment with radical causes (although not beliefs), the changed view of what people are like and the way they behave that has already been suggested in my remarks about the concentration camps.

All of these books were researched in a way that brought no critical reproach, all written with the care for the discovery of a proper vantage point that seems to me vitally important for the biographer who is trying to create a work of art which shall also be a work of truth. Let me repeat a few sentences from a lecture I gave two or three years back, "The Art of Biography":

The biographer is always personally involved in what he writes. As to the degree of his involvement, that will be a matter of an individual writer and a particular subject. A biography is a journey of discovery, and in making it you learn things about yourself as well as about your subject.

If I seem to have abandoned life for books, leaving myself stranded around the year 1951, that reflects reasonably enough the hours spent in my study. Or studies, for we have been decidedly peripatetic over the years, shuttling between pleasant houses in more or less rural Kent, and equally pleasant houses in unfashionable south London. These changes have reflected Kathleen's love of the country and my own feeling for urban life. After a time, one or other of us has said a decisive no to city or country life, and we have moved, a process we have both found exhilarating, even exciting. We have been settled for five years, as I write, at Walmer near to Dover, on the unfashionable (again) southeast coast of England. The house—really two houses joined together, with a hole or small courtyard in the middle—is perhaps the most delightful we have had, we enjoy looking at and in summer entering the sea, we are neither in city nor country. Are we settled for good? Neither of us likes to think so.

In 1975 we spent a year at Amherst College where, thanks to Bill Pritchard's advocacy, I was visiting writer. Since I had never taught (and some would add never learned), the challenge was irresistible, the experience tremendously enjoyable. The openness of America and Americans, the astonishing beauty and variety of the country (often strangely unremarked by its natives), delighted me. That innocence which Henry James and others contrasted with the sophistication of Europe seemed to me still existent, even in the academic and literary circles where I mostly moved—although I'm aware that remarks of this kind may be found both superficial and condescending. Nothing offensive, though, in saying that if we had been a few years younger we might have made a home in America, on the East rather than the West Coast. That year is also tragically marked on Kathleen's life and mine. While we were in Amherst, Sarah became ill. She spent several weeks with us in America after her recovery, but died soon after our return to England. Time, it is said, heals grief, but in the deepest sense we have both found that to be untrue. Our personal consolations have been Mark and Christine, our son and daughter-in-law, and grandchildren Daniel and Sarah. Orwell once wrote to me that one of the joys of having children is that in them you live again your own childhood, and that has been especially true for me in relation to Mark, whether I was crawling over the floor re-creating H.G. Wells's *Little Wars* with toy soldiers, or watching him play the handsome cricketing strokes that I made only in imagination. Can the same apply to grandchildren? Four-year-old Dan now has a castle and some soldiers...

In the past decade I have been surprised and amused to find my reputation changing. That candid question asked by the Canadian academic is now rarely voiced. On the contrary, academics tend to be friendly to and even admiring of somebody who has made a living in the marketplace. A number of them, especially in America, are prepared to accept that crime stories, some crime stories, are worth serious literary consideration and that a history of the genre is useful and even valuable. Many find no contradiction between the writing of such books and the production of biographies and literary criticism. All that is agreeable, although I'm well aware that the benevolent critical zephyrs blowing just now may turn to cold north winds next winter.

Some of this, now that I read it over, has an elegiac tone. That may be inevitable as one looks back over what sometimes seems a very long life but really is not intended. Ideas for books are buzzing in my head, and although some will be discarded as impracticable, others will appear between covers if I am given the luck of continuing health and energy. I even hope that I may write poetry again some day. I dislike and disapprove much that I see around me. Many of the personal freedoms we struggled for in my youth have been gained, but not with the results we hoped for and, perhaps naively, expected. Freedom in the written and spoken word, freedom in sexual activity through the pill, freedom from the restrictions of family and religion, all have been trivially or degradingly misused. In the West we live in a society of frantically greedy consumers, eager for the second car and the second home, looking always for the labour-saving devices that give more time to eat junk food, read junk literature, watch junk TV. This is the world of "freedom," and the world of dictatorships is much worse. How can one look on them cheerfully?

Yet, against all the odds, it remains exciting to be alive. Some of the lines at the end of *Notes from Another Country*, published when I was sixty, can be repeated without alteration thirteen years later:

> My prime emotion, if I knew that I was to die tomorrow, would be that "violent resentment" felt by George Orwell when shot through the throat in Spain, "at having to leave this world which, when all is said and done, suits me so well." It suits me, too, I should be crying, there is a great deal I still wish to experience and understand, postpone that coronary or street accident for another few years if you please. For one thing, there is still work to be done on my always cluttered writing desk, notes to be made, a book to organize and then to write...

Yes, it remains a pleasure, personal, profound, unquantifiable, to feel that there is still work to be done.

"How Lucky You Are..."

by
Kathleen Symons[1]

"How lucky you are to have Julian working at home", my friends have said to me over the years. Well—yes—I suppose so—but as I have no experience of any other way of life, it's difficult to know how lucky.

For instance, some years ago we had a marvelous cleaning lady, who one day said she wouldn't use the Hoover upstairs. "Oh, why not?" I asked. She answered in a quiet voice, "He's thinking." "How can you tell?" I asked—not the most complimentary way of putting it, I thought afterwards. "Well. He's not typing, is he, so he must be thinking, and when he's thinking he doesn't like any noise."

When the Thinker came down to lunch I asked whether he'd had a good morning. "Marvelous," he answered. "You know how late we were last night—well, I started to read a book for review and dropped right off. Just woke up as a matter of fact. Feel like a walk this afternoon?"

Mind you, that morning sleep is a rarity. On most days he goes up to his study immediately after breakfast, and I *know* he's working, because of the click-click of the typewriter (old-fashioned manual machine, says he can't work on any other). And then—silence. And I know he's coming down to lunch. I don't need to look at the clock, the time will be exactly one o'clock. Nothing wrong with being so punctual, of course, except—except that there are times when I'm busy with one thing or another and don't actually want to break off just then for lunch. But a measured tread is coming down the stairs....

In the afternoon he's less concerned about time-keeping. And it *is* very enjoyable to be able to go for a walk or swim, or go to London for the day or night (we now live on the Kent coast near Dover), without having to fit in with the office hours of what many people would call a REAL JOB. But I must say that when Julian goes off to London for the day or away for a week or so to do research or give some lectures, I do feel a great sense of freedom. I can do exactly what I like, eat when I like, take off myself to see my sisters. That's all very enjoyable, although after a week I'm delighted to see him back again.

---

[1] Reprinted from *Mystery Writers Annual*, 1987, published by the Mystery Writers of America, Inc. Reproduced by kind permission of the author.

Many times at parties strangers when introduced having said "And what do *you* write?" as if the ability to write a crime or mystery novel is somehow infectious, a mild and not unpleasant disease. If only it were! But to be honest, I think one crime writer in a family is enough.

I seem to have made Julian sound like the Ogre in the Upstairs Study, when almost the opposite is the truth. He is remarkably easy to live with, his writing hours really very flexible. He is perfectly able to fend for himself, with a little help from his friends, when I am away, and is a quite marvelous shopper, with a good eye for delicious and expensive food. In fact as long as he can work where and when and for as long as he likes, he's perfect. Nonsense—in the words of Joe E. Brown "Nobody's Perfect"!

Chronology

1912   Julian Gustave Symons born May 30 in London, England.

1926   Completes education in state school in England.

1927   Employed as shorthand typist and secretary at Victoria Lighting and Dynamos, London.

1929   Death of father, Morris Albert Symons.

1934   *A Quest for Corvo*, the life of Frederick Rolfe by Julian's brother, A.J.A. Symons, published.

1936   Meets Wyndham Lewis.

1937   Founds and runs single-handedly *Twentieth Century Verse*.

1938   *Confusions about X* published.

1939   Meets Kathleen Clark.

1941   Marries Kathleen Clark, October 25.

1942   Refuses conscription, plea rejected, accepts induction into British army; edits *An Anthology of War Poetry*.

1943   Meets George Orwell; *The Second Man* published; mustered out of Royal Armoured Corps with non-war related benign tumor on left arm.

1944   Employed as advertising copywriter, Rumble, Crowther and Nicholas, London.

1945   *The Immaterial Murder Case* published.

1947   Begins as full-time writer; *A Man Called Jones* published; begins weekly column in *The Manchester Evening News*.

1948   Birth of daughter, Sarah.

1949   *Bland Beginning* published.

1950   *The Thirty-First of February* and *A.J.A. Symons: His Life* are published.

1951   Birth of son, Marcus; *Charles Dickens* published.

1952   *The Broken Penny* and *Thomas Carlyle: The Life* are published.

1954   *The Narrowing Circle* published.

1955   *Horatio Bottomley: A Biography* published.

1956   *The Paper Chase* (*Bogue's Fortune* in U.S. edition) published; edits *Selected Works* by Thomas Carlyle.

1957   *The Colour of Murder* and *The General Strike* are published; *The Colour of Murder* voted Crime Writers' Association Crossed Red Herrings Award for best crime story of the year.

1958   Reviewer, *London Sunday Times*; *The Gigantic Shadow* (*The Pipe Dream* in U.S. edition) published; serves as chairman of the Crime Writers' Association.

1960   *The Progress of a Crime*, *A Reasonable Doubt*, and *The Thirties: A Dream Revolved* are published.

1961   *Murder! Murder!* published; receives Edgar Allan Poe Award from the Mystery Writers of America for *The Progress of a Crime.*

1962   *The Killing of Francie Lake* (*The Plain Man* in U.S. edition) and *The Detective Story in Britain* are published.

1963   *Buller's Campaign* published.

1964   *The End of Solomon Grundy* published.

1965   *The Belting Inheritance*, *England's Pride*, and *Francis Quarles Investigates* are published.

1966   *Critical Occasions*, *Crime and Detection* (*A Pictorial History of Crime* in U.S. edition), and *The Julian Symons Omnibus* are published; receives special award from Crime Writers' Association for *Crime and Detection.*

1967   *The Man Who Killed Himself* published.

1968   *The Man Whose Dreams Came True* published.

1969   Edits *Essays and Biographies* by A.J.A. Symons.

1970   *The Man Who Lost His Wife* published; writes introduction and appreciation for *Nineteen Eighty-Four* by George Orwell.

1972   *Bloody Murder: From the Detective Story to the Crime Novel: A History* (*Mortal Consequences: A History—from the Detective Story to the Crime Novel* in the U.S. edition), *The Players and the Game*, *Notes from Another Country* are published; edits and writes introduction to *Between the War: Britain in Photographs.*

1973   *The Plot Against Roger Rider* and *A Reflection on Auden* are published.

1974   *The Object of an Affair and Other Poems* published; edits and writes introduction to *The Woman in White* by Wilkie Collins.

1975   *A Three-Pipe Problem* published; visiting writer at Amherst College, Amherst, Massachusetts.

1976   Edits *The Angry Thirties*; death of daughter, Sarah.

1977   *Ellery Queen Presents Julian Symons' How to Trap a Crook and 12 Other Mysteries* published; awarded the Grand Master of Swedish Academy of Detection.

1978   *The Blackheath Poisonings: A Victorian Murder Mystery* and *Tell-Tale Heart: The Life and Works of Edgar Allan Poe* are published.

1979   *Portrait of an Artist: Conan Doyle* and *Seven Poems for Sarah* are published.

1980   *The Modern Crime Story* and *Sweet Adelaide: A Victorian Puzzle Solved* are published; selects and writes introductions to the twelve-volume Collins Jubilee Reprints; edits *Selected Tales* by Edgar Allan Poe.

1981   *Critical Observations, Great Detectives: Seven Original Detectives,* and *Tom Adams' Agatha Christie Cover Story (Agatha Christie, the Art of Her Crimes: The Paintings by Tom Adams* in the U.S. edition) are published.

1982   *The Tigers of Subtopia and Other Stories* and *The Detling Murders (The Detling Secret* in the U.S. edition) are published; recipient of The Grand Master Award, Mystery Writers of America.

1983   *Crime and Detection Quiz* and *The Name of Annabel Lee* are published.

1984   *1948 and 1984* published; edits *The Penguin Classic Crime Omnibus.*

1985   *The Criminal Comedy of a Contented Couple (A Criminal Comedy* in the U.S. edition), *Dashiell Hammett, Two Brothers,* and *A.J.A Symons Brother Speculator* are published.

1987   *Makers of the New* and *Criminal Acts Three* (a Book-of-the-Month Club edition of *The Narrowing Circle, The End of Solomon Grundy,* and *The Blackheath Poisonings)* are published.

1988   *The Kentish Murders, Did Sherlock Holmes Meet Hercule...,* and *Oscar Wilde: A Problem in Biography* are published.

1990   *Death's Darkest Face, The Thirties and the Nineties,* and *Somebody Else and Other Stories* are published; awarded the Cartier Diamond Dagger by the Crime Writers' Association.

1991   *Portraits of the Missing* published.

1992   *Something Like a Love Affair* published.

1993   *Does Literature Exist?* published.

1994   *Playing Happy Families* published.
         Dies November 19 in Walmer, Kent.

SECTION A

FICTION

". . .the best of the books seems to be
not only ingenious crime stories
but also good novels . . .
that is their justification."

THE IMMATERIAL
MURDER CASE

by

JULIAN SYMONS

LONDON
VICTOR GOLLANCZ LTD
1945

Title page, *The Immaterial Murder Case*, the first crime novel, Gollancz, 1945.

(a) First U.K. edition (1945)

THE IMMATERIAL MURDER CASE | by | JULIAN SYMONS | LONDON |
VICTOR GOLLANCZ | 1945

Size: 7¼ x 4¹³⁄₁₆".
Pagination: [1-6] 7-160.
Contents: 1, half title; 2, blank; 3, title page; 4, copyright page: "Copyright, 1945,
   by Julian Symons" and dedication: "FOR RUTHVEN TODD" followed by a
   four-line poem; 5, "CONTENTS"; 6, characters; 7-160, text.
Binding: Blue cloth, cream lettering on spine: THE IMMATERIAL MURDER
   CASE * JULIAN SYMONS.
Dust Jacket: "Gollancz yellow"; purple and black lettering on front, black letter-
   ing on spine and back.
Publication Date: October 1945.
Price: 7/6.
Printing: Printed in Great Britain by The Camelot Press Ltd., London and
   Southampton.
Symons's Note: The Immaterial Murder Case is an appallingly bad detective story.
   I got into such a tangle with the plot that at one point I included a four-page
   chart showing the movements of the characters, done for my own benefit rather
   than that of readers.... I've forgotten now who most of the grotesques in the
   story were meant to be, but I do remember that Ruthven [Todd] was justifiably
   angered and upset by the caricature of himself and not noticeably mollified by
   the dedication, which said in part:

> Dear murdered, see without too much rage
> Your name set here, not on the title page.[1]

(b) Second U.K. issue (1945)

THE IMMATERIAL | MURDER CASE | by | JULIAN SYMONS | LONDON |
VICTOR GOLLANCZ LTD

Same as A 1 a except for the following changes:
Contents: 2, addition of "By the same Author | A MAN CALLED JONES"; 3,
   title page: removal of publication date, 1945; 4, copyright page: addition of
   "First published October 1945 | Second impression (first cheap edition) May
   1948".
Binding: Blue cloth, gold lettering on spine: THE IMMATERIAL MURDER CASE
   * JULIAN SYMONS.
Dust Jacket: "Gollancz yellow"; purple and black lettering on front and spine,
   black lettering on back.

(c) First U.S. edition (1957)

The Immaterial | Murder Case | by | JULIAN SYMONS | COCK ROBIN | MYSTERY | [publisher's logo: COCK ROBIN • MYSTERY (two sides of a box, rule on other two sides) plus robin with arrow in breast inside box] | New York | THE MACMILLAN COMPANY | 1957

Size: 7⅓ x 5".
Pagination: [i-viii] 1-208.
Contents: i, series note and half title; ii, list of twenty titles in the "MURDER REVISITED SERIES"; iii, title page; iv, copyright page; v, dedication: "FOR RUTHVEN TODD"; vi, note; vii, "CONTENTS"; viii, characters; 1-208, text.
Binding: Gray paper over boards, red lettering on front cover: COCK ROBIN • MYSTERY. The words make up two sides of a box enclosing a picture of a robin with an arrow in its breast. Red lettering on spine: The Immaterial Murder Case SYMONS MACMILLAN.
Dust Jacket: Black and pink lettering on white front, spine, and back. Illustration is a Dali-like picture by Vera Bock.
Publication Date: November 1957
Price: $3.25.
Printing: Printed in the United States of America.
Symons's Note: My own first book, *The Immaterial Murder Case*, was turned down in the U.S. They wrote me a first paragraph about it that was full of praise, saying it was wonderfully funny, enjoyed reading it enormously, etc. Then the second part said: afraid its not right for us, can't publish it, shall we destroy the ms. or would you like it back![2]

(d) First U.K. paperback edition (1954)

THE IMMATERIAL | MURDER CASE | [rule] | JULIAN SYMONS | PENGUIN BOOKS | MELBOURNE • LONDON • BALTIMORE

Size: 7¹⁄₁₆ x 4¼".
Pagination: [1-9], 10-216, [217-224].
Contents: 1, half title; 2, blank; 3, title page; 4, copyright page: "First Published 1945 | Published in Penguin Books 1954"; 5, "CONTENTS"; 6, "NOTE"; 7, dedication: "FOR RUTHVEN TODD" followed by a four-line poem; 8, characters; 9-216, text; 217-224 list of "new fiction and crime of interest to readers of this book...".
Binding: Traditional 1950s Penguin Books wrappers. Front cover is green with white middle band that wraps to spine. Black lettering in white irregular oval on top green band of front: PENGUIN | BOOKS. Black lettering on white middle band: THE IMMATERIAL | MURDER CASE | [rule] | JULIAN SYMONS. Black lettering on bottom green band of front: COMPLETE [publisher's logo: penguin] UNABRIDGED. Black lettering bottom right corner: 2|-. Black lettering on spine: JULIAN SYMONS [in green band] | THE IMMATERIAL MURDER CASE [in

white band] | [publisher's logo] 989 [in green band]. Back is white with a green border and black lettering. It has a black and white photograph of Julian Symons by John Vickers followed by a biographical sketch in black lettering. Black lettering on green border: NOT FOR SALE IN THE U.S.A. Inside front cover has promotional blurb; inside back cover has continuation of titles.
Publication Date: 1954.
Price: 2/-.
Printing: Printed in Great Britain by Hazell, Watson and Viney Ltd, Aylesbury and London.

A 2   A MAN CALLED JONES   1947

(a) First U.K. edition (1947)

A MAN CALLED JONES | by | JULIAN SYMONS | LONDON | VICTOR GOLLANCZ LTD | 1947

Size: 7¼ x 4¾".
Pagination: [1-4] 5-192.
Contents: 1, half title; 2, "BY THE SAME AUTHOR" with one title; 3, title page; 4, copyright page: "Copyright 1947 by Julian Symons" and dedication: "For MY MOTHER"; 5-6, "CHARACTERS IN THE STORY"; 7-192, text.
Binding: Blue cloth, gilt lettering on spine: A MAN CALLED JONES * JULIAN SYMONS.
Dust Jacket: "Gollancz yellow"; purple and black lettering on front and spine, black lettering on back.
Publication Date: June 1947.
Price: 8/6.
Printing: Printed in Great Britain by Purnell and Sons, Ltd. (T.U.) Paulton (Somerset) and London.
Symons's Note: Little, and little good, to say of this. The book sprang from my years in an advertising agency from 1944 to 1947 and gives a mild, almost saccharine view of the agency game. As a crime story it is poorly devised and handled, with some humour the only redeeming feature.

(b) Second U.K. edition (1970)

A MAN CALLED JONES | [double rule] | JULIAN SYMONS | [publisher's logo: black fingerprint] | A FINGERPRINT BOOK | [rule] | HAMISH HAMILTON | LONDON

Size: 7¾ x 5⅛".
Pagination: [1-8] 9-188 [189-192].
Contents: 1, half title; 2, "by the same author" followed by a list of thirteen titles;

3, title page; 4, copyright page: "© Julian Symons, 1947 | First Published in Great Britain 1947 | First published in this edition | by Hamish Hamilton Ltd 1970 | 90 Great Russell Street London W.C. 1"; 5, dedication: "For My Mother"; 6, blank; 7, characters; 8, blank; 9-188, text; 189-192, blank.

Binding: Red paper over boards, spine stamped in gilt: A Man Called Jones JULIAN SYMONS [gilt fingerprint].

Dust Jacket: Rust and white lettering on black front and spine, black lettering on white back. Illustration is a photograph of a Smith & Wesson gun between two leather gloves. Jacket design by Bernard Higton.

Publication Date: 1970.

Price: £1.50|30s.

Printing: Printed in Great Britain by Clarke, Doble & Brendon Ltd., Plymouth.

(c) First U.K. paperback edition (1963)

JULIAN SYMONS | [rule] | A Man Called | Jones | Collins | FONTANA BOOKS

Size: 7 x 4⅛".

Pagination: [1-6] 7-192.

Contents: 1, half title and plot outline; 2, "By the Same Author in Fontana Books" followed by five titles; 3, title page; 4, copyright page: "First published by Victor Gollancz Ltd., 1947 | First issued in Fontana Books 1963"; 5, dedication: "For My Mother"; 6, "CHARACTERS IN THE STORY"; 7-192, text.

Binding: Front and back wrappers have blue and white lettering on a black background. Front has a photograph of a Smith and Wesson revolver, a pair of white gloves, and a red wig on a stand on a table in the foreground; a man is standing in the background. Blue lettering: A MAN | CALLED | JONES. White lettering: Julian | Symons | An Ad. Agency | murder...an elusive | killer...and one, | unclaimed wig! Black lettering on yellow band across bottom: fontana books 2'6. Spine is yellow with black lettering: A MAN CALLED JONES Julian Symons [publisher's logo: white fb in black oval] [two black triangles] 892. Back has detail of front photograph in a circle with a white border followed by excerpt.

Publication Date: 1963.

Price: 2'6.

Printing: Printed in Great Britain by Collins Clear-Type Press, London and Glasgow.

(d) Second U.K. paperback edition (1992)

JULIAN SYMONS | THE| ADVERTISING | MURDERS | AN OMNIBUS EDITION COMPRISING | The Thirtyfirst of February | AND | A Man Called Jones | [publisher's logo: a black diamond with a sword inside, the word PAN across the hilt] | CRIME | PAN BOOKS | LONDON, SYDNEY AND AUCKLAND

Size: 7 x 4¼".
Pagination: [i-x] [1] 2-403 [404-406].
Contents: i, biographical note; ii, "by the same author" followed by a list of twenty-seven titles; iii, title page; iv, copyright page: "*A Man called Jones* first published 1947 by Victor Gollancz Ltd | *The Thirtyfirst of February* first published 1950 by Victor Gollancz Ltd | Both titles first published in this edition 1992 by Pan Books Ltd...| © Julian Symons 1947, 1950"; v, dedication: "For my mother"; vi, blank; vii, half title: "A MAN | CALLED JONES"; viii, blank; ix, "CHARACTERS IN THE STORY"; x, blank; 1-203 text; 204, blank; 205, half title: "THE THIRTYFIRST | OF FEBRUARY"; 206, dedication: "To Kathleen"; 207, two poems by Edward Taylor; 208, blank; 209, contents; 210, blank; 211-403, text; 404-405, blank; 406, order blank for Pan Books.
Binding: Gray, blue, red, and white lettering on front illustration of a table top with a sheet of paper, a bullet, a point marker, and an exacto knife. Gray lettering: AN OMNIBUS EDITION. Blue lettering: JULIAN SYMONS | 'Incontestably the doyen of British crime writers' *SUNDAY TIMES*. Red hand lettering: The | Advertising | Murders. White lettering in lower left corner: [PAN logo in red diamond] | CRIME. Red spine with blue lettering and white hand lettering: JULIAN SYMONS The Advertising Murders [black diamond with PAN logo] | CRIME. Red, black, and blue lettering on white back includes review comments, price, ISBN. Cover illustration by Nick Cudworth.
Publication Date: 1992.
Price: £4.99.
Printing: Phototypeset by Intype, London; Printed in England by Clays Ltd. St Ives Plc.

A 3   BLAND BEGINNING   1949

(a) First U.K. edition (1949)

BLAND BEGINNING | A Detective Story | by | JULIAN SYMONS | LONDON | VICTOR GOLLANCZ LTD | 1949

Size: 7¼x 4¹³⁄₁₆".
Pagination: [1-6] 7-230 [231-232].
Contents: 1, half title; 2, "By the same author" followed by two titles; 3, title page; 4, copyright page: "Copyright 1949 by Julian Symons" and dedication: "For SARAH SYMONS" followed by a nine-line poem by Julian to his daughter; 5, contents; 6, blank; 7-9, "FROM THE BIOGRAPHICAL DICTIONARY"; 10, blank; 11-229, text; 230, POSTSCRIPT; 231-232 blank.
Binding: Red cloth, black lettering on spine: BLAND | BEGINNING | BY | JULIAN | SYMONS | GOLLANCZ.
Dust Jacket: "Gollancz yellow"; purple and black lettering on front, black lettering on spine and back.

BLAND
BEGINNING

by

JULIAN SYMONS

HARPER & BROTHERS

PUBLISHERS/NEW YORK

Title page, *Bland Beginning*, Harper & Brothers, 1949, the first U.S. appearance.

Publication Date: February 1949
Price: 8|6.
Printing: Printed in Great Britain by The Camelot Press Ltd., London and Southampton.
Symons's Note: "Whatever happened to Inspector Bland?" people sometimes ask. Or, to put it differently, why did I abandon the series detective? I've been told a hundred times that to deny myself the luxury or pleasure of a series character is commercially foolish, and I don't doubt that is true. But the other benefits for a writer (no need to describe the detective's appearance or character, the reader knows it already) and reader (the known figure is greeted with the comfortable feeling of putting on a pair of old slippers) are for me far outweighed by the fact that if you want to write a story showing people involved in emotional conflict that leads to crime, a detective of this kind is grit in the machinery. It's true also that I find the fanzine aspect of the series detective repellent—the Wimsey pedigree, Nero Wolfe's cook book. Chandler once said that the puzzle plot is a kind of crutch needed by the crime writer, and much the same is true of the series detective. A crutch is useful, no doubt, but it is better to stand on two legs.

The book is of course based on the bibliographical forgeries of Thomas J. Wise and, for reasons connected with the plot, had to be set in the Twenties, becoming, therefore, Bland's first case. Hence the title. It developed an interesting bibliographical variation when it crossed the Atlantic. It was the first book of mine to be published in the United States, and Joan Kahn at Harper felt I should indicate the detective's later career. Accordingly, the American edition contains a prologue set in 1949, in which Bland tells me the story. Joan also felt it necessary to simplify some of the terminology used in the cricket match finale. A cricket match last chapter for the American market! As I think back, Joan's courage looks like foolhardiness, but we both survived it successfully.

Author's Note: In an earlier article Julian wrote: "...*Bland Beginning*, the first of my crime stories to appear in America. Some people have liked this book, which was based on the Thomas J. Wise literary forgeries, although I don't think much of it myself."[3] Some twenty-four years later the American writer William H. Hallahen would again use the theme of T. J. Wise's literary forgeries as backdrop to his own very fine work *The Ross Forgery* (Indianapolis/New York: Bobbs-Merrill, 1973 and London: Victor Gollancz, 1977).

(b) First U.S. edition (1949)

BLAND BEGINNING | [rule] | [rule of printer's flowers] | [rule] | by | JULIAN SYMONS | [publisher's logo: oval wreath with hand passing torch to second hand] | HARPER & BROTHERS | PUBLISHERS / NEW YORK

Size: 8 x 5¼".
Pagination: [i-x] 1-236 [237-238].
Contents: i, half title; ii, blank; iii, title page; iv, copyright page: "Copyright 1949, by JULIAN GUSTAVE SYMONS....FIRST EDITION I-Y"; v, dedication: "For

Sarah Symons" followed by a nine-line poem; vi, blank; vii; contents; viii, blank; ix, half title; x, blank; 1-235, text; 236, "POSTSCRIPT"; 237-238, blank.

Binding: Black cloth, front cover blind stamped: [Harper logo] HB. Gilt lettering on spine: [leaf] I Bland I Begin- I ning I [rule] I Julian I Symons I [rule] I Harper I [leaf].

Dust Jacket: White lettering on purple, turquoise, and black front and spine, black lettering on white back. Jacket design by Thomas Ruzicka.

Publication Date: October 1949.

Price: $2.50.

Printing: Printed in the United States of America.

(c) Second U.S. (Book Club) edition (1950)

[decorative rules] I Bland Beginning I by JULIAN SYMONS I [rule] I Pebble in the Sky I by ISAAC ASIMOV I [rule] I Just for the Bride I by DOROTHY PARK CLARK I [rule] I The Owl and the Pussycat I by OWEN CAMERON I [decorative rules] I PUBLISHED FOR THE I UNICORN MYSTERY BOOK CLUB I By Unicorn Press, Publishers, Inc. • New York • 1950

Size: 7½" x 5³⁄₁₆".

Pagination: [i-viii] 1-236; [i-iv] 9-223; [i-iv] 9-222; [i-iv] 1-240; [i-ii]. (Note: Each novel is given separate pagination.)

Contents: i, "UNICORN MYSTERY BOOK CLUB"; ii, publisher's statement; iii, title page; iv, copyright page; v, half title; vi, blank; vii, title page; viii, "About Bland Beginning"; 1-5, "Prologue—1949"; 6-8, "FROM THE BIOGRAPHICAL DICTIONARY"; 9-235, text; 236, "POSTSCRIPT." Followed by three other titles as above.

Binding: Tan cloth, cover stamped in gilt and red: UNICORN MYSTERY BOOK CLUB. Words form a circle with a unicorn's head on top of a pile of books. Gilt lettering in red and black blocks on spine, alternating for each of the four titles. Gold and black decorative rules followed by gilt lettering on red background: BLAND I BEGINNING I Julian Symons.

Dust Jacket: Issued without a jacket.

Publication Date: 1950.

Price: Not given.

Printing: None given.

(d) Second U. K. issue (1975)

BLAND BEGINNING I A Detective Story I by I JULIAN SYMONS I LONDON I VICTOR GOLLANCZ LTD I 1975

A Gollancz reissue, same as A 3 a, with addition of the "Copyright 1949 by Julian Symons I First Published 1949 I Reissued 1975 I ISBN 0 575 019484" on verso of title page. Priced at £2.50, the inside front flap of the dust jacket carries the following:

"'That rare combination, a good thriller and a good, amusing book' wrote John Betjeman...when we first published *Bland Beginning* in 1949....We are delighted to be again making available this ingenious and diverting novel concerning forgery and murder."

(e) First U.K. paperback edition (1955)

Bland | Beginning | [rule] | JULIAN SYMONS | [publisher's logo: fb in oval] | COLLINS | fontana books

Size: 7¹⁄₁₆ x 4¼".
Pagination: [1-6] 7-9 [10] 11-251 [252-256].
Contents: 1, half title; 2, "Famous books and authors in the | Fontana Series" followed by twenty-four titles and authors; 3, title page; 4, copyright page: "First published 1949 | First issued in Fontana Books 1955" and dedication: "For Sarah Symons" followed by nine-line poem; 5, "CONTENTS"; 6, publisher's promotional blurb; 7-9, "From 'The Biographical Dictionary'" followed by introductory text; 10, blank; 11-252, text; 253-254, "fontana books" followed by partial list of titles; 255-256, "ALSO AVAILABLE IN FONTANA BOOKS" followed by four titles and synopses.
Binding: Cover illustration shows a couple in the foreground watching two men running across a field. White lettering: Bland | Beginning | JULIAN | SYMONS | A first-rate, original, detective story. Black lettering on blue and white striped band across bottom of front cover: [publisher's logo: black oval with "Collins" in white lettering, a dot above and below the name] fontana books [globe in halftone on black oval]. Black lettering on blue and white striped spine: BLAND BEGINNING Julian Symons [publisher's logo: fb in black oval] 72. Black lettering on white back with promotional blurb and biographical note; black and white photograph of Julian Symons. Black lettering on blue and white striped band: [publisher's logo: fb in black oval] fontana books [publisher's logo: fb in black oval]. Cover illustration by John Rose.
Publication Date: 1955.
Price: 2/-.
Printing: Printed in Great Britain by Collins Clear-Type Press, London and Glasgow.

(f) First U.S. paperback edition (1962)

BLAND BEGINNING | Julian Symons | [publisher's logo: dolphin] | DOLPHIN BOOKS | DOUBLEDAY & COMPANY, INC. | GARDEN CITY, NEW YORK

Size: 7⅛ x 4¼".
Pagination: [1-11] 12-239 [240].
Contents: 1, half title; 2, biographical note; 3, title page; 4, copyright page: "Dolphin Books edition, 1962, by | arrangement with Harper & Brothers | Copyright 1949 by Julian Gustave Symons | All Rights Reserved"; 5, dedication:

"For SARAH SYMONS" followed by nine-line poem; 6, blank; 7, "CONTENTS"; 8, blank; 9, half title; 10, blank; 11-239, text; 240, POSTSCRIPT.
Binding: Front cover has black and blue lettering on white and gold: C318 A DOLPHIN MYSTERY [price] I BLAND I BEGINNING I JULIAN SYMONS I MYSTERY. Illustration shows stylized skull and crossbones, open book, and ink stain. Black lettering on gold spine: Bland Beginning JULIAN SYMONS [publisher's logo: dolphin] C318 [star]. Black lettering on gold back has title, author, promotional blurb, reviews, logo. Cover design by George Giusti. Cover drawing by Sydney Butchkes.
Publication Date: 1962.
Price: 95¢.
Printing: Printed in the United States of America.

(g) Second U.K. paperback edition (1969)

Julian Symons I Bland Beginning I [rule] I [publisher's logo: dog in circle] CORGI-BOOKS I A DIVISION OF TRANSWORLD PUBLISHERS

Size: 7⅛ x 4⅜".
Pagination: [1-8] 9-222 [223-224].
Contents: 1, "JULIAN SYMONS" followed by reviewers' comments; 2, "Also by Julian Symons" followed by two published titles, one title to be published; 3, title page; 4, copyright page: "William Collins Edition published 1949 I Corgi Edition published 1969" and printing information; 5, contents; 6, blank; 7, half title; 8, blank; 9-221; 222, postscript; text; 223-224, "A SELECTION OF FINE READING I AVAILABLE IN CORGI BOOKS" followed by list of titles and order blank.
Binding: Black and blue lettering on gray: Julian I Symons I Bland I Beginning. Review from *The Irish Times* enclosed in oval garland. Corgi Books and publisher's logo in top right corner, 552 08080 2 in lower right corner. Illustration is a photograph of bullets, a length of rope, a gun, a palm frond, a bloody crutch, an open pocket knife, and a croquet ball on front; bullets, fireplace poker, book, and S-hook on back. Black lettering on spine: 552 I 08080 I 2 I CRIME I [publisher's logo] I BLAND BEGINNING JULIAN SYMONS [crutch wraps to back]. Black lettering on back with promotional blurb, review enclosed in garland, book number, prices.
Publication Date: 1969.
Price: U.K. 4 s 0 d 20 p; Australia 65¢;   New Zealand 60¢.
Printing: Printed in Great Britain by Richard Clay (The Chaucer Press), Ltd., Bungay, Suffolk.

(h) Second U.S. paperback edition (1971)

BLAND I BEGINNING I [rule] I BEAGLE BOOKS [bullet] NEW YORK I An Intext Publisher

Size: 7 x 4⅜".

Pagination: [i-xviii] 1-238 .

Contents: i, Review and promotional tease; ii, "Mysteries by Julian Symons" followed by six titles (Beagle editions); iii, title page; iv, copyright page: "Copyright, 1949, by Julian Gustave Symons. | Beagle edition published by arrangement with | Harper & Row, Publishers" and dedication: "For SARAH SYMONS" followed by nine-line poem; v, "CONTENTS"; vi, blank; vii-xi, "PROLOGUE—1949"; xii, blank; xiii-xv, "FROM THE BIOGRAPHICAL DICTIONARY"; xvi, blank; xvii, half title; xviii, blank; 1-237, text; 238, POSTSCRIPT.

Binding: Black lettering on light blue front: [publisher's logo: bb in white box] 94140 A BEAGLE BOXER MYSTERY 95¢ | Julian | Symons | "Delightful." | —*New York Herald Tribune* | BLAND BEGINNING. Cover photograph shows a gun, a club, a sketch of a man's face, and a noose on top of two books. White lettering on black spine: MYSTERY | [publisher's logo] | BLAND BEGINNING JULIAN SYMONS 8441 • 95140 • 095. White lettering on black back includes *New York Times* review, promotional blurb, and list of six Symons novels in Beagle editions, along with printing information and price.

Publication Date: September 1971.

Price: 95¢.

Printing: Printed in the United States of America.

(i) Third U.S. paperback edition (1987)

JULIAN SYMONS | Bland Beginning | Carroll & Graf Publishers, Inc. | New York

Size: 6¹³⁄₁₆ x 4⅛".

Pagination: [i-vi] vii-xi [xii] xiii-xv [xvi-xviii] 1-238.

Contents: i, reviews; ii, "Other Julian Symons novels published by | Carroll & Graf: | *The 31st of February;* iii, title page; iv, copyright page: "Copyright © 1949 by Julian Gustave Symons. | Copyright © renewed 1977 by Julian Gustave Symons...First Carroll & Graf edition 1987" and dedication: "For Sarah Symons" followed by nine-line poem; v, "CONTENTS"; vi, blank; vii-xi, "PRO-LOGUE—1949"; xii, blank; xiii-xv, "FROM THE BIOGRAPHICAL DICTIO-NARY"; xvi, blank; xvii, half title; xviii, blank; 1-237, text; 238, POSTSCRIPT.

Binding: Black with gold and white lettering on front: $3.95 "Entertaining...cleverly original." | —*The Chicago Sunday Tribune* | JULIAN SYMONS | Bland Beginning. Front has illustration of a woman in white dress standing over a man's body. Gold and white lettering on black spine: Carroll | & Graf | [rule] | Mystery BLAND BEGINNING JULIAN SYMONS. White and gold lettering on black back has excerpts from reviews, title, and promotional blurb, followed by publisher's logo [open book with Carroll & Graf written on endpapers], ISBN, and distributor.

Publication Date: 1987.

Price: $3.95.

Printing: Manufactured in the United States of America. Published by arrangement with Harper & Row Publishers, Inc.

A 4   THE THIRTYFIRST OF FEBRUARY   1950

(a) First U.K. edition (1950)

THE THIRTYFIRST OF | FEBRUARY | A Mystery Novel | by | JULIAN SYMONS | LONDON| VICTOR GOLLANCZ LTD | 1950

Size: 7¼ x 4¹³⁄₁₆".
Pagination: [1-10] 11-204 [205-208].
Contents: 1, half title; 2, "BY THE SAME AUTHOR" followed by three earlier Symons titles; 3, title page; 4, copyright page: "Copyright 1950 by Julian Symons"; 5, dedication "To Kathleen"; 6, blank; 7, a six-line poem by Edward Taylor followed by another Taylor quote of four lines; 8, blank; 9, "CONTENTS"; 10, blank; 11-204, text; 205-208, blank.
Binding: Red cloth, black lettering on spine: THE THIRTYFIRST OF FEBRUARY * JULIAN SYMONS.
Dust Jacket: "Gollancz yellow"; purple and black lettering on front, black lettering on spine and back.
Publication Date: February 1950.
Price: 8/6.
Printing: Made and printed in England by STAPLES PRESS LIMITED at their Rochester, Kent, establishment.
Symons's Note: This fourth crime story is the first I can look back on with satisfaction. It is one of my six best books. In some places it is based directly on my advertising experiences (as in the passage where Anderson's secretary sends letter and memo to the wrong people), and some of the characters are recognisable as advertising colleagues. I had been reading Dostoievsky before I began the book, and as one critic perceptively observed, the Inspector has some relation to the Grand Inquisitor. I should go along with those who put it among the most interesting things I have written, and it is the first piece of prose fiction that expresses a view of life and society I recognize as truly my own.

(b) First U.S. edition (1951)

THE 31ST | OF FEBRUARY | Julian Symons | HARPER & BROTHERS | [publisher's logo: oval wreath with hand passing torch to second hand] | NEW YORK

Size: 8¹⁄₁₆ x 5¼".
Pagination: [i-vii] ix [x-xii] 1-201 [202-210].
Contents: i, half title; ii, "By the same author: BLAND BEGINNING"; iii, title page; iv, copyright page: "Copyright 1950, by Julian Gustave Symons...FIRST EDITION M-Z"; vi, dedication "TO KATHLEEN"; vi, blank; vii, six-line poem by Edward Taylor followed by four-line poem by Taylor; vii, blank; ix, "CONTENTS"; x, blank; xi, half title; xii, blank; 1-201, text; 202-210, blank.
Binding: Three-quarter black paper over boards, red lettering on tan cloth spine: THE 31ST | OF | FEBRUARY | [rule] | SYMONS | Harper.

Dust Jacket: White and black lettering on orange front and spine, black lettering on white back. Illustration is a sketch of a worried-looking man. Back has reviewers' comments on *Bland Beginning.* Jacket design by Peter Fraenkel.
Publication Date: February 1951.
Price: $2.50.
Printing: Printed in the United States of America.

(c) Second U.K. edition (1995)

THE 31ST OF | FEBRUARY | Julian Symons | • BLACK • | DAGGER | • CRIME •
[the words Black Dagger Crime and a black dagger are in a box]

Size: 7¹¹⁄₁₆ x 4¾".
Pagination: [i-iv] v-vii [1-4] 5-190 [191-194].
Contents: 1, half title and brief plot description; ii, blank; iii, title; iv; copyright page: "First published 1950 | by | Victor Gollancz Ltd. | This edition 1995 by Chivers Press | published by arrangement with | the author's estate | .... © Julian Symons, 1950 | Foreword copyright © Michael Gilbert, 1995"; v-vii, "FORE-WORD"; 1, blank; 2, "THE BLACK DAGGER | CRIME Series" statement; 4, blank; 5-190, text; 191-194, blank.
Binding: Black paper over boards, gilt lettering on spine: JULIAN | SYMONS THE 31ST OF FEBRUARY [publisher's logo] • BLACK • | DAGGER | • CRIME •.
Dust Jacket: Photograph of ten black Homburg hats referred to on page 7: "...on Monday morning a small regiment of black Homburg hats marched down Bezyl Street." Background is pink, with the publisher's logo in the lower-right corner. White and black lettering on black, white, and red spine. Back illustration is three sheets of note paper pulled from a spiral notepad; list of five titles in the series is hand lettered in black.
Publication Date: 1995.
Price: £13.99.
From the Foreword: "It will be seen that, if he came late to crime writing, he came formidably well-equipped. His knowledge of the genre was exhaustive. He was a perceptive social critic, and he had developed a style which was clear-cut and readable without being tiresomely literary." — Michael Gilbert.

(d) First U.K. paperback edition

JULIAN SYMONS | The 31st of February | Collins | Fontana Books.

Not seen.

(e) First U.S. paperback edition (1953)

The 31st | of February | by JULIAN SYMONS | Bantam Books [publisher's logo: rooster] New York

Size: 6½ x 5¼".
Pagination: [i-viii] 1-198 [199-200].
Contents: i, excerpt; ii, blank; iii, title page; iv, copyright: "Copyright, 1950, by Julian Gustave Symons" and printing history; v, "CONTENTS"; vi, blank; vii, dedication: "TO KATHLEEN"; viii, two poems by Edward Taylor; 1-198, text; 199, promotional blurb for *Spin the Glass Web* by Max Ehrlich; 200, list of Bantam titles and order information.
Binding: Red, white, and light blue lettering on black front: 1059 [publisher's logo enclosed in a ring of words: A BANTAM BOOK Every Book Complete] "Brilliant, Powerful, Sordid I and Unnerving" San Francisco CHRONICLE I THE 31ST of February I JULIAN I SYMONS I Complete and Unabridged. Illustration shows painting of a man's face surrounded by smaller art spots of a couple embracing at a party, a naked man and scantily clad woman about to be discovered by another woman, and a man being led away by two policemen. Black lettering on red spine: 1059 [triangle] THE 31st OF FEBRUARY JULIAN SYMONS [publisher's logo: rooster]. Blue, red, and black lettering on white back highlighted by blue corner rule and red stripe along spine. Back has excerpt, logo, and picture of the original hardback edition published by Harper & Brothers.
Publication Date: February 1953.
Price: 25¢.
Printing: Printed in the United States of America.

(f) Second U.S. paperback edition (1958)

THE 31ST I OF FEBRUARY I Julian Symons I [publisher's logo: trefoil] I BERKLEY PUBLISHING CORP. I 145 West 57th Street •
New York, 19, N.Y.
Size: 6⅜ x 4¼".
Pagination: [1-4] 5-176.
Contents: 1, excerpt and reviews; 2, nine titles by John Dickson Carr; 3, title page; 4, copyright page: "Copyright © 1950, BY JULIAN GUSTAVE SYMONS....BERKLEY EDITION, JULY, 1958" and dedication: "TO KATHLEEN"; 5-176, text.
Binding: Black lettering over illustration, upper left corner: BERKLEY I [publisher's logo] I BOOKS I [rule] I G-137; upper right corner: 35¢. Red lettering: THE 31ST OF I FEBRUARY. Black lettering: JULIAN SYMONS I COMPLETE AND UNABRIDGED. Illustration is a painting of a woman in a red negligee lying at the bottom of a staircase; a man is standing in a doorway at the top of the stairs. Yellow and black lettering on red spine: THE 31ST OF FEBRUARY JULIAN SYMONS BERKLEY [publisher's logo] BOOKS. Red and black lettering on white calendar page on back, highlighting key dates in plot; quote from Anthony Boucher review in yellow lettering on red.
Publication Date: July 1958.
Price: 35¢.
Printing: Printed in the United States of America.

(g) Third U.S. paperback edition (1971)

THE | THIRTY-FIRST | OF FEBRUARY | A mystery novel by | JULIAN SYMONS | BEAGLE BOOKS • NEW YORK | An Intext Publisher

Size: 7 x 4¼".
Pagination: [i-vi] 1-186.
Contents: i, reviews and excerpt; ii, "Mysteries by Julian Symons" followed by six titles in Beagle editions; iii, title page; iv, copyright page: "Copyright, 1950, by Julian Gustave Symons....First printing: September 1971" and dedication: "TO KATHLEEN"; v, two poems by Edward Taylor; vi, blank; 1-186, text.
Binding: Black lettering on red front: [publisher's logo: bb in white box] 905139 A BEAGLE BOXER MYSTERY 95¢ | Julian | Symons | "Superior" | Saturday Review | THE 31st OF FEBRUARY. Illustration is a photograph of a desk at Vincent Advertising, showing a calendar opened to February 4 ("Valerie Dead"), a portfolio with a note sticking out of it ("I don't see why I didn't push her down the stairs long ago"), an open box of safety matches. White lettering on black spine: MYSTERY | [publisher's logo] | THE 31st OF FEBRUARY JULIAN SYMONS 844 • 95139 • 095. White lettering on black back includes *New Yorker* and *Saturday Review* reviews, promotional blurb, and list of six Symons novels in Beagle editions, along with printing information and price.
Publication Date: September, 1971.
Price: 95¢.
Printing: Printed in the United States of America.

(h) Fourth U.S. paperback edition (1978)

[rule] | THE 31st | OF FEBRUARY | [rule] | Julian Symons | [publisher's logo: torch] | PERENNIAL LIBRARY | Harper & Row, Publishers | New York, Hagerstown, San Francisco, London

Size: 7 x 4⅛".
Pagination: [i-viii] 1-212 [213-216].
Contents: i, half title and reviews; ii, "Other title by Julian Symons available in Perennial Library: THE COLOR OF MURDER"; iii, title page; iv, copyright page: "Copyright © 1950 by Julian Gustave Simons [sic]. First PERENNIAL LIBRARY edition published 1978"; v, two poems by Edward Taylor; vi, blank; vii, half title; viii, blank; 1-212, text; 213-216, "THE PERENNIAL LIBRARY MYSTERY SERIES" followed by titles and reviews of series authors, including Julian Symons.
Binding: Gray and white lettering on black front: P460 [publisher's logo] PERENNIAL LIBRARY | A HARPER NOVEL OF SUSPENSE | JULIAN | SYMONS | THE 31ST OF | FEBRUARY. Illustration is a photograph of a woman lying at the bottom of a flight of stairs. White lettering on black spine: P460 | [publisher's logo] | THE 31ST OF FEBRUARY Julian Symons $1.95. Black lettering on white back includes genre, title, author, excerpt, reviews, another Symons title in series, publisher, ISBN. Cover design by One + One Studio.

Publication Date: 1978.
Price: $1.95.
Printing: Printed in the United States of America; published simultaneously in Canada by Fitzhenry & Whiteside Limited, Toronto.

(i) Fifth U.S. paperback edition (1987)

JULIAN SYMONS | THE 31st of FEBRUARY | Carroll & Graf Publishers, Inc. | New York

Size: 6¹³⁄₁₆ x 4⅛.
Pagination: [1-4] 5-190 [191-192].
Contents: 1, reviews; 2, blank; 3, title page; 4, copyright page: "Copyright © 1950 by Julian Gustave Symons | Copyright © renewed 1978 by Julian Gustave Symons...First Carroll & Graf edition 1987" and dedication: "To Kathleen"; 5-190, text; 191-192, "[publisher's logo: open book with Carroll & Graf written on endpapers] | FINE MYSTERY AND SUSPENSE TITLES FROM CARROLL & GRAF" followed by titles and order blank.
Binding: Black with lavender and white lettering on front: $3.50 | "Precise and pitiless"—*Kirkus* | JULIAN SYMONS | The 31st OF FEBRUARY. Front has a photograph of a woman's body lying at the bottom of a flight of stairs. Lavender and white lettering on black spine: Carroll | & Graf | [rule] | Mystery The 31st of February JULIAN SYMONS. Lavender and white lettering on black back has excerpts from reviews and a promotional blurb, followed by publisher's logo, ISBN, and distributor.
Publication Date: 1987.
Price: $3.50.
Printing: Manufactured in the United States of America. Reprinted by arrangement with Harper & Row Publisher's, Inc.

A 5   THE BROKEN PENNY   1953

(a) First U.K. edition (1953)

THE BROKEN PENNY | by | JULIAN SYMONS | "The thing which is attempted to represent is the | conflict between the tender conscience and the world." | ARTHUR HUGH CLOUGH in 1850. | LONDON | VICTOR GOLLANCZ LTD | 1953

Size: 7¼ x 4¾".
Pagination: [1-6] 7-223 [224].
Contents: 1, half title; 2, "By the same author" followed by four fiction titles and one biography; 3, title page; 4, copyright page: "Copyright 1953 by Julian Symons"; 5, dedication "For MARCUS RICHARD JULIAN SYMONS"; 6, blank; 7, "CONTENTS"; 8, blank; 9, "Part One PLAN"; 10, blank; 11-223, text; 224, blank.

Binding: Red paper over boards, gilt lettering on spine: THE | BROKEN | PENNY | BY | JULIAN | SYMONS | GOLLANCZ | DETECTIVE.

Dust Jacket: "Gollancz yellow"; purple and black lettering on front, black lettering on spine and back.

Publication Date: April 1953.

Price: 9|6.

Printing: Printed in Great Britain by The Camelot Press Ltd., London and Southampton.

Symons's Note: The only book of mine to which the label "thriller" can be properly applied had its origin in a visit to Yugoslavia shortly after the War. My wife, her brother and I were viewed with some suspicion; ordered off a train at bayonet point; thought to be Germans, then slapped on the back and offered drinks when understood to be English. On the island of Hvar, where we spent most of our holiday, the electricity was turned off at 9 each night, breakfast was dry bread and a small square of marmalade. When we asked why one man in the breakfast room got an egg, we were told 'Partisano.' The feeling of a country in turmoil, the frontier with Italy undecided, the tenseness generated by the worsening relations with the Soviet Union that ended in Tito's break with Stalin, were all things that interested me. I went back to the country again and again in the next decade, and at one time thought of living on one of the islands for half the year, spending the rest in England.

So Yugoslavia, with its uncertainties, was the country shaped like a broken penny; the central character was vaguely based on George Orwell; the theme, of a country wavering between dictatorship and democracy, and the individual conflicts between 'the tender conscience and the world' absorbed me. Few people, however, have shared my fondness for the book, although in the U.S. Anthony Boucher gave it high praise. Like *Bland Beginning* it has a particular bibliographical interest, in the fact that because Joan Kahn found the ending implausible, I modified some of the later scenes. I am not sure that she thought the final result any better, or that it was.

Donald McCormick comments that Julian Symons is not a spy fiction writer, adding: "Be that as it may, Symons has all the talents of a skilled writer of the genre and he comes very close indeed to being included if only for *Broken Penny*...."[4]

(b) First U.S. edition (1953)

THE | BRO | KEN | PENNY | Julian Symons | [publisher's logo: oval wreath with hand passing torch to second hand] | HARPER & BROTHERS | Publishers, New York [the entire title page is broken by a vertical row of twenty-eight dots down the center]

Size: 8¹⁄₁₆ x 5⁵⁄₁₆".

Pagination: [i-x] [1-2] 3-243 [244-246].

Contents: i, half title; ii, "By the same author: BLAND BEGINNING | THE THIRTY-FIRST OF FEBRUARY"; iii, title page; iv, copyright page: "Copyright, 1953, by Julian Gustave Symons....FIRST EDITION | IC"; v, dedication; vi, blank; vii, "CONTENTS"; viii, blank; ix, quote from Arthur Hugh Clough; x, blank; 1, "1 PLAN"; 2-243, text; 244, blank; 245, colophon; 246, blank.

Binding: Purple paper over boards, black cloth spine stamped in silver: Symons | THE | BRO | [five silver dots] | KEN | PENNY | HARPER.

Dust Jacket: Black and white lettering on purple front and spine, black lettering on white back. Illustration shows three circles—black, white, and orange—with a running man in the white circle. Back has reviewers' comments on *The Thirty-first of February*. Jacket design by Jason Kirby.

Publication Date: October 1953.

Price: $2.75.

Printing: Set in Linotype Electra. Foremat by Edwin H. Kaplin. Manufactured by The Haddon Craftsmen, Inc. Printed in the United States of America.

(c) Second U.K. edition (1973)

The Broken Penny | [rule] | BY | JULIAN SYMONS | [publisher's logo: fingerprint] | A FINGERPRINT BOOK | [rule] | HAMISH HAMILTON | LONDON

Size: 7¾ x 5".

Pagination: [1-6] 7-192.

Contents: 1, half title; 2, "By the same Author" followed by a list of sixteen titles; 3, title page; 4, copyright page: "First published in Great Britain 1953 | First published in this edition 1973 | by Hamish Hamilton Ltd | 90 Great Russell Street London WC1 | Copyright © Julian Gustave Symons, 1953"; 5, dedication; 6, Clough quote; 7-192, text.

Binding: Light green paper over boards, gilt lettering on spine: The Broken Penny JULIAN SYMONS [gilt fingerprint].

Dust Jacket: Green and white lettering on black front and spine, black lettering on white back. Illustration is a photograph of a person in a gas mask, the right eye replaced by a broken English penny. Back has list of other books in the Fingerprint series. Jacket design by Graham Miller.

Publication Date: 1973.

Price: £2.00.

Printing: Printed in Great Britain by Bristol Typesetting Co., Ltd., Bristol.

(d) First U.K. paperback edition

Julian Symons | The Broken Penny | Collins | Fontana Books

Not seen.

(e) First U.S. paperback edition(1961)

THE BROKEN PENNY | BY | JULIAN SYMONS | [publisher's logo: dolphin] | Dolphin Books | Doubleday & Company, Inc. | Garden City, New York

Size: 7⅛ x 4¼".
Pagination: [1-13] 14-232 [233-240].
Contents: 1, half title; 2, blank; 3, title page; 4, copyright page: "The Dolphin edition of THE BROKEN PENNY is I reprinted by arrangement with Harper & Broth- I ers, Publishers, New York I Copyright 1953 by Julian Gustave Symons I All Rights Reserved"; 5, dedication: "FOR Marcus Richard Julian Symons"; 6, blank; 7, contents; 8, blank; 9, quotation by Arthur Hugh Clough in 1850; 10, blank; 11, "I PLAN"; 12, blank; 13-232, text; 233-239, "DOLPHIN BOOKS AND DOLPHIN MASTERS" followed by list of titles; 240, blank.
Binding: Front cover has black lettering on white and gold: A DOLPHIN BOOK [price] I The I Broken Penny I JULIAN SYMONS I MYSTERY. Illustration shows drawing of a globe on a stand with a blood stain covering North America. Black lettering on gold spine: THE BROKEN PENNY SYMONS [publisher's logo: dolphin] C227 [star]. Black lettering on gold back has title, author, review by Anthony Boucher, publisher, logo. Cover design by George Giusti. Cover drawing by Sydney Butchkes.
*Publication Date:*1961.
Price: 95¢.
Printing: Printed in the United States of America.

(f) Second U.S. paperback edition (1971)

THE BROKEN PENNY I [rule] I JULIAN SYMONS I BEAGLE BOOKS • NEW YORK I An Intext Publisher

Size: 7 x 4¼".
Pagination: [i-viii] 1-214 [215-216].
Contents: i, reviews; ii, "Mysteries by Julian Symons" followed by three titles in Beagle editions, four titles to be published; iii, title page; iv, copyright page: "Copyright, © Julian Gustave Symons, 1953....First printing: April 1971" and dedication: "For I MARCUS RICHARD JULIAN SYMONS"; v, "CONTENTS"; vi, blank; vii, quotation by Arthur Hugh Clough in 1850; viii, blank; 1-214, text; 215, "Mysteries I by I RUTH RENDELL" followed by titles, reviews, order information; 216, "Dr. Cellini Mysteries by I JOHN CREASEY I writing as Kyle Hunt" followed by titles, reviews, order information.
Binding: Black lettering on red front: [publisher's logo: bb in white box] 95064 [box rule: A BEAGLE MYSTERY 95¢] I Julian I Symons I The leading exponent and advocate I of the 'crime novel' THE TIMES LITERARY SUPPLEMENT I THE BROKEN I PENNY. Illustration is a photograph showing an open wallet containing letters, money, and notes; a pair of handcuffs; a gas mask; a photograph of a man's face in a frame with broken glass; a rifle; a tear gas canister. Blue and white lettering on black spine: [publisher's logo] I MYSTERY I THE BROKEN PENNY JULIAN SYMONS 8441 I 95064 I 095. White lettering on black back includes reviews, promotional blurb, and list of two Symons novels in Beagle editions, along with printing information and price.
Publication Date: April 1971.

Price: 95¢.
Printing: Printed in the United States of America.

(g) Third U.S. paperback edition (1980)

THE BROKEN PENNY | BY | JULIAN SYMONS | [publisher's logo: torch] | PERENNIAL LIBRARY | Harper & Row, Publishers | New York, Cambridge, Hagerstown, | Philadelphia, San Francisco | London, Mexico City, São Paulo, Sydney

Size: 7 x 4¼".
Pagination: [1-13] 14-232 [233-240].
Contents: 1, half title, promotional blurb, review excerpts; 2, "Other titles by Julian Symons available in Perennial Library:" followed by five titles; 3, title page; 4, copyright page: "THE BROKEN PENNY. Copyright 1953 by Julian Gustave Symons....First PERENNIAL LIBRARY edition published 1980"; 5, dedication: "FOR Marcus Richard Julian Symons"; 6, blank; 7, "CONTENTS"; 8, blank; 9, quotation by Arthur Hugh Clough in 1850; 10, blank; 11, "I | PLAN"; 12, blank; 13-232, text; 233, blank; 234-237, "THE PERENNIAL LIBRARY MYSTERY SERIES" followed by titles and reviews of series authors, including Julian Symons; 238-240, blank.
Binding: Black and white lettering on gray front: P480 [publisher's logo] PEREN-NIAL LIBRARY $1.95 | A HARPER NOVEL OF SUSPENSE | JULIAN | SYMONS | THE BROKEN | PENNY. Illustration is a photograph of a man's lifeless hand lying on concrete amidst shards of broken glass. White lettering on black spine: P480 | [publisher's logo] | THE BROKEN PENNY Julian Symons | $1.95. Black lettering on white back includes genre, author, title, reviews, other Symons titles in series, publisher, logo, ISBN. Cover design by One + One Studio.
Publication Date: 1980.
Price: $1.95.
Printing: Printed in the United States of America; published simultaneously in Canada by Fitzhenry & Whiteside Limited, Toronto.

(h) Fourth U.S. paperback edition (1988)

THE BROKEN PENNY | JULIAN SYMONS | Carroll & Graf Publishers, Inc. | New York

Size: 6⅞ x 4".
Pagination: [i-viii] 1-214 [215-216].
Contents: i, reviews; ii, "Other Julian Symons novels published by | Carroll & Graf" followed by two titles; iii, title page; iv, copyright page: "Copyright © 1953 by Julian Gustave Symons | Copyright © renewed 1981 by Julian Gustave Symons...First Carroll & Graf edition 1988"; v, "CONTENTS"; vi, blank; vii, quotation by Arthur Hugh Clough in 1850; viii, blank; 1-214, text; 215-216, "[publisher's logo: open book with Carroll & Graf written on endpapers] |

FINE MYSTERY AND SUSPENSE TITLES FROM CARROLL & GRAF" followed by titles and order blank.

Binding: Black with blue and white lettering on front: $3.95 | "The most exciting, astonishing and believable thriller | to appear in years."—*The New York Times Book Review* | JULIAN SYMONS | The Broken Penny. Title is white lettering on a gray band. Front has a photograph of a frightened woman clinging to a man standing on a waterfront. White and blue lettering on black spine: Carroll | & Graf | [rule] | Mystery THE BROKEN PENNY JULIAN SYMONS. Blue, gray, and white lettering on black back has excerpts from reviews and a promotional blurb, followed by publisher's logo, ISBN, and distributor.

Publication Date: 1988.

Price: $3.95.

Printing: Manufactured in the United States of America. Reprinted by arrangement with Harper & Row Publisher's, Inc.

A 6   THE NARROWING CIRCLE   1954

(a) First U.K. edition (1954)

THE NARROWING CIRCLE | A Crime Novel | by | JULIAN SYMONS | LONDON | VICTOR GOLLANCZ LTD | 1954

Size: 7³⁄₁₆ x 4¾".

Pagination: [1-4] 5-223 [224].

Contents: 1, half title; 2, "BY THE SAME AUTHOR" followed by five titles, each with a brief reviewer comment; 3, title page; 4, copyright page: "Copyright 1954 by Julian Symons"; 5-224, text.

Binding: Red paper over boards, gilt lettering on spine: THE | NARROWING | CIRCLE | BY | JULIAN | SYMONS | GOLLANCZ.

Dust Jacket: "Gollancz yellow"; purple and black lettering on front, black lettering on spine and back.

Publication Date: 1954.

Price: 10|6.

Printing: Printed in Great Britain by The Camelot Press Ltd., London and Southampton.

Symons's Note: No critic has remarked on the fact that the central idea of this story owes something to Kenneth Fearing's *The Big Clock*. Fearing's magazine syndicate Janoth Enterprises has obvious structural similarities to the Gross empire, and the idea of setting the chief character to investigate a trail that leads to himself is central to both books. So far so derivative, but at least I used the idea quite differently, and I think more interestingly, than Fearing. There are things that, then and now, please me about the book, in particular the not over-stated satire, and the husband-wife relationship. And things I'm unhappy about, like the inability to produce a satisfactory climactic scene, which I know to be a failing transcended only in a few stories. If I were marking my own crime stories I should call this Grade 2.

(b) First U.S. edition (1954)

THE | NARROWING | CIRCLE | by | JULIAN SYMONS | [publisher's logo: flaming torch] | harper & brothers | new york

Size: 8⅟₁₆ x 5⁵⁄₁₆".
Pagination: [i-vi] 1-217 [218].
Contents: i, half title; ii, "by the same author" followed by three titles; iii, title page; iv, copyright page "Copyright 1954, by | JULIAN GUSTAVE SYMONS....FIRST EDITION | C-E; v, half title; vi, blank; 1-217, text; 218, blank.
Binding: Light blue paper over boards, lower-left front cover stamped in gilt: [Harper logo] HB. Black cloth spine, gilt lettering: The | Narrow- | ing | Circle | symons | HARPER.
Dust Jacket: Black and orange lettering on light blue front, black and white lettering on light blue spine, black lettering on white back. Illustration is a drawing of three nooses superimposed from large to small. Jacket design by Thomas Harshman.
Publication Date: April 1954.
Price: $2.75.
Printing: Printed in the United States of America.

(c) Second U.K. edition (1968)

The Narrowing | Circle | [rule] | BY | JULIAN SYMONS | [fingerprint] | A FINGERPRINT BOOK | [rule] | HAMISH HAMILTON | LONDON

Size: 7¾ x 4¹⁵⁄₁₆".
Pagination: [1-4] 5-191 [192].
Contents: 1, half title; 2, "By the same Author" followed by a list of thirteen titles; 3, title page; 4, copyright page: "First published in Great Britain 1954 | First published in this edition 1968 | by Hamish Hamilton Ltd 90 | Great Russell Street London WC1 | Copyright © Julian Symons 1954"; 5-192, text.
Binding: Gray paper over boards, gilt lettering on spine: The Narrowing Circle JULIAN | SYMONS [gilt fingerprint].
Dust Jacket: Pink and white lettering on black front and spine, black lettering on white back. Illustration is a photograph a of noose around three books; a pink circle and black fingerprint are in the upper-left corner. Back has list of other books in the Fingerprint series.
Publication Date: 1968.
Price: £1.25.
Printing: Printed in Great Britain by Northumberland Press Ltd., Gateshead.

(d) Second U.S. edition (1983)

The Narrowing Circle | JULIAN SYMONS | Garland Publishing, Inc. | New York
• London | 1983

Size: 8½ x 5⅞₁₆".
Pagination: [i-xii] 1-217 [218-228].
Contents: 1, Series title page; ii, blank; iii, title page; iv, copyright page: "This edition published by arrangement with the author | Copyright © 1954 by Julian Gustave Symons | Introduction Copyright © 1983 by Jacques Barzun | and Wendell H. Taylor"; v-ix, introduction; x, blank; xi, half title; xii, "by the same author" followed by three titles; 1-217, text; 218, blank; 219-221, "50 Classics of Crime Fiction 1900-1950"; 222-224, "50 Classic of Crime Fiction 1950-1975".
Binding: Light green cloth, black lettering on spine: The Narrowing Circle SYMONS [publisher's logo] Garland.
Dust Jacket: Issued without a jacket.
Publication Date: 1982.
Price: $14.95.
Printing: Printed in the United States of America.
From the Introduction: "Mr. Symons is really himself when he depicts the world of publishing and its natural affinity with crime....Here his understanding of the motives and conditions of murder serves him particularly well and supplies the reader with an intelligent substitute for standard detection." p. ix.

(e) Second U.K. issue (1985)

JULIAN SYMONS | THE | NARROWING | CIRCLE | M | Macmillan

Size: 7¾ x 4⅞".
Pagination: [1-4] 5-224.
Contents: 1, half title and blurb: 2, by the same author followed by 24 titles: 3, title page; 4, copyright page: "Copyright © Julian Symons 1954 | First published in 1954 | Re-issued in 1985"; 5-224, text.
Binding: Black paper over boards, stamped in gilt on spine: Symons [rule] The Narrowing Circle M.
Dust Jacket: Red and gold lettering on black front, black and white lettering on red spine, black lettering on white back.
Publication Date: 1985.
Price: £8.50.
Printing: Printed and bound in Great Britain by Anchor Brendon Ltd.

(f) First U.K. paperback edition

Julian Symons | The Narrowing Circle | Collins | Fontana Books

Not seen.

(g) First U.S. paperback edition (1956)

by Julian Symons | the narrowing circle | [title inside noose] BERKLEY PUBLISHING CORP. | 145 West 57th Street • New York, 19, N.Y.

Size: 6⅚₆ x 4¼".
Pagination: [1-4] 5-158 [159-160].
Contents: 1, excerpt and reviews; 2, reviews; 3, title page; 4, copyright page: "COPYRIGHT © 1954, BY JULIAN GUSTAVE SYMONS....BERKLEY EDITION, MARCH, 1956;" 5-158, text; 159, "A MESSAGE I FROM THE PUBLISHERS I OF I BERKLEY BOOKS" followed by a letter; 160, "YOU WILL ALSO WANT TO READ I THE MAGICIAN I BY GEORGES SIMENON" followed by promotional blurb and reviews.
Binding: Green and black lettering on white front: A starling novel of suspense I by the author of I "The Thirty-first of February" I Julian Symons I the narrowing I circle. Top right corner: BERKLEY I [publisher's logo: trefoil] I BOOKS I 354. Bottom left corner: K [North America with the letters ID in white] I 25¢ I COMPLETE AND UNABRIDGED. Cover illustration shows noose in foreground with the partially clad body of a woman on a couch in the background. Black lettering on blue spine: THE NARROWING CIRCLE JULIAN SYMONS I BERKLEY I [publisher's logo] I BOOKS I 354. Black lettering on white back highlighted by stylized black noose with light blue border includes excerpt and reviews, along with the publisher's logo and printing information.
Publication Date: March 1956.
Price: 35¢.
Printing: Printed in the United States of America.

(h) Second U.K. paperback issue (1956)

The Narrowing Circle I [rule] I JULIAN SYMONS I [publisher's logo: fb in oval] I COLLINS I fontana books

Size: 7⅟₆ x 4¼".
Pagination: [1-4] 5-190 [191-192].
Contents: 1, half title; 2, "Recent Fontana Books" followed by a list of authors and titles and the address; 3, title page; 4, publishing history: "First published by Gollancz in 1954 I First issued in Fontana Books 1956 I Second Impression in Fontana Books October, 1962"; 5-190, text; 191-192, "ALSO AVAILABLE IN FONTANA BOOKS" followed by titles and reviews.
Binding: Cover illustration shows a dishevelled man holding his temple. Black and red lettering on white: "Mr. Symons has excelled himself I in this brilliant story." YORKSHIRE POST I The narrowing Circle I Julian Symons I Fontana Books [vertical rule] 2I6. Black lettering on yellow spine: THE NARROWING CIRCLE Julian Symons [publisher's logo] [two triangles] 746. Black lettering on red, black, and white back includes an excerpt, a review, and publisher. Cover illustration by Stein.
Publication Date: 1956.
Price: 2/6.
Printing: Printed in Great Britain by Collins Clear-Type Press, London and Glasgow.

(i) Second U.S. paperback edition (1961)

THE NARROWING CIRCLE | BY | JULIAN SYMONS | [publisher's logo: dolphin] | Dolphin Books | Doubleday & Company, Inc. | Garden City, New York

Size: 7⅛ x 4⅛".
Pagination: [1-7] 8-198 [199-200].
Contents: 1, half title; 2, biographical note; 3, title page; 4, copyright page: "The Dolphin Books edition of THE NARROWING | CIRCLE is published by arrangement with Harper & | Brothers, New York | Dolphin Books edition: 1961 | ....Copyright 1954, by Julian Gustave Symons | All rights in this book are reserved"; 5, half title; 6, blank; 7-198, text; 199-200, blank.
Binding: Front cover has black lettering on white and gold: A DOLPHIN MYS-TERY 95¢ | The | Narrowing | Circle | JULIAN SYMONS | MYSTERY. Illustration shows drawing of a man with a magenta target superimposed over his face; a running figure is in the bull's eye. Black lettering on gold spine: The Narrowing Circle JULIAN SYMONS | [publisher's logo: dolphin] C | 142 [star]. Black lettering on gold back has title, author, promotional blurb, publisher, logo. Cover design by George Giusti. Cover drawing by Robert Jonas.
Publication Date: 1961.
Price: 95¢.
Printing: Printed in the United States of America.

(j) Third U.K paperback edition (1987)

THE | NARROWING | CIRCLE | JULIAN SYMONS | [publisher's logo: penguin in an oval] | Penguin Books

Size: 7¾ x 5".
Pagination: [1-4] 5-223 [224].
Contents: 1, "PENGUIN CLASSIC CRIME | THE NARROWING CIRCLE" followed by a biographical note; 2, blank; 3, title page; 4, copyright page: "First published by Macmillan London Ltd 1954 | Published in Penguin Books 1987 | Copyright © Julian Symons, 1954"; 5-224, text.
Binding: Black with green spine. White, green, red, and blue lettering on front: [publisher's logo: PENGUIN | CLASSIC CRIME in rounded box rule with black smoking gun in green circle] | [script] The | NARROWING | [script] Circle | Part classic crime puzzle, part horrific | comedy, part urban nightmare | JULIAN SYMONS | 'He is very, very good' —*Guardian*. Cover illustration shows photograph of a woman's compact, powder puff, and open lipstick case beside two mystery paperbacks, a stick figure hanging from a gallows drawn on a notepad, a case file folder, and a length of rope. White and black lettering on green spine: JULIAN SYMONS THE NARROWING CIRCLE ISBN 0 14 | 00.9364 8 | [publisher's logo: penguin]. White, green, red, and blue lettering on back includes Penguin Classic Crime logo, excerpt and promotional blurb, reviews, publisher's logo, genre, price list, ISBN and bar code. Cover photograph by Carol Sharp.
Publication Date: 1987.

THE
PAPER CHASE

by
JULIAN SYMONS

Published for
THE CRIME CLUB
by COLLINS 14 ST. JAMES'S PLACE
LONDON

Title page, *The Paper Chase*, The Crime Club, Collins, 1956, a new publisher.

Price: U.K. £3.95, AUST. $12.95 (recommended), N.Z. $14.99 (inc. GST), CAN. $5.95, U.S.A. $5.95.
Printing: Printed and bound in Great Britain by Cox & Wyman Ltd, Reading.

A 7 THE PAPER CHASE 1956

(a) First U.K. edition (1956)

THE | PAPER CHASE | by | JULIAN SYMONS | [publisher's logo: hooded gunman] | Published for | THE CRIME CLUB | by COLLINS 14 ST. JAMES'S PLACE | LONDON

Size: 7¼ x 4¹³⁄₁₆".
Pagination: [1-4] 5-256.
Contents: 1, half title; 2, brief plot description followed by "By the Same Author" and one title; 3, title page; 4, copyright page: 1956; 5-256, text.
Binding: Red paper over boards, black lettering on spine: THE | PAPER | CHASE | JULIAN | SYMONS | [publisher's logo: hooded gunman] | THE | CRIME | CLUB.
Dust Jacket: Blue and white lettering on black front and spine, black lettering on white back. Back has reviewers' comments: JULIAN SYMONS HAS BEEN DESCRIBED BY THE CRITICS AS "A master of his craft. Sphere"; "One of the most talented living writers of crime stories, Christopher Pym."
Publication Date: 1956.
Price: 10s. 6d.
Printing: Printed in Great Britain, Collins Clear-Type-Press: London and Glasgow.
Symons's Note: The first page is the best!
Author's Note: See also C 4. Horatio Bottomley was the real-life model for Johnny Bogue, the lead character of the novel.

(b) First U.S. edition (1957)

BOGUE'S | FORTUNE | BY | JULIAN | SYMONS | HARPER & BROTHERS [publisher's logo: flaming torch] PUBLISHERS, NEW YORK

Size: 8³⁄₁₆ x 5½".
Pagination: [i-vi] 1-209 [210-218].
Contents: i, half title; ii, "By Julian Symons" followed by five titles; iii, title page; iv, copyright page: " Copyright © 1956 by Julian Gustave Symons | ....FIRST EDITION | B-G | This book is published in England | under the title of THE PAPER CHASE"; v, half title; vi, blank; 1-209, text; 210, blank; 211, colophon; 212-218, blank.
Binding: Light green paper over boards, lower-right front cover stamped in gilt: [publisher's logo] HB. Gilt lettering on black cloth spine: JULIAN | SYMONS | BOGUE'S FORTUNE | HARPER.

Dust Jacket: White lettering on black, green, and blue front wrapping to spine and back; white, black, and green lettering on spine. Illustration is the silhouette of a man and a woman against an open green door. Jacket design by Fred Hausman.
Publication Date: April 1957.
Price: $2.95.
Printing: Set in Linotype Granjon format by Stephen King. Manufactured by The Haddon Craftsmen, Inc. Printed in the United States of America.

(c) Second U.K (Book Club). issue (1958)

THE | PAPER CHASE | [star] | JULIAN SYMONS | [publisher's logo: white gun within black diamond] | THE MYSTERY BOOK GUILD | 178-202 GREAT PORTLAND STREET | LONDON, W. 1.

Size: 7¼ x 4¹¹⁄₁₆".
Pagination: [1-4] 5-256.
Contents: 1, half title and brief plot description; 2, "By the same author" followed by one title; 3, title page; 4, copyright page: "First published by Wm. Collins Sons & Co. Ltd., 1956 | This Edition 1958." 5-256, text.
Binding: Dark blue paper over boards, gilt lettering on spine: THE | PAPER | CHASE | [rule] | JULIAN | SYMONS.
Dust Jacket: Black and pink diamonds on front with a black gun in each pink diamond and a pink gallows in each black diamond. Black lettering on white and pink spine. Same colors are used on back.
Publication Date: 1958.
Price: Not given.
Printing: Made and printed by Litho Offsett in Great Britain at Taylor Garnett Evans & Co. Ltd., Watford, Herts.

(d) Third U.K. issue (1977)

THE | PAPER CHASE | by | JULIAN SYMONS | [publisher's logo: black bell-like dome with white box and letter SH inside] | SEVERN HOUSE | [rule]
Size: 7¾ x 5".
Pagination: [1-4] 5-256.
Contents: 1, half title, 2, blank; 3, title page; 4, copyright page: "First published in Great Britain in 1956 by Wm. Collins Sons | & Co. Ltd. This 1977 edition by Severn House Publishers Ltd | .... ©Julian Symons 1956"; 5-256, text.
Binding: Maroon paper over boards, gilt lettering on spine: THE PAPER CHASE SYMONS [publisher's logo] SEVERN | HOUSE.
Dust Jacket: Black and rust lettering on tan front and spine, black lettering on tan back. Illustration is the silhouette of eight people holding hands. Jacket design by David Pearce.
Publication Date: 1977.
Price: £3.75.

Printing: Printed in Great Britain by litho at The Anchor Press Ltd and bound by Wm. Brendon & Sons Ltd both of Tiptree, Essex.

(e) First U.K. paperback edition (1958)

The | Paper Chase | [rule] | JULIAN SYMONS | [publisher's logo: fb in oval] | COLLINS | fontana books

Size: 7¹⁄₁₆ x 4¼".
Pagination: [1-4] 5-190 [191-192].
Contents: 1, half title and excerpt; 2, "Famous books and authors in the | Fontana Series" followed by twenty-four titles and authors; 3, title page; 4, publishing history: "First published 1956 | First issued in Fontana Books 1958"; 5-190, text; 191, "THRILLING DETECTIVE STORIES | IN THE FONTANA SERIES" followed by four titles and synopses; 192, "ALSO AVAILABLE IN FONTANA BOOKS" followed by four titles and synopses.
Binding: Cover illustration shows a woman in a black strapless sheath being strong-armed by a man with a gun. Black and red lettering on white: The | Paper | Chase | Julian | Symons | Murder | in a | Co-ed | school. Black lettering on yellow band across bottom of front cover: [publisher's logo: black oval with "Collins" in white lettering, a dot above and below the name] fontana books [publisher's logo: fb in oval]. Black lettering on yellow spine: THE PAPER CHASE Julian Symons | [publisher's logo: fb in oval] | 245. White lettering on red: about the book | about the author. Black lettering on white back with excerpt and biographical note; black and white photograph of Julian Symons. Black lettering on yellow band: [publisher's logo: fb in black oval] fontana books [publisher's logo: fb in black oval].
Publication Date: 1958.
Price: 2/-.
Printing: Printed in Great Britain by Collins Clear-Type Press, London and Glasgow.

(f) First U.S. paperback edition (1961)

BOGUE'S FORTUNE | JULIAN SYMONS | [publisher's logo: dolphin] | Dolphin Books | Doubleday & Company, Inc. | Garden City, New York

Size: 7⅛ x 4⅛".
Pagination: [1-8] 9-237 [238-240].
Contents: 1, half title; 2, blank; 3, biographical note; 4, blank; 5, title page; 6, copyright: "Dolphin Edition published 1961 | Copyright © 1956 by Julian Gustave Symons"; 7, half title; 8, blank; 9-237, text; 238-240, "DOLPHIN BOOKS AND DOLPHIN MASTERS" followed by list of titles.
Binding: Front cover has black lettering on white and gold: A DOLPHIN BOOK 95¢ | Bogue's | Fortune | JULIAN SYMONS | MYSTERY. Illustration shows drawing of a man and woman silhouetted in a doorway against a magenta background as they ascend a stairway; man is holding a light. Black lettering on gold

spine: BOGUE'S FORTUNE SYMONS | [publisher's logo: dolphin] | C 290 | [star]. Black lettering on gold back has title, author, promotional blurb, reviews, publisher, logo. Cover design by George Giusti. Cover drawing by Alex Tsao.
Publication Date: 1961.
Price: 95¢.
Printing: Printed in the United States of America.

(g) Second U.K. paperback issue (1966)

JULIAN SYMONS | [rule] | The Paper Chase | Collins | FONTANA BOOKS

Size: 7 x 4¼".
Pagination: [1-4] 5-190 [191-192].
Contents: 1, half title and promotional blurb; 2, "available in Fontana by the same author" followed by six titles; 3, title page; 4, publishing history: "First published 1956 | First issued in Fontana books 1958 | Second Impression, June 1966"; 5-190, text; 191-192, "ALSO AVAILABLE IN FONTANA BOOKS" followed by eight titles.
Binding: White paper. Top half of cover has close-up photograph of a dead co-ed with a pistol beside her head. Rust, pink, and black lettering on white: [rule] | THE PAPER | CHASE | [rule] | Julian Symons | A co-ed school—with a basic | curriculum of nymphomania and murder | FONTANA BOOKS [publisher's logo: THE CRIME CLUB in white lettering on red blood stain] 3|6. Black lettering and tan rules on white spine: [rule above and below title] THE PAPER CHASE Julian Symons | [publisher's logo: fb in oval] | [three triangles] | 1278. Black lettering and rust rules on white back includes review and promotional blurb.
Publication Date: 1966.
Price: 3|6.
Printing: Printed in Great Britain by Collins Clear-Type Press, London and Glasgow.

(h) Second U.K. paperback edition (1970)

Julian Symons | The Paper Chase | [publisher's logo: dog in circle] | CORGI-BOOKS | TRANSWORLD PUBLISHERS LTD | A National General Company

Size: 7¹⁄₁₆ x 4⅜".
Pagination: [1-6] 7-189 [190-192].
Contents: 1, excerpt; 2, "Also by JULIAN SYMONS" followed by list of eight titles in Corgi Books series and one title to be published; 3, title page; 4, copyright page: "Collins Edition published 1956 | Corgi Edition published 1970 | Copyright © Julian Symons 1956"; 5, half title; 6, blank; 7-190, text; 191-192, "A SELECTION OF FINE READING | AVAILABLE IN CORGI BOOKS" followed by a list of titles and order information.
Binding: Brown front, black spine and back. White, yellow, and blue lettering on front: Julian | Symons | The leading exponent and | advocate of the 'crime novel' | THE TIMES LITERARY SUPPLEMENT | THE PAPER CHASE. Upper

right corner: Corgi | Books | [publisher's logo in white on red]. Illustration is a photograph of a stack of currency, a bloody knife, a gold cross on a chain, a parachute harness, and currency in tight rolls stuffed into gold casings. White and blue lettering on black spine: 552 | 08378 | X | CRIME | [publisher's logo: white dog on red circle] | THE PAPER CHASE JULIAN SYMONS CORGI-BOOKS. Blue and white lettering on back includes promotional blurb, review, and price list.

Publication Date: 1970.
Price: U.K 4s (20p.), AUSTRALIA 65¢, NEW ZEALAND 65¢, SOUTH AFRICA 50¢.
Printing: Made and printed in Great Britain by Richard Clay (The Chaucer Press), Ltd., Bungay, Suffolk.

(i) Second U.S. paperback edition (1971)

THE PAPER CHASE | [rule] | Julian Symons | (Originally published as "Bogue's Fortune") | BEAGLE BOOKS • NEW YORK | An Intext Publisher

Size: 7 x 4³⁄₁₆".
Pagination: [1-6] 7-192.
Contents: 1, excerpt; 2, "Mysteries by | Julian Symons" followed by five titles in Beagle Books series; 3, title page; 4, copyright page: "Copyright © 1956 by Julian Symons | ....First printing: June, 1971"; 5, half title; 6, blank; 7-192, text.
Binding: Brown front, black spine and back. White, yellow, and blue lettering on front: Julian | Symons | The leading exponent and | advocate of the 'crime novel' | THE TIMES LITERARY SUPPLEMENT | THE PAPER CHASE | Originally published as "Bogue's Fortune". Upper left corner: [publisher's logo: bb in white box] 95092. Upper right corner: A | BEAGLE | MYSTERY | 95¢. Illustration is the same photograph as A 7 h. White and blue lettering on black spine: MYSTERY | [publisher's logo: white bb in black box] | THE PAPER CHASE JULIAN SYMONS 8441 • 95092 • 095. Blue and white lettering on back includes promotional blurb, reviews, list of titles, publisher, and price.
Publication Date: JUNE 1971.
Price: 95¢.
Printing: Printed in the United States of America.

(j) Third U.S. paperback edition (1980)

BOGUE'S FORTUNE | JULIAN SYMONS | [publisher's logo: torch] | PERENNIAL LIBRARY | Harper & Row, Publishers | New York, Cambridge, Hagerstown, Philadelphia, San Francisco | London, Mexico City, São Paulo, Sydney

Size: 7 x 4⅛".
Pagination: [1-8] 9-237 [238-240].

The Colour of Murder

By

JULIAN SYMONS

Published for

THE CRIME CLUB

by COLLINS, ST JAMES'S PLACE

LONDON

Title page, *The Colour of Murder*, The Crime Club, Collins, 1957, winner of the Crime Writers Association–Best Crime Novel of 1957.

Contents: 1, half title, promotional blurb, review; 2, blank; 3, "Other titles by Julian Symons available in Perennial Library:" followed by list of five titles; 4, blank; 5, title page; 6, copyright page: "Copyright © 1956 by Julian Gustave Symons....First PERENNIAL LIBRARY edition published 1980"; 7, half title; 8, blank; 9-237, text; 238, blank; 239, "THE PERENNIAL LIBRARY MYSTERY SERIES" followed by list of authors and titles, including Julian Symons; 240, blank.

Binding: Black front and spine, white back. Gray and white lettering on front: P 481 [publisher's logo: torch] PERENNIAL LIBRARY $1.95 | A HARPER NOVEL OF SUSPENSE | JULIAN | SYMONS | BOGUE'S FORTUNE. Front illustration is a photograph of the midsection of a man's body on a bed; a kitchen knife is protruding from the stomach, and there is blood on the shirt. White lettering on black spine: P 481 | [publisher's logo: torch] | BOGUE'S FORTUNE Julian Symons | $1.95. Black lettering on white back includes genre in upper left, author and title, reviews, other Symons titles in Perennial Library, publisher, logo, ISBN. Cover design by One + One Studio.

Publication Date: 1980.

Price: $1.95.

Printing: Printed in the United States of America. Published simultaneously in Canada by Fitzhenry & Whiteside Limited, Toronto.

A 8   THE COLOUR OF MURDER   1957

(a) First U.K. edition (1957)

The Colour of | Murder | By | JULIAN SYMONS | [publisher's logo: hooded gunman] | Published for | THE CRIME CLUB | by COLLINS, ST JAMES'S PLACE | LONDON

Size: 7³⁄₁₆ x 4¾".

Pagination: [1-8] 9-256.

Contents: 1, half title and brief plot description; 2, "By the Same Author" followed by three titles; 3, title page; 4, copyright page: 1957, and also dedication "For Michael Evelyn"; 5, "Note"; 6, blank; 7, "Part One [rule] BEFORE"; 8, blank; 9-256, text.

Binding: Red paper over boards, black lettering on spine: THE | COLOUR | OF | MURDER | JULIAN | SYMONS | [publisher's logo] | THE | CRIME | CLUB.

Dust Jacket: White and red lettering on black front, black lettering on white back.

Publication Date: 1957.

Price: 10s. 6d.

Printing: Printed in Great Britain, Collins Clear-Type Press: London and Glasgow.

Symons's Note: In the Fifties I became for a while much interested in the way justice is done, or not done, through the English legal process, and the long trial scenes in this book reflect that interest. In this decade I first knew Michael Evelyn [to whom the book is dedicated], who occupied an important position in the Department of Public Prosecutions, and when in doubt about any legal matter I went to him for advice. He indulged my amateur curiosity about such things as the degree of personal involvement felt by defence barristers with their clients, and in general gave me much guidance in avoiding errors of fact and behaviour. The character of Magnus Newton owes a good deal to conversations with Michael. The book was a considerable success, and won the Crime Writers' Association Award as the best crime novel of its year. At this time my successful crime stories seemed to alternate with very poor ones, and this book was followed by *The Gigantic Shadow*.

(b) First U.S. edition (1958)

the COLOR of murder I by JULIAN SYMONS I HARPER & BROTHERS, PUBLISHERS I NEW YORK [eight rules running vertically fill top two-thirds of title page]

Size: 8⅛ x 5⅜".
Pagination: [i-vi] [1-2] 3-184 [185-186].
Contents: i, half title; ii, "By Julian Symons" followed by a list of six titles; iii, title page; iv, copyright page: "Copyright © 1957 by Julian Gustave Symons I ....E-H" [denotes FIRST EDITION]; v, "NOTE"; vi, blank; 1, "part one BEFORE"; 2, blank; 3-184 text; 185-186, blank.
Binding: Red paper over boards, lower-right front cover stamped in gilt: [double circle with torch and HB inside]. Gilt lettering on black cloth spine: julian I symons I the COLOR of murder I harper.
Dust Jacket: White, black, green, and red lettering on green, white, and red front; black and red lettering on green and white spine; black lettering on white back. Illustration shows a fully clothed woman in high heels lying on a beach; two bright red blood stains are splashed across bottom third of the picture. Back has publisher's comments about seven other titles on the Harper suspense novel list. Jacket design by Julian de Miskey.
Publication Date: 1958.
Price: $2.95.
Printing: Printed in the United States of America.

(c) Second U.K. issue (1985)

JULIAN I SYMONS I The I COLOUR I of MURDER I M I MACMILLAN

Size: 7¾ x 4¹³⁄₁₆".
Pagination: [1-8] 9-256.
Contents: 1, half title and brief description; 2, "by the same author" followed by a list of twenty-four titles; 3, title page; 4, copyright page: "Copyright © Julian Symons 1957 I First published in 1957 I Re-issued in 1985 by I MACMILLAN LONDON LIMITED"; 5, dedication; 6, "Note"; 7, "Part One [rule] BEFORE"; 8, blank; 9-256, text.

Binding: Red paper over boards, gilt lettering on spine: Symons [rule] The Colour of Murder M.

Dust Jacket: Black and gold lettering on red front; black, white, and red lettering on red and white spine; black lettering on white back. Back has excerpts from five reviews of *The Colour of Murder.*

Publication Date: 1985.

Price: £8.50.

Printing: Printed and bound in Great Britain by Anchor Brendon Ltd.

(d) Second U.K. (large print) edition (1988)

JULIAN SYMONS | [rule] | THE COLOUR | OF MURDER | Complete and Unabridged | [publisher's logo: turret of castle] | ULVERSCROFT | Leicester

Size: 8⅞₆ x 5¼".

Pagination: [i-x] [1-2] 3-399 [400-406].

Contents: i, 8 line poem by Janice James on books and reading; ii, blank; iii, half title and blurb; iv, books by Julian Symons in large print series followed by list of three titles; v, title page; vi, copyright page: "First published in Great Britain in 1957.... | First Large Print Edition | published January 1988 | ....Copyright © 1957 by Julian Symons"; vii, dedication; viii, blank; ix, Julian Symons note on blood text; x, blank; 1, "Part One, Before"; 2, blank; 3-399, text, 400, publisher's statement; 401, "Guide to Colour Coding"; 402-405, other titles in the Ulverscroft Large Print Series; 406, further publisher statement.

Binding: Plastic lamination, black and white lettering on front, spine, and back. Illustration shows the ocean and a pier with a gavel floating in the water.

Dust Jacket: Issued without a jacket.

Publication Date: January 1988.

Price: Not given.

Printing: Published by F.A. Thorpe. Set by Rowland Phototypesetting Ltd. Bury St. Edmunds, Suffolk. Printed and bound in Great Britain by T.J. Press (Padstow) Ltd., Padstow, Cornwall.

(e) First U.K. paperback edition (1959)

The Colour | of Murder | [rule] | JULIAN SYMONS | [publisher's logo: fb in oval] | COLLINS | fontana books

Size: 7 x 4¼".

Pagination: [1-6] 7-191 [192].

Contents: 1, half title and reviews; 2, "Famous books and authors in the | Fontana Series" followed by twenty-six titles; 3, title page; 4, copyright page: "First published 1957 | First issued in Fontana Books 1959 | ....© JULIAN SYMONS, 1959" and dedication: "For Michael Evelyn | with much gratitude for his patient | guidance through the legal maze"; 5, note; 6, blank; 7-191, text; 192, "ALSO AVAILABLE IN FONTANA BOOKS" followed by four titles.

Binding: Light blue front, yellow spine, white back; yellow and white striped band wraps front to back across bottom. White and black lettering on front: THE COLOUR OF | MURDER | Julian Symons | Murder breaks the web of fantasy. In band: [two triangles over Collins in black oval] fontana books [2|6 in black oval]. Cover illustration shows a man looking over his shoulder at a retreating woman. Black lettering on yellow spine: THE COLOUR OF MURDER Julian Symons | [publisher's logo: fb in oval] | [two triangles] 343. Black lettering on back includes information about the book and the author and a black and white photograph of Julian Symons. In band: [publisher's logo] fontana books [publisher's logo].

Publication Date: 1959.

Price: 2/6.

Printing: Printed in Great Britain by Collins Clear-Type Press, London and Glasgow.

(f) First U.S. paperback edition (1959)

Julian Symons | The | Color of | Murder | A DELL MYSTERY

Size: 6⅞₆ x 4¼".

Pagination: [1-4] 5-192.

Contents: 1, excerpt and review; 2, blank; 3, title page; 4, copyright page: "Copyright © 1957 by Julian Gustave Symons | ....First Dell printing June, 1959" and Author's note; 5-192, text.

Binding: Black paper. Purple, yellow, red, and white lettering on front. Upper left corner: [purple box with DELL in black lettering] | D296. Upper right corner: 35¢. Yellow lettering: She would never free him, | she said, laughing.... | He could rot with her forever, | in a marriage made in Hell. Red lettering: THE | COLOR | OF | MURDER. White lettering: "Best mystery novel of the year". Purple lettering: by JULIAN SYMONS. Cover illustrations shows the body of a woman with a bead necklace wound tightly around her neck. Purple, red, and white lettering on black spine: [D296 in black lettering on purple circle] THE COLOR OF MURDER JULIAN SYMONS | DELL. Purple, black, and red lettering on white and black back includes title and excerpt. Cover painting by Bob McGuire.

Publication Date: June 1959.

Price: 35¢.

Printing: Printed in U.S.A. Designed and produced by Western Printing & Lithographing Company. Reprinted by arrangement with Harper & Brothers New York, N.Y.

(g) Second U.K. paperback issue (1964)

The Colour | of Murder | [rule] | JULIAN SYMONS | [publisher's logo: fb in oval] | COLLINS | fontana books

Size: 7 x 4¼".

Pagination: [1-6] 7-191 [192].

Contents: 1, half title and reviews; 2, "Recent Fontana Books" followed by twenty titles; 3, title page; 4, copyright page: "First published 1957 | First issued in Fontana Books 1959 | Second Impression, October 1964 | ....© JULIAN SYMONS 1959" and dedication: "For Michael Evelyn | with much gratitude for his patient | guidance through the legal maze"; 5, note; 6, blank; 7-191, text; 192, "ALSO AVAILABLE IN FONTANA BOOKS" followed by four titles, including A MAN CALLED JONES.

Binding: White paper. Top half of cover has close-up photograph of a horrified man staring at his bloody hand. Turquoise, pink, and black lettering on white: Winner of the Crime Writers' Award | [rule] | THE COLOUR | OF MURDER | [rule] | Julian Symons | "The best thing he has done yet." Maurice Richardson | "A triumph." Pat Wallace | FONTANA BOOKS [publisher's logo: THE CRIME CLUB in yellow lettering on red blood stain] 3|6. Tan and turquoise lettering and black rules on white spine: [rule above and below title] THE COLOUR | OF MURDER | Julian Symons | [publisher's logo: white fb in black oval] | [three triangles] | 102. Black lettering and rules on white back includes an excerpt.

Publication Date: 1964.

Price: 3/6.

Printing: Printed in Great Britain by Collins Clear-Type Press, London and Glasgow.

(h) Second U.S. paperback issue (1967)

A DELL GREAT MYSTERY ["T" is a dagger] LIBRARY EDITION | The Color of | Murder | JULIAN SYMONS

Size: 7 x 4¼".

Pagination: [1-4] 5-192.

Contents: 1, excerpt and review; 2, blank; 3, title page; 4, copyright page: "Copyright © 1957 by Julian Gustave Symons | ....Previous Dell Edition D296 | New Dell Edition | First Printing — August, 1967" and "AUTHOR'S NOTE:"; 5-192, text.

Binding: White paper. Gray lettering on white top border: [DELL in box] | 1356 GREAT MYSTERY LIBRARY 60¢. White and yellow lettering in top blue box: JULIAN SYMONS | THE | COLOR OF | MURDER | "A memorably brilliant detective story." | —NEW YORK HERALD TRIBUNE.

Cover illustration in blue box is photo collage of doll's head, dart, heart, crumpled newspaper article about a murder witness, and yoyos in a decorated box. Gray, blue, and black lettering on white spine: 1356 | [rule] | 60¢ | [rule] | FIC | THE COLOR OF MURDER JULIAN SYMONS | DELL. Black and gray lettering on white back and white lettering on blue box on back includes excerpt and review. Cover illustration by Ancona|Gianakos.

Publication Date: August 1967.

Price: 60¢.

Printing: Printed in U.S.A.

(i) Second U.K. paperback edition (1969)

Julian Symons | The Colour of | Murder | [rule] | [publisher's logo: dog in circle]
CORGIBOOKS | A DIVISION OF TRANSWORLD PUBLISHERS

Size: 7⅛ x 4⅜".
Pagination: [1-9] 10-173 [174-176].
Contents: 1, "JULIAN SYMONS" followed by reviewers' comments; 2, "Also by
    Julian Symons" followed by two published titles, one title to be published; 3,
    title page; 4, copyright page: "PRINTING HISTORY | William Collins Edition
    published 1957 | Corgi Edition published 1969"; 5, dedication: "For Michael
    Evelyn | with much gratitude for his patient | guidance through the legal maze";
    6, blank; 7, "NOTE"; 8, blank; 9, "PART ONE | BEFORE"; 10-174, text;
    175-176, "A SELECTION OF FINE READING | AVAILABLE IN CORGI
    BOOKS" followed by list of titles and order blank.
Binding: Black and green lettering on gray: Julian | Symons | The | Colour of
    Murder. Review from *The Irish Times* enclosed in oval garland. Corgi Books
    and publisher's logo in top right corner, 552 08081 0 in lower right corner.
    Illustration is a photograph of a chess piece, playing cards, a bloody rock,
    brass knuckles, a knife, a liquor bottle and overturned glass, a bloody coat
    sleeve (sleeve wraps to back) coming out of a ripped-open parcel labeled
    Exhibit A, and a bloody tin can. Black lettering on spine: 552 | 08081 | 0 |
    CRIME | [publisher's logo] | THE COLOUR OF MURDER JULIAN
    SYMONS. Black lettering on back with promotional blurb, review enclosed in
    garland.
Publication Date: 1969.
Price: 4/.
Printing: Printed in Great Britain by Richard Clay (The Chaucer Press), Ltd., Bun-
    gay, Suffolk.

(j) Second U.S. paperback edition (1978)

[rule] | THE COLOR OF | MURDER | [rule] | Julian Symons | [publisher's logo: torch]
| PERENNIAL LIBRARY | Harper & Row, Publishers | New York, Hagerstown, San
Francisco, London

Size: 7 x 4⅛".
Pagination: [i-vi] [1-2] 3-215 [216-218].
Contents: i, half title and reviews; ii, "Other title by Julian Symons available in |
    Perennial Library: | THE 31st OF FEBRUARY" iii, title page; iv, copyright
    page: "Copyright © 1957 by Julian Gustave Symons....First PERENNIAL
    LIBRARY edition published 1978"; v, note; vi, blank; 1, "[rule] | PART ONE |
    [rule] | BEFORE"; 2, blank; 3-215, text; 216, blank; 217, "THE PERENNIAL
    LIBRARY MYSTERY SERIES" followed by list of authors and titles, including
    Julian Symons; 218, Department of Energy public service message about energy
    conservation.

Binding: Black spine, white back. Gray and black lettering on front: P 461 [publisher's logo: torch] PERENNIAL LIBRARY $1.95 I A HARPER NOVEL OF SUSPENSE I JULIAN I SYMONS I THE COLOR I OF MURDER. Front illustration is a photograph of a woman standing on a bridge. White lettering on black spine: P 461 I [publisher's logo: torch] I THE COLOR OF MURDER Julian Symons I $1.95. Black lettering on white back includes genre in upper left, author and title, promotional blurb, reviews, other Symons title in Perennial Library, publisher, logo, ISBN. Cover design by One + One Studio.
Publication Date: 1978.
Price: $1.95.
Printing: Printed in the United States of America.

(k) Third U.K. paperback edition (1988)

JULIAN SYMONS I THE COLOR OF MURDER [author and title in box rule] I M I PAPERMAC

Size: 7½ x 4⅞".
Pagination: [1-8] 9-256.
Contents: 1, biographical note; 2, "by the same author" followed by twelve titles; 3, title page; 4, copyright page: "Copyright ©Julian Symons 1957 I First published in the United Kingdom 1957 by I William Collins, Sons & Co Ltd I First published in paperback 1988 by I PAPERMAC"; 5, dedication: "For I MICHAEL EVELYN I with much gratitude for I his patient guidance I through the legal maze."; 6, "Note"; 7, "Part One I [rule] I BEFORE"; 8, blank; 9-256, text.
Binding: Plasticized black paper with red spine. White lettering on blue block on front: JULIAN I SYMONS I [red rule bleeds from spine] I THE COLOUR OF MURDER. At bottom: 'SO UNPUTDOWNABLE IT ALMOST MAKES I YOU LEVITATE.' I THE OBSERVER. Upper right corner: [publisher's logo: CRIME FILE superimposed on dagger]. Cover illustration shows a razor blade on a sheet of marbled paper; both have been sliced through. White and black lettering on red spine: 6 I [publisher's logo: CRIME FILE superimposed on dagger] I JULIAN SYMONS • THE COLOUR OF MURDER I [vertically] PAPERMAC M. White lettering on black back includes logo, author, title, GOLD DAGGER AWARD WINNER, excerpt, review, genre, price, ISBN and bar code. Cover photograph by Peter Aprahamian/Science Photo Library.
Publication Date: 1988.
Price: £3.95 net.
Printing: Printed in Hong Kong.

(l) Third U.K. paperback issue (1988)

Same as A 8 k except for the following changes:
Contents: 4, copyright page: "Reprinted 1988" has been added. "Printed in Hong Kong" replaced by "Printed in England by I Richard Clay, Bungay, Suffolk." Cover photograph credit has been deleted.

A 9   THE GIGANTIC SHADOW   1958

(a) First U.K. edition (1958)

The | Gigantic | Shadow | JULIAN SYMONS | [publisher's logo: hooded gunman] | Published for | THE CRIME CLUB | by COLLINS, ST JAMES'S PLACE | LONDON

Size: 7¼ x 4¹¹⁄₁₆".
Pagination: [1-4] 5-192.
Contents: 1, half title and brief description; 2, "By the Same Author" followed by four titles; 3, title page; 4, copyright page: "© Julian Symons, 1958" and dedication: "Again, for Kathleen"; 5-192, text.
Binding: Red paper over boards, black lettering on spine:
THE | GIGANTIC | SHADOW | JULIAN | SYMONS | [star] | [publisher's logo: hooded gunman] | THE | CRIME | CLUB.
Dust Jacket: White and blue lettering on black front and spine, black lettering on white back.
Publication Date: 1958.
Price: 10s. 6d.
Printing: Printed in Great Britain, Collins Clear-Type Press: London and Glasgow.
Symons's Note: The idea of a book beginning with a TV confrontation seemed to me a good one, but after the opening in which the interrogator gets his verbal comeuppance, the book trails off into a rather commonplace and improbable thriller. It taught me not to be seduced by a good opening unsupported by a plausible plot: or at least, I hope I learned the lesson.

(b) First U.S. edition (1959)

THE | PIPE | DREAM | by Julian Symons | Harper & Brothers | Publishers, New York | [publisher's logo: flaming torch]

Size: 8¹⁄₁₆ x 5⅜".
Pagination: [i-x] 1-177 [178-182].
Contents: i-ii, blank; iii, half title; iv, "BOOKS BY JULIAN SYMONS" followed by a list of seven titles; v, title page; vi, copyright page: "Copyright © 1958, Julian Symons | ....This book is published in England | under the title of *THE GIGANTIC SHADOW* | I-I"; vii, dedication: "Again, for Kathleen"; viii, blank; ix, half title; x, blank; 1-177, text; 178, blank; 179, colophon; 180-182, blank.
Binding: Dark gray paper over boards, lower right of front cover stamped in silver: [publisher's logo]. Silver lettering on black cloth spine: THE | PIPE | DREAM | [broken rule in red] | SYMONS | [broken rule in red] | HARPER.
Dust Jacket: Green, orange, and white lettering on gray front and spine; black lettering on white back. Illustration shows man looking furtively back over his shoulder. Jacket design by Saul Lambert.

Publication Date: October 1959.
Price: $2.95.
Printing: Set in Old Style, format by Ernest Haim, manufactured by McKibbin & Son. Printed in the United States of America.

(c) Second U.K. issue (1961)

The | Gigantic | Shadow | JULIAN SYMONS | [publisher's logo: hooded gunman]| Published for | THE CRIME CLUB | by COLLINS, ST JAMES'S PLACE | LONDON A Crime Club reissue, same as A 9 a, with this change on the copyright page: FIRST PUBLISHED 1958 | THIS EDITION 1961 and page 2 "By the same author" is followed by a listing of five titles, not four as found in the 1958 edition.

Price: 10s 6d.

(d) Second U.K. edition (1977)

The | Gigantic | Shadow | JULIAN SYMONS | [publisher's logo: black, bell-like dome with white box and letters SH inside] | SEVERN HOUSE | [rule]

Size: 7¾ x 5⅟₁₆".
Pagination: [1-4] 5-192.
Contents: 1, half title and brief description; 2, blank; 3, title page; 4, copyright page: "First published in 1958 by Wm. Collins Sons & Co. Ltd | This 1977 Edition from Severn House Publishers Ltd | of 144-146 New Bond Street, London W 1 | ....© Julian Symons, 1958"; 5-192, text.
Binding: Maroon paper over boards, gilt lettering on spine: SYMONS THE GIGANTIC SHADOW [publisher's logo] SEVERN | HOUSE.
Dust Jacket: White and blue lettering on front photograph of blue sky and clouds, white and blue lettering on blue spine, white lettering on blue back.
Publication Date: 1977.
Price: £3.25.
Printing: Printed in Great Britain by litho at The Anchor Press Ltd and bound by Wm Brendon & Son Ltd both of Tiptree, Essex.
Symons's Note: This was *The Pipe Dream* in the U.S., a better title.

(e) Third U.K. edition (1988)

THE GIGANTIC | SHADOW | Julian Symons | • BLACK • | DAGGER | •CRIME • [the words Black Dagger Crime and a black dagger are in a box]

Size: 7¾ x 4⅞".
Pagination: [i-iv] [1-4] 5-192 [193-194].

Contents: i, half title and brief description; ii, "Other titles in the Black Dagger Crime series"; iii, title page; iv, copyright page: "First published in 1958 | by | Collins | for the Crime Club | This edition 1988 by Chivers Press | published by arrangement with | the author | ....© Julian Symons, 1958 | Foreword copyright © 1988 by Michael Underwood"; 1, "FOREWORD"; 2, "THE BLACK DAGGER | CRIME SERIES"; 3, dedication "Again, for Kathleen"; 4, blank; 5-192, text; 193-194, blank.

Binding: Black paper over boards, gilt lettering on spine: JULIAN SYMONS THE GIGANTIC SHADOW [publisher's logo] •BLACK• | DAGGER | •CRIME•.

Dust Jacket: Illustration shows close-up of a man's face in green, gray, and purple; large red blood stain covers most of the lower third of the picture, with the publisher's logo in the lower-left corner. White and black lettering on black, white, and red spine. Back illustration is three sheets of note paper pulled from a spiral notepad; list of five titles in the series is hand lettered in black.

Publication Date: 1988.

Price: £8.50.

From the Foreword: "Symons has written extensively in various fields of literature, amongst them poetry....Thus all his books have one thing in common: they are beautifully written....He is a total professional in all his literary endeavours." Michael Underwood.

(f) First U.K. paperback edition (1960)

The Gigantic | Shadow | [rule] | JULIAN SYMONS | [publisher's logo: fb in oval] | COLLINS | fontana books

Size: 7¹⁄₁₆ x 4⅛".

Pagination: [1-4] 5-192.

Contents: 1, half title and reviews; 2, "Famous Books and Authors in the | Fontana Series" followed by twenty-one titles; 3, title page; 4, copyright page: "© JULIAN SYMONS, 1958" and dedication: "Again, for Kathleen; 5-192, text.

Binding: Red, lavender, and blue front, yellow spine, white back; yellow and white striped band wraps front to back across bottom. Black and white lettering on front: The | Gigantic | Shadow | ...of a past | he could never | escape | JULIAN | SYMONS. In band: [two triangles over Collins in black oval] fontana books [2|6 in black oval]. Cover illustration shows a furtive-looking man on the run clutching a box. Black lettering on yellow spine: THE GIGANTIC SHADOW Julian Symons | [publisher's logo: fb in oval] | [two triangles] 441. Black lettering on back includes information about the book and same illustration in cyan. In band: [publisher's logo] fontana books [publisher's logo].

Publication Date: 1960.

Price: 2/6.

Printing: Printed in Great Britain by Collins Clear-Type Press, London and Glasgow.

(g) First U.S. paperback edition (1962)

[two-page spread] [verso:] JULIAN SYMONS | THE | [publisher's logo: stylized globe surrounded by "C"] [recto:] PIPE | DREAM | COLLIER BOOKS | NEW YORK, N.Y.

Size: 7⅟₁₆ x 4¼".
Pagination: [1-6] 7-156 [157-160].
Contents: 1, half title; 2-3, title page; 4, copyright: "First Collier Books Edition 1962 | ....Copyright © 1958, Julian Symons"; 5, dedication: "Again, for Kathleen"; 6, blank; 7-156, text; 157-160, blank.
Binding: White paper; red and green band on middle of front and back; ragged red band on bottom of front wraps to back. Black and green lettering on front: [top left:] AS157V [top right:] 95¢ | The Pipe Dream | A Mystery Novel | Julian Symons | [in middle band:] [publisher's logo: white stylized globe surrounded by "C", COLLIER BOOKS in black below] The story of a man who finds | he can't run fast enough to | escape the past. Illustration on bottom front red band shows black, white, and green drawing of two men fighting in a television studio; third man in background is running toward the scene. Black lettering on spine: The Pipe Dream Symons [in white oval on red band:] AS157V. Green and black lettering on back includes title, promotional blurb, review, publisher's logo, same illustration as front.
Publication Date: 1962.
Price: 95¢.
Printing: Printed in the United States of America.

(h) Second U.K. paperback issue (1967)

The Gigantic | Shadow | [rule] | JULIAN SYMONS | [publisher's logo: fb in oval] | COLLINS | fontana books

Same as A 9 e except for the following changes:
Contents: 1, half title and review; 2, "Available in Fontan [sic] | by the same author" followed by six titles; 4, updated publishing information on copyright page. "First issued in Fontana Books 1960 | Second Impression October 1962 | Third Impression March 1967."
Binding: White front and spine, green back. White band across top has semicircle of black dots with title superimposed on circle and author and review inside. Green lettering with blue shadow: The Gigantic Shadow | ; white lettering with black shadow: Julian Symons | ; [hand-lettered in black] "Brilliant...the usual superb | Symons standard" —*SUN*; across bottom in black lettering: FONTANA BOOKS 3|6. Cover illustration shows close-up photograph of a syringe with a man's face reflected in the glass; the syringe is resting on a pound note with holes punched in it; there is blood on the needle and drops of blood on the currency. Green/blue and white/black lettering on spine: The Gigantic Shadow JULIAN SYMONS | [publisher's logo in green] | [three green triangles] 1494. Hand lettering in black on green back has *Sun* review and excerpt from book.

(i) Second U.K. paperback edition (1970)

Julian Symons | The | Gigantic Shadow | [rule] [publisher's logo: dog in circle] CORGIBOOKS | A DIVISION OF TRANSWORLD PUBLISHERS

Size: 7⅛ x 4⅜".
Pagination: [1-6] 7-189 [190-192]
Contents: 1, reviews; 2, "Also by Julian Symons" followed by seven Corgi Books titles and two titles to be published; 3, title page; 4, copyright page: "William Collins Edition published 1958 | Corgi Edition published 1970 | Copyright © 1958 by Julian Symons"; 5, dedication: "Again, for Kathleen"; 6, blank; 7-190, text; 191-192, additional titles and order information.
Binding: Purple front, black spine and back. White, yellow, and orange lettering on front: Julian Symons | The leading exponent and advocate | of the 'crime novel' THE TIMES LITERARY SUPPLEMENT | THE GIGANTIC | SHADOW | [Upper left corner:] 552 08339 9; Upper right corner: CORGI | BOOKS | [publisher's logo]. Cover illustration is a color photograph of a pair of glasses, packets of pound notes in a torn parcel, a ransom note made by pasting cut-out letters to a card, a key, a baggage claim check, a gun, a television clapboard, small envelopes with white powder spilling out of them. White lettering on black spine: 552 | 08339 | 9 | CRIME | [publisher's logo]. Turquoise lettering: THE GIGANTIC SHADOW JULIAN SYMONS. White lettering: CORGI-BOOKS. White lettering on back includes promotional blurb, reviews, prices.
Publication Date: 1970.
Price: U.K. 4 s. (20p.), Australia 65¢, New Zealand 65¢, South Africa 50¢.
Printing: Made and printed in Great Britain by Richard Clay (The Chaucer Press), Ltd., Bungay, Suffolk.

(j) Second U.S. paperback edition (1971)

THE GIGANTIC | SHADOW | [rule] | Julian Symons | (Originally published in the U.S. | as "The Pipe Dream") | BEAGLE BOOKS • NEW YORK | An Intext Publisher

Size: 7 x 4³⁄₁₆".
Pagination: [i-iv] 1-188.
Contents: 1, excerpt; 2, "Mysteries by | Julian Symons" followed by five titles in Beagle Books series; 3, title page; 4, copyright page: "Copyright © 1958 by Julian Symons | ....First printing: June, 1971"; 5-188, text.
Binding: Purple front, black spine and back. White, yellow, and orange lettering on front: Julian Symons | The leading exponent and advocate | of the 'crime novel' | THE TIMES LITERARY SUPPLEMENT | THE GIGANTIC | SHADOW | [lower left corner:] Originally published | as "The Pipe Dream". [Upper left corner:] [publisher's logo: bb in white box] 95093. Upper right corner: A | BEAGLE | MYSTERY | 95¢. Cover illustration is same as A 9 i. White lettering on black spine: MYSTERY | [publisher's logo: bb in white box] | THE GIGANTIC SHADOW JULIAN SYMONS 8441 • 95093 • 095. White lettering on back includes promotional blurb, reviews, list of titles, publisher, and price.

Publication Date: JUNE 1971.
Price: 95¢.
Printing: Printed in the United States of America.

A 10   THE PROGRESS OF A CRIME   1960

(a) First U.K. edition (1960)

The Progress of I a Crime I by I JULIAN SYMONS I [publisher's logo: hooded gunman] I Published for I THE CRIME CLUB I by COLLINS, ST JAMES'S PLACE I LONDON

Size: 7³⁄₁₆ x 4⅝".
Pagination: [1-4] 5-256.
Contents: 1, half title and brief plot description; 2, "By the Same Author" followed by a list of five titles; 3, title page; 4, copyright page: "© Julian Symons, 1960" and dedication "FOR I KATE FULLER"; 5-256, TEXT.
Binding: Red paper over boards, black lettering on spine: THE I PROGRESS I OF A I CRIME I JULIAN I SYMONS I [Crime Club logo] I THE I CRIME I CLUB.
Dust Jacket: White and orange lettering on black front and spine, black lettering on white back.
Publication Date: 1960.
Price: 12s 6d.
Printing: Printed in Great Britain, Collins Clear-Type Press: London and Glasgow.
Symons's Note: This is one of the half-dozen books of mine that I regard as really successful. The germ of this book is to be found in an actual crime, commonplace enough even in the London of the Fifties, but interesting me because it took place in Clapham, where I was born and brought up. A quarrel broke out between several boys on a bus, they fought, and one of them was stabbed by another. The stabbed boy died, but which of the others had killed him? Partly on the evidence of one of the boys, partly through a very convincing eyewitness, a boy was arrested, tried, found guilty, served a life sentence—in practice, ten years in prison. It now seems almost certain that the positive eyewitness was mistaken, and that the boy convicted was innocent.

    Some of this I knew when I wrote the book but the particular interest of the crime for me was in the way that it showed justice not being done. At the same time, life is not fiction but the raw material of fiction. I shifted the locals of the crime, changed many details, and decided to show the whole thing through the medium of a young reporter on a provincial paper. This proved difficult, because although I have worked for many papers as reviewer, I have never worked in a newspaper office. I was able to arrange this, and for a few weeks "worked" as a reporter at a morning paper in Bristol—or rather, did the kind of thing a young reporter on such a paper would have done, going to Magistrates' Court, a Valuation Court, and so on. I didn't actually write any stories.

THE

PROGRESS

OF A CRIME

by JULIAN SYMONS

HARPER & BROTHERS
PUBLISHERS
NEW YORK

Title page, *The Progress of a Crime*, Harper & Brothers, 1960, winner of the
Edgar Allan Poe Award for the Best Mystery Novel published in America in 1960.

The result was a book which won the Mystery Writers of America Edgar Allan Poe Award as the best book of the year. It had the odd corollary that one of the reporters on the Bristol paper was moved to write crime stories, the first of which was published in the U.K. and the U.S., under the name of Anthony Dekker.

(b) First U.S. edition (1960)

THE | PROGRESS | OF A CRIME | by JULIAN SYMONS | [publisher's logo: flaming torch] | HARPER & BROTHERS | PUBLISHERS | NEW YORK

Size: 8⅟₁₆ x 5½".
Pagination: [i-vi] 1-211 [212-218].
Contents: i, half title; ii, "BOOKS BY JULIAN SYMONS" followed by eight titles; iii, title page; iv, copyright page: "Copyright © 1960 by Julian Symons.... | FIRST EDITION | H-K"; v, half title; vi, blank; 1-211, text; 212-218, blank.
Binding: Black paper over boards, lower-right front cover stamped in orange: [publisher's logo]. Orange and white lettering on gray cloth spine: THE PROGRESS OF A CRIME Harper JULIAN SYMONS.
Dust Jacket: Black, white, and red lettering on blue front and spine; black lettering on white back. Illustration is the silhouette of a man with a knife through him; the book title is printed across the handle and blade of the knife. Jacket design by Lawrence Ratzkin.
Publication Date: September 1960.
Price: $3.50.
Printing: Printed in the United States of America.

(c) Second U.S. (Book Club) issue (1960)

Same as A 10 b except for the following changes:
Contents: ii, "Books by Julian Symons" deleted; iv, First edition notice and Library of Congress information removed from copyright page.
Binding: Changed to light green paper over boards. "Harper Novel of Suspense" blue endpapers replaced by plain white endpapers.
Dust Jacket: "A Harper Novel of Suspense" removed from bottom front of dust jacket, along with the removal of price, issue date, and ISBN. "BOOK CLUB EDITION" added to lower front flap of the dust jacket.

(d) Second U.K. issue (1961)

The Progress of | a Crime | by | JULIAN SYMONS | [publisher's logo: hooded gunman] | THE THRILLER BOOK CLUB | 121 CHARING CROSS ROAD | LONDON, W.C.2

A book club reissue, same as A 10 a, with the above change on the title page, along with this change on the copyright page: THIS EDITION 1961. Binding changed from red paper over boards to a light green paper over boards. Lettering on spine in black: THE | PROGRESS | OF A CRIME | Julian Symons.

Dust Jacket: New dust jacket from that used for A 10 a. Illustration shows a man carrying a knife; three racing motorcycles are in the background; drawing is superimposed on the front page of a newspaper, with the title of the book in the headline position in red, other lettering in black and gray. Black and red lettering on spine, blue lettering on white back. Jacket design by Eisner.

Author's Note: The Thriller Book Club was operated by Foyle's Bookshop, with W. A Foyle acting as president.

(e) Third U.K. issue (1971)

The Progress of | a Crime | by | JULIAN SYMONS | [publisher's logo: hooded gunman in circle] | THE CRIME CLUB | by COLLINS, ST JAMES'S PLACE | LONDON

Same as A 10 a except for the following changes:

Contents: 2, "By the Same Author" followed by a list of twelve titles; 3, title page; 4, copyright page: "First Published 1961 | This impression 1971".

Binding: Red paper over boards, black lettering on spine: THE | PROGRESS | OF A CRIME | Julian | Symons | [Crime Club logo: hooded gunman with THE CRIME CLUB inside a circle].

Dust Jacket: White and orange lettering on black front and spine, black lettering on white back.

Publication Date: 1971.

Price: 70p.

Printing: Printed in Great Britain, Collins Clear-Type Press: London and Glasgow.

(f) Fourth U.K. issue (1977)

The Progress of | a Crime | by | JULIAN SYMONS | [publisher's logo: hooded gunman] | The Crime Club | Collins, 14 St James' Place, London

Size: 7¾ x 5".

Pagination: [i-iv] [1-4] 5-256.

Contents: i-ii, blank; iii, half title and blurb; iv, "By the same author" followed by a list of twelve titles; 1, title page; 2, copyright page: "First published 1961 | Reprinted 1977, © JULIAN SYMONS, 1960"; 3, dedication; 4, blank; 5-256, text; 257-261, blank.

Binding: Red paper over boards, gilt lettering on spine: THE | PROGRESS | OF A | CRIME | JULIAN SYMONS | [Crime Club logo].

Dust Jacket: White and black lettering on red front and spine, black lettering on white back. Crime Club logo in black and gray on lower left of front and base of spine. Back has reviewers' comments on *A Three Pipe Problem* and *The Plot Against Roger Rider.*

Publication Date: 1977.

Price: £2.95.
Printing: Printed in Great Britain Collins Clear-Type Press; London and Glasgow.

(g) First U.K. paperback edition (1962)

The Progress of | a Crime | [rule] | JULIAN SYMONS | [publisher's logo: fb in oval] | COLLINS | fontana books

Size: 7 x 4⅟₁₆".
Pagination: [1-4] 5-189 [190-192].
Contents: 1, half title; 2, "Recent Fontana Books" followed by twenty titles; 3, title page; 4, copyright page: "First published 1960 | First issued in Fontana Books 1962 | ....© Julian Symons, 1960" and dedication: "For Kate Fuller"; 5-190, text; 191-192, "ALSO AVAILABLE IN FONTANA BOOKS" followed by eight titles.
Binding: Black cover, yellow spine, white back. White, yellow, and black lettering on front: "Shrewd, sardonic account of how murder quite | easily gets done. Compellingly readable." SPECTATOR | THE PROGRESS | OF A | CRIME | julian symons | Fontana books [vertical rule] 2|6. Cover illustration shows a man running from a fiery light toward the shadows; he is holding a knife. Black lettering on yellow spine: THE PROGRESS OF A CRIME julian symons | [publisher's logo: white fb in black oval] | [two triangles] | 713. Black lettering on white back includes a promotional blurb and review. Black lettering on broken black and orange band: Fontana | Books.
Publication Date: 1962.
Price: 2/6.
Printing: Printed in Great Britain by Collins Clear-Type Press, London and Glasgow.

(h) First U.S. paperback edition (1962)

THE PROGRESS | OF A CRIME | BY JULIAN SYMONS | [publisher's logo: dolphin] | Dolphin Books | Doubleday & Company, Inc. | Garden City, New York

Size: 7⅟₁₆ x 4¼".
Pagination: [1-9] 10-191 [192-200].
Contents: 1, half title; 2, blank; 3, biographical note; 4, blank; 5, title page; 6, copyright page: "Dolphin Books edition, 1962, | ....Copyright © 1960 by Julian Symons"; 7, half title; 8, blank; 9-191, text; 192, blank; 193-200, list of Dolphin titles arranged by color and genre.
Binding: Brown paper. Front has black and white lettering: C 370 [slash] A DOLPHIN MYSTERY [slash] 95¢ | THE | PROGRESS | OF A | CRIME | JULIAN | SYMONS | WINNER OF THE | EDGAR ALLAN POE | AWARD FOR THE | BEST MYSTERY NOVEL | PUBLISHED IN AMERICA | IN 1960. Cover illustration has stylized drawing of a brown-handled white switchblade with red blood on the knife point. Black lettering on spine: THE PROGRESS OF A

CRIME JULIAN SYMONS | C 370. Black lettering on back includes title, author, and reviews. Cover design by Robert Flynn.
Publication Date: 1962.
Price: 95¢.
Printing: Printed in the United States of America.

(i) Second U.K. paperback issue (1966)

The Progress of | a Crime | [rule] | JULIAN SYMONS | [publisher's logo: fb in oval] | COLLINS | fontana books

Size: 7 x 4¼".
Pagination: [1-4] 5-189 [190-192].
Contents: 1, half title; 2, "Available in Fontana | by the same author" followed by two titles; 3, title page; 4, copyright page: "First published 1960 | First issued in Fontana Books 1962 | Second Impression, January 1966 | ....© Julian Symons, 1960" and dedication: "For Kate Fuller"; 5-190, text; 191-192, "ALSO AVAILABLE IN FONTANA BOOKS" followed by eight titles.
Binding: White paper. Top half of cover has close-up photograph of a frightened woman superimposed over the face of a dead man with blood dribbling out of his mouth. Purple, turquoise, and black lettering on white: [rule] | THE | PROGRESS | OF A CRIME | [rule] | Julian Symons | A Guy Fawkes night to remember... | when somebody knifed a living guy | FONTANA BOOKS [publisher's logo: THE CRIME CLUB in white lettering on black blood stain] 3|6. Purple and turquoise lettering and black rules on white spine: [rule above and below title] THE PROGRESS| OF A CRIME | Julian Symons | [publisher's logo: white fb in black oval] | [three triangles] | 1224. Black lettering and rules on white back includes an excerpt and reviews.
Publication Date: 1966.
Price: 3|6.
Printing: Printed in Great Britain by Collins Clear-Type Press, London and Glasgow.

(j) Second U.K. paperback edition (1969)

Julian Symons | The Progress of a | Crime | [rule] | [publisher's logo: dog in circle] CORGIBOOKS | A DIVISION OF TRANSWORLD PUBLISHERS

Size: 7⅛ x 4⅜".
Pagination: [1-6] 7-189 [190-192].
Contents: 1, reviews; 2, "Also by JULIAN SYMONS" followed by three Corgi Books titles and six titles to be published; 3, title page; 4, copyright page: "Collins Edition published 1960 | Corgi Edition published 1969 | Copyright © Julian Symons, 1960"; 5, dedication: "For | Kate Fuller"; 6, blank; 7-190, text; 191-192, "A SELECTION OF FINE READING | AVAILABLE IN CORGI BOOKS" followed by a list of titles and order information.

Binding: Gray and black paper. Black lettering in upper right corner: CORGI | BOOKS | [publisher's logo: white dog in red circle]. Black and red lettering on front: Julian Symons | The leading exponent and advocate | of the 'crime novel' THE TIMES LITERARY SUPPLEMENT | THE PROGRESS | OF A CRIME. White lettering in lower right corner: 552 09229 5. Cover illustration is a photograph of a glass of liquor; a pearl-handled switchblade; a fire cracker; a wreath of laurel, daffodils, and myrtle; a jacket with an exhibit tag attached to it; a copy of the Evening Standard with headline about Guy Fawkes murder. White and blue lettering on black spine: 552 | 08229 | 5 | CRIME | [publisher's logo] | THE PROGRESS OF A CRIME [vertical rule] JULIAN SYMONS CORGIBOOKS. Red, white, and blue lettering on black back includes a headline, an excerpt, and reviews, along with a price list.

Publication Date: 1969.

Price: U.K 4s (20p.), AUSTRALIA 65¢, NEW ZEALAND 65¢, SOUTH AFRICA 50¢.

Printing: Made and printed in Great Britain by Richard Clay (The Chaucer Press), Ltd., Bungay, Suffolk.

A 11 MURDER! MURDER!   1961

(a) First U.K. paperback edition (1961)

Murder! Murder! | [rule] | Julian Symons | [publisher's logo: fb in oval] | COLLINS | fontana books

Size: 7¹⁄₁₆ x 4⅛".

Pagination: [1-6] 7-190 [191-192].

Contents: 1, half title; 2, "Famous Books and Authors in the | Fontana Series"; 3, title page; 4, copyright page: "First published in volume form in Fontana Books 1961 | © Julian Symons, 1961"; 5, contents; 6, blank; 7-8, "A Note on Francis Quarles"; 9-190, text; 191-192, list of eight Fontana titles.

Binding: Paperback original. Wrapper has green border with yellow stripes at the bottom. Red lettering on white center panel of front; black lettering on yellow spine; black lettering on yellow, green, red, and white back. Back has black and white photograph of Julian Symons.

Publication Date: 1961.

Price: 2/6.

Printing: Printed in Great Britain by Collins Clear-Type Press, London and Glasgow.

Symons's Note: During the Fifties I wrote a lot of stories, and some serials, for the London *Evening Standard*. The cliff-hanging demands of the serials and the brevity of the single stories (2,500 was the maximum number of words) made the development of character impossible, so that ingenuity was their only possible merit. They were published only in paperback, here and in the later *Francis Quarles Investigates* [see A 15], because they didn't seem to me worth putting between hard covers. They have found a number of admirers who rate them, and Francis Quarles the detective who appears in almost all of them, much more highly than they deserve.

Murder! Murder!

JULIAN SYMONS

COLLINS

fontana books

Title page, *Murder! Murder!*, Fontana Books, 1961, a paperback original,
never published in the U.S.

Back cover, *Murder! Murder!*, with photograph of Julian Symons.

A 12 KILLING OF FRANCIE LAKE   1962

(a) First U.K. edition (1962)

The Killing of | Francie Lake | by | Julian Symons | [publisher's logo: hooded gun-man] | Published for | THE CRIME CLUB | by COLLINS, ST JAMES'S PLACE | LONDON

Size: 7³⁄₁₆ x 4¼ ".
Pagination: [1-4] 5-256.
Contents: 1, half title and brief plot description; 2, "by the author" followed by six titles; 3, title page; 4, dedication: "For | GEORGE SIMS" and copyright page: "© Julian Symons, 1962"; 5-256, text.
Binding: Red cloth, black lettering on spine: THE | KILLING OF | FRANCIE | LAKE | JULIAN | SYMONS | [*] | [publisher's logo] | THE | CRIME | CLUB.
Dust Jacket: White and green lettering on black front and spine, black lettering on white back.
Publication Date: 1962.
Price: 12s 6d.
Printing: Printed in Great Britain, Collins Clear-Type Press, London and Glasgow.
Author's Note: Julian described this as "a nice idea, not carried through" and, expanding on that thought, tells of basing the character Ocky Gaye on Horatio Bottomley. "Ocky Gaye in *The Killing of Francie Lake,* whose Plain Man Enterprises was by intention an up-to-date version of Bottomley's *John Bull.*" See C 4 a for more on Bottomley-Gaye.

(b) First U.S. edition (1962)

[square] | The Plain Man | [square] | [double rule] | by Julian Symons | [rule] | Harper & Row, Publishers [dot] New York and Evanston | [rule]

Size: 8³⁄₁₆ x 5¼ ".
Pagination: [i-viii] 1-181 [182-184].
Contents: i, half title; ii, "Books by Julian Symons" followed by nine titles; iii, title page; iv, copyright page: "THE PLAIN MAN. Copyright © 1962 by Julian Symons....FIRST U.S. EDITION H-M"; v, dedication: "For George Sims"; vi, blank; vii, half title; viii, blank; 1-181, text; 182, blank; 183, colophon; 184, blank.
Binding: Three-quarter red paper over boards, lower-left front cover has publisher's logo of torch in box, year 1817 within the box. Black lettering on tan cloth spine: The | Plain | Man | [double rule] Julian | Symons | Harper | & | Row.
Dust Jacket: Patterned lettering on tan and black diagonally striped front, three red fingerprints in lower right, lettering at bottom: A Harper Novel of Suspense by Julian Symons. Black lettering on white spine and back.
Publication Date: August 1962.
Price: $3.50.

Printing: Printed in the United States of America. Colophon: Set in Linotype Granjon, ...Format by Howard Burg. Composition and printing by York Composition Co., Inc., Binding by The Haddon Craftsmen, Inc.

(c) Second U.K. issue (1977)

The Killing of | Francie Lake | by JULIAN SYMONS | [publisher's logo: black, bell-like dome with box and letters SH inside] | SEVERN | HOUSE

Size: 7¹³⁄₁₆ x 5".
Pagination: [1-4] 5-256.
Contents: 1, half title and blurb; 2, "by the same author" followed by a list of six titles: 3, title page; 4, copyright page: "First published in 1962 for The Crime Club by Wm. Collins & Co., Ltd. | This 1977 edition from Severn House Publisher Ltd. | ©Julian Symons, 1962"; 5-256, text.
Binding: Maroon paper over boards, stamped in gilt on spine: the Killing of Francie Lake Julian Symons [publisher's logo] Severn House.
Dust Jacket: Black lettering on front photograph of the right half of a woman's face, black lettering on spine, white lettering on black back.
Publication Date: 1977.
Price: £3.25.
Printing: Printed in Great Britain by Biddles Ltd. Guildford, Surrey.

(d) First U.S. paperback edition (1963)

The Plain Man | [double rule] | by JULIAN SYMONS | [publisher's logo: stylized torch] | [rule] | HARPER COLOPHON BOOKS | HARPER & ROW, PUBLISHERS • NEW YORK AND EVANSTON | [rule]

Size: 8 x 5⁵⁄₁₆".
Pagination: [i-viii] 1-181 [182-184].
Contents: i, half title; ii, "Books by Julian Symons" followed by nine titles; iii, title page; iv, copyright page: "Copyright ©1962 by Julian Symons....First HARPER COLOPHON Edition published 1963 by Harper & Row;" v, dedication: "For George Sims"; vi, blank; vii, half title; viii, blank; 1-181, text; 182, blank; 183, "HARPER COLOPHON BOOKS" followed by twenty titles; 184, blank.
Binding: Beige paper. Front has black lettering in a seven-column newspaper format, with the title as the masthead, author name as three-column headline: The Plain Man | [rule] | A HARPER NOVEL OF SUSPENSE | [rule] | by Julian Symons | [in column:] "An | exceptionally | literate | murder | mystery, | one of | the best | in years." | [rule] | Louis | Untermeyer. | [lower right corner:] [publisher's logo] | Harper | Colophon | Books | CN [slash] 20 | $1.25. Four art spots in newspaper columns: torso, pill bottle, dagger, gun. Black lettering on spine: The Plain Man by Julian Symons Harper | Colophon Books | [publisher's logo] | CN [slash] 20. Black lettering on black cover has title and author as on

front, with four reviews in newspaper columns and publisher in bottom right corner. Cover design by Milton Glaser.
Publication Date: 1963.
Price: $1.25.
Printing: Printed in the United States of America.

(e) First U.K. paperback edition (1964)

JULIAN SYMONS | [rule] | The Killing of | Francie Lake | Collins | FONTANA BOOKS

Size: 7¹⁄₁₆ x 4¼".
Pagination: [1-4] 5-256.
Contents: 1, half title, promotional blurb; 2, blank; 3, title page; 4, copyright page: "First published 1962 | First issued in Fontana Books 1964 | FOR | GEORGE SIMS | © Julian Symons, 1962"; 5-256, text.
Binding: White paper. Top half of cover has close-up photograph of a mirror reflecting the body of a woman wearing a nightgown. Pink, purple, and black lettering on white: [rule] | THE KILLING OF | FRANCIE LAKE | [rule] | Julian Symons | "Engrossing, vitriolic study of a magazine tycoon with | a magnetic personality and no morals." | Glasgow Herald | FONTANA BOOKS [publisher's logo: THE CRIME CLUB in yellow lettering on red blood stain], price of 3/6 at bottom right. Tan and turquoise lettering and black rules on white spine: [rule above and below title] THE KILLING OF | FRANCIE LAKE | Julian Symons | [publisher's logo: white fb in black oval] | [three triangles] | 985. Black lettering and rules on white back includes a promotional blurb and reviews.
Publication Date: 1964.
Price: 3/6.
Printing: Printed in Great Britain by Collins Clear-Type Press, London and Glasgow.

(f) Second U.K. paperback edition (1969)

Julian Symons | The Killing of | Francie Lake | [rule] | [publisher's logo: dog in circle] CORGIBOOKS | A DIVISION OF TRANSWORLD PUBLISHERS

Size: 7¹⁄₁₆ x 4⅜".
Pagination: [1-6] 7-159 [160].
Contents: 1, three reviews; 2, "Also by Julian Symons" followed by two Corgi Books titles and one title to be published; 3, title page; 4, copyright page: "William Collins Edition published 1962 | Corgi Edition published 1969 | © Julian Symons, 1962"; 5, dedication: "For George Sims"; 6, blank; 7-159, text; 160, "A SELECTION OF FINE READING AVAILABLE IN CORGI BOOKS" followed by list of genres and titles and order information.

Binding: Black and blue lettering on gray front: Julian | Symons | The Killing | of Francie Lake. Irish Times review enclosed in garland. Corgi Books and publisher's logo in top right corner, 552 08079 9 in lower right corner. Illustration is photograph of bullets, a telephone receiver, a gun, a bloody switchblade, black fabric, a pink bloodstained bathrobe (wraps to back), a walking stick, a camera, an indian club, and a cigar. Black lettering on spine: 552 | 08079 | 9 | CRIME | [publisher's logo] | THE KILLING OF FRANCIE LAKE JULIAN SYMONS. Black lettering on back includes a promotional blurb, an Oxford Mail review inside of garland, book number, and prices.

*Publication Date:*1969.

Price: U.K. 4s, Australia 65¢, N.Z. 60¢.

Printing: Made and printed in Great Britain by Hunt Barnard & Co. Ltd., Aylesbury, Bucks.

A 13   THE END OF SOLOMON GRUNDY   1964

(a) First U.K. edition (1964)

The End of | Solomon Grundy | by | JULIAN SYMONS | [publisher's logo: hooded gunman] | Published for | THE CRIME CLUB | by COLLINS, ST JAMES'S PLACE | LONDON

Size: 7³⁄₁₆ x 4¹¹⁄₁₆".

Pagination: [1-8] 9-255 [256].

Contents: 1, half title and short plot description; 2, "by the same author" followed by a list of seven titles ; 3, title page; 4, dedication: "FOR SARAH SYMONS | The various kinds of heaven and hell | Awaiting you will not include, I hope, The Dell" and copyright: "© Julian Symons, 1964" ; 5, "CONTENTS"; 6, "The Nursery Rhyme of Solomon Grundy"; 7, "Part One"; 8, blank; 9-256, text.

Binding: Red and black paper printed to simulate three-quarter binding, gilt lettering on spine: THE | END OF | SOLOMON | GRUNDY | JULIAN | SYMONS | [publisher's logo] | THE | CRIME | CLUB.

Dust Jacket: Black and gray lettering on white triangle on pink top half of front, black and white lettering on tan triangle on black and tan striped bottom half of front; white lettering on pink top of spine, black lettering on tan bottom of spine; black lettering on white back. Back has reviewers' comments on *The Killing of Francie Lake.*

Publication Date: 1964.

Price: 15s.

Printing: Printed in Great Britain. Collins Clear-Type Press, London and Glasgow.

Symons's Note: In Blackheath, the attractive London suburb where I lived between 1945 and 1950 in a flat above my friend Roy Fuller, then again from 1955 until 1963 in a villa facing the Heath, there sprang up in the Fifties some admirably designed new housing estates which went under the name of Span. They were later copied, less successfully, by other architects and builders, but at the time the design of Span houses was something new. They were occupied mostly by young executive couples with a child or two who were rising in the world, and if and when they succeeded would aspire to grander things. Span housing in Blackheath is the model for The Dell. Supposing, I said to myself, one put into this pleasant but slightly smug community, an outsider, Solomon Grundy.

Apart from that, the book is evidence of my continuing interest in the processes of English law, and marks the final appearance of Magnus Newton, who was in danger of becoming my abomination, a series character.

(b) First U.S. edition (1964)

THE END OF | SOLOMON GRUNDY | [rule] | by Julian Symons | HARPER & ROW, PUBLISHERS | NEW YORK AND EVANSTON

Size: 8 x 5½".
Pagination: [i-viii] [1-2] 3-241 [242-248].
Contents: i, half title; ii, "Books by Julian Symons" followed by a list of ten titles; iii, title; iv, copyright page: "Copyright ©1964 by Julian Symons....FIRST EDI-TION H-O"; v, dedication: "For Sarah Symons"; vi, blank; vii, half title; viii, blank; 1, "Part I"; 2, blank; 3-241, text; 242, blank; 243, "ABOUT THE AUTHOR"; 244, blank; 245, colophon; 246-248, blank.
Binding: Three-quarter black paper over boards, black lettering on gold cloth spine: Julian | Symons | [black triangle] | THE END | OF | SOLOMON GRUNDY [perpendicular to other words] | [black triangle] | HARPER | & ROW. Front cover has publisher's logo: torch in oval with year 1817 in the lower left corner.
Dust Jacket: Black and tan lettering on tan, white, and black front drawing of British court wrapping to spine. Black lettering on white back. Back has head-ing "Julian Symons" followed by reviewers' comments.
Publication Date: October 1964.
Price: $3.95.
Printing: Printed in the United States. Colophon: Format by Jeanne Ray | Set in Linotype Caledonia. Composed by York Composition Company, Inc. Bound by The Haddon Craftsmen, Inc.
Symons's Note: A book that's been sold a dozen (?) times for film option—but never made!

(c) Second U.K. issue (1977)

The End of | Solomon Grundy | by | JULIAN SYMONS | [publisher's logo: masked gunman in circle] | The Crime Club | Collins, 14 St James's Place, London

Size: 7¾ x 5".
Pagination: [i-ii] [1-8] 9-256 [i-ii].

Contents: i-ii, blank; 1, outline of story and half title; 2, "By the Same Author" followed by sixteen titles; 3, title page; 4, copyright page: "First published 1964 | This edition 1977 | © Julian Symons 1964"; 5, "CONTENTS"; 6, The Nursery Rhyme of Solomon Grundy with a ten-line rhyme; 7, Part One; 8, blank; 9-257, text; 258-265, blank.

Binding: Red paper over boards, gilt lettering on spine: THE | END OF | SOLOMON | GRUNDY JULIAN | SYMONS | The Crime Club | [publisher's logo].

Dust Jacket: Black and white lettering on light blue front and spine, black lettering on white back. Front shows the outline of a single hand in white. Spine has crime club logo at foot. Back has reviewers' comments on *A Three Pipe Problem*, *The Plot Against Roger Rider*, and *The Progress of a Crime*.

Publication Date: 1977.

Price: £3.50.

Printing: Made and printed in Great Britain by William Collins Sons & Co. Ltd Glasgow.

(d) First U.K. paperback edition

Julian Symons | The End of Solomon Grundy | Collins | Fontana Books

Not seen.

(e) First U.S. paperback edition (1965)

The | End | of | Solomon Grundy | by Julian Symons | [publisher's logo: torch] | PERENNIAL LIBRARY | Harper & Row, Publishers | New York

Size: 7⅛ x 4³⁄₁₆".

Pagination: [i-viii] [1-2] 3-213 [214-216].

Contents: i, half title; ii, "Books by Julian Symons" followed by list of eleven titles; iii, title page; iv, copyright page: "Copyright ©1964 by Julian Symons....First PERENNIAL LIBRARY edition published 1965...." v, dedication: "For | Sarah Symons"; vi, blank; vii, half title; viii, blank; 1, "PART ONE"; 2, blank; 3-213, text; 214, blank; 215, "ABOUT THE AUTHOR"; 216, blank.

Binding: Black lettering diagonally across turquoise top right corner: [publisher's logo: bust of stylized figure with red heart with a bullet hole in it] A HARPER NOVEL OF SUSPENSE. Black and blue lettering on white front: P 4011 B [publisher's logo: torch] A PERENNIAL BOOK 60¢ | [column one: promotional blurb] [column two: review] | BY JULIAN SYMONS. | Black lettering inside of illustration of noose with broken rope: The | End of | Solomon | Grundy. White and blue lettering on black spine: P | 4011| B | [publisher's logo: torch] | THE END OF SOLOMON GRUNDY BY JULIAN SYMONS. White and black lettering on turquoise back includes genre, title, author, promotional blurb, reviews, logo, publisher.

Publication Date: 1965.
Price: 60¢.
Printing: Printed in the United States of America.

(f) Second U.K. paperback edition (1969)

Julian Symons | The End of | Solomon Grundy | [rule] | [publisher's logo: dog in circle] CORGIBOOKS | A DIVISION OF TRANSWORLD PUBLISHERS

Size: 7⅛ x 4⅜".
Pagination: [1-8] 9-205 [206-208].
Contents: 1, reviews; 2, "Also by JULIAN SYMONS" followed by six titles published by Corgi Books and three to be published; 3, title page; 4, copyright page: "Collins edition published 1964 | Corgi edition published 1969 | Copyright © Julian Symons 1964" and dedication: "FOR SARAH SYMONS | The various kinds of heaven and hell | Awaiting you will not include, I hope, The Dell"; 5, "CONTENTS"; 6, ten-line poem "The Nursery Rhyme of | Solomon Grundy"; 7, "PART ONE"; 8, blank; 9-206, text; 207, "MORE—TOO GOOD TO MISS... | thrillers by Julian Symons" followed by three titles; 208, "MORE EXCITING CRIME FROM CORGI BOOKS" followed by thirty-one titles.
Binding: Blue front, black spine and back. Black, white, and purple lettering on front: Julian Symons | The leading exponent and advocate | of the 'crime novel' THE TIMES LITERARY SUPPLEMENT | THE END | OF SOLOMON | GRUNDY. Corgi Books and publisher's logo in top right corner, 552 08259 7 in lower right corner. Cover illustration is a color photograph of a hypodermic syringe, a length of pink ribbon, a passport, a love note, an appointment reminder, a broken ashtray, and a gun and ammunition clip. White and turquoise lettering on black spine: 552 | 08259 | 7 | CRIME | [publisher's logo: dog in red circle] | THE END OF SOLOMON GRUNDY • JULIAN SYMONS CORGIBOOKS. White lettering on back includes promotional blurb, reviews, price list.
Publication Date: 1969.
Price: U.K. 4s. (20p), Australia 65¢, N.Z. 65¢, South Africa 50¢.
Printing: Made and printed in Great Britain by Richard Clay (The Chaucer Press), Ltd., Bungay, Suffolk.

(g) Second U.S. paperback edition (1971)

THE END OF | SOLOMON GRUNDY | [rule] | JULIAN SYMONS | BEAGLE BOOKS • NEW YORK | An Intext Publisher

Size: 7 x 4³⁄₁₆".
Pagination: [i-vi] [1-2] 3-214 [215-218].

Contents: i, reviews; ii, "Mysteries by Julian Symons" followed by three titles published by Beagle Books and four to be published; iii, title page; iv, copyright page: "Copyright ©Julian Symons 1964 | ....First printing: April 1971"; v, "CONTENTS"; vi, ten-line poem "The Nursery Rhyme of Solomon Grundy"; 1, "PART ONE"; 2, blank; 3-214, text; 215, "Mysteries | by | RUTH RENDELL"; 216, "Dr. Cellini Mysteries by | JOHN CREASY | writing as Kyle Hunt"; 217-218, "Enjoyable reading from | BEAGLE BOOKS".
Binding: Same as A 13 f except for the following changes: [Upper left corner:] [publisher's logo: bb in white box] 95065. [Upper right corner:] A | BEAGLE | MYSTERY | 95¢. Cover illustration is the same. White and turquoise lettering on black spine: [publisher's logo: bb in white box] | MYSTERY | THE END OF SOLOMON GRUNDY • JULIAN SYMONS | 8441 | 95065 | 095. White lettering on back includes promotional blurb, reviews, list of titles, publisher, and price.
Publication Date: April 1971.
Price: 95¢.
Printing: Printed in the United States of America.

(h) Second U.K. paperback issue (1988)

JULIAN SYMONS | THE END OF SOLOMON GRUNDY [author and title in box rule] | M | PAPERMAC

Size: 7⅟₁₆ x 4¹³⁄₁₆".
Pagination: [1-8] 9-256.
Contents: 1, biographical note; 2, "by the same author" followed by thirteen titles; 3, title page; 4, copyright page: "Copyright ©Julian Symons 1964 | ....First published in the United Kingdom 1964 by | William Collins Sons & Co Ltd | First published in paperback 1988 by | PAPERMAC"; 5, "CONTENTS"; 6, ten-line poem "The Nursery Rhyme of | Solomon Grundy"; 7, "Part One"; 8, blank; 9-256, text.
Binding: Plasticized black paper with red spine. White lettering on blue block on front: JULIAN | SYMONS | [red rule bleeds from spine] | THE END OF SOLOMON GRUNDY. Below box: 'ONE OF THE MOST TALENTED LIVING WRITERS | OF CRIME STORIES' | CHRISTOPHER PYM. Upper right corner: [publisher's logo: CRIME FILE superimposed on dagger]. Cover illustration shows a pair of scissors on top of a tabletop that has a figure hanging from a gallows cut out of newspaper on it; figure, tabletop, and scissors have been sliced through. White and black lettering on red spine: 10 | [publisher's logo: CRIME FILE superimposed on dagger] | JULIAN SYMONS • THE END OF SOLOMON GRUNDY | [vertically] PAPERMAC M. White lettering on black back includes logo, author, title, excerpt, review, genre, price, ISBN and bar code. Cover photograph by Joe Partridge.
Publication Date: 1988.
Price: £3.95.
Printing: Printed in Hong Kong.

UNCORRECTED ADVANCE PROOFS

THE BELTING
INHERITANCE

JULIAN SYMONS

COLLINS

Cover, *The Belting Inheritance*, The Crime Club, Collins, 1975,
the uncorrected advance proof.

A 14   THE BELTING INHERITANCE   1965

(a) First U.K. edition (1965)

The Belting I Inheritance I JULIAN SYMONS I [publisher's logo: masked gunman] I Published for I THE CRIME CLUB I by COLLINS, ST JAMES'S PLACE I LONDON

Size: 7¾₆ x 4¹¹⁄₁₆".
Pagination: [1-8] 9-255 [256].
Contents: 1, half title and brief plot description; 2, "by the same author" and a list of seven titles; 3, title page; 4, Copyright page: "© Julian Symons, 1965"; 5, "Contents"; 6, blank; 7, dedication: "For Gordon Bromley"; 8, blank; 9-255 text; 256, blank.
Binding: Three-quarter black and red patterned paper, gilt lettering on red spine: THE I BELTING I INHERITANCE I JULIAN I SYMONS I [publisher's logo] I THE I CRIME I CLUB.
Dust Jacket: White and blue lettering on black front and spine, black lettering on white back. Back cover has reviewers' comments on *The End of Solomon Grundy.*
Publication: April 1965.
Price: 15s.
Printing: Printed in Great Britain by Collins Clear-Type Press, London and Glasgow.
Symons's Note: The origins here were the nineteenth century *cause célèbre* of The Tichborne claimant, a fine study of which I reviewed and wrote about in *Critical Occasions.* The book is an attempt to put the claimant story into a modern setting, or at least that was in my mind at the beginning. In any event, I found the pros and cons of the claimant's authenticity insufficient to sustain the whole of a novel, and strayed off to other things to support the plot.
So the book must be called a failure. Re-reading it recently, however, when a new paperback edition came out, I was surprised to find myself thinking the first half of the book was very fresh, Christopher an acceptable hero, and the background of Belting and the people who lived there well realized. Later on there are too many coincidences (indeed one in such a story is too many) and the story loses conviction, but it has more merit than I remembered.

(b) First U.S. edition (1965)

The I Belting I Inheritance I by JULIAN SYMONS I [publisher's logo: torch within an oval with year 1817] I Harper & Row, Publishers I New York and Evanston

Size: 8 x 5¾".
Pagination: [i-viii] 1-210 [211-216].
Contents: i, half title; ii, "Books by Julian Symons" followed by a list of eleven titles; iii, title page; iv, copyright page: "THE BELTING INHERITANCE • Copyright © 1965 by Julian Symons I ....FIRST EDITION I ....D-P"; v, dedication:

"To Gordon Bromley"; vi, blank; vii, half title; viii, blank; 1-210, text; 211 "About the Author"; 212, blank; 213, colophon; 214-216, blank.

Binding: Three-quarter black paper over boards, gold lettering on red cloth spine: JULIAN SYMONS   The Belting Inheritance I Harper I & Row • Front cover, lower right corner, has publisher's logo with year 1817.

Dust Jacket: Black and white lettering on red. Front cover illustration shows a hand in the upper-left corner holding a rectangular sign: The Belting I Inheritance. Below the sign are two hands and a skeleton of a hand reaching upward. Black lettering on white back, spine red with black and white lettering.

Publication Date: June 1965.

Price: $3.95.

Printing: Printed in the United States of America. Format by Cynthia Muser. Set in Intertype Baskerville. Composed and printed by York Composition Co., Inc.

Symons's Note: The first (and best) few thousand words were written in hospital while I was having an operation and recovering from it!

(c) First U.K. paperback edition

Julian Symons I THE BELTING INHERITANCE I CORGI BOOKS.

Not seen.

(d) First U.S. paperback edition (1966)

THE BELTING I INHERITANCE I [double rule] I by JULIAN SYMONS I [publisher's logo: N.A.L I SIGNET I BOOKS in an oval with a star dotting the "i"] I A SIGNET BOOK I Published by THE NEW AMERICAN LIBRARY

Size: 7 x 4¾₆".

Pagination: [1-6] 7-160.

Contents: 1, promotional blurb; 2, "Other SIGNET Suspense You Will Enjoy" followed by four titles and order information; 3, title page; 4, copyright page: "Copyright ©1965 by Julian Symons I ....FIRST PRINTING, NOVEMBER, 1966"; 5, dedication: "TO GORDON BROMLEY"; 6, blank; 7-160, text.

Binding: White paper. Black and blue lettering on front. Top right corner, forming two sides of a ruled box: A SIGNET I [publisher's logo: a star wearing a fedora and pointing a gun] MYSTERY • D 3013 • 50¢ [rules top, right side, and bottom to complete box. Inside box: A man returns from the dead I to claim his share in a fortune ... I THE BELTING I INHERITANCE. Outside box: Julian Symons I "Julian Symons is one of England's best I crime novelists." *Roanoke Times* at bottom. Cover illustration shows a bloody clown marionette in a green, red, yellow, orange, and blue harlequin outfit hanging by the neck from a taut blue string; strings to hands and feet are hanging limp. Blue and black lettering on white spine: [publisher's logo: SIGNET in an oval, star dotting the "i"] I D I 3013 I THE BELTING INHERITANCE • Julian Symons. Blue and black lettering and rules on white back includes title, author, review, promotional blurb, publisher.

Publication Date: November 1966.
Price: 50¢.
Printing: Printed in the United States of America.

(e) Second U.K. paperback edition (1967)

JULIAN SYMONS | [rule] | The Belting | Inheritance | Collins | FONTANA BOOKS

Size: 7 x 4¼".
Pagination: [1-6] 7-189 [190-192].
Contents: 1, half title and promotional blurb; 2, "Also in Fontana" followed by eight Symons titles; 3, title page; 4, copyright page: "First published 1965 | First issued in Fontana Books 1967 | ....©Julian Symons, 1965" and acknowledgements: "The author and publishers wish to thank T.S. Eliot and Faber and Faber Ltd., for permission to quote from "Portrait of a Lady"; 5, "Contents"; 6, dedication: "for Gordon Bromley"; 7-189, text; 190-192, "ALSO AVAILABLE IN FONTANA BOOKS" followed by twelve titles, including two by Julian Symons.
Binding: White front and spine, magenta back. White band across top has semicircle of red dots with title superimposed on circle and author and review inside. Yellow lettering with red shadow: The Belting Inheritance | ; white lettering with black shadow: Julian Symons | ; hand-lettered in black: "Keeps the reader agog from Folkestone to Paris. | Exciting...Diverting." Sunday Telegraph; | across bottom in black lettering: FONTANA BOOKS 3/6. Cover illustration shows close-up photograph of the head and strings of marionette in the form of an old woman with a photograph of five pilots and an airplane in the background. Yellowlred and whitelblack lettering on spine: The Belting Inheritance JULIAN SYMONS | [publisher's logo in red] | [three red triangles] 1489. Hand lettering in blue on magenta back has Observer review and excerpt from book.
Publication Date: 1967.
Price: 3/6.
Printing: Printed in Great Britain by Collins Clear-Type Press, London and Glasgow.

(f) Second U.S. paperback edition (1971)

THE BELTING | INHERITANCE | [rule] | Julian Symons | BEAGLE BOOKS• NEW YORK | An Intext Publisher

Size: 7 x 4³⁄₁₆".
Pagination: [i-viii] 1-184.
Contents: i, reviews; ii, "Mysteries by Julian Symons" followed by three titles published by Beagle Books and four to be published; iii, title page; iv, copyright page: "Copyright ©1965 by Julian Symons | ....First printing: April 1971"; v, "CONTENTS"; vi, blank; vii, dedication: "For Gordon Bromley"; viii, blank; 1-184, text.

Binding: Green and black paper. White, black, and red lettering on green front: Julian | Symons | "Especially brilliant...highly enjoyable" | —ANTHONY BOUCHER | THE BELTING INHERITANCE. Upper left corner: [publisher's logo: bb in white box] 95063. Upper right corner: A | BEAGLE | MYSTERY | 95¢. Cover illustration shows a row of toy soldiers, a photograph of five pilots by an airplane, an overseas letter, leg irons, and a marionette. White and turquoise lettering on black spine: [publisher's logo: bb in white box] | MYSTERY | THE BELTING INHERITANCE • JULIAN SYMONS | 8441 • 95063 •095. White lettering on back includes promotional blurb, reviews, list of titles, publisher, and price.
Publication Date: April 1971.
Price: 95¢.
Printing: Printed in the United States of America.

(g) Third U.S. paperback edition (1979)

THE BELTING | INHERITANCE | [rule] | Julian Symons | [publisher's logo: torch] | PERENNIAL LIBRARY | Harper & Row, Publishers | New York, Hagerstown, San Francisco, London

Size: 7 x 4⅛".
Pagination: [i-viii] 1-184.
Contents: i, half title and reviews; ii, "Other titles by Julian Symons available in | Perennial Library:" followed by three titles; iii, title page; iv, copyright page: "Copyright ©1965 by Julian Symons. | ....First PERENNIAL LIBRARY edition published 1979"; v, "CONTENTS"; vi, blank; vii, dedication: "For Gordon Bromley"; viii, blank; 1-184, text.
Binding: Black and white paper. Gray and white lettering on front: P468 [publisher's logo: torch} PERENNIAL LIBRARY $1.95 | A HARPER NOVEL OF SUSPENSE | JULIAN | SYMONS | THE BELTING | INHERITANCE. Cover illustration shows Punch and Judy puppets facing each other with the skeleton of a hand in between them. White lettering on black spine: P468 | [publisher's logo: torch] | THE BELTING INHERITANCE Julian Symons | $1.95. Black lettering on white back includes genre, author, title, promotional blurb, reviews, list of titles, publisher, logo, ISBN. Cover design by One + One Studio.
Publication Date: 1979.
Price: $1.95.
Printing: Printed in the United States of America.

(h) Third U.K. paperback edition (1989)

JULIAN SYMONS | THE BELTING | INHERITANCE [author and title in box rule] | M | PAPERMAC

Size: 7½ x 4⅞".

Pagination: [1-8] 9-254 [255-256].

Contents: 1, half title and biographical note; 2, "by the same author" followed by fourteen titles; 3, title page; 4, copyright page: "Copyright ©Julian Symons 1965 | ....First published in the United Kingdom 1965 by | The Crime Club, Collins | First published in paperback 1989 by | PAPERMAC"; 5, dedication, "For Gordon Bromley"; 6, "Acknowledgments | The author and publisher wish to thank T.S. | Eliot and Faber and Faber Ltd. for permission | to quote from 'Portrait of a Lady'"; 7, "Contents"; 8, blank; 9-255, text; 256, "Other titles available in Papermac Crime File" followed by twenty-two titles (one by Julian Symons), and order information.

Binding: Plasticized black paper with red spine. White lettering on blue block on front: JULIAN | SYMONS | [red rule bleeds from spine] | THE BELTING INHERITANCE. Upper right corner: [publisher's logo: CRIME FILE superimposed on dagger]. Cover illustration shows a photograph of a marionette collapsed on a stage; a jigsaw puzzle-shaped piece is missing from the red curtain in the background. White and black lettering on red spine: 24 | [publisher's logo: CRIME FILE superimposed on dagger] | JULIAN SYMONS • THE BELTING INHERITANCE | [vertically] PAPERMAC M. White lettering on black back includes logo, author, title, excerpt, reviews, genre, price, ISBN and bar code. Cover photograph by Joe Partridge.

Publication Date: 1989.

Price: £3.99.

Printing: Printed in Hong Kong.

A 15   FRANCIS QUARLES INVESTIGATES   1965

(a) First U.K. edition (1965)

Julian Symons | [rule] | FRANCIS | QUARLES | INVESTIGATES | [publisher's logo: panther's head inside double circle] | A Panther Book

Size: 6¹⁵⁄₁₆ x 4⅜".

Pagination: [1-6] 7-125 [126-128].

Contents: 1, brief plot description; 2, blank; 3, title page; 4, copyright page: "This collection first published by | Panther Books Limited as *Francis | Quarles Investigates* July 1965. Copyright ©Julian Symons 1960, 1961, 1965"; 5, "CONTENTS"; 6, blank; 7-125, text; 126-127, "PANTHER BOOKS"; 128, "Famous authors in Panther Books".

Binding: Paperbound in light blue and black with white and blue lettering. Front cover has light blue border; upper half is black with publisher's logo in upper right corner; lower half is illustrated with a picture of a desk blotter covered with photographs, newspapers, and a magnifying glass. Spine and back cover are light blue with black lettering.

Publication: July 1965.

Price: 2'6.

Printing: Printed in Great Britain by Cox & Wyman Ltd., London, Reading and Fakenham, and published by Panther Books Ltd., 108 Brompton Road, London, S.W.3.

Symons's Note: [See A 11.]

A 16   THE JULIAN SYMONS OMNIBUS   1967

(a) First U.K. edition (1967)

THE | JULIAN SYMONS | OMNIBUS | WITH AN INTRODUCTION | BY THE AUTHOR | Published for | THE CRIME CLUB | by COLLINS, ST JAMES'S PLACE | LONDON

Size: 7⅝ x 5".

Pagination: [i-vi] vii-xi [xii, 1-2] 3-216 [3-4] 5-256 [3-8] 9-255 [256].

Contents: i, half title; ii, blank; iii, title page; iv, copyright page: "©this edition Julian Symons 1967 | *The 31st of February* was first published in 1950 | *The Progress of a Crime* was first published in 1960 | *The End of Solomon Grundy* was first published in 1964"; v, "Contents"; vi, blank; vii-xi, "Introduction: Realism and the Crime Novel" by Julian Symons; xii, blank; 1, brief plot introduction for *The 31st of February*; 2, dedication: "TO KATHLEEN"; 3-216, text; 3, half title and brief plot introduction for *The Progress of a Crime*; 4, dedication: "FOR KATE FULLER"; 5-256, text; 3, half title and brief plot description for *The End of Solomon Grundy*; 4, dedication: "For Sarah Symons | The various kinds of heaven and hell | Awaiting you will not include, I hope, The Dell"; 5, "CONTENTS"; 6, poem of Solomon Grundy; 7, "Part One"; 8, blank; 9-256, text.

Binding: Green paper over boards, gilt lettering on spine: The Julian | SYMONS OMNIBUS | CRIME CLUB.

Dust Jacket: Black, light blue, and white lettering on dark green. Back has black and white photograph of Julian Symons by Jerry Bauer.

Publication Date: 1967.

Price: 21s.

Printing: Printed in Great Britain by Collins Clear-Type Press, London and Glasgow.

A 17   THE MAN WHO KILLED HIMSELF   1967

(a) First U.K. edition (1967)

THE MAN | WHO KILLED | HIMSELF | JULIAN SYMONS | [publishers logo: hooded gunman] | PUBLISHED FOR | THE CRIME CLUB | by Collins, ST JAMES'S PLACE | LONDON

Size: 7⅛ x 4½".

Pagination: [1-8] 9-223 [224].

Contents: 1, half title and brief plot description; 2, "previous works" followed by a list of eight titles; 3, title page; 4, copyright page: "© Julian Symons 1967"; 5, dedication: "For George Hardinge"; 6, note thanking Mr. A.J. Nathan of L. and H. Nathan for theatrical advice; 7, "PART ONE | Before the Act"; 8, blank; 9-223, text; 224, blank.

Binding: Red paper over boards, gilt lettering on spine: THE | MAN | WHO | KILLED | HIMSELF | JULIAN | SYMONS | [publisher's logo] | THE | CRIME | CLUB.

Dust Jacket: White and green lettering on blue background. Front has a photograph of a man's face. White lettering in lower-right corner: Crime Club Choice. Symons's note on this dust jacket: I complained bitterly about this jacket!

Publication Date: 1967.

Price: 16s.

Printing: Printed in Great Britain by Collins Clear-Type Press, London and Glasgow.

Symons's Note: A novelist's strategies, the approaches he makes to his material, change with the years; even the material changes, or seems to him to do so, those raw shapes of life he is trying to coerce into a pattern. The crime novel must be an inferior article generally to the novel (the distinction, and the inferiority, resting in the crime novel's inevitable sensationalism), but the need for a changed strategy in approaching it is no less for that reason. There is a moment when one realises that the old kind of plotting won't do, that the order which had seemed to serve well over a number of books no longer satisfies.

So, halfway through the Sixties, I realised—less consciously than I'm putting it down here—that I wanted to write something more loosely constructed, giving scope for a more casual interweaving of characters and perhaps for an increased depth in considering them. I had done with novels about the police and the administration of justice and had got Horatio Bottomley out of my system. These three *Man Who...* stories [A17, A18, A19] are the result, books in which there is no puzzle to be solved, but an attempt to show the social ironies of urban life. They are all emphatically books about town life and people, seen realistically although with a touch of exaggeration. I hope they have their ingenuities, but they are basically sophisticated comedies of the way crime was committed, or might be committed, by such people in that decade. Some passages in them—the death of Claire in *The Man Who Killed Himself*, the dinner party in *The Man Who Lost His Wife*—seem to me as good as anything I have written. With these three books completed I appear to have worked out the vein, and have never returned to it.

(b) First U.S. edition (1967)

The | Man | Who | Killed | Himself [at left margin] | by Julian Symons | HARPER & ROW, PUBLISHERS | NEW YORK | AND | EVANSTON [at right margin]

Size: 8 x 5⅜".

Pagination: [i-vi] [1-2] 3-186.

Contents: i, half title; ii, "Books by Julian Symons" with list of twelve titles; iii, title
page; iv, copyright page: "Copyright ©1967 by Julian Symons | ....FIRST EDI-
TION | ....C-R"; v, "NOTE" thanking Mr. A.J. Nathan of L. and H. Nathan; vi,
blank; 1, "PART ONE | BEFORE THE ACT"; 2, blank; 3-186, text.

Binding: Red paper over boards. Publisher's logo stamped in lower-right front
cover in silver. Silver lettering on black spine: The Man Who Killed Himself |
[printer's flower] [rule] | Julian Symons | HARPER & ROW.

Dust Jacket: Black lettering on white background. Title forms an arch at the top
with author's name underneath; an illustration of a man wearing a purple
jacket and striped trousers and carrying a briefcase is in the center; a black bow
is below the illustration; black lettering arches upward at the bottom: A Harper
Novel of Suspense. Back has reviewers' comments, spine lettering in black on
white.

Publication Date: April 1967.

Price: $4.50.

Printing: Printed in the United States of America.

(c) First U.K. paperback edition

Julian Symons | THE MAN WHO KILLED HIMSELF | Corgi Books

Not seen.

(d) First U.S. paperback edition (1967)

Julian Symons | THE MAN WHO | KILLED HIMSELF | POPULAR LIBRARY •
NEW YORK

Size: 6⅞ x 4¼".

Pagination: [1-6] 7-141 [142-144].

Contents: 1, "THE MAN WHO | KILLED HIMSELF IS ..." followed by reviews;
2, blank; 3, title page; 4, copyright page: "POPULAR LIBRARY EDITION |
Copyright ©1967 by Julian Symons" and note thanking A.J. Nathan for infor-
mation; 5, "PART ONE | [three flowers] | BEFORE THE ACT"; 6, blank; 7-
141, text; 142-143, order blanks for other titles; 144, blank.

Binding: Black paper. White and black lettering on front. Upper left corner: [pub-
lisher's logo: white pine tree on red circle] 445-02476-060. Upper right corner:
60¢. Black lettering in red box: [publisher's logo: gun] A JOAN KAHN -
HARPER NOVEL OF SUSPENSE. White lettering: Julian Symons | THE MAN
WHO | KILLED HIMSELF | A brilliant novel of high-tension terror— | of a
man who devised the perfect murder... | "THE BEST MYSTERY OF THIS
YEAR AND A FEW OTHERS AS WELL" | —Stanley Ellin. Cover illustration
shows a bearded man with a collage of scenes superimposed on his head: the
same man clean shaven; the same man, clean shaven, embracing a blonde; a
brunette in a seductive pose; and a gun being fired. White and yellow lettering

on black spine: [publisher's logo: pine tree in red circle] I POPULAR I LIBRARY I THE MAN WHO KILLED HIMSELF Julian Symons 445-02476 -060. Yellow, white, and black lettering on back includes a promotional blurb, reviews, publisher, logo.
Publication Date: 1967.
Price: 60¢.
Printing: Printed in the United States of America.

(e) Second U.S. paperback edition (1977)

Julian Symons I The Man Who Killed I Himself I Penguin Books

Size: 7⅟₁₆ x 4¾₆".
Pagination: [1-8] 9-167 [168-176].
Contents: 1, "Penguin Crime Fiction I Editor: Julian Symons I The Man Who Killed Himself" followed by a biographical note; 2, blank; 3, title page; 4, copyright page: "First published in the United States of America I by Harper & Row, Publishers, Inc., 1967 I First published in Great Britain I by William Collins Sons & Co in their Crime Club 1967 I ....Published in Penguin Books 1977 I Copyright ©Julian Symons, 1967"; 5, dedication: "For George Hardinge"; 6, note thanking A.J. Nathan for information; 7, "PART ONE I Before the Act"; 8, blank; 9-167, text; 168, blank; 169, "More about Penguins I and Pelicans" followed by information and logo; 170-176, information about individual Penguin titles.
Binding: White with green spine. Black and magenta lettering: JULIAN SYMONS I THE MAN WHO KILLED HIMSELF. Green lettering in upper right corner: [publisher's logo: penguin in green circle] I CRIME. Cover illustration is a photograph of a bearded man wrapped in a shroud and lying in a pink satin-lined casket; the man is winking at the camera. White and black lettering on green spine: JULIAN SYMONS THE MAN WHO KILLED HIMSELF ISBN 0 14 I 00.4143 5 I [publisher's logo: penguin in green circle] I CRIME. Black lettering on white back includes promotional blurb and reviews, prices, genre, ISBN. Logo in upper right corner. Cover photograph by Philip Webb.
Publication Date: 1977.
Price: U.K. 70p, Canada $1.95, U.S.A. $1.95.
Printing: Printed in the United States of America by Offset Paperback Mfrs., Inc., Dallas, Pennsylvania. Set in Monotype Plantin.

A 18   THE MAN WHOSE DREAMS CAME TRUE   1968

(a) First U.K. edition (1968)

JULIAN SYMONS I The Man Whose I Dreams Came True I [publisher's logo: hooded gunman inside circle] I PUBLISHED FOR I The Crime Club I BY COLLINS, ST JAMES'S, LONDON I 1968

Size: 7¹¹⁄₁₆ x 4⅞".
Pagination: [1-8] 9-255 [256].
Contents: 1, half title and brief plot description; 2, "previous works" with list of nine title; 3, title page; 4, copyright page: "© Julian Symons 1968"; 5, "Contents"; 6, blank; 7, "PART ONE | Misfortunes of a Young Man"; 8, blank; 9-255, text; 256, blank.
Binding: Light blue paper over boards. Gilt lettering on spine: THE MAN | WHOSE | DREAMS | CAME TRUE | JULIAN | SYMONS | [publisher's logo].
Dust Jacket: Black lettering on gray background. Illustration is a photograph of a white ceramic bust with photographs covering the cranium and a bloody hammer leaning against it. Jacket design by George Coral.
Publication Date: 1968.
Price: 21s.
Printing: Printed in Great Britain Collins Clear-Type Press London and Glasgow.
Symons's Note: [See A 17.]

(b) First U.S. edition (1969)

THE MAN WHOSE | DREAMS | CAME TRUE | by Julian Symons | HARPER & ROW, PUBLISHERS | New York and Evanston

Size: 8¹⁄₁₆ x 5⅜".
Pagination: [i-iv] [1-3] 4-229 [230-234].
Contents: i, half title; ii, "Books by Julian Symons" with list of thirteen titles; iii, title page; iv, copyright page: "Copyright ©1968 by Julian Symons | ....FIRST U.S. EDITION | ....A-T"; 1, "ONE Misfortunes of | a Young Man"; 2, blank; 3-229, text; 230, blank; 231, colophon; 232-234, blank.
Binding: Three-quarter tan paper, lower-right front cover stamped in black: [torch in box, year 1817 below box]. Gilt lettering on black cloth spine: SYMONS | THE MAN WHOSE | DREAMS CAME TRUE | HARPER | & ROW.
Dust Jacket: Purple and black lettering on white front. Front illustration shows three circular images in purple and yellow and a roulette wheel on a purple background. Purple and black lettering on white and purple spine. Black lettering on white back. Back has reviewers' comments on *The Man Who Killed Himself.* Jacket design by David Holzman.
Publication Date: April 1969.
Price: $4.95.
Printing: Colophon page: Format by Vivian Ostrow. Set in 11|13 Granjon. Composed, printed and bound by The Haddon Craftsmen, Inc. Printed in the United States of America.

(c) First U.S. paperback edition (1968)

THE MAN WHOSE | DREAMS CAME TRUE | [rule] JULIAN SYMONS [rule] | POPULAR LIBRARY • NEW YORK

Size: 6⅞ x 4¼".
Pagination: [1-6] 7-191 [192].
Contents: 1, reviews; 2, blank; 3, title page; 4, copyright page: "POPULAR LIBRARY EDITION | Copyright ©1968 by Julian Symons"; 5, "ONE | [rule] | Misfortunes of | a Young Man"; 6, blank; 7-191; 192, order blank for other titles.
Binding: Black paper. White lettering over cover illustration: [publisher's logo: pine tree in blue oval] 445-01390-075 | [publisher's logo: gun] A JOAN KAHN - HARPER NOVEL OF SUSPENSE | [rule] | THE MAN WHOSE | DREAMS CAME TRUE | [rule] JULIAN SYMONS [rule] | A man's dream becomes a lethal nightmare. Yellow lettering in top right corner: 75¢. Cover illustration shows a couple throwing a body over the side of a boat. White lettering on black spine: [publisher's logo: pine tree in blue oval] | POPULAR LIBRARY | THE MAN WHOSE DREAMS CAME TRUE Julian Symons 445-01390-075. White lettering on back includes promotional blurb, review, publisher, logo.
Publication Date: 1968.
Price: 75¢.
Printing: Printed in the United States of America.

(d) First U.K. paperback edition (1977)

Julian Symons | The Man Whose | Dreams Came True | Penguin Books

Size: 7⅛ x 4⅜".
Pagination: [1-8] 9-236 [237-240].
Contents: 1, "Penguin Crime Fiction | Editor: Julian Symons | The Man Whose Dreams Came True" followed by a biographical note; 2, blank; 3, title page; 4, copyright page: "Published in Penguin Books 1977 | Copyright ©Julian Symons, 1968"; 5, "Contents"; 6, blank; 7, "PART ONE | Misfortunes of a Young Man"; 8, blank; 9-237, text; 238, blank; 239, "More about Penguins | and Pelicans" followed by information and logo; 240, blank.
Binding: White with green spine. Black and orange lettering: JULIAN SYMONS | THE MAN WHOSE DREAMS | CAME TRUE. Upper right corner: [publisher's logo: penguin in green circle] | CRIME. Cover illustration is a photograph of a woman with an armload of bank notes. White and black lettering on green spine: JULIAN SYMONS THE MAN WHOSE DREAMS CAME TRUE ISBN 0 14 | 00.4347 0 | [publisher's logo: penguin in green circle] | CRIME. Black lettering on white back includes promotional blurb and reviews, prices, genre, ISBN. Logo in upper right corner. Cover photograph by Philip Webb.
Publication Date: 1977.
Price: U.K. 75p, Canada $1.95, U.S.A. $1.95.
Printing: Made and printed in Great Britain by Richard Clay (The Chaucer Press) Ltd, Bungay, Suffolk. Set in Monotype Plantin.

A 19   THE MAN WHO LOST HIS WIFE   1970

(a) First U.K. edition (1970)

The Man Who I Lost His Wife I [rule] I Julian Symons I [publisher's logo: hooded gunman inside circle] I The Crime Club I Collins, 14 St. James's Place, London

Size: 7¾ x 4⅞".
Pagination: [1-6] 7-222 [223-224].
Contents: 1, half title and brief plot description; 2, "by the same author" with list of ten titles; 3, title page; 4, copyright page: "© Julian Symons, 1970"; 5-6, contents page; 7-222, text; 223-224, blank.
Binding: Red paper over boards, gilt lettering on spine: THE I MAN I WHO I LOST I HIS I WIFE I JULIAN I SYMONS I [publisher's logo].
Dust Jacket: Black and white lettering on purple front and spine. Illustration on bottom half of front shows three suitcases: one has a picture of a woman on it, and one has the round, green Collins Crime Club emblem on it. Black lettering on white back. Back has reviewers' comments on *The Man Whose Dreams Came True*. Spine has black and white lettering with green Crime Club emblem at the bottom.
Publication Date: 1970.
Price: 25s.
Printing: Printed in Great Britain Collins Clear-Type Press London and Glasgow.
Symons's Note: [See A 17.]

(b) First U.S. edition (1971)

THE I MAN I WHO I LOST I HIS I WIFE I [printer's logo of two hands with finger pointing to the right] I Julian Symons I HARPER & ROW, PUBLISHERS I NEW YORK AND EVANSTON I [publisher's logo: torch in box, year 1817 below box]

Size: 8¹⁄₁₆ x 5⁷⁄₁₆".
Pagination: [i-vi] [1-3] 4-214 [215-218].
Contents: i-ii, blank; iii, half title; iv, "Books by Julian Symons" followed by a list of fourteen titles; v, title page; vi, copyright page: "Copyright © 1970 by Julian Symons I ....FIRST U.S. EDITION" ; 1, "Part One [broken rule] Wife Going"; 2, blank; 3-214, text; 215, colophon; 216-218, blank.
Binding: Three-quarter purple paper, lower-right front cover blind stamped: [publisher's logo]. Silver lettering on brown cloth spine: THE MAN WHO LOST HIS WIFE I JULIAN SYMONS I HARPER & ROW.
Dust Jacket: Cream background with black lettering on front, spine, and back. Illustration of a framed wedding photograph takes up most of the cover. Back has reviewers' comments on *The Man Whose Dreams Came True*. Jacket design by Ed Soyka.
Publication Date: January 1971.
Price: $4.95.

Printing: Colophon page: Design by Sidney Feinberg. Set in Intertype Garamond. Composed by York Composition Company, Inc. Printed and bound by The Haddon Craftsmen, Inc. Printed in the United States of America.

(c) Second U.S./U.K. (large print) edition (1992)

The Man Who Lost His Wife Oxford, England and Santa Barbara, California: Clio Press, 1992.

Not seen.

(d) First U.K. paperback edition (1972)

THE MAN WHO | LOST HIS WIFE | JULIAN SYMONS | [publisher's logo: circle over open book with silhouette of Pan playing his pipes] | UNABRIDGED | PAN BOOKS LTD : LONDON

Size: 7 x 4³⁄₁₆".
Pagination: [1-8] 9-206 [207-208].
Contents: 1, half title and biographical note; 2, "By the same author in Pan Books | THE MAN WHOSE DREAMS CAME TRUE" and conditions of sale; 3, title page; 4, copyright page: "First published 1970 by William Collins Sons and Company Ltd. | This edition published 1972 by Pan Books Ltd, | ....©Julian Symons 1970"; 5, "Contents"; 6, blank; 7, "PART I | Wife Going"; 8, blank; 9-207, text; 208, "A SELECTION OF POPULAR PAN | FICTION" followed by twenty-two titles.
Binding: White with black spine. Black and orange lettering on white front: [orange, pink, and black publisher's logo] Pan Books | Julian Symons | THE MAN WHO | LOST HIS WIFE. Illustration shows a photograph of an empty birdcage with the door left open and feathers strewn about. White lettering on black spine: JULIAN SYMONS The Man Who Lost His Wife | [publisher's logo] | Pan. Black lettering on back includes a promotional blurb, reviews, genre, ISBN, price list, and photograph of the author.
Publication Date: 1972.
Price: U.K. 30p, Australia 95¢, NZ 95¢, South Africa 75¢, Canada $1.25.
Printing: Printed in Great Britain by Richard Clay (The Chaucer Press), Ltd., Bungay, Suffolk.

(e) Second U.K. paperback edition (1972)

Julian Symons | The Man Who Lost | His Wife | Penguin Books

Size: 7¹⁄₁₆ x 4⁵⁄₁₆".
Pagination: [1-8] 9-203 [204-208].

Contents: 1, half title and biographical note; 2, blank; 3, title page; 4, copyright page: "Published in Penguin Books 1977 I Copyright ©Julian Symons, 1970"; 5, "Contents"; 6, blank; 7, "PART ONE I Wife Going"; 8, blank; 9-204, text; 205, "More About Penguins I and Pelicans"; 206, blank; 207, promotional blurbs for Simenon titles; 208, blank.

Binding: White with green spine. Black and turquoise lettering: JULIAN SYMONS I THE MAN WHO LOST HIS WIFE. Green lettering in upper right corner: [publisher's logo: penguin in green circle] I CRIME. Cover illustration is a photograph of a befuddled-looking man scratching his head. White and black lettering on green spine: JULIAN SYMONS THE MAN WHO LOST HIS WIFE ISBN 0 14 I 00.4348 9 I [publisher's logo: penguin in green circle] I CRIME. Black lettering on white back includes promotional blurb and reviews, prices, genre, ISBN. Logo in upper right corner. Cover photograph by Philip Webb.

Publication Date: 1977.

Price: U.K. 75p, Canada $1.95, U.S.A. $1.95.

Printing: Made and printed in Great Britain by Richard Clay (The Chaucer Press) Ltd, Bungay, Suffolk. Set in Monotype Plantin.

A 20   THE PLAYERS AND THE GAME   1972

(a) First U.K. edition (1972)

The Players and I the Game I [rule] Julian Symons I [publisher's logo: hooded gunman] I The Crime Club I Collins, 14 St James's Place, London

Size: 7⅝ x 4⅞".

Pagination: [1-9] 10-224.

Contents: 1, half title and brief plot description; 2,"by the same author" followed by a list of eleven titles; 3, title page; 4, copyright: "First published 1972 I © Julian Symons 1972"; 5, "CONTENTS"; 6, blank; 7, "NOTE: This story has similarities to some of the cases mentioned in the text, in particular the Moors Murders and the American Lonely Hearts Murders"; 8, blank; 9-224, text.

Binding: Red paper over boards, gilt lettering on spine: THE I PLAYERS I AND THE I GAME I Julian I Symons I [publisher's logo].

Dust Jacket: White and orange lettering on black front and spine. Front has orange emblem of the Collins Crime Club at the top. Illustration across the bottom is a photograph of five playing cards, two face up: one shows a person with a hand gun, one shows a person with vampire-like fangs. Jacket photograph is by Margaret Murry. Black lettering on white back. Back has reviewers' comments on *The Man Who Lost His Wife*.

Publication Date: 1972.

Price: £1.50.

Printing: Set in Intertype Baskerville. Made and printed in Great Britain by William Collins Sons & Co Ltd Glasgow.

Symons's Note: The best of my masher books! The origins of this one were, as I said in a prefatory note, the horrific Moors murders, as famous in Britain as the Manson case in the U.S. In the end, though, I strayed rather far from my original plan, in part because I couldn't bring myself to write about the torture of children, in part for the less worthy reason that I wanted to make the book a puzzle. As a puzzle it seems to me ingenious, though in other respects I was not altogether pleased with it.

(b) First U.S. edition (1972)

The Players | and the Game | [broken rule] | JULIAN SYMONS | HARPER & ROW, PUBLISHERS | New York, Evanston, San Francisco, London

Size: 8" x 5⅜".
Pagination: [i-vi] 1-217 [218].
Contents: i, half title; ii, "Books by Julian Symons" followed by a list of sixteen titles; iii, title page; iv, copyright page: "Copyright © 1972 by Julian Symons....FIRST U.S. EDITION"; v, "Note"; vi, blank; 1-217, text; 218, printing statement: 72 73 10987654321.
Binding: Three-quarter black paper, lower-right front cover blind stamped: [publisher's logo: torch in box, year 1817 below box]. Black lettering on yellow cloth spine: The Players and the Game | JULIAN SYMONS | Harper | & Row.
Dust Jacket: Black lettering on yellow front and spine. Illustration shows a white dagger piercing a red-lipped mouth with fangs and a nude woman inside. Black lettering on white back. Back has reviewers' comments on *The Man Who Lost His Wife*. Jacket design by William Ingraham.
Publication Date: September 1972.
Price: $5.95.

(c) Second U.S. issue (1972)

Same as A 20 b except "First U.S. Edition" deleted from copyright page and printing statement on page 218 drops the number 1 from the printing chain.

(d) First U.K. paperback edition (1974)

Julian Symons | The Players and | the Game | Penguin Books

Size: 7 x 4³/₁₆".
Pagination: [1-8] 9-220 [221-224].
Contents: 1, "Penguin Crime Fiction | Editor: Julian Symons | The Players and the Game" followed by a biographical note; 2, blank; 3, title page; 4, copyright page: "First published by Collins 1972 | Published in Penguin Books 1974 |

Copyright ©Julian Symons, 1972"; 5-6, "Contents"; 7, "Note | This story has similarities to some of the cases | mentioned in the text, in particular the Moors | Murders and the American Lonely Hearts Murders. The similarities are deliberate, but | they extend only to details. The book is not a documentary, and no theory about any actual murder case should be read into what is | emphatically a work of fiction."; 8, blank; 9-221, text; 222, blank; 223, "More about Penguins | and Pelicans" followed by information and logo; 224, blank.

Binding: Black with black spine. White and red lettering: JULIAN SYMONS | THE PLAYERS AND THE GAME. Green lettering in upper right corner: [publisher's logo: penguin in green circle] | CRIME. Cover illustration is a photograph of a vampire with blood dripping from his fangs. White and red lettering on spine: JULIAN SYMONS THE PLAYERS AND THE GAME ISBN 0 14 | 00.3808 6. Green lettering at base of spine: [publisher's logo: penguin in green circle] | CRIME. Red and white lettering on back includes promotional blurb and review, prices, genre, ISBN. Logo in upper right corner. Cover photograph by Ray Massey. "For copyright reasons this edition is not for sale in the U.S.A."

Publication Date: 1974.

Price: U.K. 35p, Australia $1.20 (recommended), New Zealand $1.20, Canada $0.95.

Printing: Made and printed in Great Britain by Cox & Wyman Ltd, London, Reading and Fakenham. Set in Intertype Baskerville.

(e) First U.S. paperback edition (1975)

[inside of block "P"] THE | PLAYERS | AND | THE | GAME | JULIAN SYMONS | [publisher's logo: parallelograms arranged in a triangle] AVON | PUBLISHERS OF BARD, CAMELOT, DISCUS, EQUINOX AND FLARE BOOKS

Size: 7 x 4⅛".

Pagination: [1-7] 8-192.

Contents: 1, half title and reviews; 2, blank; 3, title page; 4, copyright page: "Copyright ©1972 by Julian Symons | ....First Avon Printing, July 1975"; 5, "Note"; 6, blank; 7-192, text.

Binding: Blue paper. White and red lettering on front: "BRILLIANT...THIS MAY BE JULIAN SYMONS' MASTERPIECE!" | [rule] ROSS MACDONALD | A spellbinding blend of lurking mystery, pulse-pounding | detection, and the darkest secrets of human passion! | [white lettering inside of red "P"] THE | PLAYERS | AND | THE | GAME | A NOVEL BY JULIAN SYMONS | Author of A THREE-PIPE PROBLEM. Top right corner: [publisher's logo] | AVON | 25 106 | $1.25. Cover illustration is the profile of a blonde wearing a Bonnie Parker mask facing a man wearing a vampire mask; blood is dripping down the wall behind them. White lettering on spine: [publisher's logo] | AVON | THE PLAYERS AND THE GAME [vertical rule] SYMONS 380 •25106 • 125. White lettering on back includes promotional blurb and reviews.

Publication Date: July 1975.

Price: $1.25.

Printing: Printed in the U.S.A.

(f) Second U.S. paperback issue (1984)

THE PLAYERS | AND THE GAME | [broken rule] | JULIAN SYMONS | [publisher's logo: penguin in oval] | PENGUIN BOOKS

Size: 7⅛ x 4⅜".
Pagination: [i-vi] 7-217 [218].
Contents: i, "PENGUIN CRIME FICTION | THE PLAYERS AND THE GAME" followed by biographical note; ii, "Also by Julian Symons" followed by twenty-four titles; iii, title page; iv, copyright page: "Published in Penguin Books by arrangement with | Harper & Row, Publishers, Inc., 1984 | Copyright ©Julian Symons, 1972"; v, "Note"; vi, blank; 1-217, text; 218, blank.
Binding: Green spine, black back. White lettering over cover illustration: JULIAN SYMONS | Grand Master—Mystery Writers of America | [rule forms two sides of a box around title and review] THE PLAYERS AND | THE GAME | "A brilliant combination | of psychological and | police-procedural elements, | with pure horror at the core" | —Ross Macdonald. Green lettering in lower right corner: [publisher's logo] | CRIME. Cover illustration shows a burning stake with a cross carved in it. White and black lettering on green spine: JULIAN SYMONS THE PLAYERS AND THE GAME ISBN 0 14 | 00.3808 6 | [publisher's logo] | CRIME. White lettering on black back includes promotional blurb and reviews, price list, genre, ISBN. Green logo at top center. Cover design by Neil Stuart. Cover photograph by Irvin Cook.
Publication Date: 1984.
Price: U.K. £1.95, Aust. $4.95 (recommended), N.Z. $7.95, Canada $3.95, U.S.A. $3.50.
Printing: Printed in the United States of America by George Banta Co., Inc., Harrisonburg, Virginia. Set in Caledonia.

A 21   THE PLOT AGAINST ROGER RIDER   1973

(a) First U.K. edition (1973)

The Plot Against | Roger Rider | [rule] | Julian Symons | [publisher's logo: hooded gunman] | The Crime Club | Collins, 14 St James's Place, London

Size: 7⅝ x 4¹³⁄₁₆".
Pagination: [1-9] 10-222 [223-224].
Contents: 1-2, blank; 3, half title and brief plot description; 4, "by the same author" followed by a list of twelve titles; 5, title page; 6, copyright page: "First published 1973 | © Julian Symons 1973" and dedication: "For | Alan and Winifred Eden-Green; 7, "CONTENTS"; 8, blank; 9-222, text; 223-224, blank.
Binding: Red paper over boards, black lettering on spine: THE | PLOT | AGAINST | ROGER | RIDER | Julian | Symons| [publisher's logo].
Dust Jacket: Red and black lettering on front and spine; background fades top to bottom from black to white. The illustration is a photograph of a hand gun,

airplane tickets, and dental X-rays. Jacket photograph by Graham Miller. Black lettering on white back. Back has reviewers' comments on *The Player and the Game.*

Publication Date: 1973.

Price: £1.25.

Printing: Set in Intertype Baskerville. Made and Printed in Great Britain by William Collins Sons & Co Ltd Glasgow.

Symons's Note: A good idea (or was it ever?) that went wrong. It's a very inferior book, I'm afraid.

(b) First U.S. edition (1973)

JULIAN SYMONS | [vertical center double rule] | The Plot | Against | Roger Rider | HARPER & ROW PUBLISHERS | New York, Evanston | San Francisco, London [publisher's logo: torch in box, year 1817 below box in lower left corner]

Size: 8 x 5⅜".

Pagination: [i-vi] [1-3] 4-199 [200-202].

Contents: i, half title; ii, "Books by Julian Symons" followed by a list of seventeen titles; iii, title page; iv, copyright page: "Copyright © 1973 Julian Symons | ....FIRST U.S. EDITION"; v, dedication: "For Alan and Winifred Eden-Green"; vi, blank; 1, "PART ONE The Plot | Against | Geoffrey Paradine"; 2, blank; 3-199, text; 200-201, blank; 202, printing statement: 73 74 10987654321.

Binding: Three-quarter blue paper, gilt lettering on brown cloth spine: Julian Symons The Plot Against | Roger Rider Harper & Row.

Dust Jacket: Black lettering on gray front. Illustration shows a man tied to a chain below sea level with a number five buoy marker floating on the surface of the water. Black lettering on white spine. Tan lettering on white back. Back has reviewers' comments on *The Players and the Game.* Jacket design by Michael Flanagan.

Publication Date: November 1973.

Price: $5.95.

Printing: Designed by C. Linda Dingler. Printed in the United States of America.

(c) Second U.S. issue (1973)

Same as A21b except "FIRST U.S. EDITION" deleted from copyright page and printing statement on page 202 drops the number 1 from the printing chain.

(d) Second U.K. issue (1973)

The Plot Against | Roger Rider | [rule] | Julian Symons | Book Club Associates London

Size: 7⅝ x 4⅞".

Same as A 21 a except for the following changes:

Contents: 4, copyright page: addition of: This edition published 1973 by | Book Club Associates | By arrangement with Wm. Collins Sons & Co Ltd. Dedication has been deleted.

Binding: Red paper over boards, gilt lettering on spine: THE | PLOT | AGAINST | ROGER | RIDER | Julian | Symons | [publisher's logo: bca in box].

Dust Jacket: Same as A 21 a except publisher's logo [black lettering bca in white circle] is in bottom left of front; white and black lettering on spine with publisher's logo in black on white. Back of jacket is blank.

Publication Date: This edition published 1973 by Book Club Associates by arrangement with Wm. Collins Sons & Co. Ltd.

Price: n|a.

(e) Third U.K. issue (1990)

The Plot | Against | Roger Rider | Julian Symons | M | Macmillan | London

Size: 7¾ x 4⅞".

Pagination: [1-9] 10-222 [223-224].

Contents: 1, half title and brief plot description; 2, "by the same author" followed by a list of twenty-six titles; 3, title page; 4, copyright page: "Copyright © Julian Symons 1973 | ....Reissued 1990 by | MACMILLAN LONDON LIMITED"; 5, dedication: "For Alan and Winifred Eden-Green"; 6, blank; 7, "CONTENTS"; 8, blank; 9-222, text; 223-224, blank.

Binding: Red paper over boards, gilt lettering on spine: Julian Symons [rule] The Plot Against Roger Rider | M.

Dust Jacket: Gold, black, and red lettering on white front and spine. Black lettering on white back. Back has reviewers' comments.

Publication Date: Reissue in 1990 by Macmillan London Limited. First published in Great Britain 1973 by William Collins Sons & Co. Ltd.

Price: £11.95.

(f) U.K. (large print) edition (1992)

The Plot Against Roger Rider. Lansdown, 1992.

Not seen.

A 22   A THREE-PIPE PROBLEM   1975

(a) First U.K. edition (1975)

A | THREE-PIPE PROBLEM | [short rule] | JULIAN SYMONS | 'What are you going to do then?' I asked. | 'To smoke', he answered. 'It is quite a three pipe prob-

A
THREE PIPE PROBLEM

JULIAN SIMONS

'To smoke,' he answered. 'It is quite a three pipe problem,
'What are you going to do then?' I asked.
and I beg that you won't speak to me for fifty minutes.'
The Adventures of Sherlock Holmes

COLLINS
ST JAMES'S PLACE, LONDON
1975

Title page, *A Three Pipe Problem*, The Crime Club, Collins, 1975, the uncorrected
advance proof with author's name misspelled "SIMONS."

lem, I and I beg that you won't speak to me for fifty minutes.' I *The Adventures of Sherlock Holmes* I [publisher's logo: hooded gunman inside circle] I COLLINS I ST JAMES'S PLACE, LONDON I 1975

Size: 8³⁄₁₆ x 5¼".

Pagination: [1-8] 9-223 [224].

Contents: 1, half title and brief description of the plot; 2, "by the same author" followed by a list of thirteen titles; 3, title page; 4, copyright page: "First published February 1975 I © Julian Symons, 1975"; 5, dedication: "For Ngaio Marsh I who gave me the title"; 6, blank; 7, "Contents"; 8, blank; 9-223 text; 224 blank.

Binding: Black paper over boards, gilt lettering on spine: A I THREE I PIPE I PROBLEM I Julian I Symons I [publisher's logo].

Dust Jacket: Brown and white lettering on black front and spine. Illustration shows photograph of Sherlock Holmes character smoking a pipe and leaning on a parking meter. Black lettering on white back. Back has reviewers' comments on *The Plot Against Roger Rider*. Jacket photograph by Christopher Ridley.

Publication Date: February 1975.

Price: £2.50.

Printing: Set in Monotype Imprint. Made and printed in Great Britain by William Collins Sons & Co Ltd Glasgow.

Symons's Note: The natural and obvious genesis of this book was my reading and re-reading of the Holmes saga, especially the short stories, when I was a boy. The appeal they had for me was on the edge of reality—that is, I remember thick London fogs and horse-drawn cabs, so that the Holmesian Baker Street (which I never saw physically until I was perhaps twenty years old) wasn't costume history for me, but something like present drama.

But, although this early Holmes worship stayed with me through the years, it was accompanied by an admiration for much other work by Holmes's creator. I became perhaps unwarrantably annoyed by what seemed to me the tendencies of the various Sherlock Holmes societies to denigrate Conan Doyle at the expense of Sherlock, as in the pretence that Conan Doyle was merely the agent through which the masterpieces were brought into print. I said something of this in *Bloody Murder*, and enlarged on it when invited to speak to the British Sherlock Holmes Society. They received my strictures with perfect politeness, but there is no doubt that they gave offence, and it was in an attempt to make amends that I not only removed the remarks from later editions of the book, but also embarked on a book not about Sherlock Holmes, but about an actor who when confronted with some puzzles tries to solve them by Holmesian methods.

The result seemed to me to come off pretty well, and the idea that a TV series in which the stories are played straight would be successful because they are mostly such excellent stories (excellent distinct from the mystery, sometimes distinct even from the detection) has been shown to be on the mark by the versions in which Jeremy Brett plays the detective. The completed book lacked a title, and I found it hard to think of anything suitable. In the end the title was given by Ngaio Marsh—the most beautiful and most charming woman crime writer I have ever met—on a train journey when we were sent out by our English publisher to give talks and sign books.

   I'm not usually very happy with the way in which my light novels have worked out, but I thought this one was a success within the limits of what was attempted. The decision, more than a decade later, to revive Sheridan Haynes in *The Kentish Manor Murders* [A 32] was a disaster. I should have known better than to think I could repeat such a joke successfully.

(b) Second U.K. issue (1975)

A | THREE PIPE PROBLEM | [rule] | JULIAN SYMONS | 'What are you going to do then?' I asked. | 'To smoke,' he answered. 'It is quite a three pipe problem, | and I beg that you won't speak to me for fifty minutes.' | *The Adventures of Sherlock Holmes* | [The Crime Club and hooded gunman in circle] | COLLINS | St James Place, London | 1975

This U.K. edition was "Reprinted August 1975" with no change to the text. Reviewers' comments were added to the front jacket flap. Also added was white lettering on a black band with gilt and white stripes at top and bottom: CRIME CLUB CHOICE [gilt gunman on front and spine].

(c) Third U.K. (Book Club) issue (1975)

A | THREE PIPE PROBLEM | [rule] | JULIAN SYMONS | 'What are you going to do then?' I asked. | 'To smoke,' he answered. 'It is quite a three pipe problem, | and I beg that you won't speak to me for fifty minutes.' | *The Adventures of Sherlock Holmes* | BOOK CLUB ASSOCIATES | LONDON

A reissue of A 22 a with the following changes:
Contents: 3, title page: Book Club Associates | London; 4, copyright page: "This edition published 1975 by | Book Club Associates | By arrangement with Wm Collins Sons & Co Ltd | ©Julian Symons, 1975".
Binding: publisher's logo on spine: [bca in a square].
Dust Jacket: publisher's logo [bca in white circle] on lower-left corner of front and on spine. Price has been removed from front jacket flap; the blurb for *The Players and the Game* has been removed from the back jacket flap.

(d) First U.S. edition (1975)

Julian Symons | A THREE-PIPE PROBLEM [repeated three times in gradually darker letters] | Harper & Row, Publishers | New York, Evanston, San Francisco, London

Size: 8 x 5⅛".
Pagination: [i-vi] [1] 2-216 [217-218].

Contents: i, half title and "A Joan Kahn Book"; ii, "Books by Julian Symons" followed by a list of seventeen fiction and nonfiction titles; iii, title page; iv, copyright page: "A THREE-PIPE PROBLEM. Copyright © 1975 by Julian Symons.... | FIRST U.S. EDITION |....75 76 77 78 79 10 9 8 7 6 5 4 3 2 1"; v, dedication: "For Ngaio Marsh, | who gave me the title"; vi, quote from *The Adventures of Sherlock Holmes*; 1-216, text; 217-218, blank.

Binding: Three-quarter tan paper over boards, silver lettering on medium blue cloth spine: Symons A THREE-PIPE PROBLEM Harper & Row.

Dust Jacket: Black lettering on tan. Illustration is a line drawing of Sherlock Holmes character on blue. Black lettering at the bottom and black lettering on spine. Illustration is repeated on back. Back has reviewers' comments on *The Plot Against Roger Rider.*

Publication Date: April 1975.

Price: $6.95.

Printing: Printed in the United States of America. Designed by C. Linda Dingler.

(e) Fourth U.K. (Book Club) issue (1976)

A | THREE PIPE PROBLEM | [rule] | JULIAN SYMONS | 'What are you going to do then?' I asked. | 'To smoke,' he answered. 'It is quite a three pipe problem, | and I beg that you won't speak to me for fifty minutes.' | *The Adventures of Sherlock Holmes* | THE THRILLER BOOK CLUB | LONDON : 1976

A reissue of A 22 a with the following changes:

Contents: 3, title page has 1976 publication date rather than 1975; 4, copyright page: "The Thriller Book Club, | 125 Charing Cross Road, | London .... | © 1975 Julian Symons. | First published in Great Britain 1975. | This edition by arrangement with William Collins Sons & Co., Ltd."

Binding: Red paper over boards, gilt lettering on spine: The Three Pipe Problem | JULIAN SYMONS [publisher's logo: BTC].

Dust Jacket: Red and white lettering on front. Illustration is a water color of Sherlock Holmes character standing next to a television camera. Colors are predominantly gray, blue, and brown. Black lettering on white back. Back lists forthcoming selections from The Thriller Book Club.

Publication Date: 1976.

Price: Note on dust jacket: Originally published By William Collins Ltd., at £2.50, this edition only available to Foyles Group of Book Clubs.

Printing: Printed in Great Britain by Biddles Ltd, Guildford, Surrey.

(f) Second U.S. edition (1975)

[Rectangular box] | THE BIG CALL | BY | JOHN CREASEY AS GORDON ASHE | [Rectangular box] | THE BABY MERCHANTS | BY | LILLIAN O'DONNELL | [Rectangualr box] | A THREE-PIPE PROBLEM | BY | JULIAN SYMONS | Published for the | DETECTIVE BOOK CLUB [trademark] | by Walter J. Black, Inc. | ROSLYN, NEW YORK | [publisher's logo: dagger with the initials DCB] | [double rule]

Size: 7⁵⁄₁₆ x 5".
Pagination: [i-vi] [1-3] 4-126 [1-3] 4-172 [1-3] 4-176. (Note: Each novel is given separate pagination.)
Contents: i, "DCB" trademark; ii, blank; iii, title page; iv, copyright page: "A THREE-PIPE PROBLEM | Copyright © 1975 | by Julian Symons"; v, half title and brief plot description of each title, original publisher and price, (*The Three Pipe Problem* is the Harper & Row edition, selling for $6.95); vi, blank; 1, title page; 2, blank; 3-176, text.
Binding: Black and white striped paper over boards with wide band wrapping front to back for each title; each band is highlighted with green. Each title and reduced picture of its original cover appears on a band on the front cover; each title appears in a band wrapping the spine. The Detective Book Club logo is at the bottom of the spine.
Dust Jacket: Issued without a jacket.
Publication Date: None given, although Library of Congress gives the year as 1975.
Price: Not given.
Printing: Printed in the United States of America.

(g) First U.S. paperback edition (1976)

A THREE-PIPE PROBLEM | JULIAN SYMONS | [publisher's logo: three parallelograms forming a triangle| AVON | PUBLISHERS OF BARD, CAMELOT, DISCUS, EQUINOX AND FLARE BOOKS

Size: 6¹⁵⁄₁₆ x 4⅛".
Pagination: [1-8] 9-206 [207-208].
Contents: 1, promotional blurb and reviews; 2, "Avon Books by | Julian Symons" followed by one title; 3, title page; 4, copyright page: "Copyright ©1975 by Julian Symons | ....First Avon Printing, March, 1976"; 5, dedication: "For Ngaio Marsh, | who gave me the title"; 6, blank; 7, quotation from *The Adventures of Sherlock Holmes*; 8, blank; 9-206, text; 207-208, additional AVON titles.
Binding: Black paper. Beige lettering on front: THREE MURDERS SO BAFFLING THAT ONLY ONE MAN CAN SOLVE THEM— | THE REINCARNATION OF SHERLOCK HOLMES HIMSELF! | "SOMETHING SPECIAL...JULIAN SYMONS | HAS NEVER DONE A BETTER STORY!" | Dorothy B. Hughes | A THREE-PIPE PROBLEM | [rule] | JULIAN SYMONS. Bottom left corner: [publisher's logo] AVON [slash] 28225 [slash] $1.50. Cover illustration is a drawing of an pipe-smoking actor sitting at a vanity in his dressing room, reading the London *Times*. Beige lettering on black spine: [publisher's logo] | AVON | A THREE-PIPE PROBLEM | JULIAN | SYMONS 380 • 28225 • 150. Beige lettering on back includes promotional blurb, reviews, "SELECTED BY THE DETECTIVE BOOK CLUB".
Publication Date: March 1976.
Price: $1.50.
Printing: Printed in the U.S.A.

(h) First U.K. paperback edition (1977)

Julian Symons | **A Three Pipe Problem** | 'What are you going to do then?' I asked. | 'To smoke,' he answered. 'It is quite a three pipe problem, | and I beg that you won't speak to me for fifty minutes.' | The Adventures of Sherlock Holmes | [publisher's logo: penguin in oval] Penguin Books

Size: 7⅛ x 4⅜".

Pagination: [1-8] 9-191 [192].

Contents: 1, "Penguin Crime Fiction | Editor: Julian Symons | A Three Pipe Problem" and biographical note; 2, blank; 3, title page; 4, copyright page: "Published in Penguin Books 1977 | Copyright ©Julian Symons, 1975"; 5, dedication: "For Ngaio Marsh who gave me the title"; 6, blank; 7, contents; 8, blank; 9-192, text.

Binding: Green spine, black back. Front has white and black lettering over illustration: JULIAN SYMONS | A THREE PIPE PROBLEM. Green lettering in upper right corner: [publisher's logo] | CRIME. Cover illustration is a photograph of a pipe-toting Sherlock Holmes character leaning on a parking meter. White and black lettering on green spine: JULIAN SYMONS A THREE PIPE PROBLEM ISBN 0 14 |00.4330 6 | [publisher's logo] | CRIME. White letter on black back includes promotional blurb and review, price, genre, ISBN, logo. Cover photograph by Paul Wakefield.

Publication Date: 1977.

Price: U.K. 60p, Canada $1.95.

Printing: Made and printed in Great Britain by Hazell Watson & Viney Ltd, Aylesbury, Bucks. Set in Monotype Plantin.

(i) Second U.K. paperback edition (1981)

JULIAN SYMONS | A | THREE PIPE | PROBLEM | [publisher's logo: heron in marsh] | HERON BOOKS

Size: 7⅜ x 4½".

Pagination: [1-8] 9-222 [223-224].

Contents: 1, half title and promotional blurb; 2, drawing of Julian Symons; 3, title page; 4, copyright page: "©1975, Julian Symons | ©1981, Illustration, Edito-Service S.A., Geneva"; 5, quotation from *The Adventures of Sherlock Holmes*; 6, dedication: "For Ngaio Marsh | who gave me the title"; 7, contents; 8, blank; 9-223, text; 224, printing information.

Binding: Black embossed paper. Red and gilt lettering on front, with gilt decorative border: JULIAN SYMONS | A | THREE PIPE | PROBLEM | LIBRARY | OF CRIME | [blood stain]. Gilt and red lettering on spine: [gilt border] A THREE PIPE PROBLEM [double gilt border] JULIAN SYMONS [gilt border]. Back is blank.

Publication Date: 1981.

Price: Not given.

Printing: Production Edito-Service S.A., GENEVA. Printed in Italy.

90   A. *Fiction*

(j) Second U.S. paperback edition (1984)

A THREE-PIPE | PROBLEM | JULIAN SYMONS | [publisher's logo: penguin in oval] | PENGUIN BOOKS

Size: 7⅛ x 4⅜".
Pagination: [1-8] 9-191 [192].
Contents: 1, "PENGUIN CRIME FICTION" and half title with biographical note; 2, "Also by Julian Symons" followed by twenty-four titles; 3, title page; 4, copyright page: "Published in Penguin Books in Great Britain 1977 | Published in Penguin Books in the United States of America | by arrangement with Harper & Row, Publishers, Inc., 1984 | Copyright ©Julian Symons, 1975" and "Copyright ©Philip Larkin, 1974" for poem "Going, Going" from *High Windows* (p. 124); 5, dedication: "For Ngaio Marsh, | who gave me the title" and quotation from *The Adventures of Sherlock Holmes*; 6, blank; 7, contents; 8, blank; 9-192, text.
Binding: Green and black paper. White lettering over illustration: JULIAN SYMONS | Grand Master—Mystery Writers of America | A THREE-PIPE | PROBLEM | "Mr Symons has never done | anything so wholly delightful." | — Edmund Crispin. Green lettering in lower right corner: [publisher's logo] | CRIME. Cover illustration is a photograph of a brown and tan houndstooth deerstalker and a lit pipe. Black and white lettering on green spine: JULIAN SYMONS A THREE-PIPE PROBLEM ISBN 0 14 | 00.4330 6 | [publisher's logo] | CRIME. White lettering on black back includes promotional blurb and reviews, prices, genre, ISBN, logo. Cover design by Neil Stuart. Cover photograph by Irvin Cook.
Publication Date: 1984.
Price: U.K. £1.75, Aust. $5.95 (recommended), N.Z. $6.95, Canada $3.95, U.S.A. $2.95.
Printing: Printed in the United States of America by George Banta Co., Inc., Harrisonburg, Virginia. Set in Monotype Plantin.

(k) Second U.K. paperback issue (1988)

A THREE-PIPE | PROBLEM | JULIAN SYMONS | [publisher's logo: penguin in an oval] | PENGUIN BOOKS

Same as A 22 i except for the following changes:
Size: 7¾ x 5¹⁄₁₆".
Contents: 1, half title, biographical note changed; 2, blank; copyright page, added 1988.
Binding: Black paper with green spine. White, green, and cream lettering on front: [publisher's logo: PENGUIN | CLASSIC CRIME in rounded box rule with black smoking gun in green circle] | A Three-Pipe | Problem | [decorative rule] JULIAN SYMONS [decorative rule]. Cover photograph shows two men wearing hats and overcoats standing under a street lamp. Headlights of approaching car illuminate the weapons they are holding. White and black lettering on green

spine: JULIAN SYMONS • A THREE-PIPE PROBLEM | ISBN 0 14 | 01.0903 X | [publisher's logo]. Green, red, and white lettering on back includes classic crime logo, promotional blurb, and reviews. Black lettering in white box on back includes penguin logo, genre, price list, ISBN, and bar code. Cover photograph by Martin Riedl.
Publication Date: 1988.
Price: U.K. £3.99, Aust., $12.99 (recommended) N.Z. $14.99 (incl. GST), Canada, $6.95, U.S.A. $4.95.
Printing: Printed and bound in Great Britain by Hazell Watson & Viney Limited, Member of BPCC plc, Aylesbury, Bucks, England. Set in Monotype Plantin.

A 23   HOW TO TRAP A CROOK   1977

(a) First U.S. edition (1977)

ELLERY QUEEN | PRESENTS | JULIAN SYMONS'| HOW TO | TRAP | A | CROOK | AND 12 OTHER | MYSTERIES | Edited and with introduction by ELLERY QUEEN | DAVIS PUBLICATIONS, INC., | 229 Park Avenue South | New York, New York 10003

Size: 7¹¹⁄₁₆ x 5³⁄₁₆".
Pagination: [1-3] 4-190 [191-192].
Contents: 1-2, ads; 3, title page; 4, copyright page: "Copyright ©1977 Davis Publications, Inc. | ....Stories Copyright © 1957, 1960, 1961, 1963, 1965, 1966, 1967, 1968, 1971, 1972, by Julian Symons"; 5, "CONTENTS"; 6, ad.; 7-9, "INTRODUCTION"; 10, ad., 11-190, text; 191-192, ads.
Binding: Paperbound in light green on front and spine, white on back. Front cover has red, dark green, and black lettering and an illustration of a man's face inside a black ruled box. Back cover has black and blue lettering, along with an order form for Ellery Queen's Mystery Magazine and reduced reproduction of the magazine cover in black and gray.
Publication Date: February 1977.
Price: $1.35, UK 75p.
Printing: Printed in the United States of America.

A 24   THE BLACKHEATH POISONINGS: 1978
A VICTORIAN MURDER MYSTERY

(a) First U.K. edition (1978)

JULIAN SYMONS | [rule] | The Blackheath | Poisonings | A Victorian Murder Mystery | [publisher's logo: hooded gunman inside circle] | COLLINS, ST JAMES'S PLACE, LONDON

Size: 7¹¹/₁₆ x 5".

Pagination: [1-9] 10-266.

Contents: 1, half title and short plot description; 2, "by the same author" followed by a list of fourteen titles; 3, title page; 4, copyright page: "First published 1978 | © Julian Symons 1978"; 5, "ACKNOWLEDGEMENTS"; 6, blank; 7, "CONTENTS"; 8, blank; 9-266, text.

Binding: Red paper over boards, gilt lettering on spine: THE | BLACKHEATH | POISONINGS | Julian | Symons | [publisher's logo].

Dust Jacket: Red and white lettering on black. Illustration is a photograph of a Victorian doorway at night. Black lettering on white back. Back has heading "Also by Julian Symons" followed by reviewers' comments for *A Three Pipe Problem*. Jacket photograph by Dave Fairman. Photograph of Julian Symons on back flap is by Jerry Bauer.

Publication Date: 1978.

Price: £4.25.

Printing: Set in Baskerville. Made and printed in Great Britain by William Collins Sons & Co. Ltd Glasgow.

Symons's Note: The need I've felt at various times to change styles, shift gears, think again about my approach to the material of my work, is in part responsible for these stories with a Victorian setting. They also owe their existence to a conversation in which somebody said to me that it was nowadays impossible to write a successful period crime story.

So I began on what became *The Blackheath Poisonings*. I wrote something like a third of the book in 1975, put it aside when I spent a year at Amherst College, returned to it when I came back to England, and was horrified by the proliferation of characters. I scrapped most of what I'd done, eliminated some minor figures, and built on the slender foundations that remained. The basis of the book was the Croydon Poisonings (which I wrote about in *A Reasonable Doubt* [C 7]). I shifted this story of three deaths back in time, added a good many Victorian trappings to it, and enjoyed writing the book, in particular the period dialogue which seemed (and seems) to me convincing.

In *Sweet Adelaide* [A 25] I attempted, with similar period detail, to translate a real life case into fiction. I thought it less successful than *The Blackheath Poisonings* but was still interested enough in the period and its criminal possibilities to write a third story. *The Detling Murders* [A 27] (in the U.S. *The Detling Secret*) proved much more difficult to write, and I was unsatisfied with the final result. The critics were indulgent, but it seemed to me that I'd exhausted the Victorian mode, or background. Since then I've thought of setting a crime story in rich self-satisfied Edwardian England, the time around 1910, but haven't yet found a suitable subject.

(b) First U.S. edition (1978)

THE | BLACKHEATH | POISONINGS | [decorative rule] | A Victorian Murder Mystery | by Julian Symons | [decorative rule] | HARPER & ROW, PUBLISHERS | NEW YORK, HAGERSTOWN, SAN FRANCISCO, | LONDON

Size: 8 x 5¼".
Pagination: [i-xii] 1-302 [303-308].
Contents: i-ii, blank; iii, half title and "A I Joan I Kahn I Book"; iv, blank; v, "Other Books by Julian Symons" followed by a list of two nonfiction and seventeen fiction titles; vi, blank; vii, title page; viii, copyright page: "THE BLACKHEATH POISONINGS. Copyright © 1978 by Julian Symons.... I FIRST U.S. EDITION I ....78 79 80 81 82 10 9 8 7 6 5 4 3 2 1"; ix, "ACKNOWLEDGMENTS"; x, blank; xi, half title; xii, blank; 1-302, text; 303-308, blank.
Binding: Three-quarter medium blue paper, lower-right front cover blind stamped: [publisher's logo: torch in box, year 1817 below box]. Gilt lettering on black cloth spine: THE BLACKHEATH POISONINGS I Julian Symons I HARPER I & ROW.
Dust Jacket: Yellow-tan lettering on medium blue. Illustration is black ink drawing of English manor house; the silhouette of a person can be seen in the one illuminated window (same color as the lettering). Photograph of Julian Symons by Jerry Bauer on back. Jacket design by Edgar Blakely.
Publication Date: December 1978.
Price: $9.95.
Printing: Printed in the United States of America. Designed by Sidney Feinberg.

(c) Second U.S. issue (1978)

Same as A 24 b except for the following changes:
Dust Jacket: Price and publication date removed from front jacket flap; addition of "Printed in the U.S.A." at bottom of back jacket flap; ISBN removed from the bottom of the jacket back. A blind stamped square appears at the lower right hand corner of the back cover, "HB2J" added to lower right hand corner of page 308.

(d) Second U.K. issue (1990)

The I Blackheath I Poisonings I Julian Symons I M I MACMILLAN I LONDON

Size: 7¾ x 4⅞".
Pagination: [1-9] 10-266 [267-272].
Contents: 1, half title and short plot description; 2, "by the same author" followed by a list of twenty-six titles; 3, title page; 4, copyright page: "Copyright © Julian Symons 1978 I ....First published in Great Britain 1978 by William Collins Sons & Co Ltd. I Reissued in 1990 by I MACMILLAN LONDON LTD"; 5, Acknowledgements; 6, blank; 7, "CONTENTS"; 8, blank; 9-266, text; 267-272, blank.
Binding: Black cloth, gilt lettering on spine: Julian Symons [rule] The Blackheath Poisonings M.
Dust Jacket: Tan, black, and red lettering on white front. Spine has black and white lettering on red; white lettering on black at bottom. Black lettering on white back. Back has reviewers' comments.

Publication Date: 1990.

Price: £11.95.

Printing: Printed and bound in Great Britain by The Camelot Press Ltd, Southampton.

(e) First U.K. paperback edition (1980)

THE | BLACKHEATH | POISONINGS | [ornament] | A Victorian Murder Mystery | by Julian Symons | [publisher's logo: penguin in oval] | PENGUIN BOOKS

Size: 7¹⁄₁₆ x 4³⁄₁₆".

Pagination: [i-xii] 1-302 [303-308].

Contents: i, half title and biographical note; ii, blank; iii, "Other Books by Julian Symons" followed by two nonfiction and seventeen fiction titles; iv, blank; v, title page; vi, copyright page: "Published in Penguin Books 1980 | Reprinted 1980, 1981 | Copyright ©Julian Symons, 1978"; vii, "CONTENTS"; viii, blank; ix, "ACKNOWLEDGMENTS"; x, blank; xi, half title; xii, blank; 1-302, text; 303, order information; 304-308, list of titles.

Binding: Black paper with green spine. White lettering on front: THE BLACKHEATH | POISONINGS | A VICTORIAN MURDER MYSTERY | BY JULIAN SYMONS. Green lettering in top right corner: [publisher's logo: penguin in oval] | CRIME. Cover illustration is a photograph of a table with a framed portrait in the background, a book, a walking stick, a clock, a bottle of poison with the cork stopper beside it. Black and white lettering on green spine: Julian Symons The Blackheath Poisonings | ISBN 0 14 | 00.5171 6 | [publisher's logo] | CRIME. Back has white lettering on black back that includes promotional blurb, reviews, price, genre, ISBN. Green lettering in upper right corner: [publisher's logo] | CRIME. Cover design by Neil Stuart. Cover photograph by Irvin Cook.

Publication Date: Published in Penguin Books 1980, Reprinted 1980, 1981.

Price: $3.50.

Printing: Printed in the United States of America by Offset Paperback Mfrs., Inc., Dallas, Pennsylvania. Set in Caledonia.

(f) Second U.K. paperback issue (1988)

THE | BLACKHEATH | POISONINGS | [ornament] | A Victorian Murder Mystery | by Julian Symons | [publisher's logo: penguin in oval] | PENGUIN BOOKS

Size: 7¹⁄₁₆ x 4⅜".

Pagination: [i-x] 1-302 [303-310].

Contents: i, half title and biographical note; ii, blank; iii, title page; iv, copyright page: "Published in Penguin Books 1980 | Reprinted 1980, 1981 (twice), 1984 (twice), 1985 (three times), 1988 | Copyright ©Julian Symons, 1978"; v, "CONTENTS"; vi, blank; vii, "ACKNOWLEDGMENTS"; viii, blank; ix, half title; x, blank; 1-302, text; 303, addresses and order information; 304-308, list of titles; 309-310, blank.

Binding: Orange and white paper. White, cream, and red lettering on front illustration: JULIAN SYMONS | [rule] THE [rule] | BLACKHEATH | POISONINGS | A VICTORIAN MURDER MYSTERY | 'HIS BEST'—*OBSERVER* [publisher's logo: penguin in orange oval]. Cover illustration is a photograph of a blue bottle of poison. Black and white lettering on orange spine: JULIAN SYMONS • THE BLACKHEATH POISONINGS | ISBN 0 14 | 00.5171 6 | [publisher's logo]. Orange and black lettering on white back includes promotional blurb and reviews, logo, genre, price list, ISBN, and bar code. Cover photograph by Tony Hutchings.

Publication Date: Published in Penguin Books 1980, Reprinted 1980, 1981 (twice), 1984 (twice), 1985 (three times), 1988.

Price: U.K. £3.50, Aust. $9.95 (recommended), N.Z. $12.99 (including GST), Canada $4.95, U.S.A. $3.95.

Printing: Printed and bound in Great Britain by Cox & Wyman Ltd, Reading. Set in Caledonia.

(g) Third U.K. paperback issue [1992]

THE | BLACKHEATH | POISONINGS | [ornament] | A Victorian Murder Mystery | by Julian Symons | [publisher's logo: penguin in oval] | PENGUIN BOOKS

Same as A 24 f except for the following changes:

Contents: i, half title and biographical note [updated]; iv, copyright page: Published in Penguin Books 1980 | 11 13 15 17 19 20 18 16 14 12; 303, order information and addresses; 304, blank; 305-310, list of titles, including *A Three Pipe Problem*.

Binding: Black and white paper. White and red lettering on front: A Victorian murder mystery | The | BLACKHEATH | POISONINGS | Now a | compelling | ITV series | Julian Symons. Publisher's logo in orange oval in top right corner. Cover illustration is a photograph of the cast of the ITV series. White and red lettering on spine: JULIAN SYMONS THE BLACKHEATH POISONINGS | ISBN 0 14| 01.7142 8 | [publisher's logo: penguin in orange oval]. Black lettering on white back includes promotional blurb and reviews; information about the ITV production, along with Central Independent Television logo; Penguin logo and genre; price list, ISBN, bar code.

Publication Date: [1992].

Price: U.K. £4.99, Can. $6.99.

Printing: Printed in England by Clays Ltd, St. Ives Pl.

A 25 SWEET ADELAIDE   1980

(a) First U.K. edition (1980)

JULIAN SYMONS | [rule] | Sweet Adelaide | A Victorian Puzzle Solved | [publisher's logo: hooded gunman inside circle] | COLLINS, ST JAMES'S PLACE, LONDON

Size: 8⅛₆ x 5⅛₆".
Pagination: [1-9] 10 [11] 12-284 [285-288].
Contents: 1, half title and brief plot description; 2, "by the same author" followed
  by a list of fifteen titles; 3, title page; 4, copyright page: "First published | ©
  Julian Symons, 1980"; 5, dedication: "For | Elizabeth Doherty | and | Diana
  Jagoda"; 6, "ACKNOWLEDGMENT"; 7, "CONTENTS"; 8, Victorian Street
  Ballad, sung at Adelaide Bartlett's trial; 9-10, "AFTERWARDS (I)"; 11-284,
  text; 285-288, blank.
Binding: Red paper over boards, stamped in gilt on spine: SWEET | ADELAIDE |
  Julian | Symons | [publisher's logo].
Dust Jacket: Green, yellow, and white lettering on black front and spine. Illustra-
  tion shows the edge of a table with an oval-shaped photograph of a woman, a
  green bottle labeled Chloroform Poison, and a single puzzle piece. The round
  Collins Crime Club logo is at the base of the spine. Back has reviewers' com-
  ments on *The Blackheath Poisonings.*
Publication Date: 1980.
Price: £5.95.
Printing: Made and printed in Great Britain by William Collins Sons & Co Ltd,
  Glasgow.
Symons's Note: [See A 24.]

(b) First U.S. edition (1980)

SWEET | ADELAIDE | [ornament] | Julian Symons | [publisher's logo: torch in box,
year 1817 below box] | HARPER & ROW, PUBLISHERS, New York | Cambridge,
Hagerstown, Philadelphia, San Francisco, | London, Mexico City, São Paulo, Sydney

Size: 8⅛₆ x 5¼".
Pagination: [i-xviii] [1] 2 [3] 4-263 [264-270].
Contents: i-ii, blank; iii, half title and "A | Joan | Kahn | Book"; iv, blank; v,
  "Other books by Julian Symons" followed by a list of two nonfiction and eigh-
  teen fiction titles; vi, blank; vii, title page; viii, copyright page: "SWEET ADE-
  LAIDE. Copyright © 1980 by Julian Symons.... | FIRST U.S. EDITION | 80 81
  82 83 84 10 9 8 7 6 5 4 3 2 1"; ix, dedication: "For | Elizabeth Doherty | and |
  Diana Jagoda"; x, blank; xi, Victorian Street Ballad; xii, blank; xiii-xiv, "CON-
  TENTS"; xv, "ACKNOWLEDGMENT"; xvi, blank; xvii, half title; xviii,
  blank; 1-2, "AFTERWARDS (I)"; 3-263, text; 264-270, blank.
Binding: Three-quarter green paper over boards, lower-right front cover blind
  stamped: [publisher's logo: torch in box, year 1817 below box]. Silver lettering
  on blue cloth spine: Julian Symons SWEET ADELAIDE | HARPER & ROW.
Dust Jacket: White lettering on cover and spine. Illustration shows a woman sit-
  ting in a train car, reading a book and holding a small bottle. Black lettering on
  white back. Back has reviewers' comments on *The Blackheath Poisonings.*
Publication Date: October 1980.
Price: $11.95.
Printing: Designed by Sidney Feinberg. Printed in the United States of America.

(c) Second U.K. (large print) edition (1982)

JULIAN SYMONS | [rule] | SWEET | ADELAIDE | A VICTORIAN PUZZLE
SOLVED | Complete and Unabridged | [publisher's logo: castle turret] | ULVER-
SCROFT | Leicester

Size: 8⅜ x 5¼".
Pagination: [i-xiv] 1-537 [538-546].
Contents: i, poem by Janice James on reading books; ii, blank; iii, half title and
brief plot description; iv, blank; v, title page; vi, copyright page: "First pub-
lished in 1980 by | William Collins Sons & Co Ltd. | London | First Large Print
Edition | published March 1982 | ....© Julian Symons 1980"; vi, dedication;
viii, blank; ix, "ACKNOWLEDGEMENT"; x, blank; xi, "CONTENTS"; xii-
xiii, Victorian Street Ballad; xix, blank; 1-538, text; 539, publisher's statement;
540, Guide to Colour Coding; 541-545, "List of Titles in Ulverscroft Large
Print Series"; 546, publisher's statement.
Binding: Plastic lamination, black and white lettering on front, spine, and back.
Illustration shows an orchid, a string of pearls, and a blue bottle of poison.
Dust Jacket: Issued without a jacket.
Publication Date: March 1982.
Price: None given.
Printing: Printed and bound in Great Britain by T.J. Press (Padstow) Ltd., Pad-
stow, Cornwall.

A 26 THE GREAT DETECTIVES 1981

(a) First U.K. edition (1981)

THE GREAT DETECTIVES | SEVEN ORIGINAL INVESTIGATIONS | JULIAN
SYMONS | ILLUSTRATED BY | TOM ADAMS | ORBIS PUBLISHING | LONDON

Size: 10⅝ x 8⅜".
Pagination: [1-6] 7-143 [144].
Contents: 1, half title with illustration of a smoking gun; 2, full page color illustra-
tion of two men; 3, title page; 4, copyright page: "First published 1981 in |
Great Britain by Orbis Publishing Limited | ....Text © 1981 by Julian Symons |
Illustrations ©1981 by Tom Adams"; 5, "CONTENTS"; 6, full page color
illustration of a man with his back to a tape recorder; 7-8, "INTRODUC-
TION" by Julian Symons, along with black and white photo; 9, "ARTIST'S
NOTE" by Tom Adams, along with black and white photo; 10, full-page color
illustration for "How a Hermit Was Disturbed in His Retirement"; 11-144,
text.
Binding: Cream paper over boards, gilt lettering on spine: THE GREAT DETECTIVES
SYMONS/ADAMS | [publisher's logo: circle within a circle, rule], and the
word ORBIS.

Dust Jacket: Black lettering on yellow. Illustration shows seven oval-shaped pictures of characters in detective novels. Jacket spine is same as binding spine. Illustration on back shows a hand holding a diamond ring under a magnifying glass.
Publication Date: 1981.
Price: None given.
Printing: Typeset in Linotron 11 on 13pt Horley Old Style by Tradepools Limited, Frome, Somerset. Illustrations originated on a Magnascan 460 by Barrett Berkeley, London. Printed in Italy by I.G.D.A. Novara.
Symons's Note: The GREAT DETECTIVES are creatures of myth, and deserve the capital letters I have given them. They belong to the world of Don Quixote and Sancho Panza.... I must say something about...the most exciting and controversial part of the book, Tom Adams's illustrations.... The word *controversial* comes into play in relation to the depiction of the Great Detectives. Most of them remain unpictured in books, and have been shown only by grotesquely inaccurate figures on stage and screen.... The artist here has gallantly attempted the impossible and has gone a long way towards squaring the circle. [From the introduction.]

(b) First Canadian edition (1981)

THE GREAT DETECTIVES | SEVEN ORIGINAL INVESTIGATIONS | JULIAN SYMONS | ILLUSTRATED BY | TOM ADAMS | Van Nostrand Reinhold Ltd., Toronto | New York, Cincinnati, London, Melbourne [with VNR in a box to the left of the publisher's name and place of publication]

Same as A 26 a except for the following changes:
Contents: 3, title page has Van Nostrand Reinhold Ltd at the bottom;4, copyright page: "Text © 1981 by Julian Symons | Illustrations © by Tom Adams | Published in Canada by Van Nostrand Reinhold Ltd., Toronto | First Edition 1981."
Binding: Publisher's name and VNR logo at base of spine.
Publication Date: 1981.
Price: $16.95.

(c) First U.S. issue (1981)

GREAT DETECTIVES | SEVEN ORIGINAL INVESTIGATIONS | JULIAN SYMONS | ILLUSTRATED BY | TOM ADAMS | HARRY N. ABRAMS, INC., PUBLISHERS, NEW YORK

Same as A 26 a except for the following changes:
Contents: 3, title page identifies ABRAMS as the publisher; 4, copyright page: "Published in 1981 by Harry N. Abrams, Incorporated, New York | ....Text © 1981 by Julian Symons | Illustrations © 1981 by Tom Adams."
Binding: ABRAMS added to spine.
Dust Jacket: Jacket has a black background instead of yellow.

Publication Date: 1981.
Price: Published at $16.95 in 1981.
Price increased to $18.50 on January 1, 1982.

A 27 THE DETLING MURDERS 1982

(a) First U.K. edition (1982)

THE DETLING | MURDERS | Julian Symons | M | Macmillan

Size: 7¾ x 4¾".
Pagination: [1-8] 9-224.
Contents: 1, half title and brief plot description; 2, "by the same author" followed
  by a list of twenty-one titles; 3, title page; 4, copyright page: "Copyright ©
  Julian Symons 1982 | ....First published 1982 by MACMILLAN LONDON
  LIMITED"; 5, dedication: "To Christine Symons. | The mysterious stranger
  arrives. Is his roaring meant | To tell us that a Daniel's come to judgement?"; 6,
  "Contents"; 7, "PRELUDE"; 8, blank; 9-224, text.
Binding: Gray paper, silver lettering on spine: Symons [rule] The Detling Murders M.
Dust Jacket: Black and white lettering on front. Illustration shows trees, a town,
  and pink sunset reflecting on water. Black and white lettering on red spine; red
  M on white at base of spine. Back has photograph of Julian Symons by Mark
  Gerson. Jacket illustration by Martin White.
Publication Date: April 1982.
Price: £5.95.
Symons's Note: [See A 24.]
Author's Note: The publication of *The Detling Murders* marks a major change in
  Julian Symons's choice of publisher. From 1945 to 1954, his mysteries were pub-
  lished by Victor Gollancz Ltd. From 1956 to 1980, his publisher was Collins—
  The Crime Club. Then on December 12, 1981, in a double-page spread of *The
  Bookseller (pp. 2020-2021)* Macmillan London announced that Julian would be
  joining Macmillan. Later, on the back cover of a proof copy of *The Detling Murders*, the publisher wrote: "Macmillan London is delighted to announce that in
  April 1982 Julian Symons joined the Suspense list with *The Detling Murders*, his
  third Victorian Crime novel....At the same time, a collection of Julian Symons's
  outstanding short stories also becomes available in *The Tigers of Subtopia*."

(b) First U.S. edition (1983)

THE DETLING | SECRET | JULIAN SYMONS | THE VIKING PRESS | NEW
YORK

Size: 8⅛ x 5¼".
Pagination: [i-ii] [1-8] 9-225 [226].

*Jack
from
Julian —
This is what we call a
proof copy!*

THE DETLING
MURDERS

Julian Symons

To Christine Symons
The mysterious stranger arrives. Is his roaring meant
to tell us that a Daniel's come to judgement?

M

Title Page, *The Detling Murders*, Macmillan London Limited, 1982, the first
crime novel published by Macmillan, from the uncorrected proof, inscribed
"Jack from Julian—This is what we call a proof copy!'

Contents: i, half title; ii, "Also by Julian Symons" followed by a list of twenty-two titles; 1, title page; 2, copyright page: "Copyright © 1982 by Julian Symons | ....Published in 1983 by The Viking Press | ....Originally published in Great Britain under the title *The Detling Murders.*"; 3, dedication: "To Christine Symons | The Mysterious stranger arrives. Is his roaring meant | To tell us that a Daniel's come to judgement?"; 4, blank; 5, "Contents"; 6, blank; 7, "PRELUDE"; 8, blank; 9-225, text; 226, blank.

Binding: Three-quarter yellow-orange paper boards, copper-colored lettering on black paper spine: JULIAN SYMONS THE DETLING SECRET VIKING.

Dust Jacket: Orange and white lettering on black. Illustration shows Victorian woman playing piano for an audience of five men. Orange, red-orange, and white lettering on spine. Back has reviewers' comments on *The Detling Secret.* Jacket design by Jackie Schuman.

Publication Date: February 8, 1983.

Price: $14.75.

Printing: Printed in the United States of America.

(c) Second U.S. issue (1983)

Same as A 27 b except for the following change
Contents: 2, copyright page: "Second printing February 1983."

(d) Second U. K. (large print) edition (1983)

JULIAN SYMONS | [rule] | THE DETLING | MURDERS | Complete and Unabridged | [publisher's logo: castle turret] | ULVERSCROFT | Leicester

Size: 8⅞₆ x 5¼".

Pagination: [i-x] [1-2] 3-322 [323-326].

Contents: i, eight-line poem by Janice James on the wonderful world of books; ii, blank; iii, half title and story outline; iv, "Books by Julian Symons in the | Ulverscroft Large Print Series" followed by a list of two titles; v, title page; vi, copyright page: "First published 1982 by | Macmillan London Ltd. | ....Published in the United States | under the title | *The Detling Secret.* First Large Print Edition | published December 1983 | ....Copyright © Julian Symons 1982"; vii, dedication: "To CHRISTINE SYMONS"; viii, blank; ix, "Contents"; x, blank; 1, "Prelude"; 2, blank; 3-323, text; 324, publisher's statement; 325, Guide to the Colour Coding of covers in the large print series; 326, publisher's statement.

Binding: Plastic lamination, black and white lettering on front and spine. Color illustration on front cover shows silhouette of London in background and two women in Victorian boating dresses in foreground.

Dust Jacket: Issued without a jacket.

Publication Date: December 1983.

Price: Not given.

Printing: Printed and Bound in Great Britain by T. J. Press (Padstow) Ltd., Padstow, Cornwall.

THE TIGERS OF SUBTOPIA

and
Other Stories

Julian Symons

THE VIKING PRESS   NEW YORK

Title page, *The Tigers of Subtopia and Other Stories*, The Viking Press, the first title from Viking.

(e) First U.S. paperback edition (1984)

THE DETLING SECRET I JULIAN SYMONS I [publisher's logo: penguin in oval] I PENGUIN BOOKS

Size: 7⅛ x 4³⁄₁₆".
Pagination: [i-iv] [1-8] 9-225 [226-236].
Contents: i, half title and biographical note; ii, blank; iii, "Also by Julian Symons" followed by twenty-four titles; iv, blank; 1, title page; 2, copyright page: "Published in Penguin Books 1984 I Copyright ©Julian Symons, 1982"; 3, dedication: "To Christine Symons I The mysterious stranger arrives. Is his roaring meant I To tell us that a Daniel's come to judgement?"; 4, blank; 5, "Contents"; 6, blank; 7, "PRELUDE"; 8, blank; 9-225, text; 226, blank; 227, order information; 228-236, blank.
Binding: Black and green paper. White lettering on front: JULIAN SYMONS I Grand Master—Mystery Writers of America I THE DETLING SECRET I "No one today practices the classical I English detective story more skillfully I than Julian Symons." —*Newsweek*. Bottom right corner: [publisher's logo: penguin in green oval] I CRIME. Cover illustration is a piano keyboard, rosary beads, a necklace, and a silver tray. Double-framed old-fashioned photographs of a man and a woman are laying on the keyboard. Black and white lettering on green spine: JULIAN SYMONS THE DETLING SECRET I ISBN 0 14 I 00.6467 I 2 [publisher's logo] I CRIME. White lettering on back includes promotional blurb, reviews, price list, genre, ISBN, and logo. Cover design by Neil Stuart. Cover photograph by Irvin Cook.
Publication Date: 1984.
Price: U.K. £1.95, Aust. $5.95 (recommended), N.Z. $7.95, Canada $3.95, U.S.A. $2.95.
Printing: Printed in the United States of America by George Banta Co., Inc., Harrisonburg, Virginia. Set in Caslon.

A 28   THE TIGERS OF SUBTOPIA AND OTHER STORIES.   1982

(a) First U.K. edition (1982)

THE TIGERS OF I SUBTOPIA I and I Other Stories I Julian Symons I M I Macmillan

Size: 7¾ x 4⅞".
Pagination: [1-8] 9-221 [222-224].
Contents: 1, blank; 2, "by the same author" followed by a list of twenty-two titles; 3, title page; 4, copyright page: "This collection first published 1982 by I MACMILLAN LONDON LIMITED"; 5, dedication: "To Daniel James Symons"; 6, continuation of the copyright page with individual list of copyrights for the stories in this collection; 7, "Contents"; 8, blank; 9-221, text; 222-224, blank.

Binding: Maroon paper over boards, silver lettering on spine: Symons [rule] The Tigers of Subtopia M.

Dust Jacket: Yellow lettering on maroon. Black and white lettering on red spine; red M on white at base of spine. Back has photograph of Julian Symons by Mark Gerson. Jacket design by Ace.

Publication Date: April 1982.

Price: £6.95.

Printing: Typeset in Great Britain by MB GRAPHIC SERVICES LIMITED Bovingdon, Hertfordshire. Printed in Great Britain by THE ANCHOR PRESS LIMITED Tiptree, Essex.

Symons's Note: This story ["A Theme for Hyacinth"] has two points of origin. One is Wallace Stevens's marvellous poem 'Le Monocle de Mon Oncle,' much of which has stayed in my mind ever since I first read it many years ago.... The setting for the story was provided by Lokrum, that attractive little island very near to Dubrovnik.... These two elements, Stevens's poem and the little islands outside Dubrovnik, certainly shaped the story, and could even be said to bear responsibility for it. I just wrote it down.

(b) First U.S. edition (1983)

THE TIGERS OF | SUBTOPIA | and | Other Stories | Julian Symons | THE VIKING PRESS NEW YORK

Size: 8⅛ x 5⅛".

Pagination: [i-ii] [1-8] 9-221 [222-226].

Contents: i, [publisher's logo: Viking ship]; ii, blank; 1, half title; 2, "Also by Julian Symons" followed by a list of twenty-two titles; 3, title page; 4, copyright page: "Copyright © 1965, 1968, 1969, 1971, 1979, 1982 by Julian | Symons | ....Published in 1983 by The Viking Press"; 5, dedication: "To Daniel James Symons"; 6, blank; 7, "Contents"; 8, blank; 9-221, text; 222-226, blank.

Binding: Three-quarter goldenrod paper, gilt lettering on black cloth spine: Julian Symons THE TIGERS OF SUBTOPIA VIKING.

Dust Jacket: White and gilt lettering on black front, back, and spine. At bottom of front: Julian Symons | 1982 Grand Master—Mystery Writers of America. Back has heading "Praise for *The Tigers of Subtopia*" and reviewers' comments. Jacket design by George W. Sanders, Jr.

Publication Date: February 8, 1983.

Price: $14.75.

Printing: Printed in the United States of America. Set in Baskerville.

(c) First U.K. paperback edition (1984)

JULIAN SYMONS | THE TIGERS OF | SUBTOPIA | *and other stories* | [publisher's logo: penguin in oval] | PENGUIN BOOKS

Size: 7⅟₁₆ x 4⁵⁄₁₆".

Pagination: [1-8] 9-221 [222-224].

Contents: 1, half title and biographical note; 2, blank; 3, title page; 4, copyright page: "Published in Penguin Books 1984 | Copyright © Julian Symons, 1965, 1967, 1968, 1969, 1971, 1979, 1982"; 5, dedication: "To Daniel James Symons"; 6, blank; 7, "Contents"; 8, blank; 9-31 [The Tigers of Subtopia]; 32, blank; 33-50 [The Dupe]; 51-76 [Somebody Else]; 77-97 [The Flowers that Bloom in the Spring]; 98, blank; 99-112 [The Boiler]; 113-126 [The Murderer]; 127-152 [A Theme for Hyacinth]; 153-163 [The Last Time]; 164, blank; 165-186 [The Flaw]; 187-199 [Love Affair]; 200, blank; 201-221 [The Best Chess Player in the World]; 222, blank; 223, order information; 224, titles by Julian Symons.

Binding: Green and black paper. White lettering on front illustration: JULIAN SYMONS | Grand Master—Mystery Writers of America | [box rule top and left side] THE TIGERS OF | SUBTOPIA and Other Stories | "Ingenious, unbalancing, ironic, and witty" | —*The New Yorker.* Green lettering in bottom right corner: [publisher's logo] | CRIME. Cover illustration is a photograph of a chess set made of exposed aggregate reflected in a gazing globe. White and black lettering on green spine: JULIAN SYMONS THE TIGERS OF SUBTOPIA and Other Stories | ISBN 0 14 | 00.6693 4 | [publisher's logo] | CRIME. White lettering on back includes promotional blurb, reviews, price list, genre, ISBN, logo. Cover design by Neil Stuart. Cover photograph by Irvin Cook.

Publication Date: 1984.

Price: U.K. £1.75, Aust. $4.95 (recommended), Canada $3.50, U.S.A. $3.50.

Printing: Made and printed in Great Britain by Richard Clay (The Chaucer Press) Ltd, Bugay, Suffolk.

(d) Limited edition (1990)

Julian Symons | SOMEBODY ELSE | and other stories | Eurographica | Helsinki

Size: 8¹⁄₁₆ x 5¹¹⁄₁₆".

Pagination: [1-10] 11-33 [34-36] 37-70 [71-72] 73-106 [107-112].

Contents: 1-2, blank; 3, "Mystery and Spy Authors | in | Signed Limited Editions | 14"; 4, blank; 5, title page; 6, copyright page: "Copyright ©Julian Symons 1990"; 7, contents; 8, blank; 9, "The Dupe"; 10, blank; 11-106, text; 107-108, blank; 109, colophon; 110-112, blank.

Binding: Rust-red wrappers over light board with black lettering: Julian Symons | SOMEBODY ELSE | AND OTHER STORIES | EUROGRAPHICA. Black lettering on spine: Julian Symons SOMEBODY ELSE e. The ISBN is printed in black at the bottom of the back cover.

Dust Jacket: Issued without a jacket.

Publication Date: May 1990.

Price: nla.

Printing: Tipografia Nobili.

Author's Note: From the colophon: "This book, edited by Rolando Pieraccini, has been printed in 350 copies by Tipografia Nobili, established in Pesaro in 1823, on special Michelangelo paper made at the Magnani Paper Mills in Pescia,

THE NAME OF
ANNABEL LEE

Julian Symons

Macmillan London

Title page, *The Name of Annabel Lee*,
Macmillan London Ltd., 1983.

Italy. All the copies are numbered and signed by the author. Printing completed in May 1990. This is one of 20 additional copies printed for personal use of the author."

These three stories—"The Dupe," "Somebody Else," and "A Theme for Hyacinth"—along with eight others were first published in book form in 1982 under the title *The Tigers of Subtopia and Other Stories.*

A 29   THE NAME OF ANNABEL LEE   1983

(a) First U.K. edition (1983)

THE NAME OF | ANNABEL LEE | Julian Symons | M | Macmillan London

Size: 7¾ x 4¾".

Pagination: [1-12] 13-190 [191-192].

Contents: 1, half title and brief plot description; 2, "by the same author" followed by a list of twenty-three titles; 3, title page; 4, copyright page: "Copyright © Julian Symons 1983 | ....First published 1983 by MACMILLAN LONDON LIMITED, London and Basingstoke"; 5, dedication: "For Harald and Kirsten Mogensen"; 6, blank; 7, excerpts from Poe's *Annabel Lee* and a quote from Conrad Aiken; 8, blank; 9, "Contents"; 10, blank; 11, PART ONE; 12, blank; 13-191, text; 192, blank.

Binding: Medium blue paper over boards, silver lettering on spine: Symons [rule] The Name of Annabel Lee M.

Dust Jacket: White and red lettering on dark background. Illustration shows an over-turned bust, labeled with the initials E. A. P., next to a telephone with its receiver off the hook. Jacket illustration by Robert Adams.

Publication Date: 1983.

Price: £6.95.

Printing: Typeset by Messengertype, Chatham, Kent. Printed in Great Britain by The Anchor Press Limited, Tiptree, Essex.

Symons's Note: I spent a happy year from August, 1975, onwards, teaching at Amherst College in Massachusetts. It was the only time in my life that I have ever done any teaching, and almost from the first day I enjoyed it. I had some curiosity value for the students, in the sense that I was that rarity among teachers, somebody who made his living in the marketplace. I felt afterwards that I should put the experience to some kind of use, and did so in this book, although of course Graham College is not Amherst. I asked American friends to check my dialogue, my usages and my places, but still feel that I got some things subtly—or perhaps not so subtly—wrong. The atmosphere is not quite right, the climactic scene in New York is sensational but doesn't have the note of horror I intended. There are successful individual scenes and characters, but Annabel Lee herself is, I fear, a fictional character who seems drawn from other fiction.

Fly leaf, *The Name of Annabel Lee*, inscribed "Julian for Jack—nice to see him again—and Bonnie! Walmer, September, 1984."

(b) Second U.K. issue (1983)

THE NAME OF | ANNABEL LEE | Julian Symons | BOOK CLUB ASSOCIATES | LONDON

A reissue of A 29 a with the following changes:
Contents: 3, title page; Book Club Associates; 4, "This edition published 1983 by Book Club Associates by arrangement with Macmillan London Limited."
Binding: Spine: [publisher's logo: bca in a square].
Dust Jacket: Back of jacket is blank; publisher's logo added to spine; price and ISBN removed from inside front flap; "CN5686" added to inside back flap.

(c) First U.S. edition (1983)

THE | NAME OF | ANNABEL | LEE | JULIAN SYMONS [rule underlining Julian Symons's name] | [publisher's logo: Viking ship] | THE VIKING PRESS NEW YORK

Size: 8½ x 5⅛".
Pagination: [1-12] 13-190 [191-192].
Contents: 1, half title; 2, "Also by Julian Symons" followed by a list of twenty-three titles; 3, title page; 4, copyright page: "Copyright © 1983 by Julian Symons"; 5, dedication: "For Harald and Kirsten Mogensen"; 6, blank; 7, excerpts from Poe's *Annabel Lee* and a quote by Conrad Aiken; 8, blank; 9, "Contents"; 10, blank; 11, "PART ONE"; 12, blank; 13-191, text; 192, blank.
Binding: Three-quarter light blue paper over boards, silver lettering for title and red lettering for author and publisher on spine: THE NAME OF ANNABEL LEE JULIAN SYMONS VIKING.
Dust Jacket: Lavender and white lettering on black front and spine. Illustration shows the heads of three long-haired women. Red lettering on light blue back: "From the File on Julian Symons." Back has reviewers' comments in black lettering. Jacket design by Jack Ribik.
Publication Date: November 1983.
Price: $ 13.95.
Printing: Printed in the United States of America. Set in Plantin.

(d) Second U.K. (large print) edition (1984)

THE NAME OF | ANNABEL LEE | JULIAN SYMONS | [publisher's logo: crescent shaped building] | A New Portway Large Print Book | [rule] | CHIVERS PRESS | BATH

Size: 8⁷⁄₁₆ x 5⅛".
Pagination: [i-xii] 1-276.

Contents: i, half title and brief plot description; ii, blank; iii, title page; iv, copyright page: "First published 1983 by Macmillan London Limited This Large Print edition published by Chivers Press....1984. Copyright © Julian Symons 1983; v, dedications; vi, blank; vii, poems by E.A. Poe and Conrad Aiken; viii, blank; ix, contents, x, blank, xi, half title; xii, blank, 1-276, text.

Binding: Blue paper over boards, stamped in gilt on spine: LARGE PRINT [circled] THE NAME OF ANNABEL LEE Julian Symons New Portway [circled].

Dust Jacket: Pink and white lettering on front. Illustration is a photograph of a Jack-in-the-Box with the face of a woman, borders are pink and green. Black lettering on white and maroon spine and back.

Publication Date: 1984.

Price: Not given.

Printing: Photoset, printed and bound in Great Britain by Redwood Burn Ltd. Trowbridge, Wiltshire.

(e) First U.K. paperback edition (1984)

Julian Symons | [decorative rule] | THE NAME | OF ANNABEL LEE | [publisher's logo: penguin in oval] | Penguin Books

Size: 7⅛ x 4⅜".

Pagination: [1-12] 13-171 [172-176].

Contents: 1, half title and biographical note; 2, blank; 3, title page; 4, copyright page: "Published in Penguin Books, 1984 | Copyright ©Julian Symons, 1983" 5, dedication: "For Harald and Kirsten Mogensen; 6, blank; 7, excerpt from poem by Edgar Allan Poe, excerpt from poem by Conrad Aiken; 8, blank; 9, "CONTENTS"; 10, blank; 11, "[decorative rule] | PART ONE"; 12, blank; 13-172, text; 173, addresses and order information; 174, blank; 175, more titles by Julian Symons; 176, edited by Julian Symons.

Binding: Black and green paper. White lettering on illustration: JULIAN SYMONS | Grand Master—Mystery Writers of America | [top and side rule of box] THE NAME OF ANNABEL LEE | "Symons is one of the few | remaining practitioners | of the pure British | cerebral mystery." | —*The Wall Street Journal*. Green lettering in lower right corner: [publisher's logo] | CRIME. Cover illustration shows a photograph of a spool of audiotape and a packet of white powder resting on a copy of *The Poems of Edgar Allan Poe* opened to "Annabel Lee." White and black lettering on green spine: JULIAN SYMONS THE NAME OF ANNABEL LEE | ISBN 0 14 | 00.6913 5 | [publisher's logo] | CRIME. White lettering on black back includes promotional blurb, reviews. price list, genre, ISBN, logo. Cover design by Neil Stuart. Cover photograph by Paul Wakefield.

Publication Date: 1984.

Price: U.K. £1.95, Aust. $4.95 (recommended), N.Z. $7.95, Canada $3.95, U.S.A. $3.50.

Printing: Filmset in Monophoto Photina by Northumberland Press Ltd, Gateshead, Tyne and Wear. Printed and bound in Great Britain by Cox & Wyman Ltd, Reading.

A 30   THE JULIAN SYMONS OMNIBUS   1984

(a) First U.K. paperback edition (1984)

The | Julian Symons | Omnibus | THE MAN WHO KILLED HIMSELF | THE
MAN WHOSE DREAMS CAME TRUE | THE MAN WHO LOST HIS WIFE |
[publisher's logo: a penguin in an oval] | Penguin Books

Size: 7¾ x 5".
Pagination: [1-10] 11-169 [170-176] 177-405 [406-412] 413-608.
Contents: 1, half title and brief plot description; 2, blank; 3, title page; 4, copy-
   right page: "This collection published as *The Julian Symons Omnibus* 1984 |
   Copyright © Julian Symons, 1984"; 5, "Contents"; 6, blank; 7, "The Man
   Who Killed Himself"; 8, "Note"; 9, "Contents"; 10, blank; 11-169, text; 170,
   blank; 171, "The Man Whose Dreams Came True"; 172, blank; 173, "Contents"; 174, blank; 175, "PART ONE"; 176, blank; 177-405, text; 406, blank;
   407, "The Man Who Lost His Wife"; 408, blank; 409, "Contents"; 410,
   blank; 411, "PART ONE"; 412, blank; 413-608, text.
Binding: Paperbound in black with a green and white spine. Front cover has white
   and pink lettering. Bottom half of front shows silhouettes of three men: one in
   bed, one in a casket, and one on a gaming table. Spine is green at the top and
   bottom and white with black lettering in the center. Back cover is black with
   white lettering. Cover design is by George Hardie.
Dust Jacket: Issued without a jacket.
Publication Date: 1984.
Price: £3.50 | $8.95.
Printing: Made and printed in Great Britain by Richard Clay (The Chaucer Press)
   Ltd, Bungay, Suffolk. Set in Plantin.

A 31   THE CRIMINAL COMEDY OF
THE CONTENTED COUPLE   1985

(a) First U.K. edition (1985)

JULIAN | SYMONS | THE | CRIMINAL | COMEDY | OF THE | CONTENTED |
COUPLE | M | MACMILLAN

Size: 7¾ x 4¾".
Pagination: [1-10] 11-220 [221-224].
Contents: 1, half title and brief plot description; 2, "by the same author" followed
   by a list of twenty-four titles; 3, title page; 4, copyright page: "Copyright ©
   Julian Symons 1985 | ....First published 1985 by MACMILLAN LONDON
   LIMITED"; 5, "Contents"; 6, "Acknowledgements"; 7, "From The *Sunday
   Banner Colour Magazine,* | December 1979"; 8, blank; 9, PART ONE | The
   Letters, The Revolver, The Drink; 10, blank; 11-220, text; 221-224, blank.

Binding: Black paper over boards, gilt lettering on spine: Symons [rule] The Criminal Comedy of the Contented Couple M.

Dust Jacket: Black and tan lettering on white front with a hand gun pictured at the bottom. Black and white lettering on red spine; red M on white at base of spine. Black lettering on white back. Back has reviewers' comments on *The Name of Annabel Lee.*

Publication: 1985.

Price: £7.95.

Printing: Typeset by Bookworm Typesetting. Printed and bound in Great Britain by Anchor Brendon Ltd., Tiptree.

Symons's Note: This title was too much for my U.S. publisher, and in the end I consented to *A Criminal Comedy* for its American public, although I liked it less than the British original. The story itself was one of those rarities that went smoothly in the writing from beginning to end, with none of my customary back-tracking and elimination of what seem otiose characters. The uncomfortable train journey to Venice was based on one endured by my wife and myself (Jason's indignation at the lack of a restaurant car was our own), nothing in the book seems to be really unlikely, the quest for D.M. Cruddle bears a distant resemblance to my brother A.J.'s *Quest for Corvo,* and Cruddle himself is more or less a Corvine figure; the solution will I hope have baffled most readers as it did Ruth Rendell. It's inevitable that with age one should worry about flagging powers, but I felt cheerful when I had completed this book, thinking it among the best and sharpest of those I have written in the last few years.

(b) First U.S. edition (1986)

[double rule] A [double rule] | CRIMINAL | COMEDY | [double rule] | JULIAN SYMONS | [publisher's logo: Viking ship] | VIKING

Size: 8¼ x 5⅛".

Pagination:[i-ii] [1-10] 11-220 [221-222].

Contents: i, half title plus box in lower right-hand corner: A VIKING NOVEL OF MYSTERY AND SUSPENSE; ii, "by the same author" followed by a list of twenty-five titles; 1, title page; 2, copyright page: "First American Edition | Published in 1986 | Copyright © Julian Symons, 1985 | .... First published in Great Britain under the title | *The Criminal Comedy of the Contented Couple.*"; 3, "Contents"; 4, "Acknowledgements"; 5, half title; 6, blank; 7, "From The *Sunday Banner Colour Magazine,* | December 1979"; 8, blank; 9, "PART ONE | The Letters, The Revolver, The Drink"; 10, blank; 11-220, text; 221-222,blank.

Binding: Black paper over boards, gilt lettering on spine: Julian | Symons A CRIMINAL COMEDY [rule] VIKING [rule].

Dust Jacket: White lettering on black front and spine. Illustration is a photograph of a hand gun, two wedding rings, and an Italian postage stamp. White and tan lettering on black back. Back has reviewers' comments. Jacket photograph by Thomas Lindley. Jacket design by Neil Stuart.

Publication Date: January 1986.
Price: $14.95.
Printing: Printed in the United States of America by R.R. Donnelley & Sons Company, Harrisonburg, Virginia. Set in Baskerville.

(c) First U.S. paperback edition (1987)

[offset double rule] A [offset double rule] I CRIMINAL I COMEDY I [offset double rule] I JULIAN SYMONS I [publisher's logo: penguin in oval] ; PENGUIN BOOKS

Size: 6⅞ x 4³⁄₁₆".
Pagination: [i-ii] [1-10] 11-220 [221-222].
Contents: i, half title and biographical note; ii, "Also by Julian Symons" followed by twenty-five titles; 1, title page; 2, copyright page: "Published in Penguin Books 1987 I Copyright ©Julian Symons, 1985"; 3, "Contents"; 4, "Acknowledgments"; 5, half title; 6, blank; 7, feature from The *Sunday Banner Colour Magazine*; 8, blank; 9, "PART ONE I The Letters, The Revolver, The Drink"; 10, blank; 11-220, text; 221-222, blank.
Binding: Black and red paper with a gold band across top of front. Black, white, and red lettering on illustration: [in gold band] GRAND MASTER—MYSTERY WRITERS OF AMERICA I JULIAN SYMONS I [offset double rule] A [offset double rule] I Criminal I Comedy I "Superlative... I A master at the top of his form" — Ruth Rendell. White lettering parallel to spine: SELECT PENGUIN • ISBN 0 14 00.9621 3 • $3.50 U.S. White lettering in lower left corner: [publisher's logo] I CRIME. Cover illustration is a photograph of a hand gun, two wedding rings, and an Italian postage stamp. White lettering on red spine: JULIAN SYMONS A CRIMINAL COMEDY I IN U.S. I $3.50 I [rule] I ISBN 014 I 00.9621 3 I [publisher's logo] I CRIME. White lettering on red back includes review and promotional blurb. Black lettering in white box includes logo, ISBN, price, bar code.
Publication Date: 1987.
Price: $3.50.
Printing: Printed in the United States of America by Offset Paperback Mfrs., Inc., Dallas, Pennsylvania. Set in Baskerville.

A 32   CRIMINAL ACTS   1987

(a) First U.S. edition (1987)

CRIMINAL I ACTS I THREE I BY I JULIAN I SYMONS I THE I NARROWING I CIRCLE I THE I END OF I SOLOMON GRUNDY I THE I BLACKHEATH I POISONINGS I BOOK-OF-THE-MONTH CLUB I SPECIAL EDITION I BOOK-OF-THE-MONTH CLUB I NEW YORK [rule down the center of page]

Size: 8³⁄₁₆ x 5½".
Pagination: [i-xii] 1-217 [i-iii] [1-2] 3-241 [i-iii] 1-302 [303-308].

Contents: i-ii, blank; iii, half title with photograph of gun, bullets, knife and bottle of poison; iv, blank; v, "ALSO BY JULIAN SYMONS" followed by a list of thirty-one titles; vi, blank; vii, title page; viii, copyright page; "THE NAR-ROWING CIRCLE I Copyright © 1954 by Julian Gustave Symons, renewed 1982 I Published 1955 by Harper & Row, Publishers, Inc. I THE END OF SOLOMON GRUNDY I © 1964 by Julian Symons I Published 1964 by Harper & Row, Publishers, Inc. I THE BLACKHEATH POISONINGS I © 1978 by Julian Symons I Published 1979 I by Harper & Row, Publishers, Inc. I Published in one volume by I arrangement with Harper & Row, I Publishers and the author"; ix, repeat of edition title; x, blank, xi, half title; xii, blank, 1-217, text; i, blank; ii, half title; iii, blank; 1, "Part 1"; 2, blank; 3-241, text; i, blank, ii, half title; iii, "ACKNOWLEDGEMENTS"; 1-302, text; 303-308, blank.

Binding: Gray paper over boards, silver lettering on black cloth spine: CRIMINAL I ACTS I THREE I BY I JULIAN I SYMONS I [BMC logo].

Dust Jacket: Pink and white lettering on front, spine, and back. Illustration is photograph of a gun, knife, two cartridges, and a bottle of poison, wrapping front to back. Jacket photograph by Richard Chestnut. Jacket design by Steven Max Singer.

Publication Date: Not given; circa October, 1987.

Price: $17.95.

Printing: Manufactured in the United States of America.

A 33   DID SHERLOCK HOLMES MEET HERCULE   1988

(a) First U.S. limited edition (1988)

Did I Sherlock Holmes I Meet Hercule... I by JULIAN SYMONS I [red rule] I Wood Engravings by I John DePol I [red rule] I The Yellow Barn Press I Council Bluffs

Size: 8⅞ x 5¾".

Pagination: [1-6] 7-21 [22-24].

Contents: 1, blank; 2, frontispiece: wood engraving by John DePol; 3, title page; 4, copyright page: "Copyright 1987 by Julian Symons"; 5, blank; 6, text; 7, text with illustrations; 8, text; 9, text with illustration; 10-19, text; 20, text with illustration; 21, text; 22, blank; 23, colophon with illustration; 24, blank.

Binding: case bound, gray and white DePol pattern paper over boards with red cloth spine. Black lettering on gray rectangular spine label with black double rule border: Did Sherlock Holmes Meet Hercule... Symons.

Dust Jacket: Issued without a jacket.

Publication Date: February 15, 1988.

Price: $35.00.

Printing: Printed at the Yellow Barn Press, Council Bluffs, Iowa.

Author's Note: From the colophon: "This book was printed at the Yellow Barn Press, Council Bluffs, Iowa in the winter of 1987-88. Neil Shaver was the pressman using a Vandercook Universal. The paper is Rives mould-made. The text

Did
Sherlock Holmes
Meet Hercule...

by JULIAN SYMONS

Wood Engravings by
JOHN DE POL

The Yellow Barn Press
Council Bluffs

Title page, *Did Sherlock Holmes Meet Hercule...*, The Yellow Barn Press, 1988.

January 1987   Julian Symons

DID SHERLOCK HOLMES MEET....?

[Did Sherlock Holmes ever meet Hercule Poirot? This
is not so unlikely a supposition as it might seem. The last
recorded Sherlock Holmes case takes place in 1914 on the eve of
World War I, after which he retired to bee-keeping on the
Sussex downs. At that time Poirot, according to the best
information we have, was fifty and still active, (the account of his
of his retirement in 1904 (in The Mysterious Affair at Styles)
being no doubt a printing error.
The following account   It is this possibility that
gives peculiar interest to the following story, even though it
is regrettably not quite complete. particularly as it does not
come from the batch Dr Watson's battered dispatch-box
containing details of many important cases of Sherlock which
he placed "somewhere in the vaults of the bank of Cox & Company
at Charing Cross." where it presumably remains.   It was
found, instead, rather, among the papers of Poirot's friend
Captain Arthur Hastings, who recorded a number of the
great Belgian detective's cases. /   The narration is unfortunately
not quite complete,   but there can be only a few lines
                                    and narration by Dr Watson
why should a case involving Sherlock Holmes / be among the Hastings the
Hastings papers?   Perhaps the narrative itself answere that
question.
missing at the end.   Of course, no absolute guarantee of
its authenticity, I can be given < or of its relevance to the
                                     two great detectives,

Manuscript page, *Did Sherlock Holmes Meet Hercule...*, January, 1987,
showing Julian Symons's corrections to the original manuscript.

was set in 12-point Monotype Bulmer at the Los Angeles Type Founders with refinements by hand at the Press. John DePol created the pattern paper for the cover. Jack Walsdorf, an admirer of Julian Symons, made this edition possible. Finished on the 15th day of February, 1988. This is copy number ____ of 200 copies." Numbered by hand in black ink. This story first appeared in the April, 1987, edition of "The Illustrated London News," which carried a full-color front cover illustration of Holmes and the headline: "SHERLOCK HOLMES SENSATION Edwardian spy scandal: Poirot Link exposed FULL STORY INSIDE."

A 34   THE KENTISH MANOR MURDERS   1988

(a) First U.K. edition (1988)

The Kentish Manor | Murders | Julian Symons | M | MACMILLAN | LONDON

Size: 7¾ x 4¹³⁄₁₆".
Pagination: [1-6] 7-191 [192].
Contents: 1, half title and brief plot description; 2, "by the same author" followed by a list of twenty-five titles; 3, title page; 4, copyright page: "Copyright © Julian Symons 1988 | ....First published in 1988 by MACMILLAN LONDON LIMITED"; 5, "Contents"; 6, blank; 7-191, text; 192, blank.
Binding: Burnt-orange paper over boards with gilt lettering on spine: Symons [rule] The Kentish Manor Murders M.
Dust Jacket: White lettering on front. Illustration is photograph of book shelves and a person holding a typewritten sheet of paper. Black and white lettering on red spine; red M on white at base of spine. Black lettering on white back. Back has reviewers' comments on *The Criminal Comedy of the Contented Couple* and *The Name of Annabel Lee.* Jacket photograph by Marcus Wilson-Smith.
Publication Date: April 1988.
Price: £9.95.
Printing: Typeset by Matrix, 21 Russell St., London SC2. Printed by Anchor Brendon Ltd. Tiptree, Essex.
Symons's Note: [See A 22.]

(b) First U.S. edition (1988)

[rule] |THE [rule] | KENTISH MANOR [rule] | MURDERS [rule] | Julian Symons | [publisher's logo: Viking ship] | VIKING

Size: 8¼ x 5⅛".
Pagination: [1-6] 7-191 [192].
Contents: 1, half title; 2, "by the same author" followed by a list of twenty-five titles; 3, title page; 4, copyright page: "First American Edition | Published in

DEATH'S DARKEST FACE

Julian Symons

Death's darkest face is murder, murder that comes
Subtle and cruel and secret.
Vortigern, *William Ireland*

MACMILLAN
LONDON

Title page, *Death's Darkest Face*, Macmillan London Ltd., 1990.

1988 by Viking Penguin Inc. | Copyright © Julian Symons, 1988"; 5, "Contents"; 6, blank; 7-191, text; 192, blank.

Binding: Three-quarter tan paper, gilt lettering on black cloth spine: Julian Symons THE KENTISH MANOR MURDERS [rule] VIKING [rule].

Dust Jacket: Red and white lettering on front. Illustration is photograph of a lamp with a green shade, a syringe, and a pistol on a table. Gilt border extends to spine and back border. White lettering on spine. White lettering on black back: "Praise for JULIAN SYMONS." Back has reviewers' comments. Jacket photograph by Thomas Lindley. Jacket design by Neil Stuart.

Publication Date: July 1988.

Price: $15.95.

Printing: Printed in the United States of America by Arcata Graphics, Fairfield, Pennsylvania. Set in Plantin.

(c) Second U.S. (Book Club) edition (1988)

[double rule box surrounding each title and author] THE KENTISH MANOR MURDERS | BY | JULIAN SYMONS | THE RELUCTANT RONIN | BY | JAMES MELVILLE | BERNHARDT'S EDGE | BY | COLLIN WILCOX | Published for the | DETECTIVE BOOK CLUB [trademark] | by Walter J. Black, Inc. | ROSLYN, NEW YORK | [publisher's logo: DBC]

Size: 7⁵⁄₁₆ x 5".

Pagination: [i-iv] [1-6] 7-191 [192] [3-8] 9-206 [i-iv] [1-2] 3-311 [312-316]. (Note: each novel is given separate pagination.)

Contents: i, publisher's logo: DBC; ii, blank; iii, title page; iv, copyright page: "THE KENTISH MANOR MURDERS | Copyright © 1988 by Julian Symons | THE RELUCTANT RONIN | Copyright © 1988 | by James Melville | BERNHARDT'S EDGE | Copyright © 1988 | by Collin Wilcox"; 1, publisher's statement; 2, blank, 3, half title for THE KENTISH MANOR MURDERS; 4, blank; 5, "Contents"; 6, blank, 7-191, text; 192, blank; other two novels as above.

Binding: Black and white striped paper over boards with wide band wrapping front to back. Each title and reduced picture of its original cover appears on a band on the front cover; each title also appears in a band wrapping the spine. The Detective Book Club logo is at the bottom of the spine.

Dust Jacket: Issued without a jacket.

Publication Date: 1988.

Price: $16.00.

Printing: Printed in the United States of America.

(d) Third U.S. (large print) edition (1989)

The Kentish | Manor Murders | Julian Symons | G.K. Hall & Co. | Boston, Massachusetts | 1989

Size: 8⅞₆ x 5¼".
Pagination: [i-vi] 1-288 [289-290].
Contents: i, half title; ii, blank; iii, title page; iv, copyright page: "Copyright © Julian Symons, 1988 I ....Published in Large Print by arrangement with I Viking Penguin, a division of Penguin books USA Inc."; v, "Contents"; vi, blank; 1-288, text; 289, colophon; 290, blank.
Binding: Paperbound with black and white borders on front, black spine, and black border on white back. Illustration shows a castle and full moon within an outline of Sherlock Holmes on a lavender background. Purple lettering on front cover, white lettering on spine. Black lettering on back: A Nightingale Mystery in Large Print. Cover illustration by Fritz.
Dust Jacket: Issued without a jacket.
Publication Date: 1989.
Price: $13.95.
Printing: Set in 16 pt. Plantin. From the colophon: Large print edition designed by Kipling West. Composed in 16 pt Plantin on a Xyvision 300/Linotron 202N by Marilyn Ann Richards of G.K. Hall & Co.

(e) Second U.K. issue (1989)

The Kentish Manor I Murders I Julian Symons I M I MACMILLAN I LONDON 1989 Reprint of A 34 a. Not seen.

(f) First U.S. paperback edition (1989)

[rule] I THE I [rule] I KENTISH MANOR I [rule] I MURDERS I [rule] I Julian Symons I [publisher's logo: penguin in oval] I PENGUIN BOOKS

Size: 6⅞ x 4⅛".
Pagination: [1-6] 7-191 [192].
Contents: 1, half title and biographical note; 2, blank; 3, title page; 4, copyright page: "Published in Penguin Books 1989 I 13579108642 I Copyright ©Julian Symons, 1988"; 5, "Contents"; 6, blank; 7-191, text; 192, order information.
Binding: Green paper. Green lettering, top left corner: [publisher's logo] I CRIME. White lettering in red band across top of front: Grand Master—Mystery Writers of America. Tan and light green lettering: JULIAN SYMONS I [red rule] I THE KENTISH I MANOR MURDERS. Black writing over lime green desk lamp in illustration: "Wry and intelligent and I marvelously complex—further proof I of why the Mystery Writers of America I named him a Grand Master" I —*Chicago Sun Times.* Cover illustration is a photograph of a hypodermic syringe, a desk lamp, and a handgun on a desk. Black and white lettering on light green spine: Julian Symons THE KENTISH MANOR MURDERS I ISBN 0 14 I 01. 0872 6 I [publisher's logo] I CRIME. Tan and white lettering on back with a red decorative box includes a review and a promotional blurb, logo, genre, price, ISBN. Cover design by Melissa Jacoby. Cover photograph by Thomas Lindley.

Publication Date: 1989.
Price: $3.95.
Printing: Printed in the United States of America. Set in Plantin.

(g) First U.K. paperback edition (1990)

The Kentish Manor | Murders | Julian Symons | publisher's logo: penguin in oval] | PENGUIN BOOKS

Size: 7⅛ x 4⅜".
Pagination: [1-6] 7-191 [192].
Contents: 1, half title and biographical note; 2, blank; 3, title page; 4, copyright page: "Published in Penguin Books 1990 | 1 3 5 7 9 10 8 6 4 2 | Copyright ©Julian Symons, 1988"; 5, "Contents"; 6, blank; 7-191, text; 192, blank.
Binding: Green paper with a white band wrapping to spine, white box on back. Black lettering on white patch in green band: PENGUIN BOOKS. Black lettering on white band: THE KENTISH | MANOR MURDERS | JULIAN SYMONS. Black lettering parallel to spine: CLASSIC. Black lettering parallel to right edge: CRIME. Cover illustration shows a drawing of a pipe-smoking man reading a book in the foreground, with a castle in the background. Black lettering on white part of spine: JULIAN SYMONS • THE KENTISH MANOR MURDERS. Black lettering on green band of spine: ISBN 0 14 | 01.2714 3 | [publisher's logo]. Back has black lettering on white box with green border and includes a photograph of Julian Symons. Cover illustration by Tony McSweeney.
Publication Date: 1990.
Price: U.K. £3.99, Austr. $10.99 (recommended) Canada $5.95, N.Z. $15.95 (incl. GST).
Printing: Printed and bound in Great Britain by Cox and Wyman Ltd, Reading, Berks.

A 35   DEATH'S DARKEST FACE   1990

(a) First U.K. edition (1990)

[black and white drawing of lips and chin] DEATH'S | DARKEST | FACE | Julian Symons | Death's darkest face is murder, murder that comes | Subtle and cruel and secret. | *Vortigen* William Ireland | M | MACMILLAN | LONDON

Size: 8¾ x 5⅜".
Pagination: [1-8] 9-272.
Contents: 1, half title; 2, "by the same author" followed by a list of twenty-six titles; 3, title page; 4, copyright page: "Copyright © Julian Symons 1990 | ....First published 1990 | by MACMILLAN LONDON LIMITED"; 5, dedication: "For Kathleen | again and always"; 6, blank; 7-8, "CONTENTS"; 9-272, text.

Binding: Maroon paper over boards, gilt lettering on spine: JULIAN I SYMONS I DEATH'S I DARKEST FACE M.
Dust Jacket: Maroon lettering on yellow and green patterned front, spine, and back. Illustration is black and white drawing of a mouth and chin. Back cover repeats the William Ireland quote found on the title page.
Publication Date: May 1990.
Price: £12.95.
Printing: Typeset by Wyvern Typesetting Limited, Bristol. Printed and bound in Great Britain by Billings Book Plan, Worcester.
Symons's Note: This is Class 1!
Author's Note: This title also became a Chivers Audio Book, read by Edward De Souza.

(b) First U.S. edition (1990)

Julian Symons I [rule] I Death's I Darkest Face I [rule] I Death's darkest face is murder, murder that comes I Subtle and cruel and secret. I *Vortigern*, William Ireland I VIKING

Size: 8⅛ x 5".
Pagination: [1-8] 9-272.
Contents: 1, half title; 2, "By the same author" followed by a list of twenty-six titles; 3, title page; 4, copyright page: "First American Edition I Published in 1990 by Viking Penguin, I a division of Penguin Books USA Inc. I 10 9 8 7 6 5 4 3 2 1 I Copyright © Julian Symons, 1990"; 5, dedication: "For Kathleen I again and always"; 6, blank; 7-8, "CONTENTS"; 9-272, text.
Binding: Three-quarter navy blue paper over boards, pink lettering on black cloth spine: Julian Symons [underlined] Death's Darkest Face [rule] VIKING [rule].
Dust Jacket: White lettering shadowed in pink on black front and spine. Illustration is a right-facing mask with a human face on the outside and green countryside on the inside. Pink lettering on black back with heading "Praise for Julian Symons" at the top and "Praise for *Death's Darkest Face*" at the bottom. Jacket illustration by Phillip Singer. Jacket design by Neil Stuart.
Publication Date: October 1990.
Price: $17.95.
Printing: Printed in the United States of America. Set in Trump Mediaeval.

(c) Second U.S. issue (1991)

Julian Symons I [rule] I Death's I Darkest Face I [rule] I Death's darkest face is murder, murder that comes I Subtle and cruel and secret. I *Vortigern*, William Ireland I Viking

A reissue of A 35 b with the following changes:
Contents: 4, delete "First American Edition" and printing line.

Binding: circle blind stamped on bottom righthand corner of back cover.
Dust Jacket: Price deleted from inside front flap.

(d) Second U.S. (large print) edition (1991)

Death's Darkest Face | Boston, Mass.: G.K. Hall, 1991.

Not seen.

(e) Second U.K. (large print) edition (1992)

DEATH'S | DARKEST FACE | JULIAN SYMONS | Death's darkest face is murder, | murder that comes | Subtle and cruel and secret. | *Vortigern,* William Ireland | [publisher's logo: crescent building within bold ovoid] | A New Portway Large Print Book | [rule] | CHIVERS PRESS | BATH

Size: 9³⁄₁₆ x 5¹⁵⁄₁₆".
Pagination: [i-ii] [i-vi] vii-viii [ix-x] 1-381 [382-386].
Contents: i-ii, blank; i, half title and plot description; ii, blank; iii, title; iv, copyright page: "This Large Print edition published by | Chivers Press | ....1992 | ....Copyright © Julian Symons 1990"; v, dedication: "For Kathleen | again and always"; vi, blank; vii-viii, "CONTENTS"; ix, half title; x, blank; 1-381, text; 382-386, blank.
Binding: Three-quarter navy blue paper over boards, metallic green lettering on blue cloth spine: LARGE | PRINT | Death's Darkest Face Julian Symons CHIVERS | PRESS.
Dust Jacket: Maroon lettering on yellow and green patterned front and spine. Illustration is black and white drawing of a mouth and chin. Back cover is yellow with black lettering.
Publication Date: 1992.
Price: £12.95.
Printing: Not given.

(f) First U.K. paperback edition (1991)

Julian Symons | [rule] | Death's | Darkest Face [rule] | Death's darkest face is murder, murder that comes | Subtle and cruel and secret. | *Vortigern,* William Ireland | [publisher's logo: penguin in oval] | PENGUIN BOOKS

Size: 6⅞ x 4³⁄₁₆".
Pagination: [1-8] 9-272.
Contents: 1, half title and biographical note; 2, blank; 3, title page; 4, copyright page: "Published in Penguin Books 1991 | 1 3 5 7 9 10 8 6 4 2 | Copyright ©Julian Symons, 1990"; 5, dedication: "For Kathleen | again and always"; 6, blank; 7-8, "CONTENTS"; 9-272, text.

Binding: Gray paper with green spine. White lettering with yellow rules on black across top third of front: Death's | [rule] | DARKEST FACE |[rule]. Gray lettering in top right corner: "A complex, moody tale of | death and redemption that | weaves first-rate fiction into | the framework of detection." | —Kevin Moore, *Chicago Tribune* [three short rules]. White lettering over illustration in bottom two-thirds of cover: JULIAN SYMONS | TWICE GRAND MASTER, | MYSTERY WRITERS OF AMERICA. Bottom left corner: [publisher's logo] | CRIME. Illustration shows a formally dressed couple in the foreground watching a man approach from across the lawn of a red house where a party is taking place. Black and white lettering on spine: JULIAN SYMONS DEATH'S DARKEST FACE ISBN 0 14 | 01.3263 5 | [publisher's logo] | CRIME. White lettering on black back with yellow wavy rules includes reviews, promotional blurb, logo, genre, ISBN and bar code. Black lettering in white box: Export only | U.K. £3.50 | U.S.A. $4.95. Cover design by Todd Radom. Cover illustration by Mark Oldroyd.
Publication Date: 1991.
Price: U.K. £3.50, U.S.A. $4.95.
Printing: Printed in the United States of America, set in Trump Mediaeval.

A 36   PORTRAITS OF THE MISSING   1991

(a) First U.K. edition (1991)

Portraits | of the Missing | Imaginary Biographies | Julian Symons | [publisher's logo: a bow and three arrows in a circle] | ANDRE DEUTSCH

Size: 8⅜ x 5¼".
Pagination: [i-viii] ix-x [xi-xii] 1-137 [138-140].
Contents: i, half title; ii, "ALSO BY JULIAN SYMONS" followed by six biography and autobiography titles, three poetry titles, three history titles, seven literature and criticism titles; iii, title page; iv, copyright page: "First published in 1991....| Copyright ©Julian Symons, 1991"; v, dedication: "In memory of Geoffrey and Jan Grigson"; vi, blank; vii, "Contents"; viii, blank; ix-xi, "Preface"; xii, blank; 1-138, text; 139-140, blank.
Binding: Black paper over boards, gilt lettering on spine: Julian Symons PORTRAIT OF THE MISSING | [publisher's logo] | Andre | Deutsch.
Dust Jacket: White lettering in red band across top of front: Julian Symons. Cream lettering in torn black band across bottom of front: PORTRAITS OF | THE MISSING. Illustration on front shows a variety of caricatures in shades of black, gray, and white, including Julian Symons, who is shown in the upper right corner having a pint. White and cream lettering on red spine: Julian Symons PORTRAITS OF THE MISSING | [publisher's logo] Andre | Deutsch. Cream lettering on black back includes a promotional blurb and the ISBN and bar code in bottom right corner. Cover illustration by Russell Davies. Cover design by Peter Rozycki.

Publication Date: 1991.

Price: £12.99.

Printing: Phototypset by Falcon Graphic Art Ltd, Wallington, Surrey. Printed by Billing & Sons Worcester.

Author's Note: In February of 1992 this edition of *Portraits of the Missing* was offered for sale in the U.S. for $22.95 from Trafalgar Square Publishing of Vermont. They affixed a label to the title page of the U.K. edition which read: Distributed by I Trafalgar Square I North Pomfret, Vermont 05053. They also covered the U.K. price on the inside front flap with a label which reads: Distributed by Trafalgar Square N. Pomfret, VT 05053.

A 37   SOMETHING LIKE A LOVE AFFAIR   1992

(a) First U.K. edition (1992)

JULIAN SYMONS I Something Like I a Love Affair I M I MACMILLAN I LONDON

Size: 8⅜ x 5¼".

Pagination: [i-viii] 1-179 [180-184].

Contents: i, half title; ii, "by the same author" followed by twenty-seven titles; iii, title page; iv, copyright page: "Copyright ©Julian Symons 1992 I ....First published 1992...."; v, dedication: "For Gavin Ewart I 'Tomorrow for the young the poets exploding like bombs'. I Like many tomorrows, that one never came.I Yet still, in this elderly today, you smilingly I Give poetry a shape, a rhyme, name."; vi, blank; vii, "CONTENTS"; viii, blank; 1-179, text; 180-184, blank.

Binding: Cream paper over boards, black lettering on spine: JULIAN SYMONS Something Like I a Love Affair I M.

Dust Jacket: Gold, black, and maroon lettering on background of white crumpled paper that wraps to back: JULIAN SYMONS I WINNER OF THE CARTIER DIAMOND DAGGER AWARD 1990. Front illustration shows the body of a semi-naked woman face down on a black leather couch. Gold, maroon, and black lettering on spine. Black and maroon lettering on back includes reviews; ISBN and bar code are in a white box. Jacket illustration by James Bradley.

Publication Date: 1992.

Price: £14.99.

Printing: Typeset by Macmillan Production Limited. Printed by Billing and Sons Limited, Worcester.

Author's Note: This title became a Sterling Audio Book read by Diana Quick.

(b) First U.S. edition (1993)

SOMETHING I LIKE A LOVE I [six rules] AFFAIR I JULIAN SYMONS I [trademark: "MYSTERIOUS PRESS" on sign board shaped like an open book] I THE MYSTERIOUS PRESS I New York • Tokyo • Sweden I Published by Warner Books I [publisher's logo: stylized W in oval] A Time Warner Company

Size: 8¼ x 5¼".
Pagination: [i-viii] 1-199 [200].
Contents: i, half title; ii, "mystery novels by Julian Symons" followed by twenty-seven titles; iii, title page; iv, copyright page: "First published in 1992 by Macmillan London Limited.... | Copyright ©1992 by Julian Symons | ....First U.S. printing: February 1993 | 10 9 8 7 6 5 4 3 2 1"; v, dedication: "For Gavin Ewart | 'Tomorrow for the young poets exploding like bombs.' | Like many tomorrows, that one never came. | Yet still, in this elderly today, you smilingly | Give poetry a shape, a rhyme, a name"; vi, blank; vii, "CONTENTS"; viii, blank; 1-199, text; 200, blank.
Binding: Blue paper over boards, gilt lettering on rose spine: JULIAN SYMONS SOMETHING LIKE A LOVE AFFAIR | [publisher's logo].
Dust Jacket: Red-to-orange lettering on blue. Cover illustration is a stylized line drawing of an embracing couple in white and shades of yellow-green. Red-to-orange lettering on spine; [publisher's logo]. Gold and orange lettering on back includes reviews; ISBN and bar code are in box. Jacket design and illustration by Daniel Pelavin.
Publication Date: February 1993.
Price: $17.95.
Printing: Printed in the United States of America.

(c) First U.S. paperback edition (1994)

JULIAN SYMONS | SOMETHING | LIKE A | LOVE | AFFAIR | [trademark: "MYSTERIOUS PRESS" on sign board shaped like an open book] | THE MYSTERIOUS PRESS | Published by Warner Books | [publisher's logo: stylized W in oval] | A Time Warner Company

Size: 6¾ x 4⅛".
Pagination: [i-viii] 1-200.
Contents: i-iii, reviews; iv, biographical note and publisher's note; v, title page; vi, copyright page: "Copyright © 1992 by Julian Symons | First Printed in Paperback: January, 1994 | 10 9 8 7 6 5 4 3 2 1 | " and dedication: "For Gavin Ewart | 'Tomorrow for the young poets exploding like bombs.' | Like many tomorrows, that one never came. | Yet still, in this elderly today, you smilingly | Give poetry a shape, a rhyme, a name." vii, "CONTENTS"; viii, blank; 1-200, text.
Binding: Black paper. Gold lettering on front: JULIAN SYMONS | SOMETHING | LIKE A | LOVE | AFFAIR. White lettering in bottom left corner: "Spare and elegant | ...Mr. Symons is | properly admired | for the immaculate | craftsmanship of | his novels." | —*New York Times* | *Book Review*. [Trademark]. Parallel to spine: 0-446-40192-7 $4.99 U.S.A. Illustration is a stylized line drawing of an embracing couple in white and shades of yellow. White and gold lettering on spine: [rule] | SUSPENSE | [trademark] | JULIAN SYMONS SOMETHING LIKE A LOVE AFFAIR | 0-446- | 40192 - 7 | 499 U.S.A. Gold and white lettering on back includes reviews, promotional blurb, ISBN and bar code, price, trademark. Cover design and illustration by John Martinez.

Publication Date: January 1994.
Price: $4.99.
Printing: Printed in the United States of America.

A 38   PLAYING HAPPY FAMILIES   1994

(a) First U.K. edition (1994)
JULIAN SYMONS | [double rule] | Playing | Happy Families | M | MACMILLAN | LONDON

Size: 8½ x 5¼".
Pagination: [i-viii] 1-264.
Contents: i, half title; ii, "ALSO BY JULIAN SYMONS" followed by twenty-nine titles; iii, title page; iv, copyright page: "Copyright © Julian Symons 1994 | .... 1 3 5 7 9 8 6 4 2"; v, dedication: "For | Harry and Sheila Keating"; vi, "Acknowledgements"; vii, "Contents"; viii, blank; 1-264, text.
Binding: Teal green paper over boards, gold lettering on spine: JULIAN | SYMONS | PLAYING HAPPY | FAMILIES | M.
Dust Jacket: Front illustration shows the right half of a woman's face with a dangling earring of a naked man. Cover is teal green; illustration is black; gold lettering. Spine has black and gold lettering with naked man illustration in teal. Back has reviews of *Death's Darkest Face* and *Something Like a Love Affair*. Jacket illustration by Fernando Mercedez.
Publication Date: 1994.
Price: £14.99.
Printing: Typeset by CentraCet Limited, Cambridge. Printed by Mackays of Chatham PLC, Chatham, Kent.

(b) First U.S. edition (1995)

JULIAN SYMONS | [rule] | PLAYING | HAPPY | FAMILIES | [logo: Mysterious Press hanging sign board] | THE MYSTERIOUS PRESS | [publisher's logo: white W in black box] | A Time Warner Company

Size: 8¼ x 5⅛".
Pagination: [i-ix] x [xi-xii] [1] 2-308.
Contents: 1, half title; ii, "mystery novels by Julian Symons" followed by twenty-eight titles; iv, copyright page; "First published in 1994 Macmillan London Limited.... | Copyright ©1994 by Julian Symons | First U.S. printing: January 1995"; v, dedication: "For | Harry and Sheila Keating"; vi, blank; vii, "Acknowledgements"; viii, blank; ix-x, Contents; xi, floating title; xii, blank; 1-308, text.
Binding: Purple paper over boards, purple lettering on gray spine: JULIAN SYMONS PLAYING HAPPY FAMILIES [logo: Mysterious Press]. Logo is also blind stamped on back lower right corner.

Dust Jacket: Silver paper wraps to back. Illustration shows a woman's face super-imposed on a living room scene with a picture on the wall and a couple standing by a table containing a vase of flowers. Purple lettering on front. Author, title, and logo on spine in purple lettering. Back cover has reviewer's comments. Jacket design by Daniel Pelavin, jacket illustration by John Martinez.
Publication Date: January 1995.
Price: $19.95.
Printing: Printed in the United States of America.

(c) Second U.K./U.S. (large print) edition (1995)

PLAYING | HAPPY | FAMILIES | Julian Symons | Thorndike Press • Chivers Press| Thorndike, Maine USA Bath, Avon, England

Size: 8⅜ x 5⅞6".
Pagination: [1-8] 9-473 [474-480]
Contents: 1, half title; 2, blank; 3, title page; 4, copyright page: "Published in 1995 in the U.S. by arrangement with | Warner Books, Inc. | Published in 1995 in the U.K. by arrangement with Macmillan London Ltd. | Copyright © 1994 by Julian Symons"; 5, dedication: "For | Harry and Sheila Keating"; 6, "Acknowledgements"; 7, "Contents"; 8, blank; 9-473, text; 474, blank; 475, information about large print titles; 476-480, blank.
Binding: Blue paper over boards. Cover has black lettering on gray-blue: Julian Symons | Playing | Happy | Families | A Novel of Suspense. Abstract illustration in gray tones on white of a couple at a table. Black lettering on spine: Large Print | Julina Symons Playing Happy Families | Thorndike Chivers. Back cover has book title, synopsis, ISBN numbers, and bar code in black lettering on white. Cover illustration by John Martinez.
Dust Jacket: Issued without a jacket.
Publication Date: 1995.
Price: nla.
Printing: Set in 16 pt. News Plantin by Rick Gundberg. Printed in the United States.

(d) First U.K. paperback edition (1995)

JULIAN SYMONS | [double rule] | Playing | Happy Families | PAN BOOKS

Size: 7 x 4⅜".
Pagination: [i-viii] 1-264.
Contents: i, half title with biographical note; ii, "ALSO BY JULIAN SYMONS" followed by twenty-nine titles; iii, title page; iv, copyright page: "First Published 1994 by Macmillan | This edition published 1995 by Pan Books.... | Copyright © Julian Symons 1994"; v, dedication: "For | Harry and Sheila Keating"; vi, "Acknowledgements"; vii, "Contents"; viii, blank; 1-264, text.

Binding: Black paper. Red and white lettering on front: Playing | Happy |Families | Cartier Diamond | Dagger Award Winner | JULIAN SYMONS. Front illustration shows a photograph, picture frame, and car keys superimposed over a silhouette of a woman. White and red lettering on spine: JULIAN SYMONS Playing Happy Families [publisher's logo] PAN. White and black lettering on back includes teases about the plot and reviews, along with genre, price, ISBN, and bar code. Cover illustration by Etan Lee Al.
Publication Date: 1995.
Price: U.K. £4.99, Australia $12.95
Printing: Typeset by CentraCet Limited, Cambridge. Printed and bound in Great Britain by Cox & Wyman, Ltd, Reading, Berkshire.

(e) First U.S. paperback edition (1995)

PLAYING | HAPPY | FAMILIES | [rule] | JULIAN SYMONS | ["Mysterious Press" on signboard shaped like an open book] | THE MYSTERIOUS PRESS | Published by Warner Books | [publisher's logo: stylized W in oval] | A Time Warner Company.

Size: 6 ¾ x 4 ⅛".
Pagination: [i-xi] xii [1] 2-273 [274-276].
Contents: i-iii, reviews; iv, "mystery novels by Julian Symons" followed by twenty-eight titles and publisher's note; v, title page; vi, copyright page: "Copyright © 1994 by Julian Symons | ....First Printed in Paperback: December, 1995 | 10 9 8 7 6 5 4 3 2 1"; vii, dedication: "For | Harry and Sheila Keating"; viii, blank; ix, "Acknowedgements"; x, blank; xi-xii, "Contents"; 1-273, text; 274, blank; 275, Ad Council Coalition for Literacy advertisement; 276, blank.
Binding: Silver paper. Purple and blue lettering on front: JULIAN SYMONS | PLAYING | HAPPY | FAMILIES. Review note and publisher's logo in black on lower left front corner. Logo, author, and title on spine. Illustration shows a woman's face superimposed on a living room scene with a picture on the wall and a couple standing by a table containing a vase of flowers. Back cover has reviews, plot tease, price code. Inside front cover has price code and reviews, inside back cover has a photo of Symons by Alex Morrison and a biographical note. Cover design by Daniel Palavin. Cover illustration by John Martinez.
Publication Date: December 1995.
Price: $5.50
Printing: Printed in the United States of America.

A 39   THE MAN WHO HATED TELEVISION AND OTHER STORIES   1995

(a) First U.K. edition (1995)

JULIAN SYMONS | The Man | Who Hated | Television | and other stories | MACMILLAN

Size: 8½ x 5¼".

Pagination: [1-6] 1-184 [185-186]

Contents: 1, half title; 2, "ALSO BY JULIAN SYMONS" followed by thirty titles; 3, title page; 4, copyright page: "First published 1995 by Macmillan London | ....This collection copyright © Julian Symons 1995"; 5, "Contents"; 6, blank; 1-184, text; 185-186, blank.

Binding: Black paper over boards, gilt lettering on spine: JULIAN SYMONS The Man Who Hated Television | ...and other stories [publisher's logo].

Dust Jacket: White lettering on photograph of a woman with television test-pattern background in blue and purple; photo wraps to spine. White lettering and red logo on spine. Black and red lettering on white back includes reviews of *Playing Happy Families* and *Death's Darkest Face*, along with ISBN and bar code. Jacket photo by Paul Postle.

Publication Date: 1995

Price: £14.99

*Printing:*Typeset by CentraCet Limited, Cambridge. Printed by Mackays of Chatham PLC, Chatham, Kent.

ENDNOTES

1 Julian Symons, "Progress of a Crime Writer," in *The Mystery and Detection Annual: 1973*, ed. Donald K. Adams (Beverly Hills, Calif.: Donald Adams, 1974), p. 240.

2 *Rotten Rejections: A Literary Companion*, ed. André Bernard (Wainscott, New York: Pushcart Press, 1990), p. 62

3 Julian Symons, "Progress of a Crime Writer," in *The Mystery and Detection Annual: 1973*, ed. Donald K. Adams (Beverly Hills, Calif.: Donald K. Adams, 1974), p. 240.

4 *Who's Who in Spy Fiction*, Donald McCormick (New York, Taplinger Publisher Co., 1977), p. 168.

SECTION B

POETRY

*"I cannot pretend—I wish I could believe otherwise—
that I was more than a minor poet
of the thirties and forties."*

TWENTIETH   CENTURY   VERSE

January 1937   Sixpence   Twice Quarterly

Twentieth Century Verse is edited by Julian Symons, 17 The
Waldrons, Croydon, and printed and published by The
Noble Fortune Press, 1191 Finchley Road, London, N.W.11

EDITORIAL	**Twentieth Century Verse**

POEMS

DYLAN THOMAS	**Poem, Part One**
GEOFFREY TAYLOR	**Portrait 1936, To the Builder, In The Street, Epigram**
A. S. J. TESSIMOND	**To a Lover of Living, In that cold Land**
NORMAN HALL	**The Last Hero, The Whispering Gallery, Particular Face,**
REX WARNER	**Sonnet, Truth**
H. B. MALLALIEU	**Renewal, Poem from a Sequence**
RUTHVEN TODD	**Offering for November, Poem for F.M.**
JULIAN SYMONS	**The Romantic Speaking**

REVIEWS

HUGH GORDON PORTEUS	**Look, Stranger and The Ascent of F.6**
JULIAN SYMONS	**Mr. Thomas's Poems**

Title page, *Twentieth Century Verse*, Noble Fortune Press, 1937, Vol. 1, No. 1.

Note: For a complete listing of contributions to *Twentieth Century Verse*, see Section D. For poems that have appeared in anthologies, see Section F. For complete information about poetry collections, see B 10 and B 23 below.

1937

B 1 "The Romantic Speaking." *Twentieth Century Verse*, No. 1 (January 1937), p. [11].

B 2 "Poem," "Prologue" and "This Year." *Twentieth Century Verse*, No. 5 (September 1937), pp. [12-13].

1938

B 3 "The Place You Cannot Leave." *Purpose*, Vol. X, No. 1 (January-March 1938), pp. 47-48.

B 4 "Prelude to Poems (For A.J.A.S., S.M.S., M.A.S.)." *Twentieth Century Verse*, No. 9 (March 1938), pp. 16-17.

B 5 "Two English Poems: 'Country Weekend' and 'Musical Box Poem'." *Partisan Review*, Vol. V, No. 1 (June 1938), pp. 33-34.

B 6 "Poem (for W.E.L.)" *Twentieth Century Verse*, No. 14 (December 1938), p. 128.

B 7 "Poem." Life and Letters Today, Vol. 18, No. 12 (Summer 1938), p. 55.

B 8 "Two Poems: About Streets." *Life and Letters Today*, Vol. 20, No. 16 (December 1938), pp. 42-44.

B 9 *Confusions About X*

CONFUSIONS | ABOUT X | by | JULIAN SYMONS | THE FORTUNE PRESS | 12 BUCKINGHAM PALACE ROAD | LONDON

Size: 7½ x 5".
Pagination: [1-6] 7-47 [48].
Contents: 1, half title; 2-3, blank; 4, frontispiece drawing of Julian Symons by Wyndham Lewis; 5, title page; 6, acknowledgements; 7, "CONTENTS"; 8, blank; 9-47, text; 48, printing statement.
Binding: Green cloth or blue paper over boards. Spine stamped in gilt: CONFUSIONS ABOUT X • Julian Symons.
Dust Jacket: Light green. Front, spine, and back lettered in rust-red. Back lists thirty-three books from The Fortune Press.
Publication Date: Not given, circa December 1938.
Price: 3s.6d.

TWENTIETH CENTURY VERSE

9, CEDARS ROAD, S.W.4.

Macaulay 4628

6th December, 1939

Dear Mr. Umpleby,

Many thanks for your letter. I am afraid
present conditions have made it inevitable that
publication of the next number of TWENTIETH CENTURY
VERSE should be postponed for the present; but I
hope to be able to bring out another number, and
resume regular publication, before very long.

Yours sincerely,

Julian Symons

A. Stanley Umpleby Esq.,
Didbrook,
Linden Grove,
West Hartlepool, CO. DURHAM.

Letter signed by Julian Symons to a subscriber, 6 December, 1939, stating that
"present conditions have made it inevitable that publication of the
next number . . . should be postponed. . . ."

Printing: The Knole Park Press Limited at Sevenoaks.

Symons's Note: I can't remember how I first got in touch with R.A. Caton of the Fortune Press. It may be that I went round to the basement in Buckingham Palace Road from which he operated, to ask if he would advertise in *Twentieth Century Verse*. I already knew of the Fortune Press as a firm that published what would now be thought very mild homosexual pornography, many volumes of which were stacked round the cellar.

The upshot of this first meeting, and later conversations, was that Caton agreed to publish a collection of my poems, and also to publish other volumes recommended by me, under the title of the Fortune Poets. There was, he told me, no money in poetry, and so far as I remember, our arrangement was that I bought fifty copies of my book, *Confusions About X*, at two shillings each, the published price being three shillings and sixpence. I advertised the book in the magazine and sold all, or almost all, of the fifty copies. Later Caton published some of the magazine's other leading contributors, Roy Fuller and Gavin Ewart among them. We parted company when he began to publish other volumes of poems without consulting me, probably because the poets paid money toward the books' publication. When I remonstrated with him he replied that we had no written agreement, which was perfectly true.

Afterward, I saw him occasionally over the years in the street, often unshaven, always with a half-smile on his face. At our last meeting, just outside the London Library, he said with that half-smile: "I'm doing something in the autumn that might interest you" and produced from within the dingy raincoat he wore a copy of (I won't swear to the title's literal correctness) *Torture Through the Ages.*

And *Confusions About X* itself? I can't look at the poems now without blushing for them. No more than three or four seem other than feebly imitative of other people. How many were printed, how many sold? Caton never revealed such things, never sent royalty statements to me, or perhaps to other authors. My guess is that he printed several hundred and bound them up in batches of a hundred at a time. Certainly the book exists in two bindings, one of green cloth, the other black buckram. I think the green cloth was the first—all my fifty copies had that binding—but Caton's ways were so devious that it is impossible to be sure.

1939

B 10 "Sonnet." *Life and Letters Today*, Vol. 22, No. 26 (September 1939), p. 403.

1940

B 11 "Clapham Common." *Life and Letters Today*, Vol. 28, No. 43 (February 1940), pp. 178-180.

B 12 "The Clock." *Kingdom Come*, Vol.1, No.3 (Spring 1940), p. 77.

B 13 "Ventnor." *Kingdom Come*, Vol. 1, No. 3 (Spring 1940), p. 78.

CONFUSIONS
ABOUT X

by
JULIAN SYMONS

THE   FORTUNE   PRESS
12 BUCKINGHAM PALACE ROAD
LONDON

Title page, *Confusions About X*, The Fortune Press, 1939,
Julian Symons's first book.

DEDICATION

(FOR A.J.A.S., S.M.S, M.A.S.)

FROM the green the toy aeroplanes at morning
Swung over sea and returned like gulls.
My wilderness days were marked; you rescued me
From the ascending hills and dying valleys.
One evening I misspelt the word *several*
But concealed the mistake by subterfuge.

You are the ones who told the astonishing stories,
The cricket ball pitched on a sixpence, the experiment
With the glass bowl that was dangerous at ninety,
The dramatic words recited in darkness.
For me then too the country was chequered, trees
Moved, I saw dead men walking, Wylder's hand;

It was this to be youngest brother, to be nine
And reticent, to admire the roaring dandy
Seeking death on an Indian motor-bike
Or the industrious student saying " I propose "
Or Maurice in the evening talking of Turner the Terror.

With this purpose I write you these lines.
Things are no longer mythical : I am undoubtedly
On the beach at Clacton, my incalculable feet
On a time's quicksand dizzying the air,
I am undoubtedly in my Croydon room, waiting for
The house to fall. I am steady though unstable :
And for the moment I am not able to be afraid.

And horror begins now, it is with horror I see
All your faces are like mine, you are
Puppets like me in the iron fist of money,
Taking the financiers' heavy downward step.
This time expanding is my demon Time,
My horror sea where no one ever is
But the endless man who is afraid to weep.

But I am not afraid to weep, I raise a flood with my tears,
For you to whom brotherhood's deadly hand

9

Text page, *Confusions About X*, with corrections in Julian Symons's hand which were made, according to his inscription on the front flyleaf, "for a non-existent second edition."

B 14 "Spring 1940." *NOW*, No. 3 (Fall 1940), pp. 1-2.

B 15 "Three War Poems: 'End of a Year,' 'Pub,' 'Poem.'" *Poetry: A Magazine of Verse*, Vol. LVI, No. VI (September 1940), pp.301-304.

1941

B 16 "Poem About My Father." *Life and Letters Today*, Vol. 28, No. 43 (March 1941), p. 237.

B 17 "The Clock." *Modern Reading*, No. 1 (April 1941), p. 31.

B 18 "The Moral Nature of Man." *NOW*, No. 4 (Easter 1941), pp. 11-12.

B 19 "The Statues in Parliament Square." *NOW*, No. 6 (Summer 1941), p. 23.

B 20 "Whitsun, 1940." *Poetry (London)*, Vol. 1, No. 6 (May-June 1941), pp. 170-171.

1942

B 21 "Four Poems: 'Hart Crane,' 'Spring Poem,' 'Eleven Meetings,' 'The Clock.'" *Poetry: A Magazine of Verse*, Vol. LIX, No. V (February 1942), pp. 248-251.

B 22 "The Statues in Parliament Square" and "Reflections in Bed." *Partisan Review*, Vol IX, No. 5 (September-October 1942), pp. 386-387.

B 23 "The Intellectuals." *Poetry (London)*, Vol. 2, No. 7 (Oct.-Nov. 1942), pp. 41-42.

1943

B 24 *The Second Man*

Julian Symons | THE SECOND MAN | POEMS | ROUTLEDGE LONDON

Size: 7⅜ x 4¹⁵⁄₁₆".
Pagination: [1-4] 5-48.
Contents: 1, half title; 2, "By the Same Author" with one title listed; 3, title page; 4, copyright page: "First published 1943"; 5, dedication: "For ROY FULLER" followed by a 16-line poem; 6, blank; 7-8, "CONTENTS"; 9-47, text.
Binding: White paper over boards, black cloth spine. Spine stamped in gilt: Routledge THE SECOND MAN • Julian Symons.
Dust Jacket: Off-white paper. Front, spine, and back lettered in black and pale green. Back has list of seven other titles by various authors.
Publication Date: 1943.
Price: 5s.
Printing: Printed in Great Britain by T. and A. Constable Ltd. at the University Press, Edinburgh.

Symon's Note: This second collection of my poems was published by Routledge, for whom Herbert Read was then the poetry editor. I had said hard things about one or two of Read's books, but he generously ignored, or perhaps was unaware of them. This is certainly a much better collection than *Confusions About X* and contains my most anthologised poem, "Pub," written during a period of depression in 1940. The book sold 1200 copies, a very reasonable number for a small book of poems, then or now.

Author's Note: Interestingly, "Pub" was used as recently as 1981 in *Victims, a True Story of the Civil War* by Phillip Shaw Paludan (University of Tennessee Press, Knoxville). Paludan used these lines as the opening for Chapter 1: "Look now in the faces of those you love and remember I That you are not thinking of death."

B 25 "Mr. Symons at Richmond, Mr. Pope at Twickenham." *NOW*, Vol. 1 (1943—stamped July 28, 1943, by Bodleian), pp. 39-40.

B 26 "Writing in the Desert." *Partisan Review*, Vol X, No. 5 (September-October 1943), pp. 421-428.

B 27 "Elegy on a City." *Modern Reading*, No. 6 (1943), p. 20.

1944
B 28 "Catterick Revisited." *Poetry Quarterly*, Vol. 6, No. 1 (Spring 1944), p. 11.

B 29 "Elegy on a City." *Selected Writing*, (Winter, 1944), p. 85.

1947
B 30 "Villanelle." *The Windmill*, Vol. 2, No. 6 (1947), p. 21.

1970
B 31 "The Object of an Affair." Shenandoah, Vol. XXI, No. 3 (Spring 1970), pp. 194-195.

1973
B 32 *A Reflection on Auden*

A Reflection on Auden by Julian Symons published by Poem-of-the-Month Club Ltd. 27 Brynmaer Road, S.W. 11.

Size: 15 x 11⅛"
Pagination: [1].
Contents: 1 page broadside.
Binding: Broadsides were loosely inserted in a white half calf and buff board portfolio with cotton-tie, the front cover lettered in black.

Dust Jacket: None.
Publication Date: 1973.
Price: none given.
Printing: Printed by John Roberts Press Ltd.
Note: In 1991, Blackwell's Rare Books of Oxford, England in their catalogue
A102 offered for sale a set of 48 broadsides with the following catalogue entry:
"A collection of work by many of the most important of post-war poets, com-
missioned by the Poem of the Month Club, and each contribution signed by its
contributor. Included in the collection are poems by Stevie Smith, Robert
Graves, Stephen Spender, W.H. Auden, John Betjeman, Brian Patten, Kathleen
Raine and many others....Accompanying the Broadsheets are short biographies
of a number of the contributors, a table of contents and general information
about the Poem of the Month Club, on 19 A4 sheets." The set was published
between 1970 and 1974, and the man behind this production is the brother of
Kathleen Symons, J. "Jack" H. Clark.

1974
B 33   *The Object of an Affair and Other Poems*

THE OBJECT OF AN AFFAIR | and other poems | Julian Symons | THE
TRAGARA PRESS | EDINBURGH | 1974

Size: 9⁹⁄₁₆ x 6¹⁄₁₆"
Pagination: [28].
Contents: 1-2, blank; 3, title; 4, copyright page: "Copyright by Julian Symons
1974"; 5, a short note on the poems written by Julian Symons; 6, blank; 7-21,
text; 22-24, blank; 25, colophon; 26-28, blank.
Binding: Pale greenish blue paste batik wrappers, with geometric pattern. Cover
label applied with glue, black letters against cream background: THE OBJECT
OF AN AFFAIR and other poems | by JULIAN SYMONS inside a single rule
rectangle border.
Dust Jacket: None.
Publication Date: 1974.
Price: £3.00 for unsigned copies, signed copies unpriced.
Printing: The Tragara Press, Edinburgh.
Note: From the colophon: "Edition limited to 90 copies, of which numbers 1-25
on brown Sheepstor hand-made paper have been signed by the author. Num-
bers 26-90 are printed on a Saunders cream mould-made paper. This is number
____." Numbered by hand in black ink. Copies 26-90 are bound in green
wrappers, with black printing on the front.

1979
B34   *Seven Poems for Sarah*

SEVEN POEMS | FOR SARAH | JULIAN SYMONS | Privately Printed | 1979

THE OBJECT OF AN AFFAIR

and other poems

Julian Symons

THE TRAGARA PRESS

EDINBURGH

1974

Title page, *The Object of an Affair and Other Poems,* The Tragara Press, 1974, the first of six limited editions from this press.

Size: 9⁹⁄₁₆ x 6¹³⁄₁₆".

Pagination: [20].

Contents: 1-2, blank; 3, title; 4, copyright page: "© Julian Symons 1979"; 5, dedication page "Sarah Louise Symons born 3rd September 1948 died 11th September 1976"; 6, blank; 7-14, text; 15-16, blank; 17, colophon; 18-20, blank.

Binding: Dark green wrappers, with title in black letters on front cover: Seven Poems | for Sarah.

Dust Jacket: None.

Publication Date: 1979.

Price: N/A.

Note: From the colophon: "Fifty copies have been printed at the Tragara Press, Edinburgh." This edition was done as a memorial to Symons's daughter.

1980

B 35   "A Dark Day." *London Magazine*, Vol. 19, No. 12 (March 1980), pp. 70-71.

1982

B 36   "Albufeira: On a Balcony," "For Roy Fuller," "Questions and Answers." *London Magazine*, Vol. 22, Nos. 1 & 2 (April|May 1982), pp. 84-85.

B 37   "Hedgehog Rhyme." *Times Literary Supplement* (June 25, 1982), p. 695.

SECTION C

NONFICTION

"My crime stories . . . have been used to finance the writing of other books. . . . None of them could I have afforded to write if I had not been financially bolstered by the crime stories."

C 1 A.J.A. SYMONS: HIS LIFE AND SPECULATIONS 1950

(a) First U.K. edition (1950)

A.J.A. | Symons | HIS LIFE AND SPECULATIONS | JULIAN SYMONS | EYRE & SPOTTISWOODE | London

Size: 8⅜ x 5".

Pagination: [i-xiv] 1-283 [284].

Contents: i, half title; ii-iii, blank; iv, frontispiece photo of A.J.A. Symons; v, title page; vi, copyright page: "This book, first published in 1950, is printed in Great Britain for Eyre & Spottiswoode (Publishers) Ltd., 15 Bedford Street, London, W.C. 2"; vii-vii, "ACKNOWLEDGEMENTS"; ix, "CONTENTS;" x, "LIST OF ILLUSTRATIONS"; xi, twelve-line poem by W.H. Auden and brief quotation from A.J.A. Symons on the art of biography; xii, blank; xiii, half title; xiv, blank; 1-14, text; [15], illustration: The Race Game; 16-52, text; 53, illustration: A Decorative Envelope; 54-57, text; 58, illustration: Specimen of Amateur Forgery; 59-73, text; 74, illustration: A Letter Heading; 75-124, text; 125, illustration: Invitation to a Corvine Banquet in A.J.A. Symons's hand; 126-198, text; 199, illustration: Calligraphic Specimen of letter; 200-240, text; 241, illustration: Guide for Wine Drinkers in A.J.A. Symons's hand; 242-278, text; [279], "INDEX"; 280, blank; 281-283, index; [284], blank.

Binding: Maroon cloth with stamped gilt reproduction of A.J.A. Symons's signature on front cover. Spine blocked in 1⅛" gilt box with blue insert and gilt lettering: A.J.A. | SYMONS [decorative mark] | JULIAN | SYMONS. Gilt lettering at bottom of spine: EYRE & | SPOTTISWOODE.

Dust Jacket: Maroon border on top and bottom of front and spine wrapping to back. Front and spine have seven photographs of A.J.A. Symons in various poses, reproduced in gray half-tone. Maroon lettering on front and spine. The back is white with a maroon border and black lettering: "Recently Published Novels" followed by a list of six titles from Eyre & Spottiswoode.

Publication Date: March 1950.

Price: 15 shillings.

Printing: Printed at the Chiswick Press, New Southgate, London, N.11.

Symons's Note: Sometime in 1946 I wrote the opening chapter of what was intended as a full-length biography of my brother AJ. "Intended"....but it is not at all certain that I should have gone on with it without the encouragement offered by Graham Greene. He was at that time a director of Eyre & Spottiswoode, and the firm was offering a prize of (as I remember) $10,000, in collaboration with Houghton Mifflin, as an advance on a biography. I submitted the opening chapter and later saw the note written by Greene to his counterpart at Houghton Mifflin, saying that he would be inclined to award me the prize but for the fact that my brother was little known in the U.S.

No doubt Houghton Mifflin endorsed that view. Greene, however, commissioned the book with an advance of £250, at that time a sizeable sum. In fact, I never received any more money because the printing was 3,500, sales stopped at just over 3,000, and the last copies were remaindered. The book then

A. J. A. Symons

HIS LIFE AND SPECULATIONS

JULIAN SYMONS

EYRE & SPOTTISWOODE
London

Title page, *A.J.A. Symons: His Life and Speculations*, Eyre & Spottiswoods, 1950, the first nonfiction book.

remained out of print until O.U.P. reissued it in paperback as a "Twentieth Century Classic," with an afterword by me, in 1986.

The book's reception surprised me. It received long, laudatory reviews almost everywhere. One or two friends of AJ said I had blackened his name, some enemies said that I had whitewashed a literary villain of the period, but the consensus was almost embarrassingly friendly. Even today some friends think it is the best book I have written. I am a little dismayed by this, thinking I have written better books and even better biographies, but perhaps that is one of the illusions writers tend to nurse about their early as opposed to later writing. The book's style is a little too much like Victorian veneered mahogany for me to be happy with it.

Its publication made me painfully aware that what a family wants of a biography is almost always a portrait in a stained glass window. All the members of my family were upset by it in varying degrees, and on the two later occasions when a family suggested that I should write a biography, I made clear to them that there must be no censorship of the completed work. In one case, relating to the famous legal family of Curtis-Bennett, the family said they would prefer not to have a book written when I told them something of what I had learned in the course of research. In the other, Sonia Orwell refused to authorize me to write a biography of George Orwell unless she had a right of veto relating to material she did not approve. An appeal to her from Orwell's English publisher, Secker and Warburg, had no effect, and to my lasting regret I was denied the freedom which seemed to me essential in dealing with a subject I know I could have handled well.

Author's Note: At one point the publisher, Eyre and Spottiswoode, had suggested to Julian that the book should carry the title *The Quest For A.J.A. Symons,* a take-off on A.J.A.'s Corvo title. To this George Orwell wrote Julian: "I am glad (your publishers) are pleased with the biography, but don't let them get away with *The Quest for A.J.A. Symons* as the title. It is true that if a book is going to sell no title can kill it, but I am sure that is a bad one. Of course I can't make suggestions without seeing the book, but...something like *A.J.A. Symons: A Memoir* is always inoffensive."[1]

Although there is no change in text, this title was also bound in red paper over boards, without the gilt signature on the front and with black lettering on the spine: A.J.A. | SYMONS | HIS LIFE AND | SPECULATIONS | JULIAN | SYMONS | Eyre & Spottiswoode.

(b) First U.K. paperback edition (1986)

A.J.A. | Symons | HIS LIFE AND SPECULATIONS | [decorative rule] | JULIAN SYMONS | Oxford New York | Oxford University Press | 1986

Size: 7¾ x 5⅛".
Pagination: [i-x] 1-284 [285-286] 287-289 [290-294].
Contents: i, half title; ii, blank; iii, title page; iv, copyright page: "Afterword © Julian Symons 1985 | ....First issued, with Julian Symons's Afterword, as an |

Oxford University Press paperback 1986"; v-vi, "ACKNOWLEDGEMENTS"; vii, "CONTENTS"; viii, "LIST OF ILLUSTRATIONS"; ix, poem by W.H. Auden, quotation by A.J.A. Symons; x, blank; 1-284, text; 285, "INDEX"; 286, blank; 287-289, index; 290, blank; 291-293, additional titles by Oxford University Press; 294, blank.

Binding: White paper. Tan, yellow, and white lettering on dark blue block on cover: [publisher's logo: decorative "O"] | OXFORD | A.J.A. SYMONS | His Life & Speculations | [illustration] | JULIAN SYMONS | 'Julian Symons has composed this full-length | portrait with skill, humour and complete | truthfulness. . . a portrait of an individual and a | criticism of life.' Harold Nicolson, *Observer.* Cover illustration is brown-on-tan sketch by Wyndham Lewis, drawn in 1932. Black lettering on spine: JULIAN SYMONS A.J.A. Symons | [photograph of A.J.A. Symons] | [publisher's logo] | OXFORD. Black lettering on back includes logo, title, promotional blurb, excerpts from reviews, ISBN, bar code, cover credits, price. Spine photograph by Howard Coster.

Publication Date: 1986.

Price: £4.95.

Printing: Printed in Great Britain by Richard Clay (The Chaucer Press) Ltd, Bungay, Suffolk.

C 2   CHARLES DICKENS   1951

(a) First U.K. edition (1951)

CHARLES DICKENS | by | JULIAN SYMONS | ENGLISH NOVELISTS SERIES | [rule] | ARTHUR BARKER LTD. | 30 MUSEUM STREET, LONDON, W.C. 1

Size: 7¼ x 4¾".

Pagination: [1-4] 5-94 [95-96].

Contents: 1, half title; 2, "Uniform with this Volume:" followed by 20 other titles; 3, title page; 4, copyright page: "First published 1951"; 5, "CONTENTS"; 6, blank; 7-92, text; 93-94, "INDEX"; 95-96, a list of nineteen titles in The English Novelist Series with two additional titles listed as forthcoming.

Binding: Red cloth over boards, red lettering in a gilt rectangle stamped on the front: CHARLES | DICKENS. Gilt lettering on spine: [two rules] CHARLES | DICKENS | * | JULIAN | SYMONS | * | [two rules] | [two rules] ARTHUR | BARKER | [two rules].

Dust Jacket: White dots on a purple background form three white oval on the front. There is green lettering in the top oval. A purple line drawing in the middle oval shows a man leaning against a small monument in a garden. There is purple lettering in the bottom oval. The spine is purple with rows of white dots, broken by a top and bottom panels that are white with green lettering. The back cover is white with purple lettering, giving reviewers comments on the English Novelists Series and noting that it is under the general editor, Herbert Van Thal. Cover illustration by Felix Kelly.

Publication Date: 1951.
Price: 7 shillings, 6 pence.
Printing: Made and printed in Great Britain by Morrison and Gibbs Limited, London and Edinburgh.
Symons's Note: A good little book this, although there aren't many other people who think so!

(b) First U. S. edition (1961)

CHARLES DICKENS | by | JULIAN SYMONS | Denver | [rule] | ALAN SWALLOW

The same as C 2 a with the following changes:
Contents: 3, title page; 4, copyright page: BOUND BY THE FRANKLIN BINDERY, CHICAGO.
Binding: Red paper over boards with black lettering on spine.
Price: Not given.
Author's Note: LC-NUC, p. 350, gives the A. Swallow edition a date of [1961].

(c) Second U.S. issue (N.A.)

CHARLES DICKENS | by | JULIAN SYMONS | New York | [rule] | ROY PUBLISHERS

This edition is the same as C 2 a except for the following changes:
Contents: 2, copy deleted; 3, title page; 4, copyright page: "Copyright, 1951, by Julian Symons | All rights reserved | First published 1951".
Binding: Gilt lettering on bottom of spine: ROY | PUBLISHERS.
Dust Jacket: Green lettering on spine: ROY | Publishers. The back of the dust jacket gives a blurb for four titles in the series, priced at $2.50 each. This title is priced at $2.00.

(d) Second U.K. issue (1969)

CHARLES DICKENS | JULIAN SYMONS | ARTHUR BARKER LIMITED | 5 WINSLEY STREET LONDON WI

Size: 7¼ x 4¹³⁄₁₆".
Pagination: [1-4] 5-94 [95-96]
Contents: 1, Series note, half title; 2, "Uniform with this Volume" followed by 9 titles; 3, title page; 4, copyright page: "Copyright © 1951 by Julian Symons | First published 1951 | Second edition July 1969"; 5, "CONTENTS"; 6, blank; 7-92, text; 93-94, "INDEX"; 95-96, blank.
Binding: Cream paper over boards, stamped in black on spine: Charles Dickens [rule] Julian Symons Arthur | Barker.

Dust Jacket: Front and spine are pink with black and white lettering. Back is white with pink and black lettering listing other authors in the series along with the titles of the volumes.
Publication Date: July 1969.
Price: 15 s.
Printing: Printed in Great Britain by Loew & Brydone (Printers) Ltd., London.

(e) Third U.S. issue (1974)

CHARLES DICKENS | by | JULIAN SYMONS | NEW YORK | HASKELL HOUSE PUBLISHERS

This edition, published in 1974, is a reprint of the 1951 edition published by A. Barker, London.

C 3   THOMAS CARLYLE: THE LIFE AND IDEAS OF A PROPHET   1952

(a) First U.K. edition (1952)

THOMAS CARLYLE | The Life and Ideas of a Prophet | by | JULIAN SYMONS | In a century or less all Europe will be republican—democratic; | nothing can stop that. And they are finding their old religions, | too, to be mere putrid heaps of lies. | Thomas Carlyle to | William Allingham in 1878. | LONDON | VICTOR GOLLANCZ LTD. | 1952

Size: 8½ x 5¼".
Pagination: [1-9] 10-308.
Contents: 1, half title; 2, "BY THE SAME AUTHOR" followed by four titles; 3, title page; 4, copyright page: "Copyright © 1952 by Julian Symons"; 5, "ACKNOWLEDGEMENTS"; 6, blank; 7, "CONTENTS"; 8-295, text; 296, blank; 297-299, "SELECT BIBLIOGRAPHY"; 300, blank; 301-308, "INDEX."
Binding: Dark blue paper over boards, stamped gilt on spine: THOMAS | CARLYLE | BY JULIAN | SYMONS | GOLLANCZ.
Dust Jacket: White with black lettering on front and spine; photograph of Carlyle on front. Back has continuation of blurb.
Publication Date: February 1952.
Price: 21s.
Printing: Printed in Great Britain by the Camelot Press Ltd., London and Southampton.
Symons's Note: Why did I want to write about Carlyle when I had read little except *The French Revolution* and *Sartor Resartus*? One spur was certainly the fact that he was a radical turned conservative, from my point of view a good man gone wrong. Another no doubt was the good reception given to my biography of AJ, which gave me encouragement to attempt another subject. And a third

was the belief that failure is more interesting than success. Looking back, I see that all my biographical subjects—AJ, Carlyle, Horatio Bottomley, Edgar Allan Poe, even the Victorian generals Wolseley and Buller—can be regarded as failures if one contrasts their hopes and their achievements.

But I really knew very little about Carlyle when I began research and became fascinated by him both as writer and personality in the months I spent at desks in the London Library, the British Museum, and the Royal Library of Scotland. A good deal of new material has been turned up since my book was published, but I don't think any of it greatly changes the biographical account I gave of him, although of course my view of his merits as writer and thinker is personal. The book received a good deal of critical praise and was chosen as its Book of the Month by the *Daily Mail*, something that had little effect on the sales.

(b) First U.S. edition (1952)

THOMAS CARLYLE | The Life and Ideas of a Prophet | by | JULIAN SYMONS | In a century or less all Europe will be republican—democratic; | nothing can stop that. And they are finding their old religions, | too, to be mere putrid heaps of lies. | Thomas Carlyle to | William Allingham in 1878. | NEW YORK | OXFORD UNIVERSITY PRESS | 1952

This edition is the same as C 3 a with the following changes:

Contents: 3, title page.
Binding: Green cloth.
Dust Jacket: Not seen.
Publication Date: July 1952.
Price: $3.50.

(c) Second U.S. issue (1970)

THOMAS CARLYLE | The Life and Ideas of a Prophet | JULIAN SYMONS | In a century or less all Europe will be republican—democratic; | nothing can stop that. And they are finding their old religions, | too, to be mere putrid heaps of lies. | Thomas Carlyle to | William Allingham in 1878. | [publisher's logo: house made of books] BOOKS FOR LIBRARIES PRESS | FREEPORT, NEW YORK

This edition is the same as C 3 a with the following changes:
Size: 8⁷⁄₁₆ x 5⅜".
Binding: Greenish-blue cloth stamped in gilt on spine: SYMONS | [gilt dot] | THOMAS CARLYLE | [B | F | L inside of an oval]. Blind stamped publisher logo front cover, lower right hand corner.
Dust Jacket:: None.
Publication Date: "Reprinted 1970 by arrangement with Julian Symons and his literary agent John Cushman Associates, Inc."

Printing: Printed in the United States of America.

Author's Note: The first U.S. edition published by O.U.P. in 1952 contained the following biographical statement:

Mr. Symons is a well known literary critic and biographer as well as a writer of successful detective stories. The latter are widely read in the United States and have won him an established reputation in this field. His biographies include a life of Charles Dickens which was published in 1951. He is a regular contributor to various literary magazines and has also written two collections of poems. His home is in a small Kentish hamlet in the South of England where he works in an attic study overlooking the village green.

C 4   HORATIO BOTTOMLEY: A BIOGRAPHY   1955

(a) First U.K. edition (1955)

HORATIO | BOTTOMLEY | A BIOGRAPHY BY | JULIAN SYMONS | LONDON | [rule] | THE CRESSET PRESS | 1955

Size: 8½ x 5¾".

Pagination: [i-x] 1-287.

Contents: i, half title; ii, "By the same author" followed by a list of three biography and criticism titles and six crime novels; iii, blank; iv, frontispiece photograph of Bottomley; v, title page; vi, copyright page: "First published in 1955"; vii, "ACKNOWLEDGEMENT"; viii, "IN MEMORY OF COLIN YOUNG"; ix, "CONTENTS"; x, "ILLUSTRATIONS"; 1-277, text; 278, blank; 279-287, index. Photographs: Two-page spread between pp. 32 and 33; two-page spread between pp. 176 and 177; two-page spread between pp. 192 and 193.

Binding: Maroon paper over boards stamped in gilt on spine:[double rules] | HORATIO | BOTTOMLEY | JULIAN | SYMONS | [double rules] | CRESSET | PRESS.

Dust Jacket: Front and spine are red with white and black lettering. Front shows two black-and-white photographs of Bottomley. Back has red and black lettering on white background. Jacket design by S.A. Garrad.

Publication Date: 1955.

Price: 21/-.

Printing: Printed in Great Britain by Western Printing Services Ltd. Bristol.

Symons's Note: Horatio Bottomley was, I thought when I set out to research his life fully, another good man gone wrong, a radical who had been pushed by events and his own weakness into crooked dealings. As I dipped and delved and talked to people who had known Bottomley, even one or two who had worked for and with him, it became clear that this impression wasn't the right one, that he had been a villain from the beginning. Oddly, this discovery didn't bring disillusionment. Instead, I became almost as fascinated by Bottomley as those seduced by his siren schemes. His career, in its audacity, vulgarity, use of patriotism for commercial ends, is for me an image of the worst of Britain in the first quarter of the twentieth century. One or two people connected with theatre and film, Kenneth Tynan and John Wells among them, have been tempted by the idea of making him the central figure in a panoramic view of Britain during those years, but nothing has come of it. Bottomley needs a Brecht to do him justice.

He has haunted some of my fiction, or rather, the attempt to make a similar figure the center of a crime story has done. The first and weakest attempt to do this was the Bottomleyesque Johnny Bogue of *The Paper Chase*, but another figure derived from him is Ocky Gaye in *The Killing of Francie Lake*, whose Plain Man Enterprises was by intention an up-to-date version of Bottomley's *John Bull*. Ocky Gaye is marginally more successful than Johnny Bogue, but Bottomley was a figure so much larger than life that the fictional characters swamped the books in which they appeared.

C 5   THE GENERAL STRIKE: A HISTORICAL PORTRAIT   1957

(a) First U.K. edition (1957)

THE GENERAL | STRIKE | [rule] | A HISTORICAL PORTRAIT BY | JULIAN SYMONS | THE CRESSET PRESS | 1957

Size: 8⁷⁄₁₆ x 5⁵⁄₁₆".
Pagination: [i-iv] v-xi [xii] [1-2] 3-259 [260].
Contents: i, half title; ii, "By the same author:" followed by four biography and criticism titles and eight crime novels; iii, title page; iv, copyright page: " © Julian Symons, 1957 | First published in 1957"; v-viii, "PREFACE"; ix-x, "CONTENTS"; xi, "LIST OF ILLUSTRATIONS"; xii, blank; 1, "PART ONE | THE YEARS BEFORE"; 2, blank; 3-233, text; 234, blank; 235-247, "APPENDIX"; 248, blank; 249-251, "BIBLIOGRAPHY"; 252, blank; 253-259, "INDEX"; 260, blank. Photographs: Two-page spread between pp. 52 and 53; two-page spread between pp. 84 and 85; two-page spread between pp. 180 and 181; two-page spread between pp. 212 and 213.
Binding: Maroon paper over boards with gilt stamped on spine: [double rules] | THE | GENERAL | STRIKE | JULIAN | SYMONS | [double rule] | CRESSET | PRESS.
Dust Jacket: Front is yellow with black lettering with overlay of three white flags and three black-and-white checkered flags wrapping to spine. Spine is yellow with black lettering. Back is white with black lettering giving reviewers' comments on earlier title, *Horatio Bottomley*.
Publication Date: 1957.
Price: 21l-.
Printing: Printed in Great Britain by the Shenval Press Ltd, London, Hertford and Harlow.
Symons's Note: One further instance of my interest in thwarted social radicalism. I saw, and still see, the General Strike of 1926 in two lights. Had it succeeded, the whole of social life in Britain would have been changed, at least for many

years; but to regard it as a potential source of revolutionary change is to ignore the fact that only a tiny proportion of the trade unionists who obeyed the strike call had anything of the kind in mind. Such ambiguities, such gaps between ideas and action, have been the essential stuff of British politics in this century.

I did more and better organized research for this book than for the biographies of Carlyle and Bottomley, and the result is an adequate though strongly individual portrait of the Strike. Much of it is based on firsthand accounts of individual experiences, although collation of the hundreds of letters I received left me permanently distrustful about the veracity of personal stories about the past and skeptical of eyewitness views of any incident, a skepticism I turned to use in two crime stories, *The Colour of Murder* and *The Progress of a Crime*.

Author's Note: Called by Julian "a fragment of very un-American history," which clearly led to this title not being released by an American publisher, the work nevertheless drew praise from English reviewers, as evidenced by comments reprinted on the dust jacket on his next Cresset Press title, *A Reasonable Doubt*.

(b) Second U.K. edition (1957)

JULIAN SYMONS | THE | GENERAL | STRIKE | A HISTORICAL PORTRAIT | [publisher's logo: heron standing in water] DISTRIBUTED BY | HERON BOOKS

Size: 8½ x 5⅚₁₆".
Pagination: [1-viii] ix-xii 1-260.
Contents: i, blank; ii, THE MARCH OF HISTORY, A Collection distributed by Heron Books: iii, half title; iv, blank; v, title page; vi, copyright page: " © 1957, Julian Symons"; vii, contents; viii, contents continued; ix-xii, preface; 1, "PART ONE THE YEARS BEFORE"; 2, blank; 3-233, text; 234, blank; 235-240, appendix I; 241-247, appendix II; 248, blank; 249-251, bibliography; 252, blank; 253-259, index; 260, colophon.
Binding: Blue leatherette stamped in gilt on spine: JULIAN | SYMONS | THE | GENERAL | STRIKE | THE MARCH | OF HISTORY.
Dust Jacket: Issued without dust jacket.
Publication Date: 1957.
Price: None given.
Printing: Designed by Werner Schelling, production by Edito-Service S.A. Geneva. Printed Switzerland.

(c) Third U.K. (Book Club) edition (1959)

THE | GENERAL STRIKE | [decorative rule] | A Historical Portrait | by | JULIAN SYMONS | With 8 pages | of plates | READERS UNION | THE CRESSET PRESS | LONDON 1959

Size: 7½ x 4⅞₁₆".
Pagination: [1-5] 6-251 [252].

C. *Nonfiction* 155

Contents: 1, half title; 2, blank; 3, title page; 4, copyright page: " © JULIAN SYMONS, 1957 | This RU edition was produced in 1959...." and "By the same author:" followed by four titles of biography and criticism and nine crime novels; 5-8, "PREFACE"; 9-10, "CONTENTS"; 11, "LIST OF LLUSTRATIONS"; 12, blank; 13-233, text; 234, blank; 235-247, "APPENDIX"; 248, blank; 249-251, "BIBLIOGRAPHY"; 252, blank. Photographs: Eight pages between pp. 192 and 193.

Binding: Gold paper over boards with gilt lettering on spine: [decorative rule] | THE | GENERAL | STRIKE | by | JULIAN | SYMONS | [decorative rule] | [publisher's logo] at bottom of spine in gilt.

Dust Jacket: Maroon front and spine with white lettering. Front has a photograph of a bus. Back is white with maroon lettering, listing four titles in the Readers Union series.

Publication Date: 1959.

Price: 21s. RU member's price: 5s 9d.

Printing: The book has been reset in 10 point Baskerville, and printed by The Aldine Press, Letchworth.

(d) First U.K. paperback edition (1987)

THE | GENERAL STRIKE | A HISTORICAL PORTRAIT | Julian Symons | [in box rule] THE CRESSET LIBRARY | London Melbourne Sydney Auckland Johannesburg

Size: 8½ x 5¼".

Pagination: [i-iv] v-vii [viii-ix] x-xviii [1-2] 3-259 [260-262].

Contents: i, half title; ii, list of Cresset Library titles; iii, title page; iv, copyright page: " © Julian Symons 1957 | Preface to the Cresset Library edition © Julian Symons 1987"; v-vi, "CONTENTS"; vii, "LIST OF ILLUSTRATIONS"; viii, blank; ix-xiv, "Preface to the Cresset Library Edition; xv-xviii, preface; 1, "PART ONE THE YEARS BEFORE"; 2, blank; 3-233, text; 234, blank; 235-247, "APPENDIX"; 248, blank; 249-251, "BIBLIOGRAPHY"; 252, blank; 253-259, "INDEX"; 260-261, blank; 262, Cresset Library note. Photographs: Two-page spread between pp. 52 and 53; two-page spread between pp. 84 and 85; two-page spread between pp. 180 and 181; two-page spread between pp. 212 and 213.

Binding: Photograph showing mounted police armed with batons clearing strikers from the road is printed on light blue and wraps to back. White lettering on black box: THE CRESSET LIBRARY. White lettering on double-ruled box on front: THE GENERAL | STRIKE | [decorative rule] | Julian Symons. White lettering on black band on spine: THE GENERAL STRIKE Julian Symons THE CRESSET LIBRARY | [publisher's logo: stylized horned animal head]. White lettering on black box on back includes promotional blurb. ISBN number, bar code, and price printed in white.

Publication Date: 1987.

Price: £5.95.

Printing: Made and printed in Great Britain by Richard Clay Ltd, Bungay, Suffolk.

Author's Note: Although long out of print and difficult to find on the o.p. market (price range $25-$35), this title was reprinted in 1987 as part of the Cresset Library series designed to bring back books that the publisher, Century Hutchinson, felt should be widely available in attractively designed and reasonably priced paperback editions.

C 6   THE HUNDRED BEST CRIME STORIES   1959

(a) First U.K. edition (1959)

THE | HUNDRED BEST | CRIME | STORIES | PUBLISHED BY | [heraldic design] | THE SUNDAY TIMES

Size: 9½ x 7".
Pagination: [1] 2-20 [21].
Contents: 1, title page, plus first page of text; 2-21, text. Photographs on pages 2, 3, 5, 6, 9, 10, 12, 13, 15, 17, 18, and 19. Photograph of Julian Symons and brief text on inside of front cover.
Binding: Maroon paper covers with black and white lettering on front. Back is white with black lettering.
Dust Jacket: None.
Publication Date: Not stated, but Library of Congress date is 1959.
Price: 2s. 6d.
Printing: Printed by Withy Grove Press Limited Manchester 4.
Author's Note: Julian noted that this selection of 100 best crime stories was first published in The *Sunday Times* in "six or seven weekly installments." In the introduction he writes: "This list...has been compiled with the help of distinguished critics and crime novelists....American critics and crime novelists who have helped...are Mr. Anthony Boucher and Mr. James Sandoe...Mr. Howard Haycraft, an historian of the detective story; Mr. Frederic Melcher, editor of *Publisher's Weekly*; and a trio of crime novelists, Mr. Raymond Chandler, Mr. Ellery Queen and Mr. Rex Stout....In Britain, Mrs. Agatha Christie made lively comments on her favorite books; and Mr. Nicholas Blake, Mr. Henry Cecil, the late Cyril Hare...Miss Dilys Powell and Sir Charles Snow all put forward valuable ideas and criticisms."

    The work is divided into four sections: "The Begetters," "The Age of the Great Detective," "Novels of Action," and "The Modern Crime Novel." Each section contains an introduction by Julian, along with annotations of each title discussed.

C 7   A REASONABLE DOUBT   1960

(a) First U.K. edition (1960)

A REASONABLE | DOUBT | Some Criminal Cases Re-examined | by | JULIAN SYMONS | LONDON | THE CRESSET PRESS | MCMLX

Size: 8½ x 5⁷⁄₁₆".
Pagination: [1-6] 7-223 [224].
Contents: 1, half title; 2, "By the same author" followed by five titles in biography and criticism and nine crime novels; 3, title page; 4, copyright page: " © 1960 by Julian Symons | ....First published in 1960"; 5, "Contents"; 6, blank; 7-8, "Preface"; 9-223, text; 224, blank.
Binding: Maroon paper over boards stamped in gilt on spine: [double rules] | A | REASONABLE | DOUBT | [star] | JULIAN | SYMONS | [double rules] | CRESSET | PRESS.
Dust Jacket: Gray and white front and spine with white, black, and maroon lettering. Front shows a man standing behind prison bars superimposed with two question marks, one white, one maroon. Back is white with black lettering, giving reviewer's comments on *Horatio Bottomley* and *The General Strike*. Jacket design by HW.
Publication Date: 1960.
Price: 18s.
Printing: Printed in Great Britain by The Camelot Press Ltd. London and Southampton.
Symons's Note: The magazine *Lilliput*, now long defunct, asked me to write a study of an unsolved murder case and make some conjectures about what might have happened. It appeared [under the heading "True Crime Reconstruction"], lavishly illustrated, and led on to others. With some further additions, the collection made a book. Except in the case of Evelyn Foster, I did no first-hand investigating, and the solutions offered are those of an armchair detective.
Author's Note: It should be noted that one of the stories in this book, Chapter IX, "The Unknown Poisoner" later became the basis of the Victorian mystery, *The Blackheath Poisonings* [See A 24].

(b) First U.K. paperback edition (1962)

A REASONABLE | DOUBT | Some Criminal Cases Re-examined | JULIAN SYMONS | [publisher's logo: Pan playing his pipes inside box rule] | UNABRIDGED | PAN BOOKS LTD : LONDON

Size: 7 x 4⅜".
Pagination: [1-6] 7-248 [249-256].
Contents: 1, half title and promotional blurb; 2, "CONDITIONS OF SALE"; 3, title page; 4, copyright page: " First published 1960 by the Cresset Press Ltd. | This edition published 1962 by Pan Books Ltd. | .... © 1960 by Julian Symons"; 5, "Contents"; 6, blank; 7-249, text; 250-256, list of titles in series.
Binding: Black paper wraps to back. Orange lettering in upper left corner: PAN GIANT. Upper right corner: [logo, black in cream box]. Black lettering on cream block: A Reasonable | Julian | Symons | Doubt. Blue lettering: A brilliant | crime-writer's | startling analysis | of some famous | true murder cases | and

unsolved | mysteries | [box rule] 3'6. Photograph of British judge printed with an orange screen. Cream lettering on black spine: A REASONABLE DOUBT Symons | [three stars] | PAN | [logo] | X150. Black lettering on white back with yellow rules includes promotional blurbs and review excerpt along with logo.

Publication Date: 1962.

Price: 3/6.

Printing: Printed in Great Britain by Richard Clay and Company, Ltd., Bungay, Suffolk.

C 8   THE THIRTIES: A DREAM REVOLVED   1960

(a) First U.K. edition (1960)

Julian Symons | THE THIRTIES | A Dream Revolved | THE CRESSET PRESS • LONDON • 1960

Size: 8⁷⁄₁₆ x 5⅜".

Pagination: [i-ii] [i-vi] vii [viii] ix [x] xi-xii [1] 2-186 [187-188].

Contents: i, half title; ii, "By the same author" followed by six titles of biography and criticism and ten crime novels; i, blank; ii, frontispiece drawing and caption: "Julian Symons in 1938, by Wyndham Lewis"; iii, title page; iv, copyright page: "© 1960 by Julian Symons | ....First published in 1960"; v, dedication: "FOR MARCUS SYMONS", followed by an eight-line poem; vi, blank; vii, "Acknowledgements"; viii, blank; ix, "Contents": xi-xii, "List of illustrations"; 1-178, text; 179-181, "APPENDIX I"; 182-186, "APPENDIX II", 187-188, blank. Seventeen pages of photographs bound between pp. 84-85: SOCIAL AND POLITICAL: I-VI; PEOPLE: VII-XI; THEATRE: XII-XIII; and ART: XIV-XVII.

Binding: Dark blue paper over boards, gilt lettering on spine: THE | THIRTIES | [gilt star] | JULIAN | SYMONS | CRESSET | PRESS.

Dust Jacket: Front has pink lettering superimposed on five black-and-white 30's photographs. Spine is pink with black lettering. Back is white with black lettering giving reviews of three earlier Julian Symons books. Design by S.A Garrad.

Publication Date: 1960.

Price: 25s.

Printing: Printed in Great Britain by the Shenval Press, London, Hertford and Harlow.

Symons's Notes: In what Roy Fuller called my *annus mirabilis*, 1960, I published three books, *The Progress of a Crime, A Reasonable Doubt* and *The Thirties*, and it was the last that gave me most pleasure.

To be a man of the Thirties, the literary Thirties, in Britain marks one as somebody with certain preconceptions about the nature of society and about the connections between literary works and the world in which they are written. "A poem, a fiction, a piece of criticism, is first of all an event in society, secondarily a work of words"—such an idea, unique to the decade, seems absurd or mistaken or simply irrelevant to those brought up on the anything-goes atmosphere of the Sixties or the world of conspicuous consumption and conspicuous greed marking the Eighties.

The Thirties is a pie cut of the decade by one whose thinking still adheres by and large to its tenets. It was by design personal and impressionistic, and I sometimes wish that I had attempted a book with a wider scope and less consciously individual, more on the lines of Holbrook Jacksons's *Eighteen Nineties*. But those are later thoughts, and the book as it stands reflects my ideas and feelings. The subtitle, which some have questioned, "A Dream Revolved," is meant to suggest that the Thirties, as conceived by the typical men (and women) of the decade were in many respects a dream rather than reality.

Author's Note: This edition was imported into the United States by Dufour Editions. The U.K. price has been clipped, and the price $5.00 has been stamped on the lower left side of the front fold of the dust jacket. Also, a green adhesive label with white lettering has been added to the front paste-down endpaper: PUBLISHED IN THE UNITED STATES BY | DUFOUR EDITIONS | CHESTER SPRINGS, PENNSYLVANIA.

(b) First U.S. edition (1973)

Julian Symons, THE THIRTIES; A DREAM REVOLVED Greenwood Press, Westport, Connecticut 1973

Pagination:: [xii] 186.

Not seen.

(c) Second U.K. edition (1975)

THE THIRTIES | A Dream Revolved | [rule] | JULIAN SYMONS | FABER AND FABER | 3 Queen Square | London

Size: 7¾ x 5".

Pagination: [1-10] 11-160.

Contents: 1-2, blank; 3, half title; 4, blank; 5, title page; 6, copyright page: "First published in 1960 | by The Cresset Press | This revised edition first published 1975 | by Faber and Faber Limited | ....© Julian Symons 1975"; 7, dedication: "FOR MARCUS SYMONS," followed by an eight-line poem; 8, blank; 9, "A NOTE FOR THE 1975 EDITION" by Julian Symons; 10, "Acknowledgements"; 11, "Contents"; 12, blank; 13-14, "Illustrations"; 15-153, text; 154-156, "Appendix I"; 157-160, "Appendix II." Twenty-eight photographs reproduced on sixteen pages between pp. 96 and 97.

Binding: Red cloth with gilt lettering on spine: The Thirties JULIAN SYMONS Faber.

Dust Jacket: Front has a black-and-white photograph of police clearing way for car carrying Fascist officers, October 1936, with black and pink lettering at

top. Spine is white with black and pink lettering. Back is a black-and-white reproduction of Wyndham Lewis's illustration of Julian Symons, 1938.
Publication Date: 1975.
Price: £ 4.50.
Printing: Printed Great Britain by Butler & Tanner Ltd., Frome and London.
Author's Note: See entry C 25 for the 1990 re-issue of this title with an added thirty-nine page postscript, "The Thirties and the Nineties."

(d) First U.K. paperback edition (1975)

This edition is the same as C 8 c except for the following changes:
Size: 7¾ x 5¹⁄₁₆".
Binding: Cover of paperback edition is identical to dust jacket of C 8 c. On back cover, below the Lewis drawing: Julian Symons · The Thirties I £1.50 net I [rule] Faber Paperbacks I [rule]. Inside front cover gives promotional blurb, inside back cover lists additional Faber titles.
Publication Date: 1975.
Price: £1.50.
Printing: Printed in Great Britain by Butler & Tanner Ltd, Frome and London.

C 9   THE DETECTIVE STORY IN BRITAIN   1962

(a) First U.K. edition (1962)

THE DETECTIVE I STORY IN BRITAIN I by JULIAN SYMONS I PUBLISHED FOR I THE BRITISH COUNCIL I and the NATIONAL BOOK LEAGUE I by LONGMANS, GREEN & CO.

Size: 8⁷⁄₁₆ x 5⁷⁄₁₆".
Pagination: [1-7] 8-48.
Contents: 1, series note; 2, blank; 3, title page; 4, copyright page: "First published in 1962 I © Julian Symons 1962"; 5, "CONTENTS" and "ILLUSTRATIONS"; 6, blank; 7-36, text; 37-48, "A Select Bibliography." Drawing of 221b Baker Street by Robert Searle is on page 14 and four photographs are bound between pp. 24 and 25: I, Wilkie Collins; II, Sir Arthur Conan Doyle; III, Dorothy Sayers; IV, Agatha Christie.
Binding: Goldenrod paper covers with maroon and black lettering on front and black lettering on back. Back cover has a list of other titles in this series.
Dust Jacket: Issued without a jacket.
Publication Date: 1962.
Price: Two shillings and sixpence.
Printing: Printed in Great Britain by F. Mildner & Sons, London, E.C.1.

(b) Second U.K. edition (1969)

THE | DETECTIVE STORY | IN BRITAIN | by | JULIAN SYMONS | PUBLISHED FOR | THE BRITISH COUNCIL | AND THE NATIONAL BOOK LEAGUE | BY LONGMANS, GREEN & CO

Size: 8⅞₁₆ x 5½".
Pagination: [i-ii] [1-6] 7-48.
Contents: i, half title; ii, blank; 1, blank; 2, frontispiece illustrations of Collins, Doyle, Sayers, and Christie; 3, title page; 4, copyright page : "First published 1962 | Reprinted with minor amendments to the text and a revised bibliography | 1969 | ©Julian Symons 1962"; 5, "CONTENTS"; 6, blank; 7-36, text; 37-48, " Select Bibliography."
Binding: Goldenrod paper covers with maroon and black lettering on front and black lettering on back. Back cover has a list of other titles in this series.
Dust Jacket: Issued without a jacket.
Publication Date: 1969.
Price: Twenty New Pence.
Printing: Printed in Great Britain by F. Mildner & Sons, London, EC1.
Symons's Note: This is the reprint, with very minor amendments to the original text.
Author's Note: This title also appeared with a plasticized hardcover. The cover is cream with maroon borders along the top and bottom wrapping front to back. The cover reproduces, in changed form, the paper covers, which are bound inside. The cover reads: WRITERS AND THEIR WORK NO. 145 | [rule] | The Detective | Story in Britain | by JULIAN SYMONS | [rule] | Published for The British Council | and The National Book League | by Longmans, Green & Co. A row of oak leaves and acorns and a row of spool-like designs that have flowers in the center of each spool are printed in maroon and wrap from front to back at the top and bottom of the covers.

(c) Second U.K. issue (1969)

This is the same as C 9 b, with the following changes:
Binding: Slick gold paper with white and black lettering on front and back. List of titles in the series has been moved from the back cover to the inside back cover, where it appears in shortened form.
Price: 40 p.

C 10   BULLER'S CAMPAIGN   1963

(a) First U.K. edition (1963)

BULLER'S | CAMPAIGN | BY | JULIAN SYMONS | [rule] | LONDON | THE CRESSET PRESS

Size: 8⁷⁄₁₆ x 5¼".

Pagination: [i-ii] [i-viii] ix-xi [xii] xiii-xvi [1-2] 3-312.

Contents: i-ii, blank; i, half title; ii, "By the same author" followed by a list of seven titles of biography and criticism and eleven crime novels; iii, blank; iv, frontispiece photograph of Sir Redvers Buller; v, title page; vi, copyright page: "COPYRIGHT ©1963 BY JULIAN SYMONS | First published...in 1963"; vii, dedication: "FOR | FREDA BOARD"; viii, blank; ix-xi, "Preface"; xii, blank; xiii-xiv, "Contents"; xv-xvi, "Illustrations"; 1-293, text; 294, reproduction of a letter written from General Buller's Headquarters; 295-299, maps; 300, blank; 301-304, "Bibliography"; 305-312, "Index." Twelve pages of photographs are bound between pp. 160 and 161.

Binding: Green paper over boards with black rectangle at top of spine and gilt lettering: [rule] BULLER'S | CAMPAIGN | Julian | Symons [rule] | CRESSET | PRESS.

Dust Jacket: Gray with black lettering on front, spine, and back. Illustration of fighting soldiers on horseback is reproduced in maroon on bottom front wrapping to spine. Advertisements for four earlier Julian Symons's titles on back.

Publication Date: 1963.

Price: 30s.

Printing: Printed in Great Britain by Western Printing Services, Limited, Bristol.

Symons's Note: Difficult now to recapture my absorption in Victorian military history—which lasted for something like a decade from the late Fifties onwards—or to account for it. A reversion to childhood games with lead soldiers? A further step in the disillusionment of a radical, turning from present to past? I leave others to speculate. For two or three years I gathered materials for a book about the origins and nature of the Boer, or South African, War, beginning with Amery's remarkable *History* and going on to immersion in the multifold literature. I had a book in mind, a comprehensive one; but, I think in 1960, this field which had been fallow for years, brought forth several books, and one of them, Rayne Kruger's *Goodbye Dolly Gray,* seemed good and comprehensive enough to make my projected one otiose. But still I wanted to write something, and in the course of my researches had come across the remarkably frank letters written by Field Marshal Wolseley to his wife, letters which reflected on the quality of the whole of the British military establishment, on Wolseley's Lieutenant Buller, and on the replacement for Buller when he failed, Wolseley's bête noire Roberts. This was the origin of *Buller's Campaign,* which treated one small part of the War in macrocosm and was succeeded by a book about Wolseley's attempt to save General Gordon at Khartoum, *England's Pride.* [See C 11.] (Both Buller and Wolseley, now that I think of it, could be said to exemplify my preference for ultimate failure over success.) I contemplated then a life of Wolseley, but—fortunately, as I now think—was forestalled. And with that, I seem to have done with Victorian military history.

I have spent few happier hours than in researching the material for these books, particularly in the library of the RUSI (Royal United Services Institute), where the librarian bent the rules to admit me, since the library was open only to officers and I never advanced beyond the rank of Trooper; and in the War Office library, where I found material relating to Wolseley's advance up the

Nile that had never been written about in a book, and I daresay not even looked at for half a century or more. The books themselves are obviously the work of an amateur, though professional military historians dealt with them kindly.

(b) Second U.K. edition (1974)

BULLER'S | CAMPAIGN | BY | JULIAN SYMONS | [rule] | [publisher's logo: a white lion] | WHITE LION PUBLISHER | London • New York •Sydney • Toronto

Size: 8½ x 5⁵⁄₁₆".
Pagination: [i-viii] ix-xvi [1-2] 3-312.
Contents: i-ii, blank; iii, half title; iv, "By the Same Author" followed by list of ten titles of biography and criticism and thirteen crime novels and the notation, at the end of the list, "ETC., ETC."; v, title page; vi, copyright page: "COPY-RIGHT ©JULIAN SYMONS, 1963 | First published...by The Cresset Press, 1963 | White Lion edition, 1974"; vii, dedication: "FOR | FREDA BOARD"; vii, blank; ix-xi, "Preface"; xii, blank; xiii-xiv, "Contents"; xv-xvi, "Illustrations"; 1-293, text; 294, reproduction of letters; 295-299, maps; 300, blank; 301-304, "Bibliography"; 305-312, "Index." Twelve pages of photographs are bound between pp. 160 and 161.
Binding: Black paper over boards with gilt lettering on spine: BULLER'S | CAMPAIGN | Julian | Symons | [publisher's logo: a lion within a small gilt rectangle].
Dust Jacket: Dark brown with black and blue lettering. Front has black and white photograph of Sir Redvers Buller in full uniform (also used for frontispiece in C 10 a). Back has blurb in black lettering.
Publication Date: May 1974.
Price: £3.50.
Printing: Printed in Great Britain by The Anchor Press Ltd., Tiptree, Essex.

C 11   ENGLAND'S PRIDE: THE STORY OF THE GORDON RELIEF EXPEDITION   1965

(a) First U.K. edition (1965)

ENGLAND'S PRIDE | [rule] THE STORY OF THE | GORDON RELIEF EXPEDITION | [rule] | BY | JULIAN SYMONS | Illustrated | [publisher's logo: oak tree growing out of the pages of an open book with the letter "h" printed on each open page] | HAMISH HAMILTON | LONDON

Size: 8½ x 5⅜".
Pagination: [i-ii] [i-vi] vii [viii] ix-xi [xii] [1-2] 3-299 [300].
Contents: i, half title; ii, "By the Same Author" followed by a list of thirteen crime novels and eight general books; i, blank; ii, frontispiece reproduction of the

painting General Lord Wolseley by A. Besnard; iii, title page; iv, copyright page: "First published....1965 | ....Copyright © 1965 by Julian Symons"; v, four lines from a popular song after Gordon's death; vi, blank, vii, "ACKNOWLEDGE-MENTS"; viii, blank; ix-x, "CONTENTS"; xi, "LIST OF ILLUSTRATIONS"; xii, blank; 1, "PART ONE: | THE MISSION"; 2, blank; 3-288, text; 289-292, "BIBLIOGRAPHY"; 293-299, "INDEX"; 300, blank. Photographs: Two-page spread between pp. 20 and 21; two-page spread between pp. 36 and 37; two-page spread between pp. 148 and 149; two-page spread between pp. 164 and 165; two-page spread between pp. 196 and 197, two-page spread between pp. 212 and 213. Maps are bound between pp. 68 and 69 and between pp. 116 and 117.

Binding: Pale green paper over boards with spine stamped in gilt: ENGLAND'S | PRIDE | [rule] | JULIAN | SYMONS | [publisher's logo].

Dust Jacket: White with black lettering on front, spine, and back. Front illustration is a drawing of three soldiers on camels, each holding a gun. Illustration is divided into thirds, with the different blocks colored green, gray, and red.

Publication Date: 1965.

Price: 30s.

Printing: Printed in Great Britain by Latimer Trend and Co. Ltd., Plymouth.

Symons's Note: This book was much praised when it was published, and in some ways it is a source for other people writing about Gordon—but it earned no more than its original £750 advance. [See C 10 a, *Buller's Campaign*, for additional notes.]

(b) Second U.K. (Book Club) issue (1966)

ENGLAND'S PRIDE | The story of the | Gordon Relief expedition | by JULIAN SYMONS | THE HISTORY BOOK CLUB • LONDON

Size: 8⁷⁄₁₆ x 5⁷⁄₁₆".

Pagination: [i-ii] [i-vi] vii [viii] ix-xi [xii] [1-2] 3-299 [300].

Contents: i, half title; ii, "By the Same Author" followed by a list of thirteen crime novels and eight general books; i, blank; ii, frontispiece portrait of General Wolseley by Besnard; iii, title page; iv, copyright page: "© JULIAN SYMONS | This edition published 1966 by | The History Book Club Ltd | for sale only to its members | Originally published 1965"; v, four lines from a song written after Gordon's death; vi, blank; vii, "ACKNOWLEDGEMENTS"; viii, blank; ix-x, "CONTENTS"; xi, "LIST OF ILLUSTRATIONS"; xii, blank; 1, "PART ONE | THE MISSION"; 2, blank; 3-288, text; 289-292, "BIBLIOGRAPHY"; 292-299, "INDEX"; 300, blank. Photographs: Two- page spread between pp. 20 and 21; two-page spread between pp. 36 and 37; two-page spread between pp. 148 and 149; two-page spread between pp. 164 and 165; two-page spread between pp. 196 and 197; two-page spread between pp. 212 and 213. Maps are bound between pp. 68-69 and pp. 116-117.

Binding: Rust-red paper over boards, gilt lettering on spine: ENGLAND'S | PRIDE | [rule] | JULIAN | SYMONS | h | BC.

Dust Jacket: Tan with black and tan lettering on front and spine and black lettering on back, with rust printer's flower. Cover illustration of fighting men on horseback and on foot.
Publication Date: 1966.
Price: None given.
Printing: Printed in Great Britain by Latimer Trend & Co Ltd, Plymouth.

(c) Third U.K. issue (1974)

JULIAN SYMONS | England's Pride | The story of the Gordon Relief Expedition | [publisher's logo: a white lion] | WHITE LION PUBLISHERS | London, New York, Sydney and Toronto

Size: 8⁷⁄₁₆ x 5⁵⁄₁₆".
Pagination: [i-vi] vii [viii] ix-xi [xii] [1-2] 3-299 [300].
Contents: i, half-title: ii, "By the same author" followed by a list of twelve general books and fifteen crime novels; iii, title page; iv, copyright page: "Copyright © Julian Symons, 1965 | First published....1965 | White Lion edition, 1974"; v, four lines from a popular song written after Gordon's death; vi, blank; vii, "ACKNOWLEDGEMENTS"; viii, blank; ix-x, "CONTENTS"; xi, "LIST OF ILLUSTRATIONS"; xii, blank; 1, "PART ONE: THE MISSION"; 2, blank; 3-288, text; 289-292, "BIBLIOGRAPHY"; 293-299, "INDEX"; 300, blank. Thirteen pages of illustrations and two pages of maps are bound between pp. 148 and 149.
Binding: Black paper over boards, gilt lettering on spine: ENGLAND'S PRIDE | Julian Symons | [publisher's logo].
Dust Jacket: Blue with white and yellow lettering. Illustration on cover in light brown shows troops arriving at Jakdul wells.
Publication Date: November 1974.
Price: £3.50.
Printing: Printed in Great Britain by Biddles Ltd., Guildford, Surrey.

C 12   CRIME AND DETECTION: AN ILLUSTRATED HISTORY FROM 1840   1966

(a) First U.K. edition (1966)

Crime and detection | an illustrated history from 1840 | by Julian Symons [vertical rule] Studio Vista

Size: 11 x 8¼".
Pagination: [1-5] 6-9 [10-11] 12-288.
Contents: 1, half title; 2, frontispiece photograph of "Wanted" posters; 3, title page; 4, copyright page: "© Julian Symons 1966 | Published in 1966 by Studio

Vista Limited"; 5-7, "Contents"; 8-9, "Introduction" and "Acknowledgements"; 10, blank; 11, "Up to 1900"; 12-279, text; 280, blank; 281-282, "Bibliography"; 283-288, "INDEX"; More than 750 photographs accompany the text.

Binding: Gray paper over boards, gilt lettering on spine: Crime and detection Julian Symons | S | V.

Dust Jacket: Dark gray front and spine with white, black, and orange lettering. The front illustration shows a man looking out from behind bars. The back is white with a single finger print enlarged to nine inches. Jacket design by Tim Jaques.

Publication Date: 1966.

Price: 50s.

Printing: Printed by NV Drukkerij Koch en Knuttel, Gouda, Holland.

(b) First U.S. edition (1966)

a pictorial history of | Crime | by Julian Symons | Crown Publishers Inc. New York

This edition is the same as C 12 a except for the following changes:

Contents: title page [title change]; copyright page: "© Julian Symons 1966 | First published 1966 in the United States by | Crown Publishers Inc."

Binding: Gilt lettering on spine: Crime Julian Symons | Crown.

Publication Date: 1966.

Price: $10.00

(c) Second U.S. issue (N.A.)

a pictorial history of | Crime | by Julian Symons | Bonanza Books • New York

This edition is the same as C 12 b except for the following changes:

Contents: copyright page: "© Julian Symons MCMLXVI | First published 1966 in the United States by | Crown Publishers Inc | ....Printed in the U.S. | ....This edition published by Bonanza Books, a division of Crown Publishers, Inc."

Binding: Gray cloth over boards, gilt lettering on spine: CRIME | A | PICTORIAL | HISTORY | OF CRIME | by | Julian Symons | BONANZA.

Dust Jacket: Same as C 12 a and C 12 b except that color has been changed from dark gray to light gray.

Publication Date: Not given.

Price: Not given. The $10.00 price noted in C 12 b has been removed; no price listed.

(d) First U.K. paperback edition (1968)

Crime and detection | an illustrated history from 1840 | by Julian Symons [vertical rule] Panther

This is the same as C 12 a except for the following changes:

Size: 8¹⁵/₁₆ x 6⅝".

Contents: 4, copyright page: "Panther edition published 1968 | Copyright © Julian Symons 1966".

Binding: Yellow lettering on color photograph: Crime and Detection | An illustrated history | by Julian Symons | A Panther Book 24506. Cover illustration shows a pair of thirties-style gangsters, the hit man about to make a getaway and the victim lying in the street. White and black lettering on yellow spine: Crime and Detection Julian Symons Panther Books 24506. White and black lettering on red back includes promotional blurb and prices below an etching from page 15 "Police wear beards." Cover by Larkin|Rolfe.

Publication Date: 1968.

Price: U.K. 17/6, Australia $2.60, New Zealand $2.50, South Africa r2.10.

Printing: Printed in Great Britain by Offset Lithography by Billing & Sons Ltd., Guildford and London.

C 13   CRITICAL OCCASIONS   1966

(a) First U.K. edition (1966)

CRITICAL OCCASIONS | [rule] | BY | JULIAN SYMONS | [publisher's logo: oak tree growing out of the pages of an open book with the letter "h" printed on each open page] | HAMISH HAMILTON | LONDON

Size: 8½ x 5¼".

Pagination: [i-viii] [1-2] 3-213 [214-216].

Contents: i, half title; ii, "By the same Author" followed by a list of nine general books and thirteen crime novels; iii, title page; iv, copyright page: "First published in Great Britain, 1966 | ....Copyright © 1966 by Julian Symons" and dedication: "FOR | JACK AND CHRISTINE CLARK"; v, "Contents; vi, blank; vii, "Note"; viii, blank; 1, half title; 2, blank; 3-213, text; 214-216, blank.

Binding: Lime green paper over boards stamped in silver on spine: Critical | Occasions | [printer's flower] | JULIAN | SYMONS | [publisher's logo].

Dust Jacket: Burnt orange with black lettering. Front lists contents of book; back gives reviewer's comments for *England's Pride.* Jacket design by George Mayhew.

Publication Date: 1966.

Price: 30s.

Printing: Printed in Great Britain by Western Printing Services Ltd, Bristol.

Symons's Note: Many of these articles have appeared in the *Times Literary Supplement.* I have made only small textual changes in them and have added one or two footnotes where they seemed necessary. [From "Note", p. vii.]

C 14   BETWEEN THE WARS:
BRITAIN IN PHOTOGRAPHS   1972

(a) First U.K. edition (1972)

Between the Wars I BRITAIN I in Photographs I Introduction and commentaries by I JULIAN SYMONS I B.T. Batsford Ltd I London

Size: 9¾ x 7⁵⁄₁₆".
Pagination: [1-156; unpaginated].
Contents: 1, photograph; 2, frontispiece photograph; 3, title page; 4, copyright page: "First published 1972 I Text © Julian Symons 1972"; 5, "CONTENTS"; 6, "ACKNOWLEDGEMENTS"; 7, "INTRODUCTION"; 8-9, photograph; 10-12, introduction continued, 13, blank; 14-155, text accompanied by 188 photographs, 156 blank.
Binding: Light tan paper over boards stamped in gilt on spine: Symons I Between the Wars I Britain in Photographs I BATSFORD.
Dust Jacket: Sepia photographs reproduced on front, spine, and back, with black and brown lettering.
Publication Date: 1972.
Price: £2.50.
Printing: Printed in the Netherlands by Grafische Industrie, Haarlem.
Symons's Note: Every picture tells a story, and every story may be true, but the truth it tells is partial and single, not general and total....What follows, then, is personal: a personal portrait of Britain between the Wars seen through the eyes of non-party Leftist....When one thinks of the resources Britain possessed at this time, and then of the refusal or inability to use them to achieve any measure of social equality, one can only marvel at the timidity and imperceptiveness of the politicians who held power. [From the Introduction.]

(b) Second U.K. issue (1985)

Between the Wars I BRITAIN I in Photographs I Introduction and commentaries by I JULIAN SYMONS I B.T. Batsford Ltd I London

This edition is the same as C 14 a except for the following changes:
Contents: copyright page: "© Julian Symons 1972 I First published 1972 I Second impression 1985I ....Printed and bound in Great Britain by Anchor Brendon Ltd, Tiptree, Essex."
Binding: Gray paper over boards with gilt lettering on spine: Symons Between the Wars Britain in Photographs [publisher's logo: outline of a window] BATSFORD.
Dust Jacket: Light and dark pink vertical stripes with black lettering. The front has one color and two black-and-white photographs; the back has one large photograph taking up most of the cover space.
Publication Date: 1985.
Price: £9.95.

C 15 MORTAL CONSEQUENCES : A HISTORY 1972

(a) First U.S. edition (1972)

MORTAL | CONSEQUENCES | A HISTORY— | From the Detective Story | to the Crime Novel | JULIAN SYMONS | HARPER & ROW, PUBLISHERS | [publisher's logo: torch in box with the year 1817 below box] NEW YORK, EVANSTON, | SAN FRANCISCO, LONDON

Size: 8⅟₁₆ x 5½".
Pagination: [i-ii] [i-viii] ix-x [xi-xii] 1-269 [270-274].
Contents: i-ii, blank; i, half title; ii, "Novels by Julian Symons" followed by a list of fourteen titles; iii, title page; iv, copyright page: "Copyright © 1972 by Julian Symons | ....FIRST U.S. EDITION."; v, dedication: "For Joan Kahn | with respect, gratitude, | affection"; vi, blank; vii-viii, two-page poem by Julian Symons, "The Guilty Party"; ix-x, "Contents"; xi, half title; xii, blank; 1-253, text; 254, blank; 255-269, "Index"; 270-273, blank; 274, edition|printing notation.
Binding: Tan paper over boards, black cloth spine with silver lettering: SYMONS | MORTAL CONSEQUENCES | Harper | & Row.
Dust Jacket: Gray on front and spine with black lettering. Front shows two smoking guns, one pointing right, the other left. Back is white with black lettering, giving the contents of the book. Jacket design by One Plus One Studio.
Publication Date: March 1972.
Price: $6.95.
Printing: Printed in the United States of America.
Symons's Note: This is the true first edition, preceding the English edition by about three weeks. It also contains the poem ["The Guilty Party"], which is not in the English edition.

(b) First U.K. edition (1972)

BLOODY MURDER | From the Detective Story to the Crime Novel: | A History | [rule] | JULIAN SYMONS | FABER AND FABER | 3 Queen Square | London

Size: 8½ x 5⅟₁₆".
Pagination: [1-6] 7-254 [255-256].
Contents: 1, half title; 2, blank; 3, title page; 4, copyright page: "First published in 1972 | ....© Julian Symons, 1972"; 5, dedication: "For Joan Kahn | with respect, gratitude, affection"; 6, blank; 7, "Contents"; 8, blank; 9-243, text; 244-249, "Index of Books and Short Stories"; 250-254, "Index of Authors and Names"; 255-256, blank.
Binding: Red cloth over boards, gilt lettering on spine; Julian | Symons | Bloody Murder | From the Detective Story to the Crime Novel: a History | FABER.
Dust Jacket: Red with white and black lettering on the front and spine, along with a single black fingerprint on the lower right front and a single white fingerprint on the upper left back.

BLOODY MURDER

From the Detective Story to the Crime Novel:
A History

JULIAN SYMONS

FABER AND FABER
3 Queen Square
London

Title page, *Bloody Murder: From the Detective Story to the Crime Novel: A History*, Faber and Faber, 1972, winner of a special Edgar awarded by the Mystery Writers of America.

Publication Date: April 1972.

Price: £2.75.

Printing: Printed in Great Britain by Latimer Trend & Co., Ltd. Plymouth.

Author's Note: A handwritten note by Julian Symons in the front of *The Saturday Book* 14 (1954) refers to his article "The Great Detective": "An early sketch of material later embodied in *Bloody Murder.*" It should also be noted that the U.K. edition was reprinted in 1972 with no changes to the text or dust jacket. The only noticeable change is the addition of the words "Reprinted 1972" to the copyright page.

(c) Second U.K. edition (1985)

[double rule] I JULIAN SYMONS I [rule] I BLOODY I MURDER I [double rule] I FROM THE DETECTIVE STORY I TO THE CRIME NOVEL: I A HISTORY I VIKING

Size: 8⅞₆ x 5¼".

Pagination: [1-10] 11-261 [262-264].

Contents: 1, [publisher's logo: ship at full sail]; 2, blank; 3, title page; 4, copyright page: "First published in the United States of America under the title *Mortal Consequences* by I Harper & Row, Publisher, Inc., 1972 I This revised and updated edition published by Viking 1985 I Copyright © Julian Symons, 1972, 1985"; 5, dedication: "FOR JOAN KAHN..."; 6, blank; 7, "Contents"; 8, blank; 9, "Preface to the Revised Edition" by Julian Symons, 1984; 10, blank; 11-12, "Prologue, The Guilty Party"; 13-239, text; 240, blank; 241-262, "Index"; 263-264, blank.

Binding: Black paper over boards, red lettering on spine: JULIAN I SYMONS I BLOODY I MURDER I [splash of red] I VIKING.

Dust Jacket: Black front and spine with white and red lettering, along with red splashes designed to look like blood. Back photograph of Julian Symons by Mark Gerson.

Publication Date: July 1985.

Price: This edition carried both a U.S. and a U.K. price on front jacket flap: U.S. $14.95 on the upper edge, U.K. £10.95 on the lower edge.

Printing: Printed in Great Britain by Richard Clay (The Chaucer Press) Ltd, Bungay, Suffolk.

(d) Third revised U.S. edition (1993)

bloody I murder I Third Revised Edition [in white letters against thick black rule with blood spot below rule] I From the Detective Story to the I Crime Novel I [rule] I Julian Symons I [logo: Mysterious Press hanging sign board] I THE MYSTERIOUS PRESS I New York • Tokyo • Sweden I Published by Warner Books I [publisher's logo: white W in black box] A Time Warner Company

Size: 8³⁄₁₆ x 5⁵⁄₁₆".
Pagination: [i-xiv] 1-249 [350-354].
Contents: i, half title; ii, blank; iii, title page; iv, coyright page: "First published in England in 1992 by Penguin Books Ltd. | Copyright © 1972, 1985, 1992 by Julian Symons | ....First U.S. printing: February 1993 | 10 9 8 7 6 5 4 3 2 1"; v, dedication "For JOAN KAHN | with respect, gratitude, affection"; vi, blank; vii, "Contents"; viii, blank; ix, "Preface | to the Third Edition—1993" by Julian Symons; x, blank; xi-xii, "Prologue" poem "The Guilty Party"; xiii, half title; xiv, blank; 1-326, text; 327-349, "Index"; 350-354, blank.
Binding: Three quarter black paper over boards, spine red paper with silver lettering: bloody murder Julian | Symons | [logo: Mysterious | Press].
Dust Jacket: White on front, spine and back with black and red lettering. Front shows blood drops wrapping around to spine. Back gives reviewer's comments under heading "Writers and Critics Cheer for Julian Symons and Bloody Murder."
Publication Date: February 1, 1993.
Price: $21.95.
Printing: Book designed by Giorgetta Bell McRee. Printed in the United States of America.

(e) First U.S. paperback edition (1973)

MORTAL | CONSEQUENCES | A HISTORY— | From the Detective Story | to the Crime Novel | JULIAN SYMONS | SCHOCKEN BOOKS · NEW YORK

*Size:*7 x 4½".
Pagination: [i-ii] [i-viii] ix-x [xi-xii] 1-253 [254] 255-269 [270-274].
Contents: i, excerpts from reviews; ii, blank; i, half title; ii, blank; iii, title page; iv, copyright page: "First SCHOCKEN PAPERBACK edition 1973 | Copyright © 1972 by Julian Symons"; v, dedication: "For Joan Kahn | with respect, gratitude, affection"; vi, blank; vii-viii, poem: "THE GUILTY PARTY"; ix-x, "Contents"; xi, half title; xii, blank; 1-253, text; 254, blank; 255-269, "Index"; 270-274, blank.
Binding: White, green, and red lettering on black paper. Front cover illustration shows a skull and crossbones with red eyeballs; one of the crossbones is a pen. White and green lettering on front: JULIAN | SYMONS | MORTAL | CONSEQUENCES | [illustration] | A History from the Detective Story to the Crime Novel. Green lettering in top right corner: $1.95. Green lettering in bottom right corner: SCHOKEN SB404. Green and red lettering on spine with white illustration repeated: MORTAL | CONSEQUENCES | [illustration from front cover] | JULIAN | SYMONS | [publisher's logo: geometric `S'] | SB404. Back repeats title, author and illustration; review excerpt; publisher, logo, address; designer; ISBN. Cover design by Wendell Minor.
Publication Date: 1973.
Price: $1.95.
Printing: Manufactured in the United States of America.

(f) First U.K. paperback edition (1974)

Julian Symons | Bloody Murder | From the Detective Story to the | Crime Novel: a History | Penguin Books

Size: 7 x 4⅜".
Pagination: [1-6] 7-270 [271-272].
Contents: 1, half title and biographical note; 2, blank; 3, title page; 4, dedication and copyright page: "Published with revisions in Penguin Books 1974 | Copyright © Julian Symons, 1972"; 5, "Contents"; 6, blank; 7-257, text; 258-270, "Index"; 271-272, blank.
Binding: Orange and white lettering on black paper. Top right corner: [publisher's logo: penguin in green oval] | CRIME. Julian Symons | BLOODY | MURDER | From the Detective Story | to the Crime Novel: | A History. Photograph on cover wraps to back, with British detective paraphernalia on front (deerstalker cap, candlestick, pipe, magnifying glass, bottle of poison, guns and daggers) and U.S. detective paraphernalia on back (fedora, cigarette butts, martini, pills and capsules, pearls, guns and shivs). White and orange lettering on spine: Julian Symons Bloody Murder ISBN 014 | 00.3794 2 | [logo] | CRIME. Orange and white lettering on back includes excerpts from reviews, logo, price, genre, ISBN. Cover photograph by Humphrey Sutton.
Publication Date: 1972.
Price: UK 40p, Australia $1.35, NZ $1.35, Canada $1.25.
Printing: Made and printed in Great Britain by Hunt Barnard Printing Ltd, Aylesbury, Bucks.

(g) Second U.K. paperback issue (1975)

This reprint is identical to C 15 f except for the following changes:
Size: 6¹³⁄₁₆ x 4¼".
Publication Date: 1975.
Price: UK 75p, NZ $2.55, Canada $2.95.

(h) Third U.K. paperback edition, revised (1985)

JULIAN SYMONS | [rule] | BLOODY MURDER | From the Detective Story | to the Crime Novel: | A History | [publisher's logo: penguin in oval] | PENGUIN BOOKS

Size: 7¾ x 5¹⁄₁₆".
Pagination: [1-10] 11-238 [239-240] 241-261 [262-272].
Contents: 1, half title and biographical note; 2, blank; 3, title page; 4, copyright page: "Published in Penguin Books 1985 | Copyright © Julian Symons, 1972, 1985"; 5, dedication; 6, blank; 7, "Contents"; 8, blank; 9, "Preface to the Revised Edition"; 10, blank; 11-12, "Prologue"; 13-239, text; 240, blank; 241-262, index; 263-272, Penguin titles and order information.

Binding: Black paper with orange spine. Gold and white lettering on front cover: BLOODY | MURDER | [in red band] FROM THE DETECTIVE STORY TO THE CRIME NOVEL | "Heartily recommended" | —Kingsley Amis | JULIAN SYMONS. Penguin logo in upper right corner. Cover illustration is a photograph of a selection of crime novels on a table. White and black lettering on spine: JULIAN SYMONS · BLOODY MURDER ISBN 0 14 | 00.7263 2 | [publisher's logo]. White lettering on back includes promotional blurb, excerpts from reviews, price, genre, bar code, ISBN. Cover illustration by Gary Millican.
Publication Date:: 1985.
Price: £3.95, $6.95.
Printing: Made and printed in Great Britain by Richard Clay (The Chaucer Press) Ltd, Bungay, Suffolk.

(i) Fourth U.K. paperback edition, revised (1992)

BLOODY | MURDER | [rule] | From the detective story | to the crime novel: | a history | [rule] | JULIAN SYMONS | [rule] | M | PAPERMAC.

Size: 8½ x 5⅜".
Pagination: [1-10] 11-296.
Contents: 1, half title; 2, "by the same author" followed by a list of twenty-eight titles; 3, title page; 4, copyright page: "Copyright © Julian Symons 1972, 1985, 1992 | ....This revised and updated edition with a new postscript published in paperback 1992 by | PAPERMAC"; 5, dedication; 6, blank; 7, "Contents"; 8, blank; 9, "Preface to the Third Edition"; 10, blank; 11, "Prologue"; 13-272, text; 273-296, index.
Binding: White and red lettering over illustration: JULIAN SYMONS | FROM THE DETECTIVE STORY TO THE CRIME NOVEL | Bloody | Murder. Illustration shows a formally dressed man sitting at a writing desk in a library. He is using a quill pen; the paper on the desk is illuminated, but the man's face is in shadow. An ice pick and a bottle of red ink are on the desk. Black and red lettering on cream spine: JULIAN SYMONS Bloody Murder PAPERMAC | M. Black and red lettering on cream back includes promotional blurb, biographical note, review, price, ISBN, bar code. Cover illustration by Nick Cudworth.
Publication Date: 1992.
Price: £10.99.
Printing: Printed in Hong Kong.

(j) Fifth U.K. paperback edition (1994)

Bloody Murder | [rule] | FROM THE DETECTIVE STORY | TO THE CRIME NOVEL: | A HISTORY | JULIAN SYMONS | PAN BOOKS | LONDON, SYDNEY AND AUCKLAND

Size: 7 x 4⅜".
Pagination: [1-11] 12-365 [366-368].

Contents: 1, half title and biographical note; 2, "BY THE SAME AUTHOR" followed by twenty-nine titles; 3, title page; 4, copyright page: "This edition published in 1994 by Pan Books Ltd | ....Copyright © Julian Symons 1972, 1985, 1992"; 5, dedication; 6, blank; 7, "Contents"; 8, blank; 9, "Preface to the Third Edition"; 10, blank; 11-12, "Prologue"; 13-336, text; 337-365, index; 366-368, blank.

Binding: Front, spine, and back in black. White and red lettering on front: JULIAN | SYMONS | Bloody | Murder | THE CLASSIC | CRIME FICTION REFERENCE | FULLY REVISED AND | UPDATED. Author, title, and publisher's logo on spine. Back has promotional blurb, biographicla note, reviews, price, ISBN, and bar code.

Publication Date: 1994.

Price: £4.99.

Printing: Phototypeset by Intype, London. Printed and bound in Great Britain by Cox & Wyman Ltd., Reading, Berkshire.

C 16   NOTES FROM ANOTHER COUNTRY   1972

(a) First U.K. edition (1972)

NOTES FROM | ANOTHER COUNTRY | JULIAN SYMONS | [publisher's logo: single leaf] | L M | LONDON MAGAZINE EDITIONS

Size: 7¼ x 4¾".

Pagination: [1-8] 9-147 [148].

Contents: 1, half title; 2, blank; 3, title page; 4, copyright page: "First published in Great Britain 1972 | ....© Julian Symons"; 5, dedication: "For Alan Ross"; 6, blank; 7, "Contents"; 8, blank; 9-147, text; 148, blank.

Binding: Light green paper over boards, gilt lettering on spine: NOTES FROM ANOTHER COUNTRY Julian Symons | [publisher's logo] LM.

Dust Jacket: A photograph of Clapham Common printed in a pale green wraps from front to back with purple lettering on the front and spine.

Publication Date: 1972.

Price: £1.80.

Printing: Printed in Great Britain by Billing & Sons Ltd., Guildford and London.

Symons's Note: I should have found it difficult to write a "straight" autobiography, but these autobiographical stories and sketches about my life up to the age of around thirty-five came easily. My wife, Kathleen, says they're untrue. My response is that they may not all be accurate in detail, but they are all basically true. Reactions to them have confirmed my belief that when two or three people are present on the same occasion, each of them sees something different. An example: in the book, my view of the friend I've called Rita was not at all the same as that of Kathleen and other people who knew her. My Rita, however, is as "true" as their's, just as the "Julian Symons" known to one person— friendly, helpful, easy-going—is not the truculent, awkward, and intellectually snobbish person known to another.

Author's Note: A rarity in the lifetime of Julian Symons's published works, *Notes from Another Country* is one of the few major works that has neither been published in paperback nor published in the United States. Yet, as he points out in his notes, this is a series of "autobiographical stories and sketches about my life up to the age of around thirty-five" and does give wonderfully funny and sometimes sad insights into his early life. For the most part (8 out of 9), these stories originally appeared in the *London Magazine* and appear here with minimal changes. "A Glimpse of Thirties Sunlight" appeared in *The Times Literary Supplement* in a slightly different form.

C 17   THE ANGRY 30s   1976

(a) First U.K. edition (1976)

The | ANGRY | 30s [title within a double-rule rectangle] | JULIAN SYMONS [within a double-rule rectangle] | EYRE METHUEN LONDON [within a single rule rectangle] [The entire front page is comprised of a black-and-white photograph of a police baton charge against unemployed demonstrators in Bristol in 1932.]

Size: 9⁷⁄₁₆ x 7¼".
Pagination: [1-128 unpaginated].
Contents: 1, half title; 2, frontispiece photograph; 3, title page; 4, copyright page: "First published 1976 by Eyre Methuen Ltd | ....© 1976 Julian Symons" and also picture credits; 5, photograph; 6-7, "A TIME OF MARCHES," introduction by Julian Symons; 8-128, text accompanied by 129 photographs.
Binding: Paperbound original. The front cover is yellow with black borders around four color reproductions of photographs used in the book. Orange and black lettering on cover, black lettering on spine: THE ANGRY 30s JULIAN SYMONS EYRE | METHUEN. Back cover has a photograph of a man carrying a sandwich board: "I KNOW 3 TRADES; I SPEAK 3 LANGUAGES; FOUGHT FOR 3 YEARS; HAVE 3 CHILDREN AND NO WORK FOR 3 MONTHS; BUT I ONLY WANT ONE JOB." Also on the back cover is a blurb for the book.
Dust Jacket: Issued without a jacket.
Publication Date: 1976.
Price: £1.95.
Printing: Printed in Great Britain by Hazell Watson & Viney Ltd, Aylesbury, Bucks.
Symons's Note: When you look at some of the photographs in this book, it is easy to see why the Thirties was the angry decade of this century, a time of marches and protests. The misery of slum houses, the wretchedness of men unemployed for years and often without hope of work, the indifference of government—that is what the Thirties meant for many people. [From the introduction.]

C 18   THE TELL-TALE HEART: THE LIFE AND WORKS OF EDGAR ALLAN POE   1978

(a) First U.S. edition (1978)

THE | TELL-TALE | HEART | The Life and Works of Edgar Allan Poe | [printer's flower] | JULIAN SYMONS | HARPER & ROW, PUBLISHERS | NEW YORK, HAGERSTOWN | SAN FRANCISCO | LONDON

Size: 9¼ x 6".
Pagination: [i-vi] vii-x [1-2] 3-259 [260-262].
Contents: i, half title; ii, "Other Books by Julian Symons" followed by a list of one nonfiction and seventeen fiction titles; iii, title page; iv, copyright page: "Copyright | © 1978 by Julian Symons. | ....FIRST EDITION"; v, dedication: "To Bill and Marietta Pritchard"; vi, blank; vii-viii, "CONTENTS"; ix-x, "INTRODUC-TION"; 1, "PART ONE | THE LIFE"; 2, blank; 3-241, text; 242-245, "SELECT BIBLIOGRAPHY"; 246, blank; 247-259, "INDEX"; 260-262, blank.
Binding: Black paper over boards, maroon cloth spine with gilt lettering: JULIAN SYMONS THE TELL-TALE HEART HARPER | & ROW. Lower right of front cover has blind stamp of publisher's logo: torch within rectangular box and date 1817.
Dust Jacket: Black with red lettering on front, red and white lettering on spine. Front and back have the same illustration, which shows a picture of Poe, his heart removed and fixed to the center of his chest, with the chest opening filled in with a raven. Cover construction by John Klammer, typography by Kim Kasow.
Publication Date: June 1978.
Price: $10.95.
Printing: Printed in the United States of America.
Symons's Note: This book springs from a dissatisfaction with existing biographies of Poe. In almost all of them the life is fused with the work, so that an account of what he was doing in a given year will be interrupted by long analyses and discussions of poems and stories....For the sake of showing Poe's life as it was actually lived, I have separated it as much as possible from the work. Complete separation is not possible and would not be desirable, but I have confined comment in the biographical part of the book to a necessary minimum. [From the introduction.]

(b) First U.K. edition (1978)

THE | TELL-TALE | HEART | The Life and Works of Edgar Allan Poe | [printer's flower] | JULIAN SYMONS | FABER & FABER | 3 Queen Square | London

Size: 9⅛ x 6".
Pagination: [i-vi] vii-x [1-2] 3-259 [260-262].

This edition is the same as C 18 a, with the following changes:

Contents: i, half title [deletion of "A Joan Kahn Book"]; ii, "By the Same Author" followed by *Bloody Murder* and *The Thirties: A Dream Revolved; iv,* copyright page: "First published in 1978 | by Faber and Faber Limited | 3 Queen Square London WC1 | ....© Julian Symons, 1978."

Binding: Maroon paper over boards with gilt lettering on spine: [double rules] | THE TELL-TALE HEART | The Life and Works of EDGAR ALLAN POE | [double rules] JULIAN | SYMONS | FABER.

Dust Jacket: Maroon with white lettering on front, white and black lettering on spine. Front has a black-and-white photograph of Poe.

Publication Date: October 1978.

Price: £6.95.

Printing: Printed in the United States of America. Bound in England.

(c) First U.S. paperback edition (1981)

THE | TELL-TALE | HEART | The Life and Works of Edgar Allan Poe | [printer's flower] | JULIAN SYMONS | [publisher's logo: penguin in oval] | PENGUIN BOOKS

Size: 7¹¹⁄₁₆ x 5¹⁄₁₆".

Pagination: [i-vi] vii-x [1-2] 3-259 [260-262].

Contents: i, half title and biographical note; ii, blank; iii, title page; iv, copyright page: "Published in Penguin Books 1981 | Copyright © Julian Symons, 1978"; v, dedication: "To Bill and Marietta Pritchard"; vi, blank; vii-viii, "CONTENTS"; ix-x, "INTRODUCTION"; 1-241, text; 242-245, "SELECT BIBLIOGRAPHY"; 246, blank; 247-259, "INDEX"; 260-262, blank.

Binding: White lettering on purple paper: [publisher's logo: penguin in orange oval] | JULIAN SYMONS | [rule] | THE TELL-TALE | HEART | "Outstanding" — *Sunday Times* | THE LIFE AND WORDS OF | EDGAR ALLAN POE. Cover illustration shows raven superimposed over portrait of Poe so that the two figures share an eye. Black and white lettering on orange spine: JULIAN SYMONS THE TELL-TALE HEART ISBN 0 14 | 00.5371.9 | [logo]. White lettering on purple back includes logo, excerpts from reviews, prices, genre, ISBN. Cover illustration by Daniel Kleinman.

Publication Date: 1981.

Price: UK £1.95, Australia $6.95, Canada $3.95, USA $3.95.

Printing: Printed in the United States of America by Offset Paperback Mfrs., Inc., Dallas, Pennsylvania. Set in Caledonia.

C 19   CONAN DOYLE, PORTRAIT OF AN ARTIST   1979

(a) First U.K. edition (1979)

Portrait of an Artist | CONAN DOYLE | by | Julian Symons [title and author are enclosed in a rectangular box made up of thin outer rule and a very thick inner rule] | [publisher's logo: man sitting in chair, reading a book] | Whizzard Press/Andre Deutsch

Size: 8¹³⁄₁₆ x 5⁵⁄₁₆".
Pagination: [5-11] 12-138 [138-140].
Contents: [pp. 1-4 not present]; 5, title page; 6, copyright page: "© Julian Symons 1979"; 7-8, blank; 9, "CONTENTS"; 10, blank; 11, "AUTHOR'S NOTE"; 12, photograph of Doyle; 13-123 text accompanied by 11 color and 79 black-and-white illustrations; 124, blank; 125-126, "BIBLIOGRAPHY"; 127-130, "CHRONOLOGY"; 131-134, "LIST OF ILLUSTRATIONS", 135, blank; 136-138, "INDEX"; 139-140, blank.
Binding: Black paper over boards stamped in silver on front: Portrait of an Artist | CONAN DOYLE | by | Julian Symons [all within a heavy, silver ruled rectangular box]. Silver lettering on spine: CONAN DOYLE Julian Symons Whizzard Press/Andre Deutsch | [publisher's logo].
Dust Jacket:: Front has a photograph of Doyle sitting in a chair, reading a book; back has a black-and-white reproduction of *Beeton's Christmas Annual* cover for "A Study in Scarlet." Box in upper right of front has title in red lettering on yellow background. Spine is yellow with black lettering.
Publication Date: 1979.
Price: £4.95.
Printing: Color separation, Printing House Reproduction Ltd. Typesetting by South Bucks Typesetters Ltd, made and printed in Great Britain by Waterlow Ltd, Dunstable.
Symons's Notes: To write a new biography of Sir Arthur Conan Doyle when several books about him are already on library shelves...may seem both presumptuous and foolhardy. I can only say that there seemed to me room for a short study which looked at the life rather differently from the way it is generally seen today....for some time now we have heard perhaps too much about Sherlock Holmes, and certainly too little about the other achievements of his creator. I finished writing the book...with more admiration for its subject than when I began it. [Author's Note, p. 11.]
Author's Note: A year after the publication of this title, Julian Symons wrote a very fine, brief study of the Holmes|Doyle connection for *The New York Times Book Review* entitled "Holmes Was a Sideline" (August 3, 1980, p. 3).

(b) First U.S. edition (1987)

CONAN | [rule] | PORTRAIT of an ARTIST | [rule] | DOYLE | [rule] | JULIAN SYMONS [title and author enclosed in a rectangular box comprised of an inner rule and an outer saw-tooth rule] | [publisher's logo: signboard hanging from a pole] MYSTERIOUS | PRESS | THE MYSTERIOUS PRESS | New York • London

Size: 8¼ x 5¼".
Pagination: [1-14] 15-137 [138-144].
Contents: 1-2, blank; 3, half title; 4, blank; 5, title page; 6, copyright page: " Originally published by G. Whizzard, London | Copyright © 1979 by Julian Symons | ....First Mysterious Press Printing: November 1987 | "; 7, "CONTENTS"; 8, blank; 9, "AUTHOR'S NOTE"; 10, blank; 11, half title; 12, photograph of Doyle; 13-123, text with illustrations throughout; 124, blank; 125-126, "BIB-

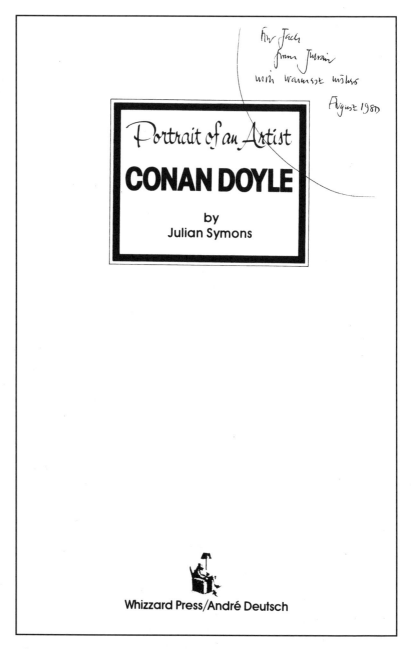

Title Page, *Conan Doyle: Portrait of an Artist*, Whizzard Press/Andre Deutsch, 1979, inscribed: "For Jack from Julian with warmest wishes August 1980."

LIOGRAPHY"; 127-130, "CHRONOLOGY"; 131-134, "LIST OF ILLUS-
TRATIONS"; 135-137, "INDEX"; 138-144, blank.
Binding: Pale green paper over boards with gilt lettering on black cloth spine:
CONAN DOYLE JULIAN SYMONS [author's name overlined with a single
rule] | publisher's logo.
Dust Jacket: Cream with maroon and black lettering. Front has a portrait photo-
graph of Doyle, back has a drawing of Sherlock Holmes and another picture of
Sir Arthur Conan Doyle. Jacket design by Louise Fili.
Printing: Printed in the United States of America.
Publication Date: November 1987.
Price: $15.95.

(c) First U.S. paperback edition (1988)

CONAN | [rule] | PORTRAIT of an ARTIST | [rule] | DOYLE | [rule] | JULIAN
SYMONS [title and author enclosed in a rectangular box comprised of an inner rule
and an outer saw-tooth rule] | [publisher's logo: signboard hanging from a pole]
MYSTERIOUS | PRESS | THE MYSTERIOUS PRESS | New York • London • Tokyo

Size: 8¼ x 5½".
Pagination: [1-14] 15-137 [138-144].
Contents: 1-2, blank; 3, half title; 4, blank; 5, title page; 6, copyright page: " Originally
published by G. Whizzard, London | Copyright © 1979 by Julian Symons | ....First
Mysterious Press Trade Paperback Printing: November 1988"; 7, "CONTENTS";
8, blank; 9, "AUTHOR'S NOTE"; 10, blank; 11, half title; 12, photograph of
Doyle; 13-123, text with illustrations throughout; 124, blank; 125-126, "BIBLIOG-
RAPHY"; 127-130, "CHRONOLOGY"; 131-134, "LIST OF ILLUSTRA-
TIONS"; 135-137, "INDEX"; 138-141, blank; 142-144, list of titles in series.
Binding: White and orange lettering on purple front: Mysterious | LIBRARY | [black
silhouette of Sherlock Holmes character on orange circle] | CONAN | DOYLE |
Portrait of an | Artist | JULIAN SYMONS. Top right corner: [Mysterious Press
logo] | 0-89296-926-1 $9.95 USA | (0-89296-927-X $13.50 CAN). Cover illus-
tration shows a hurricane lamp on a gray-and-black checked background. White
and orange lettering on purple spine: [logo] | CONAN DOYLE: PORTRAIT OF
AN ARTIST Julian Symons | [rule] | BIOGRAPHY | [rule]. Black lettering on pur-
ple back includes review, promotional blurb, logo, ISBN, price, address.
Publication Date: November 1988.
Price: $9.95.
Printing: Printed in the United States of America.

C 20   THE MODERN CRIME STORY   1980

(a) First U.K. edition (1980)

JULIAN SYMONS [rule] | The Modern Crime Story [printer's flower] | The Tragara
Press | EDINBURGH | 1980

Julian Symons

THE MODERN CRIME STORY

Eurographica
Helsinki

Title page, *The Modern Crime Story*, Eurographica, 1980.

Size: 8¹⁵⁄₁₆ x 5½"
Pagination: [i-ii] [1-4] 5-25 [26-30].
Contents: i-ii, blank; 1, half title; 2, blank; 3, title; 4, copyright page: "© Julian
  Symons 1980"; 5-25, text; 26, blank; 27, colophon; 28-30, blank.
Binding: Bluish green and tan marbled wrappers with label in black letters against
  a white background, applied with glue; Julian Symons [rule] | THE MODERN
  CRIME STORY inside a thin rule and thick rule rectangle border.
Dust Jacket: None.
Publication Date: July, 1980.
Price: n/a.
Printing: The Tragara Press, Edinburgh.
Notes: From the colophon: "Edition limited to one hundred and twenty-five copies
  set in 12 point Barbou type and printed on Glastonbury antique laid paper.
  Numbers 1 to 25 have been signed by the author. July 1980 This is number
  ____" (numbered by hand in ink) followed by Julian Symons's signature. This is
  the text of a lecture first delivered to York University, Toronto, in December,
  1975. It is printed with some minor revisions.

(b) Second Printing (1980)

Same as C20 a, but with this change on the colophon page: "Edition limited to
one hundred and twenty-five copies set in 12 point Barbou type and printed on
Glastonbury antique laid paper. July 1980 This is one of twenty-five additional
copies printed for the use of the author." This edition is un-numbered.

(c) Third Printing (1980)

Same as C20 a, with the same colophon, but bound in a solid green wrapper with
white glued-on label.

(d) Second Limited Edition (1986)

Julian Symons | THE MODERN CRIME STORY | Eurographica | Helsinki

Size: 8¹⁄₁₆ x 5¾".
Pagination: [1-8] 9-41 [42-48].
Contents: 1-2, blank; 3, "Mystery and Spy Authors in Signed Limited Editions 1";
  4, blank; 5, title; 6, copyright page: "Copyright © Julian Symons 1980"; 7, half
  title; 8, blank; 9-41, text; 42-44, blank; 45, colophon; 46-48, blank.
Binding: Rust-red wrappers over light board with title on front in black lettering:
  Julian Symons | THE MODERN CRIME STORY | Eurographica. The spine
  reads, again in black lettering: Julian Symons | THE MODERN CRIME
  STORY | c. The ISBN is printed in black at the bottom of the back cover.
Dust Jacket: None.

Publication Date: February, 1986.
Price: None given.
Printing: Tipografia Nobili.
Note: From the colophon: "This book, edited by Rolando Pieraccini, has been
printed in 350 copies by Tipografia Nobili, established in Pasaro in 1823, on
special Michelangelo paper made at the Magnani Paper Mills in Pescia, Italy.
All the copies are numbered and signed by the author. Printing completed in
February, 1986. This is one of 20 additional copies printed for the personal use
of the author." This title is the first in a series which, through 1990, has
resulted in a total of 14 books by such writers as John Fowles, Ed McBain,
Patricia Highsmith, Eric Ambler and Ruth Rendell.

C 21   TOM ADAMS' AGATHA CHRISTIE COVER STORY   1981

(a) First U.K. edition (1981)

TOM ADAMS' | AGATHA CHRISTIE | COVER STORY | Commentary by Julian
Symons | Introduction by John Fowles | Paper Tiger | [publisher's logo: tiger's face
within a circle]

Size: 11⁵⁄₁₆ x 8⁷⁄₁₆".
Pagination: [1-5] 6-144.
Contents: 1, half title; 2, color frontispiece reproduction of the cover for *The Moving
    Finger*; 3, title page; 4, copyright page: "© Copyright text Tom Adams & Julian
    Symons 1981"; 5, "CONTENTS"; 6, color illustration; 7-8, "INTRODUCTION |
    BY | JOHN FOWLES"; 9-10, "FOREWORD" by Tom Adams; 11, statement by
    Virgil Pomfret, Tom Adams agent; 12, dedication; 13-142, text by Tom Adams
    and Julian Symons, with 101 color reproductions of Adams' paintings; 143,
    "INDEX"; 144, "LIST OF OWNERS."
Binding: Dark blue paper over boards, silver lettering on cover: TOM ADAMS' |
    AGATHA CHRISTIE | COVER STORY. Author and title repeated on spine
    with publisher's logo.
Dust Jacket: White with black and red lettering on front, black lettering on spine
    and back. Front has a color reproduction of Adams' cover for *The Mirror
    Crack'd from Side to Side*, which shows an eye peering out form a cracked mir-
    ror that has a Victorian lady in a white dress reflected in it.
Publication Date: 1981.
Price: £8.95.
Printing: Designed by Steve Henderson. Printed in Hong Kong.

(b) First U.S. edition (1981)

AGATHA CHRISTIE | THE ART OF HER CRIMES | THE PAINTINGS OF
TOM ADAMS | Commentary by Julian Symons | Introduction by John Fowles |
[publisher's logo: a mountain] | New York EVEREST HOUSE Publishers

Size: 11⅚ x 8⅜".
Pagination: [1-5] 6-144.

This edition is the same as in C 21 a, except for the following changes:
Contents: title page: [title change]; copyright page: "First published in the United States of America in 1981 by Everest House....By arrangement with Dragon's World Ltd."
Binding: [publisher's logo on spine]
Dust Jacket: [publisher's logo on spine]
Publication Date: December 1981.
Price: $24.95.

C 22   CRITICAL OBSERVATIONS   1981

(a) First U.K. edition (1981)

Critical Observations | JULIAN SYMONS | FABER AND FABER | London • Boston

Size: 8½ x 5¼".
Pagination: [1-12] 13-213 [214-216].
Contents: 1, half title; 2, by the same author followed by only two non-fiction titles; 3, title page; 4, copyright page: "This collection first published in 1981 | by Faber and Faber Limited | ....This collection © Julian Symons 1981"; 5-6, "Contents": 7, dedication: "FOR ROBERT CONQUEST"; 8, blank; 9, "Preface" by Julian Symons; 10, blank; 11, chapter heading; 12, blank; 13-213, text; 214-216, blank.
Binding: Black paper over boards with silver lettering on spine: Julian Symons [rule] Critical Observations [rule] | Faber.
Dust Jacket: Black front and spine with white lettering. Front has a black-and-white photograph of Julian Symons, dark orange back has reviewers' comments on *The Thirties* and *The Tell-Tale Heart* in black.
Publication Date: 1981.
Price: £9.75.
Printing: Printed in Great Britain by Redwood Burn Ltd, Trowbridge, Wiltshire.
Symons's Note: These essays, articles and reviews are a selection from a much larger number written over the past fifteen years. They have appeared in the *London Magazine,* the *New York Review of Books, The Times,* and the *Times Literary Supplement.*...The pieces appear as they were first printed, with a very few minor textual amendments to take account of errors pointed out to me. [From the Preface.]

(b) First U.S. edition (1981)

Critical Observations | JULIAN SYMONS | TICKNOR & FIELDS | New Haven and New York | 1981

Size: 8³⁄₁₆ x 5⅜".
Pagination: [1-12] 13-213 [214-216].

This edition is the same as C 20 a except for the following changes:
Contents: 1, half title includes "A Joan Kahn Book" inscribed within an oval; 3, title page: [new publisher, cities, and date]; 4, copyright page: "This collection copyright © 1981 by Julian Symons | First published in the USA in 1981 by Ticknor & Fields | Published in Great Britain by Faber and Faber Limited | ....Printed in the United States of America | s 10 9 8 7 6 5 4 3 2 1."
Binding: Red paper over boards with black lettering on spine: Symons CRITICAL OBSERVATIONS | Ticknor | & | Fields.
Dust Jacket: Red front and spine and black and white lettering. The back is white with a black-and-white photograph of Julian Symons by Mark Gerson. Jacket design by John O.C. McCrillis.
Publication Date: November 11, 1981.
Price: $12.95.

C 23   THE MYSTIQUE OF THE DETECTIVE STORY   1981

(a) Limited Edition (1982)

THE MYSTIQUE OF THE DETECTIVE STORY | BY JULIAN SYMONS | [double rule] | THE ALCUIN SOCIETY

Size: 8½ x 5½".
Pagination: [i-ii] [1] 2-18.
Contents: i, copyright page: "Cpyright Julian Symons, 1981"; ii, title page running over onto page 1; 1, title plus first page of text; 2-18, text; inside back cover serves as colophon page.
Binding: Gray wrappers with black lettering on front cover: THE | MYSTIQUE | OF THE | DETECTIVE | STORY inside a double rule rectangle border.
Dust Jacket: None.
Publication Date: January, 1982.
Price: Not given.
Printing: Don Atkins, printer.
Note: A speech delivered under the auspices of the Vancouver Institute at the University of British Columbia on March 14, 1981. From the colophon: "The Mystique of the Detective Story, a speech by Julian Symons is the second in a series of chapbooks published by The Alcuin Society. It has been printed by Don Atkins in Trump Medieval on Carlyle Japan paper in an edition of 126 copies, of which 26, lettered, have been signed by the author and are for his own use and 100 have been numbered and are for sale. Alcuin Chapbook Number Two First Edition, January 1982. This is copy ____." Numbered by hand in black ink.

C 24   CRIME & DETECTION QUIZ   1983

(a) First U.K. edition (1983)

Julian | Symons | CRIME & | DETECTION | QUIZ [each word is enclosed by a single box rule] | WEIDENFELD AND NICOLSON | LONDON [title page has a double-ruled border]

Size: 7⁷⁄₁₆ x 3½".
Pagination: [1-10] 11-123 [124-128].
Contents: 1, half title; 2, blank; 3, title page; 4, copyright page: "Copyright © Julian Symons 1983 | ....First published in Great Britain in 1983"; 5-6, "Contents"; 7, introduction; 8, blank; 9, "Quizzes"; 10, blank; 11-99, text questions; 100, blank; 101, "Answers"; 102, blank; 102-123, text answers; 124-128, blank.
Binding: Plasticized paper over boards. Front and back cover are blue, author and title in bold, black lettering on yellow. Back cover has promotional blurb and lists five other titles in the Weidenfeld Quiz Book series, including Brian Aldiss on *Science Fiction Quiz.*
Dust Jacket: Issued without a jacket.
Publication Date: 1983.
Price:£2.95.
Printing: Printed in Great Britain by Butler & Tanner, Ltd., Frome and London.
Symons's Note: The quiz is meant for all those who read crime fiction, an umbrella phrase which here covers tales of detection, thrillers, spy stories, psychological mysteries, and any other category that occurs to you. It goes back to Edgar Allan Poe, who was the founding father of the crime story, and comes up to date with questions relating to newly risen stars of the last decade. [from Introduction, page 7]
Author's Note: The same year, 1983, saw the publication of this quiz in software from by Ivan Berg Software Ltd. and sold by Acornsoft Ltd. of Cambridge, England. The cover title is Julian Symons Crime & Detection Quiz for the BBC Microcomputer and Acorn Electron. Ref. No. XBX02. Along with two cassettes is a four-page pamphlet reproducing Julian Symons's introduction and instructions.

C 25   1948 AND 1984   1984

(a) First U.K. edition (1984)

1948 and 1984 | by Julian Symons | [line of three asterisks] | The Second Orwell Memorial Lecture | The Tragara Press | EDINBURGH | 1984

Size: 8³⁄₁₆ x 5½".
Pagination: [i-ii] [1-4] 5-32 [33-38].

Contents: i-ii, blank; 1, half title; 2, blank; 3, title; 4, copyright page: "© Julian Symons 1984"; 5-32, text; 33-34, blank; 35, colophon; 36-38, blank.

Binding: Bright blue wrappers over lightweight boards with white geometric design, pasted title in black letters against a white rectangular background, within a single black rectangular rule border: JULIAN SYMONS | [rule] | 1948 and 1984.

Dust Jacket: None.

Publication Date: 1984.

Price: Not given.

Notes: From the verso of the title page: "The title of George Orwell's book is *Nineteen Eighty-Four*, but because of the comparison being made with 1948, the solecism of using figures rather than letters seemed excusable." From the colophon page: "This lecture was delivered at London University on 25 February 1983. The edition is limited to 135 copies hand-set in Centaur type. Numbers 1 to 25 have been printed on Barcham Green handmade paper and signed by the author. This is number ___." Numbered in black ink by hand and signed by the author in ink.

C 26   DASHIELL HAMMETT   1985

(a) First U.S. edition (1985)

DASHIELL | HAMMETT | [rule] | by JULIAN SYMONS | HARCOURT BRACE JOVANOVICH, PUBLISHERS | San Diego New York London [title superimposed on reverse contrast photograph of Hammett at his typewriter and enclosed by single box rule]

Size: 9⅛ x 7⅛".

Pagination: [i-vi] vii [viii-x] xi-xiii [xiv] 1-178.

Contents: i, half title; ii, blank; iii, "ALSO BY JULIAN SYMONS" followed by twelve fiction and eight criticism titles; iv, a list of five other titles in the HBJ Album Biographies series, edited by Matthew J. Bruccoli; v, title page; vi, copyright page: "Copyright © 1985 by Julian Symons | ....First edition | ABCDE"; vii, "CONTENTS"; viii, blank; ix, "ACKNOWLEDGEMENTS"; x, blank; xi-xiii, "CHRONOLOGY"; xiv, blank; 1-155, text; 156, blank; 157-165, "NOTES"; 166, blank; 167-171, "BIBLIOGRAPHY COMPILED BY JUDITH BAUGHMAN"; 172, blank; 173-178, "INDEX." Text accompanied by 98 illustrations.

Binding: Light yellow paper covers over boards stamped on center front in gilt: DH | [underscore]. Dark blue cloth spine with gilt lettering: JULIAN | SYMONS DASHIELL HAMMETT | HBJ [within oval] | HARCOURT | BRACE | JOVANOVICH. ISBN appears in gilt on the lower right of the back cover.

Dust Jacket: Light blue front, spine and back with dark blue and gold lettering. Front shows the back of a closed book with a photograph of Hammett on its jacket. Back has comments on this work by Stanley Ellin and Thomas Chastain. Jacket design by Bob Silverman.

Publication Date: March 1985.

Price: $24.95.

Printing: Printed in the United States of America.

(b) First U.S. paperback edition (1985)

This edition is the same as C26 a except for the following changes:

Binding: Cover (front and spine) same as dust jacket of C26 a with one addition, "A Harvest/HBJ Book" added to lower left corner of the front cover. Back cover totally changes with blurb, reviewer comments and biography of Symons. *Price:* $12.95.

C 27   TWO BROTHERS
FRAGMENTS OF A CORRESPONDENCE   1985

(a) Limited edition (1985)

JULIAN SYMONS | [rule] | TWO BROTHERS | Fragments of a Correspondence | The Tragara Press | EDINBURGH | 1985

Size: 9¹³⁄₁₆ x 6½".
Pagination: [i-vi] 1-12 [13-18].
Contents: i-iii, blank; iv, frontispiece portrait of Julian Symons by Windham Lewis done in 1938; v, title; vi, copyright page: "© Julian Symons 1985"; 1-12, text; 13-14, blank; 15, colophon; 16-18, blank.
Binding: Dark red wrappers with title on front cover in black lettering: JULIAN SYMONS | [rule] | TWO BROTHERS | Fragments of a Correspondence.
Dust Jacket: None.
Publication Date: 1985.
Price: Not given.
Printing: The Tragara Press, Edinburgh.
Note: From the colophon: "Edition limited to one hundred and thirty copies hand-set in Bembo type. Numbers 1 to 25, signed by the author, have been printed on paper made by Amatruda of Amalfi. This is number ____." Hand numbered in blue ink.

(b) Second printing (1985)

Two Brothers Fragments of a Correspondence

Same as C27a, but with this change: Colophon reads as in C27a, but the last line, which reads "This is number ____" is dropped, replaced by: "This is one of thirty additional copies printed for the use of Julian Symons."

C 28   A.J.A. SYMONS BROTHER SPECULATOR   1985

(a) Limited edition (1985)

Julian Symons | A.J.A. SYMONS | BROTHER SPECULATOR

Size: 8¾ x 5½".

Pagination: 1-16.

Contents: 1, title, plus first page of text; 2, text; 3, photograph of A.J.A. Symons holding a glass of wine; 4-6, text; 7, a reproduction of signatures with A.J.A.'s forgeries below the original, bottom photo of the opening of the First Edition Club, with ex-King Manoel of Portugal and A.J.; 8-9, reproduction of the double-spread title page from Baron Corvo's *The Songs of Meleager*; 10-16, text.

Binding: Light green wrappers with eight yellow vertical rules on front and back cover, divided into rows of four rules left, four rules right, with the center of the page filled with horizontal, yellow rules (67 in all) giving a railroad tie effect. At center, middle of the front cover, in yellow lettering, is the title: A.J.A. SYMONS | [rule] BROTHER SPECULATOR | [rule] | JULIAN SYMONS.

Dust Jacket: None.

Publication Date: 1985.

Price: Not given.

Printing: No information given.

Note: "Preprinted from *The Book Collector* Autumn 1985 issue for presentation to members of the Double Crown Club." This after dinner speech was delivered on the 18th of October, 1984 and in it Julian pays tribute to his brother, not only for his fine biography of Corvo and his founding of the First Edition Club and co-editorship of *The Book Collector's Quarterly*, but also as "a dandy, a wit, a gourmet, an elegant calligrapher and a skillful amateur forger. He collected many things from books to musical boxes to Victorian card cases....and he managed to do all these things without, in a serious sense, having any money."

C 29   MAKERS OF THE NEW: THE REVOLUTION IN LITERATURE, 1912-1939   1987

(a) First U.K. edition (1987)

JULIAN SYMONS | MAKERS OF THE NEW | The revolution in Literature, | 1912-1939 | [publisher's logo: circle around bow with three arrows] | ANDRE DEUTSCH

Size: 8½ x 5⅜".

Pagination: [1-8] 9-11 [12-14] 15-295 [296].

Contents: 1, half title; 2, blank; 3, title page; 4, copyright page: "First published in 1987 by | Andre Deutsch Limited | ....© Julian Symons, 1987; 5-6, "Contents"; 7, quotes from Pound, Joyce and Lewis; 8, blank; 9-11, "INTRODUCTION"; 12, blank; 13, "PART ONE | The Founding Fathers"; 14, blank; 15-275, text; 276-287, "NOTES"; 288, "ACKNOWLEDGEMENTS"; 289-295, "INDEX;" 296, blank.

Binding: Brown paper over boards, gilt lettering on spine: MAKERS OF THE

NEW | The revolution in Literature, 1912-1939 | Julian Symons | [publisher's logo] | arrows] ANDRE | DEUTSCH.

Dust Jacket: Cream with blue and black lettering. Front is divided by two rules into fourths, each section containing reproductions of sketches by Wyndham Lewis of Pound, Joyce, Eliot, and Lewis himself. The back cover has a drawing of Symons done by Lewis in 1938.

Publication Date: 1987.

Price: £12.95.

Printing: Phototypeset by Falcon Graphic Art Ltd., printed in Great Britain by Ebenezer Baylis & Son, Worcester.

Symons's Note: This book is a blend of biography, literary history and criticism designed to show the course of literary modernism, as it developed in Britain and America between 1912 and 1939. It is shaped as a narrative, which tells what happened, why it happened, how it happened, and it is also an account of the principal figures involved and the ways in which they affected the movement. [from the Introduction, page 9]

(b) First U.S. edition (1987)

Makers of the New | The Revolution in Literature, | 1912-1939 | JULIAN SYMONS | [publisher's logo: a house] | Random House New York

Size: 9⅛ x 5¹⁵⁄₁₆".

Pagination: [i-ii] [1-8] 9-11 [12-14] 15-295 [296-302].

Contents: i-ii, blank; 1, half title; 2, blank; 3, title page; 4, copyright page: "First American Edition | Copyright © 1987 Julian Symons"; 5-6, "Contents"; 7, quotes from Pound, Joyce and Lewis; 8, blank; 9-11, "INTRODUCTION"; 12, blank; 13, "PART ONE | The Founding Fathers"; 14, blank; 15-275, text; 276-287, "NOTES"; 288, blank; 289-295, "INDEX"; 296, blank; 297, "About the Author"; 298-302, blank.

Binding: Light yellow paper over boards stamped on the front cover in gilt: J | S. Spine is dark brown cloth with gilt lettering: Makers of the New | The Revolution in Literature, 1912-1939 JULIAN SYMONS [publisher's logo] | Random House.

Dust Jacket: Light green and light yellow with black lettering. Illustrations of Eliot, Lewis, Pound and Joyce by Wyndham Lewis are reproduced on the front and back.

Publication Date: October 1987.

Price: $ 19.95.

Printing: Manufactured in the United States of America.

C 30   OSCAR WILDE:
A PROBLEM IN BIOGRAPHY   1988

(a) Limited edition (1988)

OSCAR WILDE: [in red] | A PROBLEM IN BIOGRAPHY | by JULIAN SYMONS | [decorative rule] | WOOD ENGRAVINGS BY | JOHN DEPOL | "I was a problem for which | there was no solution." | YELLOW BARN PRESS | COUNCIL BLUFFS | 1988

Size: 9½ x 6¼".

Pagination: [i-xii] 1-27 [28-32].

Contents: i-vi, blank; vii, half title; viii, frontispiece wood engraving of Wilde by John DePol; ix, title; x, copyright page: "Copyright 1988 by Julian Symons"; "THIS IS THE TEXT OF THE LUCY LECTURE DELIVERED AT AMHERST COLLEGE ON THE SEVENTH OF APRIL 1988."; xii, blank; 1-2, text; 3, text with illustration of Lord Alfred Douglas; 4-15, text; 16, text with illustration of Reading Gaol; 17-21, text; 22, text with illustration of Wilde's cell in Reading Gaol; 23-27, text; 28, blank; 29, colophon; 30-32, blank.

Binding: Case bound, with maroon cloth spine, front and back cover of maroon paste paper over boards. Gray rectangular spine label, within a double rule maroon border, reading: Oscar Wilde: A Problem in Biography [printer's flower] Symons also in maroon.

Dust Jacket: None.

Publication Date: October, 1988.

Price: $45.00.

Printing: Printed at the Yellow Barn Press, Council Bluffs, Iowa.

Note: Published with erratum slip, 3⁵⁄₁₆ x 3⁵⁄₁₆", with John DePol wood engraving showing a distraught printer (Neil Shaver) which reads: "ERRATUM The correct title for the Amherst lecture as seen in the opening pages is THE LURCY LECTURE The mistake occurred at the typecase causing the printer, as you can see [from the illustration] much consternation." The colophon note reads, in part: "Printed...during September and October 1988. The text composition is set in 12 point Monotype Bulmer and the display lines are set in Baskerville. The text was keyboarded by Mackenzie-Harris with refinements by hand at the Press. The paste paper for the cover was handmade by Molly Green and Greg Campbell at the Campbell-Logan Bindery where the book was bound. Neil Shaver was the pressman using a Vandercook Universall III. Of 200 copies, this is copy number ____." Numbered by hand in black ink.

C 31   THE THIRTIES AND THE NINETIES   1990

(a) First U.K. edition (1990)

JULIAN SYMONS | The Thirties | and the Nineties | CARCANET

Size: 8½ x 5⅜".

Pagination: [1-11] 12-184.

Contents: 1, half title; 2, blank; 3, title page; 4, copyright page: "This edition first published in Great Britain in 1990 by | Carcanet Press | ....Copyright © Julian

Symons 1975, 1990"; 5, dedication poem: FOR MARCUS SYMONS; 6, blank; 7, "Contents"; 8, blank; 9, "THE THIRTIES I A DREAM REVOLVED"; 10, blank; 11-184, text [see Author's Note].

Binding: Black paper over boards, gilt lettering on spine: JULIAN SYMONS I The Thirties and the Nineties CARCANET.

Dust Jacket: White and red lettering on blue with light blue insert on front: *The 30's and the 90's.* White lettering on spine and back. Back has review by Norman Shrapnel from the *Guardian.* Jacket design by Stephen Raw.

Publication Date: 1990.

Price: £14.95.

Printing: Set in 10 pt. Baskerville by Bryan Williamson, Darwen. Printed and bound in England by SRP Ltd., Exeter.

Author's Note: The first 135 pages of this edition are the same as the first 178 pages of C 8 a. Appendix I has been deleted, but Appendix II, Notes on Sources, has been retained. Pages 143-184 are entirely new to this edition. To this new edition Symons has added the following P.S. on page 147: A personal view like this one may still retain a flavour lacking in purely factual or academic accounts, but some details are inaccurate, other inevitably not up-to-date, yet to reissue the book with changes and corrections silently made would have been implicitly dishonest, robbing the original work of any quality it possesses as a document of its times. It seems better, then, to leave the printed pages as they stand, a piece about the period written by a period piece, and keep corrections for this postscript.

C 32   CRIMINAL PRACTICES: SYMONS ON CRIME WRITING 60s TO 90s   1994

(a) First U.K. edition (1994)

JULIAN SYMONS I Criminal Practices I Symons on Crime Writing 60s to 90s I MACMILLAN

Size: 8½ x 5⅛".

Pagination: [i-vii] viii-ix [x] [1] 2-229 [230].

Contents: i, half title; ii, "ALSO BY JULIAN SYMONS" followed by a list of thirty titles; iii, title page; iv, copyright page: "First published 1994 by Macmillan London I ....This collection copyright © Julian Symons 1994"; v, "Acknowledgements"; vi, blank; vii-ix, "Contents"; x, blank; 1-229, text; 230, blank.

Binding: Paperbound original. The front cover is black and white at top one-third, botton in orange and brown. Top illustration of man holding left hand to head, bottom illustration shows head of woman in prone position. White and black lettering on cover, black letter on orange background on spine and back. Cover reads in white lettering: JULIAN SYMONS I Criminal Practices I Symons on Crime Writing 60s to 90s in black lettering. Spine JULIAN SYMONS Criminal Practices [Publisher's logo] MACMILLAN. Back cover has blurb for the book, biography of Julian Symons, one illustration, upper right corner, price, ISBN

and this note: "The cover shows details from crime book jackets © Mary Evans Picture Library."
Dust Jacket: Issued without a jacket.
Publication Date: 1994.
Price £7.99.
Printing: Typeset by CentraCet Limited, Cambridge. Printed by Mackays of Chatham plc, Chatman, Kent.

ENDNOTES

1   *The Collected Essays, Journalism and Letters of George Orwell*, ed. by Sonia Orwell and Ian Angus (New York, Harcourt, Brace & World, Inc., 1968), vol. IV, p. 422.

SECTION D

WORKS

EDITED BY

JULIAN SYMONS

1937

D 1   *TWENTIETH CENTURY VERSE*, Number 1 (January 1937).
Edited by Julian Symons. London: The Noble Fortune Press.
"Twentieth Century Verse," editorial, p. [2]
"The Romantic Speaking," p. [11]
"Mr. Thomas's Poems," review of *Twentyfive Poems* by Dylan Thomas,
pp. [17-19]

D 2   *TWENTIETH CENTURY VERSE*, Number 2 (March 1937).
Edited by Julian Symons. London: The Noble Fortune Press.
"Exclusiveness, Politics, etc.," editorial, p. [2]
"Aiken, Pitter," review of *Time in the Rock* by Conrad Aiken and *A Trophy
of Arms* by Ruth Pitter, pp. [16-17]

D 3   *TWENTIETH CENTURY VERSE*, Number 3 (April/May 1937).
Edited by Julian Symons. London: The Noble Fortune Press.
"Against Surrealism," editorial, p. [2]
"The Ascent of F.6," review of play by W.H. Auden and Christopher
Isherwood, pp. [19-20]

D 4   *TWENTIETH CENTURY VERSE*, Number 4 (June/July 1937).
Edited by Julian Symons. London: The Noble Fortune Press.
Very short reviews signed J.S., reviews of *The Lemon Tree* by Margot
Ruddock and *Euripides' Ion* by H.D, p. [23]

D 5   *TWENTIETH CENTURY VERSE*, Number 5 (September 1937).
Edited by Julian Symons. London: The Noble Fortune Press.
"Poem," p. [12]
"Prologue," pp. [12-13]
"This Year," p. [13]
"BRIEFLY" signed J.S., review of "The Southern Review" and "Wales No.
1," p. [19]

D 6   *TWENTIETH CENTURY VERSE*, Number 6/7 (November/December 1937).
Edited by Julian Symons. London: The Noble Fortune Press.
"Mr. Wyndham Lewis," editorial, p. [2]
"Notes on One-Way Song," article, pp. [27-29]
Author's Note: This double number was devoted to Wyndham Lewis, with
works by, among others, T.S. Eliot, A.J.A. Symons, Rex Warner, and
Ruthven Todd.

1938

D 7   *TWENTIETH CENTURY VERSE*, Number 8 (January/February 1938).
Edited by Julian Symons. London: The Noble Fortune Press.
"Programme 1938," editorial, p. [2]
"Hart Crane," review of *Hart Crane: The Life of an American Poet* by
Philip Horton, pp. [20-23]

D 8   *TWENTIETH CENTURY VERSE*, Number 9 (March 1938).
Edited by Julian Symons. London: The Noble Fortune Press.
"Prelude to Poems (for A.J.A.S., S.M.S., M.A.S.),", pp. 16-17
"BRIEFLY," review of "The Southern Review" and *The Year's Poetry,
1937*; announcement of Samuel French Morse as the American Editor,
pp. 19-20

D 9   *TWENTIETH CENTURY VERSE*, Number 10 (May 1938).
Edited by Julian Symons. London: The Noble Fortune Press.
"BRIEFLY," editorial on libel, obscenity, alterations to announced future
article, cancellations by "naive or vicious intellectuals" who disagreed
with the special Lewis number, and a reprint of a haughty letter writ-
ten by Edith Sitwell's secretary to another magazine, pp. 44-45
Symons's Note: This is much too good to be lost.
Review of *Trial of a Judge*, signed "X," pp. 53-54

D 10   *TWENTIETH CENTURY VERSE*, Number 11 (July 1938).
Edited by Julian Symons. London: The Noble Fortune Press.
"EVERYMAN'S POEMS," review of *I Crossed the Minch* and *The Earth
Compels* by Louis MacNiece, pp. 69-71 "X Y and Z" signed J.S.,
review of three volumes of poetry: *Poems* by C.H. Peacock, *News
Reel* by Margaret Stanley-Wrench, and *The Garden of Disorder* by
Charles Henri Ford, p. 78

D 11   *TWENTIETH CENTURY VERSE*, Number 12-13 (September/October 1938).
Edited by Julian Symons. London: The Noble Fortune Press.
"HOW WIDE IS THE ATLANTIC? OR DO YOU BELIEVE IN
AMERICA?" editorial, pp. 80-84
Author's Note: Although not so stated, this double issue was referred to in
Number 11 as the "American Number." Some of the poets included are
Allen Tate, Conrad Aiken, Wallace Stevens, John Berryman and Theodore
Roethke.

D 12   *TWENTIETH CENTURY VERSE*, Number 14 (December 1938).
Edited by Julian Symons. London: The Noble Fortune Press.
"Poem (for W.E.L.)," p. 128
"BRIEFLY," reviews of new issues of "Partisan Review," "The Southern
Review," "Poetry," and "New Verse" magazines and a mild rebuke of
"Delta" and "Wales" magazines for reprinting "To Caitlin" by Dylan
Thomas without giving credit to "Twentieth Century Verse, January,
1938," pp. 141-142

1939

D 13   *TWENTIETH CENTURY VERSE*, Number 15-16 (February 1939).
"ABOUT FRONTIERS," reviews of *Collected Essays in Literary Criticism*
by Herbert Read, *The Mysterious Mr. Bull* by Wyndham Lewis, *On
the Frontier* by W.H. Auden, *Collected Poems* by Robert Graves,

Being Geniuses Together by Robert McAlmon, and *The Year's Poetry,*
1938, edited by D.K. Roberts and Geoffrey Grigson, pp. 163-167
Author's Note: The last five pages of this issue, numbered i-v, are the index
to Numbers 9-16, March 1938 to February 1939.

D 14 *TWENTIETH CENTURY VERSE,* Number 17 (April/May 1939).
Edited by Julian Symons. London: The Noble Fortune Press.
"Tuttifruitti: Or the Worse for Poetry," unsigned editorial, p. 19
"CONSTRUCTION AND INVENTION," review of the *Hawk Among*
the Sparrow by Desmond Hawkins, *Over the Mountain* by Ruthven
Todd, and *Happy Valley* by Patrick White, pp. 22-23
Author's Note: Pages 24-25 contain a review by Roy Fuller of Julian
Symons's first published book, *Confusions About X.*

D 15 *TWENTIETH CENTURY VERSE,* Number 18 (June/July 1939).
Edited by Julian Symons. London: The Noble Fortune Press. [Special issue
cover title: "The Poet and the Public."]
"Conversations after Dinner," article by Julian Symons and H.B. Mallalieu,
pp. 28-31
"THE FAMILY REUNION," review of *The Family Reunion* by T.S.
Eliot, pp. 44-48

1949
D 16 *SELECTED WRITINGS OF SAMUEL JOHNSON.*
Edited and introduced by Julian Symons. Falcon Press Classics Series. London:
Falcon Press, 1949.
Introduction, 9-16.

1955
D 17 *CARLYLE: Selected Works, Reminiscences, and Letters.*
Edited by Julian Symons. London: Rupert Hart-Davis, 1955.
Introduction, pp. 9-14.
Notes on pp. 18, 46, 60, 124, 258, 296, 344, 372, 404, 450, 468, 514, 698.
Author's Note: Also published in the U.S. with the same title by Harvard
University Press in 1957.

1969
D 18 *ESSAYS AND BIOGRAPHIES* by A.J.A. Symons.
Edited by Julian Symons. London: Cassell & Company, 1969.
Introduction, pp. [v-ix].

1974
D 19 *THE WOMAN IN WHITE* by Wilkie Collins.
Edited with an introduction and notes by Julian Symons. Harmondsworth,
Middlesex: Penguin Books, 1974.
Introduction, pp. 7-21.
Notes, pp. 647-648.

Author's Note: "Television edition" reprinted twice in 1982 to go with what the cover blurb calls a "stunning TV serial."

D 20   *GREAT EXPECTATIONS* by Charles Dickens.
London: Pan Books, 1974.

1980

D 21   *THE WORLD'S CLASSICS: EDGAR ALLAN POE SELECTED TALES.*
Edited with an introduction and notes by Julian Symons.
Oxford: Oxford University Press, 1980.
Introduction, pp. vii-xiii.
Notes, pp. 301-316.
World's Classics paperback published by Oxford University Press, 1980.
Reprinted in 1982 and 1984.
Published as a Borders Books edition in 1993.

1982

D 22   *A.J.A. SYMONS TO WYNDHAM LEWIS: TWENTY-FOUR LETTERS.*
Comments by Julian Symons. Edinburgh: The Tragara Press, 1982.
Author's Note: From the colophon: For permission to print these letters thanks are accorded to Julian Symons and to the Department of Rare Books at Cornell University Library. The frontispiece drawing of A.J.A. Symons by Wyndham Lewis is from the original in the possession of Julian Symons. The edition is limited to one hundred & twenty copies, hand-set in Bembo type and printed by Alan Anderson at the Tragara Press. This is number ___. [Numbered by hand in black ink.] Twenty-five additional copies were printed for the use of Julian Symons, as noted in the colophon in those editions.

1984

D 23   *THE PENGUIN CLASSIC CRIME OMNIBUS.*
Edited by Julian Symons. Harmondsworth, Middlesex: Penguin Books, 1984.
Introduction, pp. 9-12.
Author's Note: Reprinted in 1988 under the title *Penguin Classic Crime.*

1989

D 24   *THE ESSENTIAL WYNDHAM LEWIS, AN INTRODUCTION TO HIS WORK.*
Edited by Julian Symons. London: Andre Deutsch, 1989.
Introduction, pp. 1-14.
Notes on pp. 17-18, 30, 43-44, 46, 48, 59, 61-62, 83-84, 99-100, 103-104, 112, 115-116, 123-124, 126, 131, 147, 151, 171, 175, 189-190, 206, 228, 239, 242, 256, 259-261, 274-275, 288-289, 305-306, 308-309, 312-316, 324-325, 334, 339, 344-345, 363-364, 374, 380.
Published in the U.S. by Vintage, 1991 (Not seen).

SECTION E

CONTRIBUTIONS

TO BOOKS

1952

E 1 *THE QUEST FOR CORVO* by A.J.A. Symons with Introductions by Sir Norman Birkett and Sir Shane Leslie. London: The Folio Society, 1952.
Contribution: "Rolfe at Holywell," p. 256.

1955

E 2 *THE QUEST FOR CORVO* by A.J.A. Symons with an introduction by Julian Symons. East Lansing, Michigan: Michigan State University Press, 1955.
Introduction, pp. 1-4.

E 3 *THE QUEST FOR CORVO: AN EXPERIMENT IN BIOGRAPHY* by A.J.A. Symons with an introduction by Julian Symons. London: Cassell and Company Ltd, 1955. First published in 1934.
Introduction, pp. vii-x.

1963

E 4 *THE CONCISE ENCYCLOPEDIA OF MODERN WORLD LITERATURE.*
Edited by Geoffrey Grigson. New York: Hawthorn Books Inc., 1963.
A second edition was published in 1971. Symons's contributions to entries are not identified in the text.

E 5 *ORWELL'S NINETEEN EIGHTY-FOUR: TEXT, SOURCES, CRITICISM.*
Edited by Irving Howe. New York: Harcourt Brace Jovanovich, Inc., 1963.
Contribution: "George Orwell's Utopia," pp. 293-294. See also p. 287 for a letter from Orwell to Symons.
See E46.

E 6 *THE MENTOR BOOK OF MAJOR BRITISH POETS FROM WILLIAM BLAKE TO DYLAN THOMAS.*
Edited by Oscar Williams with an introduction by Julian Symons. New York: A Mentor Book published by The New American Library, 1963.
Introduction "The Two Revolutions," pp. xiii-xxii.

1966

E 7 *THE QUEST FOR CORVO: AN EXPERIMENT IN BIOGRAPHY.* By A.J.A. Symons with an introduction by Julian Symons. Harmondsworth, Middlesex: Penguin Books, Ltd, 1966.
Introduction, pp. 9-12.
This paperback edition reprinted in 1969 and 1979.

1967

E 8 *AUTHORS TAKE SIDES ON VIETNAM. Two questions on the war in VietNam answered by authors of several nations.* Edited by Cecil Woolf and John Bagguley. London: Peter Owen, 1967.
Contribution, pp. 46-47.

1968

E 9   *DOCTOR THORNE* by Anthony Trollope. Introduction by Julian Symons.
Notes by Ara Calder-Marshall. London: Pan Books, Ltd., 1968.
Introduction, pp. vii-xiv.

1969

E 10   *THE FLAXBOROUGH CHRONICLE* by Colin Watson. Combining,
complete and unabridged, *Coffin, Scarcely Used*, *Bump In the Night*, and
Hopjoy Was Here. With an introduction by Julian Symons. Decorations by
Salim Patell. London: Eyre & Spottiswoode, 1969.
Introduction, pp. 7-9.
See E 14 for Book Club edition

1970

E 11   *NINETEEN EIGHTY-FOUR* by George Orwell. With an introduction and
Appreciation by Julian Symons, London: Heron Books, 1970.
Introduction, pp. xi-xiii.
Appreciation, pp. 315-344.

1971

E 12   *THE MURDER BOOK: AN ILLUSTRATED HISTORY OF THE
DETECTIVE STORY*. Compiled by Tage la Cour and Harald Mogensen,
translated from Danish by Roy Dufell with a foreword by Julian Symons.
Translation published London: George Allen and Unwin Ltd., New York:
Herder and Herder, 1971.
Foreword, p. 9.
Originally published in 1969 as *Mordbogen*. Also published in London
by Book Club Association in 1973.

E 13   *WYNDHAM LEWIS IN CANADA*. Edited by George Woodcock with an
introduction by Julian Symons. 1971.
Introduction, pp. 1-6.

E 14   *THE FLAXBOROUGH CHRONICLE* by Colin Watson.
Book Club Associates, London, 1972.
See E 10.

1973

E 15   *THE MURDER BOOK: AN ILLUSTRATED HISTORY OF THE
DETECTIVE STORY*. Compiled by Tage la Cour and Harald Mogensen,
translated from Danish by Roy Dufell with a foreword by Julian Symons.
Originally published as *Mordbogen* in 1969. Translation published Lon-
don: Book Club Association, 1973.
Foreword, p. 9.
First published in England and the U.S. in 1971.

1974

E 16   *BRITISH CRIME FICTION*. London: The British Council and the National
Book League, 1974.
"British Crime Stories Now," pp. 5-7.

E 17 *HIS LAST BOW: SOME REMINISCENCES OF SHERLOCK HOLMES*
by Sir Arthur Conan Doyle. With an introduction by Julian Symons. London:
John Murray and Jonathan Cape, 1974.
Introduction, pp. 7-12.
First published by John Murray in 1917, first published in this edition in 1974.
Also published in paperback by Pan Books, 1976.

1976

E 18 *THE BEDSIDE BOOK OF GREAT DETECTIVE STORIES.* Edited by
Herbert van Thal. Introduction by Julian Symons. London: Book Club
Associates, 1976.
Introduction, pp. [vii-x].

E 19 *THE JOHN FRANKLIN BARDIN OMNIBUS.* With an introduction by
Julian Symons. Baltimore, Md.: Penguin Books, 1976.
Introduction, pp. 7-11.

E 20 *THE WARDEN* by Anthony Trollope. Introduction by Julian Symons. Drawings
by Peter Reddick. London: Folio Society, 1976.
The Barsetshire Novels, pp 9-18.
Introduction, pp. 19-22.

1977

E 21 *BARCHESTER TOWERS* by Anthony Trollope. Introduction by Julian
Symons. Drawings by Peter Reddick. London: Folio Society, 1977.
Introduction, pp. 7-9.

E 22 *CLASSIC CRIMES: A Selection from the works of William Roughead, made
by W.N. Roughead.* With an introduction by Julian Symons. New York:
Vintage Books, a Division of Random House, 1977.
Introduction, pp. ix-xvi.
Reprint of the 1951 edition published in London by Cassel.

1978

E 23 *DOCTOR THORNE* by Anthony Trollope. Introduction by Julian Symons.
Drawings By Peter Reddick. London: Folio Society, 1978.
Introduction, pp. 7-9.

E 24 *FRAMLEY PARSONAGE* by Anthony Trollope. Introduction by Julian
Symons. Drawings by Peter Reddick. London: Folio Society, 1978.
Introduction, pp. 7-10.

1979

E 25 *THE BEDSIDE, BATHTUB AND ARMCHAIR COMPANION TO AGATHA
CHRISTIE.* Edited by Dick Riley and Pam McAllister. Introduction by
Julian Symons. New York: Frederick Ungar, 1979.
Introduction: "A Portrait of Agatha Christie," pp. xv-xix.

E 26 *FITS AND STARTS*. Collected pieces by Maurice Richardson. Introduction
by Julian Symons. London: Michael Joseph, 1979.
Introduction, pp. 9-12.

E 27 *THE SMALL HOUSE AT ALLINGTON* by Anthony Trollope. Introduction
by Julian Symons. Drawings by Peter Reddick. London: Folio Society, 1979.
Introduction, pp. 7-9.

E 28 *VERDICT OF THIRTEEN: A Detection Club Anthology*. Introduction by
Julian Symons, President of the Detection Club. London: Faber and Faber, 1979.
Introduction, pp. 9-12.

1980

E 29 *THE ABC MURDERS* by Agatha Christie. A Jubilee Reprint. Selected and
introduced by Julian Symons. London: Collins, 1980.
Introduction, pp. [5-7].
First published in 1932.

E 30 *AN AFTERNOON TO KILL* by Shelley Smith. A Jubilee Reprint. Selected
and introduced by Julian Symons. London: Collins, 1980.
Introduction, pp. [9-11].
First published in 1953.

E 31 *ENOUGH TO KILL A HORSE* by Elizabeth Ferrars. A Jubilee Reprint.
Selected and introduced by Julian Symons. London: Collins, 1980.
Introduction, pp. [5-7].
First published in 1955.

E 32 *EVEN IN THE BEST FAMILIES* by Rex Stout. A Jubilee Reprint. Selected
and introduced by Julian Symons. London: Collins, 1980.
Introduction, pp. [5-8].
First published in 1951.

E 33 *THE LAST CHRONICLE OF BARSET* by Anthony Trollope. Introduction
by Julian Symons. Drawings by Peter Reddick. London: Folio Society, 1980.
Introduction, pp. 9-12.

E 34 *THE LOSS OF THE JANE VOSPER* by Freeman Wills Crofts. A Jubilee
Reprint. Selected and introduced by Julian Symons. London: Collins, 1980.
Introduction, [7-9].
First published in 1936.

E 35 *THE MAZE* by Philip MacDonald. A Jubilee Reprint. Selected and introduced
by Julian Symons. London: Collins, 1980.
Introduction, pp. [5-7].
First published in 1932.

E 36 *MINUTE FOR MURDER* by Nicholas Blake. A Jubilee Reprint. Selected and introduced by Julian Symons. London: Collins, 1980.
Introduction, pp. [7-10].
First published in 1947.

E 37 *NO MASK FOR MURDER* by Andrew Garve. A Jubilee Reprint. Selected and introduced by Julian Symons. London: Collins, 1980.
Introduction, [5-7].
First published in 1950.

E 38 *OBELISTS FLY HIGH* by C. Daly King. A Jubilee Reprint. Selected and introduced by Julian Symons. London: Collins, 1980.
Introduction, [5-7].
First published in 1935.

E 39 *THE ODD FLAMINGO* by Nina Bawden. A Jubilee Reprint. Selected and introduced by Julian Symons. London: Collins, 1980.
Introduction, pp. [5-7].
First published in 1954.

E 40 *SPINSTERS IN JEOPARDY* by Ngaio Marsh. A Jubilee Reprint. Selected and introduced by Julian Symons. London: Collins, 1980.
Introduction, pp.[7-9].
First published in 1954.

E 41 *WHICH I NEVER* by L.A.G. Strong. A Jubilee Reprint. Selected and introduced by Julian Symons. London: Collins, 1980.
Introduction, pp. [5-7].
First published in 1950.

1981

E 42 *THE COMPLETE SHERLOCK HOLMES* by Sir Arthur Conan Doyle. With a preface by Julian Symons. London: Secker & Warburt, 1981.
Introduction, pp. 1-10.

E 43 *THE TWO HEROINES OF PLUMPLINGTON AND OTHER STORIES* by Anthony Trollope. Introduction by Julian Symons. Drawings by Peter Reddick. London: Folio Society, 1981.
Introduction, pp. 7-11.

E 44 *VERDICT OF THIRTEEN: A Detection Club Anthology.* Introduction by Julian Symons, President of the Detection Club. South Yarmouth, Mass.: J. Curley, 1981. Large print edition of 1979 title.

1982

E 45 *THE REVENGE FOR LOVE* by Wyndham Lewis. With an introduction by

Julian Symons. London: Secker & Warburg in association with the Arts Council of Great Britain, 1982.
Introduction, pp. vii-xvi.

E 46 *ORWELL'S NINETEEN EIGHTY-FOUR: TEXT, SOURCES, CRITICISM.*
Edited by Irving Howe. New York: Harcourt Brace Jovanovich, Inc., 1982.
Contribution: "George Orwell's Utopia," pp. 293-294. See also p. 287 for a letter from Orwell to Symons.
Later edition, first published in 1963. See E5.

1983
E 47 *THE MIND OF J.G. REEDER* by Edgar Wallace. Introduced by Julian Symons. London: J.M. Dent &Sons, 1983.
Introduction, pp. vii-xv.

E 48 *THE SCOOP & BEHIND THE SCREEN: AGATHA CHRISTIE, DOROTHY L. SAYERS, HUGH WALPOLE, E.C. BENTLEY, ANTHONY BERKELEY, CLEMENCE DANE, RONALD KNOX, AND FREEMAN WILLS CROFTS.* Introduction by Julian Symons. New York: Harper & Row, 1983.
Preface: "A Brief Account of the Detection Club," pp. 1-4.
Also published in paperback by Charter Books, New York, December 1984.

1984
E 49 *INWARD JOURNEY: ROSS MACDONALD.* Edited by Ralph B. Sipper. Santa Barbara, California: Cordelia Editions, 1984.
Contribution: "A Transatlantic Friendship," pp. 59-66.
Also published in paperback by Mysterious Press, New York, April 1987.

E 50 *MURDER INK.* Revived, Revised, Still Unrepentant. Perpetrated by Dilys Winn. New York: Workman Publishing, 1984.
Contribution: "Whatever Happened to Inspector Bland? Was it, Perhaps, a Merciful Death?" pp. 206-209.

E 51 *ORWELL REMEMBERED.* Edited with a Preface and Introduction by Aubrey Coppard and Bernard Crick. London: British Broadcasting Corporation, 1984.
Contribution: "Tribune's Obituary," pp. 271-275.
Also published in the U.S. by Facts On File, New York, 1984.

E 52 *THE RIDDLE OF THE SANDS* by Erskine Childers. Introduction by Julian Symons. London and Melbourne: J.M. Dent & Sons Ltd, 1984.
Introduction, pp. 7-19.

1985
E 53 *A.J.A. SYMONS: BROTHER SPECULATOR.* Julian Symons. Reprinted from *The Book Collector*, Autumn, 1985, issue for presentation to members of the Double Crown Club. London: The Book Collector, 1985.

Contribution: Speech delivered to the Double Crown Club on 18 October 1984, p. 16; five illustrations.

E 54 *GRIGSON AT EIGHTY.* Tributes from friends and admirers. Edited with an introduction by R.M. Heley. Cambridge: Rampant Lions Press, 1985.
Contribution: "Grigson the Critic," pp. 8-11.
Edition limited to 375 copies bound in limp wrappers and 75 numbered copies bound in marbled paper boards.

E 55 *LEN DEIGHTON. An Annotated Bibliography 1954-1985* by Edward Milward-Oliver. With a foreword by Julian Symons. London: The Sammler Press, 1985.
Foreword pp. 8-9.
Edition limited to 375 copies.

1986

E 56 *NEVER COME BACK* by John Mair. Introduced by Julian Symons. Oxford: Oxford University Press, 1986.
Introduction, pp. v-xiii.

E 57 *THE SHOOTING PARTY* by Anton Chekhov. Introduction by Julian Symons. London: Andre Deutsch, 1986.
Introduction, pp. 5-13.
Published in paperback by The University of Chicago Press, 1987.

1987

E 58 *THE HOUND OF THE BASKERVILLES* by Sir Arthur Conan Doyle. Introduction by Julian Symons. Lino-cuts by Edward Bawden. London: Folio Society, 1987.
Introduction, pp. ix-xv.

E 59 *THE SHOOTING PARTY* by Anton Chekhov. Introduction by Julian Symons. Chicago: The University of Chicago Press, 1987.
Introduction, pp. 5-13.
Published in London by Andre Deutsch, 1986.

1989

E 60 *HOMAGE TO CATALONIA* by George Orwell. London: Penguin Books in association with Martin Secker & Warburg Ltd., 1989.
Introduction, pp. v-xiii.
This edition first published by Martin Secker & Warburg Ltd. in the Complete Works of George Orwell series, 1986. Introduction and new note on text added for the Penguin publication of 1989.

1990

E 61 *W.H. AUDEN 'THE MAP OF ALL MY YOUTH': EARLY WORKS, FRIENDS, AND INFLUENCES.* Edited by Kathleen Bucknell and Nicholas Jenkins. Oxford: Clarendon, 1990.
"A Communist to Others: A Symposium," pp. 173-195.

1991

E 62 *THE ADVENTURE OF THE DYING DETECTIVE* by Sir Arthur Conan Doyle. Introduction by Julian Symons. Westminster Libraries: The Arthur Conan Doyle Society, 1991.
Introduction, pp. 7-8.
There is a standard edition and a deluxe limited edition of 100 signed copies.

E 63 *DETECTIVE STORIES FROM THE STRAND MAGAZINE.* Selected and introduced by Jack Adrian. Foreword by Julian Symons. Oxford: Oxford University Press, 1991.
Foreword, pp. vii-viii.

E 64 *STRANGE TALES FROM THE STRAND MAGAZINE.* Selected and introduced by Jack Adrian. Foreword by Julian Symons. Oxford: Oxford University Press, 1991.
Foreword, pp. vii-viii.

1992

E 65 *COMMUNISM: A TLS Companion.* Edited by Ferdinand Mount. Chicago: University of Chicago Press, 1992.
"From Burmese Days to Nineteen Eighty-Four," p. 76-82.

E 66 *NINETEEN EIGHTY-FOUR* by George Orwell. New York: Alfred Knopf, 1992.
Introduction, v-xix.
Published in London by David Campbell Publishers Ltd., 1992.

E 67 *THE MODERN MOVEMENT: A TLS Companion.* Edited by John Gross. Chicago: University of Chicago Press, 1992.
"The Price of Singularity," p. 106-112.
"The Defeat of Optimism," p. 112-113.
"Figures of Allegory," p. 114.

1993

E 68 *ANIMAL FARM* by George Orwell. Introduction by Julian Symons. New York: Alfred Knopf, 1993.
Introduction, pp. xi-xxiii.

E 69 *ASTA'S BOOK* by Barbara Vine. Bristol: Scorpion Press, 1993.
"An Appreciation of Barbara Vine" pp. v-vi.
A limited edition of 100 copies signed by Ruth Rendell.

1994

E 70 *A CRITICAL RESPONSE TO DASHIELL HAMMETT.* Edited by Christopher Metress. Westport, Conn.: Greenwood Press, 1994.
"From *Mortal Consequences*" pp.113

E 71 *CRITICAL ESSAYS ON NATHANAEL WEST.* Edited by Ben Siegel. New York: G.K. Hall and Company, 1994.
"Nathanael West" pp. 99-104.

SECTION F

CONTRIBUTIONS

TO

ANTHOLOGIES

1937

F 1   *THE FIRST COMMENT TREASURY.*
Selected and Introduced by Sheila Macleod and Victor B. Neuburg. London: The Comment Press, 1937.
Contribution: "Change of Season," p. 76.

1940

F 2   *SOME POEMS IN WARTIME.* London: Diemer & Reynolds, 1940.
Contributions: "Pub," p. 13; "Faces," p. 14.
Although Diemer & Reynolds, 14 John Adam St., London, is given as the publisher, Julian Symons was, in fact, the publisher. Diemer & Reynolds printed the last five numbers of "Twentieth Century Verse." The pamphlet consisted chiefly of poems sent in for the next, never-issued number of the magazine. Almost all of the poems were written after August 1939, as a preliminary note says, and the pamphlet was published in 1940.

1942

F 3   *AN ANTHOLOGY OF WAR POETRY.* Compiled by Julian Symons. Harmondsworth, Middlesex: Pelican Books published by Penguin Books, 1942.
Frontispiece photograph of Julian Symons.
Contributions: Acknowledgements and a Note on Sources, pp. v-vi; Preface, pp. vii-viii; "Eleven Meetings," p. 186.

1943

F 4   *MORE POEMS FROM THE FORCES.*
A collection of verses by serving members of the Navy, Army, and Air Force. Edited by Keidrych Rhys. London: George Routledge, 1943.
Contributions: "Sunday, July 14th: A Fine Day at the Baths," pp. 281-284; "The Statues in Parliament Square," pp. 284-285; "Pub," pp. 286-287; "Eleven Meetings," p. 287; "Conscript," pp. 288-289; "Reflections in Bed," pp. 289-290.

1944

F 5   *NEW POEMS 1944: An Anthology of American and British Verse, with a Selection of Poems from the Armed Forces.* Edited by Oscar Williams. New York: Howell, Soskin, Publishers, 1944.
Contributions: "Pub," pp. 276-277; "Reflections in Bed," pp. 277-278; "Sunday, July 14th: A Fine Day at the Baths," pp. 278-281; Photo of Julian Symons, p. 315. Biographical note, p. 326.

F 6   *POETRY LONDON X [TEN].* Edited by Tambimuttu. London: Nicholson and Watson, 1944.
Contribution: Criticism of "Under the Cliff and other poems" by Geoffrey Grigson, pp. 244-245.

F 7   *THE SATURDAY BOOK 4.* Edited by Leonard Russell with illustrations by Laurence Scarfe. London: Hutchinson, 1944.
Contribution: "A Player of Games," pp. 249-254.

1945

F 8   *FOCUS ONE.* Edited by B. Rajan and Andrew Pearse. London: Dennis Dobson Ltd, 1945.
Contributions: "A Comment" (on Kafka and Rex Warner), p. 43; "Of Crisis and Dismay, A Study of Writing in the Thirties," pp. 90-111.

F 9   *THE SATURDAY BOOK: FIFTH YEAR.* Edited by Leonard Russell. London: Hutchinson, 1945.
Contribution: "The Battle of Holywell: A Story of Baron Corvo," pp. 215-234.

F 10   *THE WAR POETS: An Anthology of the War Poetry of the 20th Century.* Edited with an Introduction by Oscar Williams. New York: The John Day Company, 1945.
Contributions: "Comments by the Poets: Julian Symons: Poetry and the War," pp. 17-18; "The Second Man," p. 258; "Reflections in Bed," p. 259; "Hospital Observation," pp. 259-260; "Mr. Symons at Richmond, Mr. Pope at Twickenham," pp. 260-262; "Pub," pp. 262-263; "And the World's Face," pp. 263- 264; "For the Depressed," p. 264; "For My Wife," p. 265; "Gladstone," pp. 266-267; "Sunday, July 14th: A Fine Day at the Baths," pp. 267- 269.
Photo of Trooper Julian Symons, p. 459.
Biographical Note: "Julian Symons (Trooper, Royal Armoured Corps, British)," p. 472.

1946

F 11   *FOCUS TWO.* Edited by B. Rajan and Andrew Pearse. London: Dennis Dobson Limited, 1946.
Contributions: "Watching Through a Flying Bomb Raid," p. 77; "The Double Man" (review of *For The Time Being* by W.H. Auden), pp. 127-137.

F 12   *THE HOLIDAY BOOK.* Edited by John Singer. Glasgow: William McLellan, 1946.
Contribution: "Early Days of the Detective," pp. 195-203.
Biographical note and photo, p.[344].

F 13   *A LITTLE TREASURY OF THE GREAT POETRY OF THE ENGLISH LANGUAGE* (2 vols.) (Volume II: *A Little Treasury of Modern Poetry English and American*). Edited with an introduction by Oscar Williams. New York: Charles Scribner's Sons, 1946.
Contributions: "Pub," pp. 197-199; "Reflections in Bed," pp. 302-303; "Hart Crane," p. 318.

F 14   *SATURDAY BOOK: SIXTH YEAR.* Edited by Leonard Russell with illustrations by Laurence Scarfe. London: Hutchinson, 1946.
Contribution: "Table Tennis," pp. 235-240.

Circa 1949

F 15   *THE NEW BRITISH POETS: An Anthology edited by Kenneth Rexroth.* New York: A New Directions Book, N.D. [circa 1949].
Contributions: "Spring Poem," pp. 237-238; "For My Wife," pp. 239-240; "Homage to our Leaders," p. 240.
Biographical Note, p. 311.

1950

F 16   *THE EVENING STANDARD DETECTIVE BOOK.* London: Victor Gollancz Ltd, 1950.
Contribution: "The Case of the Frightened Promoter," pp. 262-271.
These stories first appeared in the *London Evening Standard.*

F 17   *THE VOICE OF POETRY.* Edited with a critical introduction by Hermann Peschmann. London: Evans Brothers Limited, 1950.
Contribution: "Pub," p. 176.

1951

F 18   *THE EVENING STANDARD DETECTIVE BOOK.* Second Series. London: Victor Gollancz Ltd, 1951.
Contributions: "The Desk," pp. 256-263; "The Case of S.W.2," pp. 264-273.
These stories first appeared in the *London Evening Standard.*

F 19   *THE SATURDAY BOOK 11.* Edited by Leonard Russell, being the eleventh annual appearance of this renowned repository of curiosities and looking-glass of past and present. The book designed by Laurence Scarfe. London: Hutchinson, 1951.
Contribution: "The Death of Trotsky," pp. 56-60.

1952

F 20   *A LITTLE TREASURY OF MODERN POETRY ENGLISH AND AMERICAN.* Revised edition. Edited with an Introduction by Oscar Williams. New York: Charles Scribner's Sons, 1952.
Contributions: "Reflections in Bed," p. 700; "Pub," pp. 701-702.

F 21   *THE VOICE OF POETRY.* Edited with a critical introduction by Hermann Peschmann. London: Evans Brothers Limited, 1952.
Contribution: "Pub," p. 176.
This anthology was originally published in 1950.

1953

F 22   *NEW POEMS 1953. A P.E.N. Anthology.* Edited by Robert Conquest,

Michael Hamburger, Howard Sergeant with an introduction by C.V. Wedgewood. London: Michael Joseph Ltd, 1953.
   Contribution: "A Quiet Evening," p. 58.

1954

F 23   *THE FOURTEENTH ISSUE THE SATURDAY BOOK.* Edited by John Hadfield. New York: Macmillan Company, 1954.
   Contribution: "The Great Detective," pp. 47-53.

F 24   *THE POCKET BOOK OF MODERN VERSE.* English and American Poetry of the last hundred years from Walt Whitman to Dylan Thomas. Edited by Oscar Williams. New York: Pocket Books, 1954.
   Contribution: "Pub," pp. 438-439.

1956

F 25   *BUTCHER'S DOZEN: A Crime Writers Association Anthology.* London: Heinemann, 1956.
   Contribution: "The Dupe," pp. 237-255.

1958

F 26   *CHOICE OF WEAPONS: A Crime Writers Association Anthology.* London: Hodder and Stoughton, 1958.
   Contribution: "The Grand National Case," pp. 203-226.

F 27   *PLANNED DEPARTURES: A Crime Writers Association Anthology.* London: Hodder and Stoughton, 1958.
   Contribution: "Eight Minutes to Kill," pp. 183-205.

1959

F 28   *CRIME IN GOOD COMPANY:* Essays on Criminals and Crime-Writing by Josephine Bell, Michael Underwood, Maurice Procter, Cyril Hare, Raymond Chandler, Michael Gilbert, Julian Symons, Jacques Barzun, L.A.G. Strong, Stanley Ellin, Roy Vickers, Eric Ambler, Mary Fitt, David Alexander. Collected by Michael Gilbert on behalf of the Crime Writers' Association. London: Constable, 1959.
   Contribution: "The Face in the Mirror," pp. 126-133.

1960

F 29   *SOME LIKE THEM DEAD: A Crime Writers Association Anthology.* London: Hodder and Stoughton, 1960.
   Contribution: "The Summer Holiday Murders," pp. 177-210.

1963

F 30   *NINETEEN EIGHTY-FOUR: TEXT SOURCES AND CRITICISM.* Edited by Irving Howe. New York: Harcourt, Brace, Jovanovich, 1963. Reprinted 1982.
   Contribution: "George Orwell's Utopia," pp. 293-294.

1964

F 31   *BEST CRIME STORIES.* Edited with an introduction by John Welcome London: Faber and Faber, 1964.
      Contribution: "The Dupe," pp. 84-97.

F 32   *BEST DETECTIVE STORIES 2.* Edited with an introduction by Edmund Crispin. London: Faber and Faber, 1964.
      Contribution: "A Pearl Among Women," pp. 73-78.

F 33   *CRIMES ACROSS THE SEA: THE 19TH ANNUAL ANTHOLOGY OF THE MYSTERY WRITERS OF AMERICA.* Edited by John Creasey. Preface by Herbert Brean. New York: Harper and Row, 1964.
      British edition published 1965 by George G. Harrap & Co. Ltd.
      Contribution: "Castle in Spain," pp. 174-180.
      Biographical note: p. 235.

F 34   *CRIME WRITERS' CHOICE:* The Fifth Anthology of the Crime Writers' Association. London: Hodder and Stoughton, 1964.
      Contribution: "Strolling in the Square One Day," pp. 32-43.

F 35   *POETRY OF THE THIRTIES.* Introduced and edited by Robin Skelton. Harmondsworth, Middlesex: Penguin, 1964.
      Contribution: "Poem," pp. 188-189.

1965

F 36   *BEST DETECTIVE STORIES OF THE YEAR:* 20th Annual Collection. Edited by Anthony Boucher. New York: E.P. Dutton and Co, 1965.
      Contribution: "Credit to Shakespeare," pp. 135-142.

F 37   *CRIMES ACROSS THE SEA: The 19th Annual Anthology of the Mystery Writers of America.* Edited by John Creasey. Preface by Herbert Brean. London: Harrap, 1965.
      U.S. edition published 1964.
      Contribution: "Castle in Spain," pp. 174-180.
      Biographical note: p. 235.

F 38   *THE POETRY OF WAR 1939-1945.* Edited by Ian Hamilton. London: Alan Ross, 1965.
      Contributions: "Eleven Meetings," p. 64; "Gladstone," pp. 120-121; "Some Autobiographical Statements" (Julian Symons) pp. 170-171.

1966

F 39   *BEST RACING AND CHASING STORIES.* Edited with an introduction by Dick Francis and John Welcome. London: Faber and Faber, 1966.
      Contribution: "The Grand National Case," pp. 51-72.

F 40   *BEST POLICE STORIES.* Edited with an introduction by Roy Vickers.

London: Faber and Faber, 1966.
Contributions: "The Dupe," pp. 90-105; "The Invisible Man," pp. 106-118.

F 41   *JOHN CREASEY'S MYSTERY BEDSIDE BOOK*. Founded by John Creasey and now incorporating the anthology of the Crime Writers Association. Edited by Herbert Harris. London: Hodder and Stoughton, 1966.
Contribution: "Out of the Mouths," pp. 49-62.

F 42   *THE TERRIBLE RAIN*: The War Poets 1939-1945. Selected and arranged by Brian Gardner. London: Methuen & Co. Ltd, 1966.
Contribution: "Elegy on a City," pp. 63-64.

F 43   *21st ANNUAL ELLERY QUEEN'S CRIME CAROUSEL: 21 STORIES FROM ELLERY QUEEN'S MYSTERY MAGAZINE*. Edited by Ellery Queen. New York: The New American Library, 1966. (British edition published 1967.)
Contribution: "The Tiger's Stripe," pp. 39-57.

1967

F 44   *ELLERY QUEEN'S CRIME CAROUSEL: 21 Stories from Ellery Queen's Mystery Magazine*. Edited by Ellery Queen. London: Victor Gollancz, Ltd, 1967. (U.S. edition published 1966.)
Contribution: "The Tiger's Stripe," pp. 39-57.

F 45   *SPIES AND MORE SPIES*. Edited by Robert Arthur. New York: Random House, 1967.
Contribution: "The Case of XX-2," pp. 43-53.
Paperback edition published in New York by Windward Silverback Edition, division of Random House, 1972.

1968

F 46   *ELLERY QUEEN'S MYSTERY PARADE: 23rd EQMM Annual, 19 Stories from Ellery Queen's Mystery Magazine*. Edited by Ellery Queen. New York: The New American Library, 1968.
Contribution: "The Main Chance," pp. 175-187.

F 47   *WITH MALICE TOWARD ALL*. An Anthology of Mystery Stories by The Mystery Writers of America. Edited and with a Foreword by Robert L. Fish. New York: G.P. Putnam's Sons, 1968.
Contribution: "The Accident," pp. 181-184.
U.S. paperback edition published in Baltimore by Penguin Books, 1970.

1969

F 48   *ELLERY QUEEN'S MURDER MENU: 24th EQMM Annual, 22 Stories from Ellery Queen's Mystery Magazine*. Edited by Ellery Queen. New York: The World Publishing Company, 1969.
Contribution: "A Theme for Hyacinth," pp. 199-219.

Published in London by Victor Gollancz, 1969 and by Book Club Associates in 1972.

F 49 *ELLERY QUEEN'S MYSTERY PARADE: 23rd EQMM Annual, 19 Stories from Ellery Queen's Mystery Magazine.* Edited by Ellery Queen. London: Victor Gollancz Limited, 1969.
Contribution: "The Main Chance," pp. 175-187.
Also published in paperback by Signet Books, June 1969. "The Main Chance" appears on pp. 195-208.

F 50 *THE VOICE OF POETRY.* Edited with a critical introduction by Hermann Peschmann. London: Evans Brothers Limited, 1969.
Contribution: "Pub," pp. 176-177.
This anthology was originally published in 1950 and reprinted in 1952.

F 51 *WINTER'S CRIMES 1.* Edited by George Hardinge. London: Macmillan, 1969.
Contribution: "Somebody Else," pp. 136-158.

F 52 *WITH MALICE TOWARD ALL.* An Anthology of Mystery Stories by The Mystery Writers of America. Edited and with a foreword by Robert L. Fish. London: Macmillan, 1969.
Contribution: "The Accident," pp. 181-184.

1970
F 53 *ELLERY QUEEN'S GRAND SLAM: 25th Anniversary Annual. 25 Stories from Ellery Queen's Mystery Magazine.* Edited by Ellery Queen. New York: The World Publishing Company, 1970.
Contribution: "Love Affair," pp. 285-295.
Published in paperback by Popular Library. "Love Affair" appears on pp. 347-359.
Also published in London by Victor Gollancz Ltd., 1971.

1971
F 54 *BEST CRIME STORIES 4.* Edited and with and introduction by John Welcome. London: Faber and Faber, 1971.
Contribution: "The Woman Who Loved a Motor-Car," pp. 51-60.

F 55 *ELLERY QUEEN'S ANTHOLOGY, FALL-WINTER, 1971.* Edited by Ellery Queen. New York: Davis Publications, 1971.
Contribution: "'Twixt the Cup and the Lip," pp. 80-105.

F 56 *ELLERY QUEEN'S GRAND SLAM: TWENTY-FIFTH ANNIVERSARY ANNUAL. 25 Stories from Ellery Queen's Mystery Magazine.* Edited by Ellery Queen. London: Victor Gollancz, Ltd., 1971.
Contribution: "Love Affair," pp. 285-295.
Published in New York by The World Publishing Company, 1970.

F 57   *SOME THINGS FIERCE AND FATAL*. Edited by Joan Kahn. New York and London: Harper & Row, 1971.
Contribution: "Eight Minutes to Kill," pp. 199-229.
U.S. paperback edition published by Avon Books, 1975 and by Flare in 1982. Symons's contribution appears on pp. 144-163.

F 58   *WINTER'S CRIMES 3*. Edited by George Hardinge. London: Macmillan, 1971.
Contribution: "The Last Time," pp. 228-238.

1972
F 59   *BLOOD ON MY MIND*. A collection of new pieces by members of the Crime Writers' Association about real crimes, some notable and some obscure. Edited by H.R.F. Keating. London: Macmillan, 1972.
Contribution: "Adolf Beck Revisited," pp. 131-144.

F 60   *THE DRUGGED CORNET And Other Mystery Stories*. Chosen by Susan Dickinson. London: William Collins Sons & Co., 1972.
Contribution: "The Impossible Theft," pp. 169-174.
Published in New York by E.P. Dutton, 1973.

F 61   *ELLERY QUEEN'S MURDER MENU: 24th EQMM Annual, 22 Stories from Ellery Queen's Mystery Magazine*. Edited by Ellery Queen. London: Book Club Associates, 1972.
Contribution: "A Theme for Hyacinth," pp. 199-219.
Published in London by Victor Gollancz and in New York by World Publishing Company, 1969.

F 62   *ELLERY QUEEN'S MYSTERY BAG: 27th Mystery Annual, 25 Stories from Ellery Queen's Mystery Magazine*. Edited by Ellery Queen. New York: The World Publishing Company, 1972.
Contribution: "Experiment in Personality," pp. 121-147.
Published in London by Victor Gollancz, 1973; published in paperback by Manor Books, Inc., 1973.

F 63   *THE MYSTERY AND DETECTION ANNUAL*. Beverly Hills, California: Donald Adams, 1972.
Contribution: Review of "A Catalogue of Crime" by Jacques Barzun and Wendell Hertig Taylor, pp. 199-202.
Biographical note, p. 264.

1973
F 64   *THE DRUGGED CORNET And Other Mystery Stories*. Chosen by Susan Dickinson. New York: E.P. Dutton & Co., 1973.
Contribution: "The Impossible Theft," pp. 169-174.
Published in London by William Collins Sons & Co., 1972.

F 65   *ELLERY QUEEN'S MYSTERY BAG: 27th Mystery Annual, 25 Stories from Ellery Queen's Mystery Magazine.* Edited by Ellery Queen. London: Victor Gollancz, Ltd., 1973
Contribution: "Experiment in Personality," pp. 121-147.
Also published in New York by The World Publishing Company, 1972.

1974

F 66   *ELLERY QUEEN'S CROOKBOOK: 28th Mystery Annual, 25 Stories from Ellery Queen's Mystery Magazine.* Edited by Ellery Queen. New York: Random House, 1974.
Contribution: "Pickup on the Dover Road," pp. 78-91.

F 67   *KILLERS OF THE MIND. A Collection of Stories by the Mystery Writers of America.* Edited by Lucy Freeman. New York: Random House, 1974.
Contribution: "Experiment in Personality," pp. 38-57.

F 68   *THE MYSTERY AND DETECTION ANNUAL.* Beverly Hills, California: Donald Adams, 1974.
Contribution: "Progress of a Crime Writer," pp. 238-244.

1975

F 69   *ELLERY QUEEN'S CROOKBOOK: 28th Mystery Annual, 25 Stories from Ellery Queen's Mystery Magazine.* Edited by Ellery Queen. London: Book Club Associates, 1975.
Contribution: "Pickup on the Dover Road," pp. 78-91.

F 70   *ELLERY QUEEN'S MURDERCADE: 29th Mystery Annual, 23 Stories from Ellery Queen's Mystery Magazine.* Edited by Ellery Queen. New York: Random House, 1975.
Contribution: "How to Trap a Crook," pp. 77-85.

F 71   *OPEN AT YOUR OWN RISK.* Edited and with an introduction by Joan Kahn. Boston: Houghton Mifflin Company, 1975.
Contribution: "A Theme For Hyacinth," pp. 207-228.
Biographical note, p. 505.

1976

F 72   *THE BEDSIDE BOOK OF GREAT DETECTIVE STORIES.* Edited by Herbert van Thal. London: Book Club Associates, 1976.
Contributions: Introduction, pp.[vii-x]; "A Theme for Hyacinth," pp. 215-234.

F 73   *ELLERY QUEEN'S MAGICIANS OF MYSTERY, Volume 32.* Edited by Ellery Queen. New York: Davis Publications, 1976.
Contribution: "The Sensitive Ears of Mr. Small," pp. 293-302.
Also published as Ellery Queen's Mystery Anthology, Fall-Winter 1976, Vol. 32.

F 74   *OPEN AT YOUR OWN RISK.* Edited and with an introduction by Joan
        Kahn. London: Hamish Hamilton Ltd, 1976.
        Contribution: "A Theme For Hyacinth," pp. 207-228.
        This anthology was published in the U.S. in 1975 by Houghton Mifflin.

1977

F 75   *AGATHA CHRISTIE: First Lady of Crime.* Edited by H.R.F. Keating.
        London: Weidenfeld & Nicolson, 1977.
        Contribution: "The Mistress of Complication," pp. 25-38.
        Published in New York by Holt, Rinehart and Winston, 1977.

F 76   *ELLERY QUEEN'S ANTHOLOGY, FALL-WINTER, 1977.* Edited by
        Ellery Queen. New York: Davis Publications, 1977.
        Contribution: "The Crimson Coach Murders," pp. 277-304.
        Also published in 1977 in hardback with cover title *Ellery Queen's
        Faces of Mystery.* New York: Davis Publications.

F 77   *ELLERY QUEEN'S COPS AND CAPERS.* Edited by Ellery Queen. New
        York: Davis Publications, 1977.
        Contribution: "'Twixt the Cup and the Lip," pp. 102-131.

F 78   *ELLERY QUEEN'S SEARCHES AND SEIZURES: 31st Mystery
        Annual, 27 Stories from Ellery Queen's Mystery Magazine.* Edited by
        Ellery Queen. New York: Dial Press, 1977.
        Contribution: "Hot Summer Night," pp. 280-290.

F 79   *JOHN CREASEY'S CRIME COLLECTION 1977.* An Anthology by
        Members of the Crime Writers' Association. Edited by Herbert Harris.
        London: Victor Gollancz, 1977.
        Contribution: "Strolling in the Square One Day," pp. 7-17.

F 80   *THE TERRIBLE RAIN: The War Poets 1939-1945.* Selected and arranged
        by Brian Gardner. London: Magnum Books, Methuen Paperbacks Ltd, 1977.
        Contribution: "Elegy on a City," pp. 63-64.
        This anthology was first published in 1966.

F 81   *THE WORLD OF RAYMOND CHANDLER.* Edited by Miriam Gross.
        Introduction by Patricia Highsmith. London: Weidenfeld & Nicolson, 1977.
        Contribution: "An Aesthete Discovers the Pulps," pp. 19-29.
        Published in New York by A & W Publishers, Inc., 1977.

1978

F 82   *CRIME WRITERS.* Reflections on crime fiction by Reginald Hill, P.D.
        James, H.R.F. Keating, Troy Kennedy Martin, Maurice Richardson, Julian
        Symons, Colin Watson. Edited by H.R.F. Keating. Additional material by
        Mike Pavett. London: British Broadcasting Corporation, 1978.
        Contribution: "Dashiell Hammett: The Onlie Begetter," pp. 80-93.

F 83   *ELLERY QUEEN'S FACES OF MYSTERY: Stories from the Mystery Magazine.* Edited by Ellery Queen. London: Victor Gollancz Ltd, 1978.
Contribution: "The Crimson Coach Murders," pp. 277-304.

F 84   *GREAT CASES OF SCOTLAND YARD.* Selected by the Editors of The Reader's Digest. Pleasantville, N.Y.: The Reader's Digest Association, 1978.
Contribution: "The Siege of Sidney Street," pp. 589-690.

F 85   *I, WITNESS: PERSONAL ENCOUNTERS WITH CRIME BY MEMBERS OF THE MYSTERY WRITERS OF AMERICA.* Edited and with an introduction by Brian Garfield. New York: New York Times Books, 1978.
Contribution: "The Invisible Man," pp. 45-58.

F 86   *JOHN CREASEY'S CRIME COLLECTION 1978.* An Anthology by members of Crime Writers' Association. Edited by Herbert Harris. London: Victor Gollancz, 1978.
Contribution: "The Woman Afraid of October," pp. 120-130.

F 87   *MASTERPIECES OF MYSTERY: THE SIXTIES.* Selected by Ellery Queen. New York: Davis Publications, 1978.
Contribution: "The Tiger's Stripe," pp. 225-243.

F 88   *VERDICT OF THIRTEEN: A Detection Club Anthology.* Introduction by Julian Symons. New York: Harper & Row, 1978.
Contributions: "Introduction," pp. vii-x; "Waiting for Mr. McGregor," pp. 221-239.
The verso of the title page reads " © 1978". Publication date was April 1979. There was also a Book Club Edition of this title with a 1979 copyright date. The British edition was published in 1979.

F 89   THE POETRY ANTHOLOGY, 1912-1977. Edited by Daryl Hine and Joseph Parisi. Boston: Houghton Mifflin Company, 1978.
Contribution: "Hart Carne," pp. 226-227.

1979

F 90   *JOHN CREASEY'S CRIME COLLECTION, 1979.* An Anthology by Members of the Crime Writers' Association. Edited by Herbert Harris. London: Victor Gollancz, 1979.
Contribution: "One Little Letter," pp. 163-168.

F 91   *MASTERPIECES OF MYSTERY: More from the Sixties.* Selected by Ellery Queen. New York: Davis Publications, 1979.
Contribution: "Love Affair," pp. 342-352.

F 92   *VERDICT OF THIRTEEN: A Detection Club Anthology.* London: Faber and Faber, 1979.
Contributions: "Introduction," pp. 9-12; "Waiting for Mr. McGregor," pp. 218-234.

This book was originally published in New York by Harper & Row, 1978. The U.K. edition removed Julian Symons's name from the title page.

F 93   *WINTER'S CRIMES 11.* Edited by George Hardinge. London: Macmillan London Limited, 1979.
Contribution: "The Flaw," pp. 205-224.

1980

F 94   *JOHN CREASEY'S CRIME COLLECTION, 1980.* An Anthology by Members of Crime Writers' Association. Edited by Herbert Harris. London: Victor Gollancz, 1980.
Contribution: "The Flowers that Bloom in the Spring," pp. 207-224.

F 95   *DETECTIVE FICTION: A Collection of Critical Essays.* Edited by Robin W. Wink, [1980].
See entry F139 (1988).

F 96   *THE PENGUIN BOOK OF LIGHT VERSE.* Edited with an introduction by Gavin Ewart. Harmondsworth, Middlesex: Penguin Books, 1980.
Contributions: "Central Park," p. 492; "Harvard," pp. 493-494.
Reprinted by Penguin Books, 1981.

F 97   *WINTER'S CRIMES 11.* Edited by George Hardinge. New York: St. Martin's Press, 1980.
Contribution: "The Flaw," pp. 205-224.

1981

F 98   *ALL BUT IMPOSSIBLE! An Anthology of Locked Room and Impossible Crime Stories by Members of the Mystery Writers of America.* Edited by Edward D. Hoch. New Haven and New York: Tichnor and Fields, 1981.
Contribution: "As If By Magic," pp. 217-221.

F 99   *THE ARBOR HOUSE TREASURY OF MYSTERY AND SUSPENSE.* Introduction by John D. MacDonald. Compiled by Bill Pronzini, Barry N. Malzberg and Martin H. Greenberg. New York: Arbor House, 1981.
Contribution: "The Santa Claus Club," pp. 333-343.
Reprinted as GREAT TALES OF MYSTERY AND SUSPENSE in New York by Galahad Press 1985 and reissued in1994.

F 100 *ELLERY QUEEN'S ANTHOLOGY, FALL-WINTER 1981, VOLUME 42.* New York: Davis Publications, Inc., 1981.
Contribution: "Credit to Shakespeare," pp. 25-30.
See F102 for hardback edition with title change.

F 101 *ELLERY QUEEN'S CRIME CRUISE ROUND THE WORLD: 35th Mystery Annual, 26 Stories from Ellery Queen's Mystery Magazine.* Edited by Ellery Queen. New York: Dial Press, 1981.

Contribution: "The Boiler," pp. 117-127.
This short story was nominated by Mystery Writers of America as one of the five best new mystery stories published in American magazines and books during 1979.

F 102 *ELLERY QUEEN'S EYES OF MYSTERY.* Edited by Ellery Queen. New York: Dial Press, 1981.
Contribution: "Credit to Shakespeare," pp. 25-30.

F 103 *THE FIFTH BEDSIDE BOOK OF GREAT DETECTIVE STORIES.* Edited by Herbert van Thal. London: Arthur Barker Limited, 1981.
Contribution: "As If By Magic," pp. 147-151.

F 104 *JOHN CREASEY'S CRIME COLLECTION 1981.* An Anthology by Members of the Crime Writers' Association. Edited by Herbert Harris. London: Victor Gollancz Ltd, 1981.
Contribution: "Pickup on the Dover Road," pp. 27-38.
Published in New York by St. Martin's Press, 1981.

F 105 *LIKES AND DISLIKES.* A private anthology with contributions by John Betjeman, Cyril Connolly, Roy Fuller, Mary Gill, Alyse Gregory, Vyvyan Holland, William Plomer, Anthony Powell, John Cowper Powys, Martin Secker, Julian Symons, Helen Thomas, Sylvia Townsend Warner, Lawrence Whistler, etc. Privately printed. Edinburgh: The Tragara Press, 1981.
Contribution: "Likes: Frozen Prawns, Kathleen, Henry James, Watching professional football matches. Dislikes: Powyses, Sitwells, Musical comedies, Television advertisements. 13 May 1958," p. [13].

F 106 *THE TERRIBLE RAIN: The War Poets 1939-1945.* Selected and arranged by Brian Gardner. London: Methuen Paperbacks Ltd, 1981.
Contribution: "Elegy on a City," pp. 63-64.
This anthology was first published in 1966. The paperback edition was published in 1977 and reprinted in 1981.

F 107 *VERDICT OF THIRTEEN: A Detection Club Anthology.* Introduction by Julian Symons. South Yarmouth, Mass.: J. Curley, 1981.
This is the large print edition, originally published in 1978.

1982

F 108 *ESSAYS BY DIVERS HANDS: being the transactions of the Royal Society of Literature.* New Series: Volume XLII. Edited by Michael Holroyd. Suffolk, England: The Boydell Press for the Royal Society of Literature, 1982.
Contribution: "The Art of Biography," pp. 163-178. This lecture was read on October 22, 1981.

F 109 *JOHN CREASEY'S CRIME COLLECTION, 1982.* An Anthology by Members of the Crime Writers' Association. Edited by Herbert Harris. New York: St. Martin's Press, 1982.
Contribution: "The Sensitive Ears of Mr. Small," pp. 37-44.

F 110   *WHODUNIT? A GUIDE TO CRIME, SUSPENSE AND SPY FICTION.*
Edited by H.R.F. Keating. London: Windward, 1982.
Contribution: "The American Detective Story," pp. 37-42.

F 111   *WINTER'S CRIMES 14.* Edited by Hilary Watson. New York: St. Martin's, 1982.
Contribution: "The Dream is Better," pp. 189-206.
Published in London by Macmillan London Limited, 1982.

F 112   *POEMS FOR ROY FULLER ON HIS SEVENTIETH BIRTHDAY.*
Oxford: Sycamore Press, [1982].
Contribution: "For Roy at Seventy," p. [3].

1983

F 113   *JOHN CREASEY'S CRIME COLLECTION 1983.* An Anthology by
Members of the Crime Writers' Association. Edited by Herbert Harris.
New York: St Martin's Press, 1983.
Contribution: "The Santa Claus Club," pp. 34-45.
Published in London by Victor Gollancz, Ltd, 1983.

F 114   *SHOW BUSINESS IS MURDER.* Edited by Carol-Lynn Rössel Waugh,
Martin Harry Greenberg and Isaac Asimov with an introduction by Isaac
Asimov. New York: Avon Books, 1983.
Contribution: "Credit to Shakespeare," pp. 223-229.

F 115   *65 GREAT MURDER MYSTERIES.* Edited by Mary Danby. London:
Octopus Books, 1983.
Contribution: "A Theme for Hyacinth," pp. 578-595.

F 116   *TALES OF THE UNCANNY.* Selected by the Editors of Reader's Digest.
Pleasantville, N.Y.: Reader's Digest Association, Inc., 1983.
Contribution: "The Remarkable Daniel Dunglas Home," pp. 257-332.

F 117   *THE TERRIBLE RAIN. The War Poets 1939-1945.* Selected and
arranged by Brian Gardner. London: Methuen Paperbacks Ltd, 1983.
Contribution: "Elegy on a City," p. 63.
This anthology was first published in 1966. The paperback edition was
published in 1977 and reprinted in 1981 and 1983.

F 118   *TOP CRIME: THE AUTHOR'S CHOICE.* Selected and introduced by
Josh Pachter. London: J.M. Dent & Sons, Ltd., 1983.
Contribution: "A Theme for Hyacinth," pp. 324-343.
Published in New York by St. Martin's Press, 1983.

F 119   *THE YEAR'S BEST MYSTERY & SUSPENSE STORIES, 1983.* (Second
Annual Collection.) Edited by Edward D. Hoch. New York: Walker &
Company, 1983.
Contribution: "The Dream is Better," pp. 216-231.

1984

F 120 *JOHN CREASEY'S CRIME COLLECTION 1984*. An Anthology by Members of the Crime Writers' Association. Edited by Herbert Harris. London: Victor Gollancz Ltd, 1984.
Contribution: "The Boiler," pp. 44-54.

1985

F 121 *THE DEADLY ARTS*. Edited by Bill Pronzini and Marcia Muller. New York: Arbor House, 1985.
Contribution: "Credit to Shakespeare," pp. 38-43.

F 122 *GREAT TALES OF MYSTERY AND SUSPENSE*. Introduction by John D. MacDonald. Compiled by Bill Pronzini, Barry N. Malzberg, and Martin H. Greenberg. (Abridged from the Arbor House Treasury of Mystery and Suspense, 1981.) New York: Galahad Books, 1985.
Contribution: "The Santa Claus Club," pp. 333-343.
Reprinted in hardcover by Galahad Books, 1994.

F 123 *JOHN CREASEY'S CRIME COLLECTION 1985*. An Anthology by Members of the Crime Writers' Association. Edited by Herbert Harris. New York: St. Martin's Press, 1985.
Contribution: "Love Affair," pp. 170-180.
U.S. paperback edition published by St. Martin's Press, 1987.

F 124 *WINTER'S CRIMES 17*. Edited by George Hardinge. New York: St. Martin's Press, 1985.
Contribution: "The Birthmark," pp. 123-139.

1986

F 125 *THE BEST OF WINTER'S CRIMES, Vols 1 & 2*. Edited by George Hardinge. London: Macmillan London Ltd., 1986.
Contribution: "The Flaw," Vol. 2., pp. 180-193.
This anthology was published in London and the U.S. in 1987 as *The Mammoth Book of Modern Crime Stories* and in the U.S. in 1991 as *The Giant Book of Crime Stories*.

F 126 *DEADLY ODDS*. Crime and Mystery Stories of the Turf. Selected and introduced by Richard Peyton. London: Souvenir Press, 1986.
Contribution: "The Grand National Case," pp. 313-335.
Published in New York by Bonanza Books in 1987 under the title *At the Track*.
U.K. paperback edition published by Pan Books, 1987.

F 127 *JOHN CREASEY'S CRIME COLLECTION, 1986*. An Anthology by Members of the Crime Writers' Association. Edited by Herbert Harris, London: Victor Gollancz, 1986.
Contribution: "The Flaw," pp. 11-29.

F 128   *101 MYSTERY STORIES.* Edited by Bill Pronzini and Martin H. Greenberg. New York: Avenel Books, 1986.
Contribution: "Castle in Spain," pp. 199-203.

1987

F 129   *AT THE TRACK.* A Treasury of Horse Racing Stories. Edited with an introduction by Richard Peyton. New York: Bonanza Books, 1987.
Contribution: "The Grand National Case," pp. 313-335.
This anthology was first published in London by Souvenir Press, 1986, under the title *Deadly Odds.*
Published in paperback by Pan Books, Ltd, 1987, under the title *Deadly Odds.*

F 130   *ELLERY QUEEN MASTERS OF MYSTERY.* New York: Galahad Books, 1987.
Contribution: "The Crimson Coach Murders," pp. 514-535.
Reissued by Galahad Books in 1993.

F 131   *JOHN CREASEY'S CRIME COLLECTION 1987.* An Anthology by Members of the Crime Writers' Association. Edited by Herbert Harris. New York: St. Martin's Press, 1987.
Contribution: "The Best Chess Player in the World," pp. 30-47.
Published in London by Victor Gollancz Ltd, 1987.

F 132   *THE MAMMOTH BOOK OF MODERN CRIME STORIES.* Edited by George Hardinge. New York: Carroll and Graf, 1987.
Contribution: "The Flaw," pp. 424-437.
Published in London by Robinson Publishing, 1987.
This anthology was published in London in 1991 under the title *The Giant Book of Crime Stories.* It was originally published in London in 1986 as *The Best of Winter's Crimes, Vols. 1 & 2.*

F 133   *SOLVED.* Famous Mystery Writers on Classic True-Crime Cases. Selected with an Introduction by Richard Glyn Jones. New York: Peter Bedrick Books, 1987.
Contribution: "The Invisible Man," pp. 100-113.

F 134   *THE TERRIBLE RAIN. The War Poets 1939-1945.* Selected and arranged by Brian Gardner. London: Methuen Paperbacks Ltd, 1987.
Contribution: "Elegy on a City," p. 63.
This anthology was first published in 1966. The paperback edition was published in 1977 and reprinted in 1981 and 1983. The 1987 edition was reissued with corrections to the bibliography.

F 135   *UNSOLVED.* Classic True Murder Cases. Selected with an Introduction by Richard Glyn Jones. New York: Peter Bedrick Books, 1987.
Contribution: "The Death of Sir Harry Oakes," pp. 273-284.
U.S. paperback edition published by Peter Bedrick Books, 1987.

Symons's contribution is entitled "Death of a Millionaire" on the content page.

F 136 *WINTER'S CRIMES 19.* Edited by Hilary Hale. London: Macmillan London Ltd, 1987.
Contribution: "Has Anybody Here Seen Me?" pp. 175-188.

1988

F 137 *CLOAK AND DAGGER. A Treasury of 35 Great Espionage Stories.* Edited by Bill Pronzini and Martin H. Greenberg. New York: Avenel Books, 1988.
Contribution: "The Case of XX2," pp. 409-415.

F 138 *CRIME AT CHRISTMAS: A SEASONAL BOX OF MURDEROUS DELIGHTS.* Selected and introduced by Jack Adrian. Illustrated by Brian Denington. Northamptonshire, England: Equation, 1988.
Contribution: "The Santa Claus Club," pp. 169-180.

F 139 *DETECTIVE FICTION: A Collection of Critical Essays.* Edited by Robin W. Wink. Woodstock, Vermont: The Countryman Press, 1988.
Contribution: "The Short Story's Mutations," pp. 154-160.
The appendix, "A Personal List of Favorites," lists three titles by Symons: *The 31st of February, The Man Who Killed Himself,* and *A Criminal Comedy* (p. 271). This work is revised and expanded edition of the volume published under the same title in 1980 by Prentice-Hall.

F 140 *ELLERY QUEEN'S MEDIA FAVORITES, ANTHOLOGY #58.* Edited by Eleanor Sullivan. New York: Davis Publications, Inc., 1988.
Contribution: "The Boiler," pp. 84-93.

F 141 *GREAT MURDER MYSTERIES.* Secaucus, N.J.: Chartwell Books, Inc., 1988.
Contribution: "A Theme for Hyacinth," pp. 578-595.

F 142 *MASTERPIECES OF MYSTERY AND SUSPENSE.* Compiled by Martin H. Greenberg. Garden City, New York: Doubleday Book and Music Clubs, Inc., 1988.
Contribution: "The Dream is Better," pp. 232-245.
Also published in New York by St. Martin's Press, 1988.

F 143 *MURDER ON CUE: Stage, Screen, and Radio Favorites, Stories from Ellery Queen's Mystery Magazine.* Edited by Eleanor Sullivan. New York: Walker and Company, 1988.
Contribution: "The Boiler," pp. 69-80.

F 144 *THE YEAR'S BEST MYSTERY AND SUSPENSE STORIES 1988.* Edited by Edward D. Hoch. New York: Walker and Company, 1988.
Contribution: "Has Anybody Here Seen Me?" pp. 207-217.

F 145   *WINTER'S CRIMES 19.* Edited by Hilary Hale. New York: Published for the Crime Club by Doubleday, 1988.
Contribution: "Has Anybody Here Seen Me?" pp. 167-180.

1989

F 146   *THE ARMCHAIR DETECTIVE BOOK OF LISTS.* Edited by Edward Strosser. New York: The Armchair Detective, 1989.
Contributions: "*The Sunday Times* Hundred Best Crime Stories," pp.117-123; "Some Famous Mystery Writers Pick Their Ten Favorite Mystery Books," (Symons's list) p. 232.

F 147   *THE BEDSIDE COMPANION TO CRIME.* H.R.F. Keating. London: Michael O'Mara Books Ltd., 1989.
Contribution: "The Guilty Party," pp. 112-113.
This book was also published in New York by The Mysterious Press, 1989.

F 148   *JOHN CREASEY'S CRIME COLLECTION 1989.* An Anthology by Members of the Crime Writers' Association. Edited by Herbert Harris. London: Victor Gollancz Ltd, 1989.
Contribution: "The Murderer," pp. 49-60.

F 149   *THE MAMMOTH BOOK OF MURDER.* Edited by Richard Glyn Jones. New York: Carroll and Graf, 1989.
Contribution: "The Riddle of Burdhurst Rise," pp. 375-383.

F 150   *MURDER TAKES A HOLIDAY.* London: Michael O'Mara Books Limited, 1989.
Contribution: "The Summer Holiday Murders," pp. 10-37. This book was also published in New York by Gallery Books, 1991; U.K. paperback edition edited by Barry Pike published in London by Headline Book Publishing, 1990.

F 151   *RED HANDED: An anthology of radical crime stories.* Edited and introduced by Jon E. Lewis. London: Allison & Busby, Published by W.H.Allen & Co, 1989.
Contribution: "The Best Chess Player in the World," pp.49-68.
Paperback edition published 1989 by W.H. Allen & Co.

F 152   *THE SPORT OF CRIME.* Edited by Carol-Lynn Rössel Waugh, Martin Harry Greenberg, and Isaac Asimov. With an introduction by Isaac Asimov. New York: Lynx Books, 1989.
Contribution: "Murder on the Race Course," pp. 321-344.
A hardback reissue was done in 1994 by Barnes & Noble Books, New York.

F 153   *THE WAR DECADE: An Anthology of the 1940s.* Compiled by Andrew Sinclair. London: Hamish Hamilton Ltd, 1989.
Contributions: "Conscript," pp. 52-53; "from *Notes from Another Country*," p. 76; "Pub," pp. 176-177;and "Homage to Our Leaders," p.237.

F 154   *WINTER'S CRIMES 21*. Edited by Hilary Hale. London: Macmillan London Ltd., 1989.
Contribution: "Et In Arcadia Ego," pp. 267-280.

1990

F 155   *A CLASSIC ENGLISH CRIME*. 13 Stories for the Christie Centenary from the Crime Writers' Association. Edited by Tim Heald. London: Pavilion Books Limited, 1990.
Contribution: "Holocaust at Mayhem Parva," pp. 45-59.
Also published in New York by The Mysterious Press, 1991. Paperback edition published in London by Headline Book Publishing, 1991 ("Holocaust at Mayhem Parva" is on pp. 51-72). U.S. paperback edition published by Mysterious Press, 1992 ("Holocaust at Mayhem Parva is on pp. 45-59).

F 156   *THE HATCHARDS CRIME COMPANION*. 100 Top Crime Novels Selected by the Crime Writers' Association. Edited by Susan Moody, London: Hatchards, 1990.
Contribution: "The Ideal Crime Novel," pp. 129-130.

F 157   *JOHN CREASEY'S CRIME COLLECTION 1990*. An Anthology by members of the Crime Writers' Association. Edited by Herbert Harris. London: Victor Gollancz, 1990.
Contribution: "Waiting for Mr. McGregor," pp. 9-25.

F 158   *THE OXFORD BOOK OF ENGLISH DETECTIVE STORIES*. Edited by Patricia Craig. Oxford: Oxford University Press, 1990.
Contribution: "The Murderer," pp. 384-393.
Paperback edition published in 1992.

1991

F 159   *A CLASSIC ENGLISH CRIME*. 13 Stories for the Christie Centenary from the Crime Writers' Association. Edited by Tim Heald. New York: The Mysterious Press, 1991.
Contribution: "Holocaust at Mayhem Parva," pp. 45-59.
This book was originally published in London by Pavilion Books, Ltd, 1990. Paperback edition published in London by Headline Book Publishing, 1991 ("Holocaust at Mayhem Parva" is on pp. 51-72). U.S. paperback edition published by Mysterious Press in 1992.

F 160   *CRIME WAVES 1. The Annual Anthology of the Crime Writers' Association*. Edited by H.R.F. Keating. London: Victor Gollancz Ltd, 1991.
Contribution: "The Tiger's Stripe," pp. 149-167.
Also issued in paperback by Gollancz in 1991.

F 161   *FIFTY BEST MYSTERIES*. Edited by Eleanor Sullivan. New York: Carroll & Graf, 1991.

Contribution: "Flowers that Bloom in the Spring," pp. 448-461.
This book was also published in New York by Carroll & Graf, 1991, as *Fifty Years of the Best from Ellery Queen's Mystery Magazine*. Published in London by Robinson Publishing, 1991, as *The Omnibus of Modern Crime Stories*, edited by Eleanor Sullivan and Ellery Queen.

F 162 *FIFTY YEARS OF THE BEST FROM ELLERY QUEEN'S MYSTERY MAGAZINE*. Edited by Eleanor Sullivan. New York: Carroll & Graf, 1991.
Contribution: "Flowers that Bloom in the Spring," pp. 448-461.
This book was also published in London by Robinson Publishing, 1991, as *The Omnibus of Modern Crime Stories*. Published in paperback by Carroll & Graf, 1991, as *Fifty Best Mysteries*.

F 163 *THE GIANT BOOK OF CRIME STORIES*. Edited by George Hardinge. London: Magpie Books, 1991.
Contribution: "The Flaw," pp. 483-497.
This anthology was originally published in the U.S. in 1987 as *The Mammoth Book of Modern Crime Stories*.

F 164 *MURDER AT CHRISTMAS AND OTHER STORIES FROM ELLERY QUEEN'S MYSTERY MAGAZINE AND ALFRED HITCHCOCK'S MYSTERY MAGAZINE*. Edited by Cynthia Manson. New York: Signet, Penguin Books U.S.A., 1991.
Contribution: "'Twixt the Cup and the Lip," pp. 29-60.

F 165 *MURDER TAKES A HOLIDAY*. New York: Gallery Books, W.H. Smith Publishers Inc., 1991.
Contribution: "The Summer Holiday Murders," pp. 10-37.
Originally published in London by Michael O'Mara Books Limited, 1989.

F 166 *THE OMNIBUS OF MODERN CRIME STORIES*. Edited by Eleanor Sullivan and Ellery Queen. London: Robinson Publishing, 1991.
Contribution: "Flowers that Bloom in the Spring," pp. 448-461.
Also published in New York by Carroll & Graf, 1991, as *Fifty Years of the Best from Ellery Queen's Mystery Magazine*. Published in paperback by Carroll & Graf, 1991, as *Fifty Best Mysteries*.

F 167 *100 GREAT DETECTIVES*. Edited and introduced by Maxim Jakubowski. New York: Carroll & Graf, 1991.
Contribution: "Julian Symons on Dashiell Hammett's Sam Spade," pp. 205-206.

F 168 *SCARLET LETTERS. TALES OF ADULTERY FROM ELLERY QUEEN'S MYSTERY MAGAZINE*. Edited by Eleanor Sullivan. New York: Carroll & Graf, 1991.
Contribution: "The Flaw," pp. 197-216.

F 169 *THE YEAR'S BEST MYSTERY AND SUSPENSE STORIES 1991*. Edited by Edward C. Hoch. New York: Walker and Company, 1991.

Contribution: "The Conjuring Trick," pp. 164-186.

1992

F 170 *THE CHATTO BOOK OF OFFICE LIFE OR LOVE AMONG THE FILING CABINETS.* Edited with an introduction by Jeremy Lewis. London: Chatto & Windus Ltd, 1992.
Contributions: "A Fight to the Death," pp. 201-205; "The Public and the Private Face," pp. 283-284
Both contributions are excerpts from *Notes from Another Country.*

F 171 *A CLASSIC ENGLISH CRIME.* 13 Stories for the Christie Centenary from the Crime Writers' Association. Edited by Tim Heald. New York: The Mysterious Press, 1992.
Contribution: "Holocaust at Mayhem Parva," pp. 45-59.
Originally published in London by Pavilion Books, 1990. Also published in New York by The Mysterious Press, 1991. Paperback edition published in London by Headline Book Publishing, 1991 ("Holocaust at Mayhem Parva" is on pp. 51-72).

F 172 *CONTEMPORARY CRIME STORIES.* Edited with notes by Koichi Fujiwara, Hidenori Muramatsu, and Hideaki Ashihara. Tokyo: The Eihosha Ltd., 1992.
Contribution: "The Conjuring Trick," pp. 7-39.
English translation with notes in Japanese.

F 173 *MURDERS FOR THE FIRESIDE. THE BEST OF WINTER'S CRIMES.* Edited and introduced by Maxim Jakubowski. London: Pan Books Ltd, 1992.
Contribution: "The Birthmark," pp. 341-357.

F 174 *MURDER UNDER THE MISTLETOE AND OTHER STORIES FROM ELLERY QUEEN'S MYSTERY MAGAZINE AND ALFRED HITCHCOCK'S MYSTERY MAGAZINE.* Edited by Cynthia Manson. New York: Signet, Penguin Books U.S.A., Inc., 1992.
Contribution: "The Santa Claus Club," pp. 13-27.

F 175 *THE OXFORD BOOK OF ENGLISH DETECTIVE STORIES.* Edited by Patricia Craig. Oxford: Oxford University Press, 1992.
Contribution: "The Murderer," pp. 384-393.
Originally published in 1990.

1993

F 176 *GRIFTERS & SWINDLERS. STORIES FROM ELLERY QUEEN'S MYSTERY MAGAZINE AND ALFRED HITCHCOCK MYSTERY MAGAZINE.* Edited by Cynthia Manson. New York: Carroll & Graf Publishers, Inc., 1993.
Contribution: "How to Trap a Crook," pp. 69-77.

F 177 *MURDER BRITISH STYLE: NINETEEN CLASSIC COZY MYSTERIES.* Edited by Martin H. Greenburg. New York: Barnes and Noble Books, 1993.
Contribution: "The Dream is Better," pp. 115-128.

F 178   *MURDER MOST COZY: MYSTERIES IN THE CLASSICAL TRADITION FROM ELLERY QUEEN'S MYSTERY MAGAZINE AND ALFRED HITCHCOCK'S MYSTERY MAGAZINE.* Edited by Cynthia Manson. New York: Signet, Penguin Books U.S.A., Inc., 1993.
Contribution: "Holocaust at Mayhem Parva," pp. 239-254.

F 179   *THE PICADOR BOOK OF CRIME WRITING.* Edited by Michael Dibdin. London: Pan Books, 1993.
Contribution: "The Man Who Killed Himself," pp. 11-15; "The Thirty-First of February," pp. 303-308.

1994

F 180   *THE ANTHOLOGY OF CRIME STORIES.* Edited by George Hardinge. London: Tiger Books International, 1994.
Contribution: "The Flaw," pp. 484-497.
First published 1986 as *The Best of Winter's Crime.*

F 181   *GREAT TALES OF MYSTERY AND SUSPENSE.* Compiled by Bill Pronzini, Barry Malzberg, and Martin Greenberg. New York: Galahad Books, 1994.
Contribution: "The Santa Claus Club," pp. 333-343.
Abridged from *The Arbor House Treasury*, 1981 (F99).

F 182   *TALES FROM THE ROGUES' GALLERY.* Edited by Peter Haining. London: Little, Brown and Company, 1994.
Contribution: "The Borgia Heirloom," pp. 176-180.
Reissued in 1995 by Warner Books.

1995

F 183   *MURDER AT THE RACES.* Edited by Peter Haining. London: Artus Books, 1995.
Contribution: "Murder on the Race Course," pp. 144-166

F 184   *TALES FROM THE ROGUES' GALLERY.* Edited by Peter Haining. London:Warner Books, 1995.
Contribution: "The Borgia Heirloom," pp. 176-180.
Published in 1994 by Little, Brown and Company, London.

F 185   *MURDER BY THE BOOK.* Edited by Cynthia Manson. New York: Carrol & Graf Publishers, 1995.
Contribution: "In the Bluebell Wood," pp. 163-178.

F 186   *THE YEAR'S 25 FINEST CRIME 7 MYSTERN STORIES, FOURTH ANNUAL EDITION.* Edited by the Stafford Mystery Scene. New York: Carrol & Graf Publishers, 1995.
Contribution: "The Man Who Hated Television," pp. 269-281.

SECTION G

SELECTED

CONTRIBUTIONS

TO PERIODICALS

Note: The following entries include selected editorials, reviews and criticism, articles, obituaries, and author profiles. For contributions to *Ellery Queen's
Mystery Magazine*, see Section H.

1937

G 1   "This Quarter's Verse." [Review: *Calamiterror* by George Barker, *Poems*
by Rex Warner, *The Disappearing Castle* by Charles Madge, *Sebastian* by
Rayner Heppenstall, *Straight or Curly?* by Clifford Dyment.] *Purpose*, Vol.
IX, No. 3 (July/September 1937), pp. 179-183.

1938

G 2   "The Journey (Parts 1 & 2)." *Wales*, No. 5 (Summer 1938), pp. 162-164.

G 3   "Periodicals." [Review: Part 1—*Fact, New Verse, Partisan Review*; Part
2—*The Criterion, New Writing, Penguin Parade, Wales*; Part 3—*Spain at
War, Left Review, Direction, The Examiner, Story*; Part 4—*Poetry
(Chicago), The Booster, The Phoenix, The Townsman.*] *Life & Letters
Today*, Vol. 18, No. 12 (Summer 1938), pp. 188-191, 191-194, 194-198,
198-200.

1939

G 4   "Auden and Poetic Drama." *Life & Letters Today*, Vol. 20, No. 18 (February 1939), pp. 70-79.

G 5   "*Journey to a War* by W.H. Auden and Christopher Isherwood." *Life &
Letters Today*, Vol. 21, No. 21 (May 1939), pp. 158-162.

G 6   "*Autumn Journal* by Louis MacNiece." *Life & Letters Today*, Vol. 21 No.
22 (June 1939), pp. 152-154.

1940

G 7   "A London Letter." *The Kenyon Review*, Vol. II, No. 2 (Spring 1940), pp.
253-256.

G 8   "Our Elders: A Re-evaluation." [Review: *The Collected Poems of A.E.
Housman, The Collected Poems of Robert Frost, More People* by Edgar
Lee Masters.] *The New English Weekly*, Vol. XVI, No. 20 (March 7,
1940), pp. 295-296.

G 9   "Notes on the Poet & War." *NOW*, No. 2 (June-July 1940), pp. 12-14.

G 10   "The Cliche Masters." [Review: *Rain upon Godshill* by J.B. Priestly, *One
Way of Living* by James Bridie, *Heaven Lies About Us* by Howard Spring,
Water Music by Sir John Squire.] *The New English Weekly*, Vol. XVI, No.
23 (March 28, 1940), pp. 39-340.

G 11   "The Knowing and the Innocent." [Review: *Lament & Triumph* by George

Barker and *Portrait of the Artist as a Young Dog* by Dylan Thomas.] *The New English Weekly*, Vol. XVIII, No. 10 (June 27, 1940), pp. 121-122.

G 12   "Ben Johnson as Social Realist: Bartholomew Fair." *Southern Review*, Vol. 6, No. 2 (Fall 1940), pp. 375-386.

G 13   "Three War Poems: 'End of a Year,' 'Pub,' and 'Poem.' " *Poetry*, Vol. LVI, No. VI (September 1940), pp. 301-304.

G 14   "A Short View on Wallace Stevens." *Life & Letters Today*, Vol. 26, No. 37 (September 1940), pp. 215-224.

G 15   "Obscurity & Dylan Thomas." *The Kenyon Review*, Vol. II, No. 1 (Winter 1940), pp. 61-71.

G 16   "Progress of Auden." [Review: *Another Time*.] *Kingdom Come*, Vol. 2, No. 2 (Winter 1940-41), pp. 51-52.

1941

G 17   "The Clock." *Modern Reading*, No. 1 (April 1941, reprinted June 1941), p. 31.

G 18   "The Case of Mr. Madge." *Kingdom Come*, Vol. 2, No. 3 (Spring 1941), pp. 73-74.

G 19   "Whitsun, 1940." *Poetry (London)*, No. 6 (May-June 1941), pp. 170-171.

G 20   "The Burgher's Mind." *NOW*, No. 6 (Summer 1941), p. 32.

G 21   "A.J.A. Symons—1900-1941: Two Personal Notes." *Horizon*, Vol. IV, No. 22 (October 1941), pp. 258-264.

G 22   "Language in Seven Poets." [Review: *Inscapes* by Francis Scarfe, *The White Island* by George Woodcock, *Poems New & Old* by Edith Sitwell, *Youth in the Skies* by Herbert Asquith, *The Mind of Man* by John Gawsworth, *War Poems & Some Others* by Lord Rennell of Rodd, *Over the Edge* by Patricia Ledward.] *The New English Weekly*, Vol. XVIII, No. 21 (March 13, 1941), p. 243.

G 23   "Romanticism in Wartime." [Review: *Horizon* and *Poetry* (London).] *The New English Weekly*, Vol. XIX, No. 3 (May 8, 1941), p. 30.

G 24   "New Poems." [Review: *Plant and Phantom* by Louis MacNiece and *My Spirit Walks Alone* by Herman Ould.] *The New English Weekly*, Vol. XIX, No. 14 (July 24, 1941), p. 145.

1942

G 25 "The Quiet Voice." [Review: *Under the Cliff and Other Poems* by Geoffrey Grigson.] *Poetry London*, Vol. 2, No. 10 (n.d., 1942?), pp. 244-245.

G 26 "The Intellectuals." *Poetry (London)*, No. 7 (October-November 1942), pp. 41-42.

1943

G 27 "Elegy on a City." *Modern Reading*, No. 6 (1943), p. 20.

G 28 "A Poet in Society." [Review: *Ruins and Visions* by Stephen Spender and *Life and the Poet* by Stephen Spender.] *NOW*, Vol. 1 (1943, stamped July 28 by Bodleian), pp. 68-73.

1944

G 29 "Catterick Revisited." *Poetry Quarterly*, Vol. 6, No. 1 (Spring 1944), p. 11.

G 30 "A Lost Talent." [Review: *The Yellow Night* by Drummond Allison, *No Crown for Laughter* by Maurice Lindsay, *Fall of a City and Other Poems* by Francis Berry.] *Poetry Quarterly*, Vol. 6, No. 2 (Summer 1944), pp. 67-68.

G 31 "Elegy on a City." *Selected Writing* (Winter 1944), p. 85.

1945

G 32 "Writing and Society." *NOW*, Vol. 3 (n.d., stamped March 14, 1946, by Bodleian), pp. 14-21.

G 33 "Restoration Comedy (Reconsiderations II)." *Kenyon Review*, Vol. Vii, No. 2 (Spring 1945), pp. 185-197.

G 34 "The End of a War: 8 Notes on the Objective of Writing in our Time." *NOW*, Vol. 5 (n.d., stamped October 2, 1945, by Bodleian), pp. 5-13.

G 35 "The Condemned Playboy." [Review: *The Condemned Playground* by Cyril Connolly.] *NOW*, Vol 6 (n.d., stamped November 29, 1946, by Bodleian), pp. 66-70.

1946

G 36 "An American Poet." [Review: *The Soldier* by Conrad Aiken and *Flash and Outbreak* by John C. Whitehead.] *Poetry Quarterly*, Vol. 8, No. 4 (Winter 1946-47), pp. 240-242.

1947

G 37 "The Little Magazine." *NOW*, Vol. 8 (May-June 1947), pp. 58-60.

G 38 "George Eliot and the Crisis of the Novel." *The Windmill*, Third issue of three (1947), pp. 9-18.

G 39   "Two American, One English." *Poetry London*, Vol. 3, No. 11 (September-October 1947), pp. 68-70.

G 40   "Freedom and Reality." *NOW*, Vol. 7 (February-March,), pp. 41-52.

G 41   "Some American Critics." *The Critic*, Vol. 1, No. 1 (Spring 1947), pp. 32-37.

G 42   "Power and Corruption." *Times Literary Supplement* (June 10, 1949), pp. 55-60.

1951

G 43   "The Criss-Cross Code." *Lilliput*, Vol. 29, No. 2, Issue 171 (August-September 1951), pp. 89-120.

1953

G 44   "*Picture* by Lillian Ross." *Punch*, Vol. CCXXIV, No. 5870 (April 8, 1953), p. 446.

G 45   "*The Face Beside the Fire* by Laurens van der Post." *Punch*, Vol. CCXXIV, No. 5875 (May 13, 1953), p. 586.

G 46   "*The Life and Death of Sylvia* by Edgar Mittelholzer." *Punch*, Vol. CCXIV, No. 5876 (May 20, 1953), p. 613.

G 47   "Literary Lecture." *Punch*, Vol. CCXXIV, No. 5880 (June 17, 1953), pp. 704-705.

G 48   "*The Spectacle* by Rayne Kruger." *Punch*, Vol. CCXXIV, No. 5881, (June 24, 1953), p. 754.

G 49   "*In the Wet* by Nevil Shute." *Punch*, Vol. CCXXV, No. 5885 (July 15, 1953), p. 102.

G 50   "*The Long View of Nothing* by H.A. Mamood." *Punch*, Vol. CCXXV, No. 5886 (July 22, 1953), p. 129.

G 51   "*Too Late the Phalarope* by Alan Paton." *Punch*, Vol. CCXXV, No. 5893 (September 9, 1953), p. 332.

G 52   "The Stories of Frank O'Connor." *Punch*, Vol. CCXXV, No. 5903 (November 11, 1953), p. 588.

G 53   "*The Second Curtain* by Roy Fuller." *Punch*, Vol. CCXXV, No. 5904 (November 18, 1953), pp. 615-616.

G 54   "*The Year of the Lion* by Gerald Hanley." *Punch*, Vol. CCXXV, No. 5909 (December 23, 1953), p. 769.

G 55   "*The Long Goodbye* by Raymond Chandler." *Punch*, Vol. CCXXV, No. 5910 (December 30, 1953), p. 800.

1954

G 56   "*Christ Recrucified* by Nicos Kazantzakis." *Punch*, Vol. CCXXVI, No. 5921 (March 17, 1954), p. 361.

G 57   "Life at Clapham." [Review: *An Impossible Marriage* by Pamela Hansford Johnson.] *Punch*, Vol. CCXXVI, No. 5923 (March 31, 1954), p. 418.

G 58   "Early Realists." [Review: *Rebels and Ancestors* by Maxwell Geismar.] *Punch*, Vol. CCXXVI, No. 5927 (April 28, 1954), p. 529.

G 59   "*Something of the Sea* by Alan Ross Verschoyle." *Punch*, Vol. CCXXVI, No. 5931 (May 26, 1954), p. 649.

G 60   "*A Flame for Doubting Thomas* by Richard Llewellyn." *Punch*, Vol. CCXXVI, No. 5933 (June 2, 1954), p. 676.

G 61   "*Brother to Dragons* by Robert Penn Warren." *Punch*, Vol. CCXXVI, No. 5934 (June 9, 1954), p. 705.

G 62   "*The End of an Old Song* by J.D. Scott." *Punch*, Vol. CCXXVII, No. 5938 (July 7, 1954), p. 73.

G 63   "Aimless Hero." [Review: *Under the Net* by Iris Murdoch.] *Punch*, Vol. CCXXVII, No. 5940 (July 21, 1954), pp. 128-129.

G 64   "*A Handful of Blackberries* by Ignazio Silone." *Punch*, Vol. CCXXVII, No. 5941 (July 28, 1954), pp. 156-157.

G 65   "*Keep the Aspidistra Flying* by George Orwell." *Punch*, Vol. CCXXVII, No. 5945 (August 25, 1954), p. 269.

G 66   "*Counterparts* by Roy Fuller." *Punch*, Vol. CCXXVII, No. 5948 (September 15, 1954), p. 365.

G 67   "Over Stylized." [Review: *The Centre of the Stage* by Gerald Sykes.] *Punch*, Vol. CCXXVII, No. 5957 (November 10, 1954), pp. 608-609.

G 68   "*Beyond the Glass* by Antonia White." *Punch*, Vol. CCXXVII, No. 5958 (November 17, 1954), p. 641.

G 69   "*Ezra Pound and T.S. Eliot* by Richard Aldington." *Punch*, Vol. CCXXVII, No. 5960 (December 1, 1954), p. 705.

1955

G 70   "A Kite's Dinner." [Review: *Poems 1938-1954* by Sheila Wingfield.] *Punch*, Vol. CCXXVIII, No. 5968 (January 26, 1955), p. 156.

G 71   "*Sweet Thursday* by John Steinbeck." *Punch*, Vol. CCXXVIII, No. 5968 (January 26, 1955), p. 157.

G 72   "*Cards of Identity* by Nigel Dennis." *Punch*, Vol. CCXXVIII, No. 5971 (February 16, 1955), p. 243.

G 73   "*The Pilgrimage* by Francis Stuart." *Punch*, Vol. CCXXVIII, No. 5975 (March 16, 1955), p. 355.

G 74   "*Collected Poems* by Stephen Spender." *Punch*, Vol. CCXXVIII, No. 5978 (April 6, 1955), p. 451.

G 75   "*Pudd'nhead Wilson* by Mark Twain." *Punch*, Vol. CCXXVIII, No. 5987 (June 8, 1955), p. 718.

G 76   "*Selected Poems* by Robert Frost." *Punch*, Vol. CCXXVIII, No. 5989 (June 22, 1955), pp. 774-775.

G 77   "*Canal in the Moonlight* by Kathleen Sully." *Punch*, Vol. CCXXIX, No. 5992 (July 13, 1955), p. 53.

G 78   "*A Fable* by William Faulkner." *Punch*, Vol. CCXIX, No. 5994 (July 22, 1955), pp. 108-109.

G 79   "*The Day of the Monkey* by David Karp." *Punch*, Vol. CCXXIX, No. 5998 (August 24, 1955), pp. 225-226.

G 80   "*Collected Poems* by William Empson." *Punch*, Vol. CCXXIX, No. 6010 (November 9, 1955), pp. 557-558.

G 81   "*Confessions of Felix Krull, Confidence Man* by Thomas Mann." *Punch*, Vol. CCXXIX, No. 6013 (November 30, 1955), p. 643.

1956

G 82   "*The Straight and Narrow Path* by Honor Tracy." *Punch*, Vol. CCXXX, No. 6040 (June 6, 1956), p. 691.

G 83   "*A Word Carved on a Sill* by John Wain." *Punch*, Vol. CCXXXI, No. 6046 (July 18, 1956), p. 81.

G 84   "*John Clare: His Life and Poetry* by John and Anne Tibble." *Punch*, Vol. CCXXXI, No. 6053 (September 5, 1956), p. 287.

G 85 "Second String." [Review: *A Case of Samples: Poems, 1946-1956* by Kingsley Amis.] *Punch*, CCXXXI, No. 6065 (November 21, 1956), pp. 629-630.

G 86 "*Further Letters of Gerard Manley Hopkins*, edited by Claude Colleer Abbott." *Punch*, Vol. CCXXXI, No. 6070 (December 26, 1956), p. 798.

1957

G 87 "*Toward the Sun* by Charles Plumb." *Punch*, Vol. CCXXII, No. 6081 (March 13, 1957), p. 369.

G 88 "*Union Street* by Charles Causley." *Punch*, Vol. CCXXXII, No. 6087 (April 24, 1957), p. 545.

G 89 "*Visitation* by Louis MacNeice." *Punch*, Vol. CCXXXII, No. 6092 (May 29, 1957), p. 685.

G 90 "*Pegasus and Other Poems* by C. Day Lewis." *Punch*, Vol. CCXXXIII, No. 6101 (July 31, 1957), p. 139.

G 91 "Arabs' Friend." [Review: *The Golden Bubble* by Roderic Owen.] *Punch*, Vol. CCXXXIII, No. 6104 (August 21, 1957), pp. 222-223.

G 92 "*Collected Poems 1930-1955* by George Barker and *The True Confession of George Barker*." *Punch*, Vol. CCXXXIII, No. 6105 (August 28, 1957), pp. 250-251.

G 93 "Meeting Wyndham Lewis." *London Magazine*, Vol.4, No. 10 (October 1957), pp. 47-53.

G 94 "Summer Show." *The Saint*, Vol. 4, No. 1 (British Edition) (November 1957), pp. 108-112.

G 95 "*A Winter Talent and Other Poems* by Donald Davie." *Punch*, Vol. CCXXXIII, No. 6123 (December 25, 1957), p. 763.

1958

G 96 "*Words for the Wind* by Theodore Roethke." *Punch*, Vol. CCXXXIV, No. 6132 (February 26, 1958), p. 303.

G 97 "*To Whom it May Concern: Poems 1952-1957* by Alan Ross." *Punch*, Vol. CCXXXV, No. 6157 (August 20, 1958), p. 249.

G 98 "An Edwardian Tragedy: True Crime Reconstruction." *Lilliput*, Volume 43, No. 3 (September 1958), pp. 46-50.

G 99 "Responsibility and Judgment in Historical Writing." [Address given at Three-day London Conference of the English Centre, October 14-16.] *P•E•N News*, No. 197 (Autumn 1958), pp. 22-23.

1959

G 100 "*Women and Thomas Harrow* by John P. Marquand." *Punch*, Vol. CCXXXVI, No. 6184 (February 25, 1959), pp. 266-267.

G 101 "*The Odyssey: A Modern Sequel* by Nikos Kazantzakis, translated into English verse by Kimon Friar." *Punch*, Vol. CCXXXVI, No. 6185 (February 25, 1959), p. 299.

G 102 "*Someone Will Die Tonight in the Caribbean* by Rene Puissesseau." *Punch*, Vol. CCXXXVI, No. 6194 (April 29, 1959), p. 592.

G 103 "*The Identity of Jack the Ripper* by Donald McCormick." *Punch*, Vol. CCXXXVII, No. 6216 (November 11, 1959), p. 443.

1960

G 104 "Variation on a Theme by Homer: The Anger of Achilles." [Review: *The Iliad*, translated by Robert Graves.] *Punch*, Vol. CCXXXVIII, No. 6236 (March 30, 1960), p. 462.

G 105 "Who Lie in Gaol." [Review: *Justice in Chains: From the Galleys to Devil's Island* by Michel Bourdet-Pleville.] *Punch*, Vol. CCXXXVIII, No. 6248 (June 22, 1960), pp. 890-891.

G 106 "Take that Body out of the Library!" *Suspense,* Vol. 3, No. 7 (July 1960), pp. 2-4.

G 107 "Frying Pan into Fire." [Review: *Gentleman Convicts* by Francois Poli, translated from the French by Naomi Walford.] *Punch*, Vol. CCXXXIX, No. 6254 (August 3, 1960), p. 177.

G 108 "Psycho." [Review: *Hume: Portrait of a Double Murderer* by John Williams.] *Punch*, Vol. CCXXXIX, No. 6260 (September 14, 1960), p. 392.

G 109 "Thief-Taker." [Review: *War on the Underground* by Ex-Detective Chief Superintendent Edward Greeno.] *Punch*, Vol. CCXXXIX, No. 6267 (November 2, 1960), p. 649.

G 110 "Private Giggles." [Review: *Summoned by Bells* by John Betjeman.] *Punch*, Vol. CCXXXIX, No. 6276 (December 28, 1960), p. 951.

1961

G 111 "*Vox et Praeterea Ali Quid.*" [Review: *Sir Patrick Hastings: His Life and Cases* by H. Montgomery Hyde.] *Punch*, Vol. CCXL, No. 6280 (January 25, 1961), p. 191.

G 112 "Cashing in on Eichmann." [Review: *Minister of Death* by Quentin Reynolds, Ephraim Katz, Zwy Aldouby; *The Capture of Adolf Eichmann* by Moshe Pearlman; *The Hunter* by Tuvia Friedman.] *Punch*, Vol. CCXL, No. 6287 (March 15, 1961), pp. 442-443.

G 113 "Crime Novels and Detective Stories." *The London Magazine*, Vol. 1, No. 2 (May 1961), pp. 76-81.

G 114 "Stunt Lawyer." [Review: *Due Process: The Story of Criminal Lawyer George T. Davis* by Brad Williams.] *Punch*, Vol. CCXLI, No. 6312 (September 6, 1961), page 368.

G 115 "Actor-Agents." [Review: *Anatomy of Spying* by Ronald Seth.] *Punch*, Vol. CCXLI, No. 6320 (November 1, 1961), p. 661.

1962

G 116 "She Poisoned the Grocer." [Review: *Poison and Adelaide Bartlett* by Yeseult Bridges.] *Punch*, Vol. CCXLLII, No. 6340 (March 14, 1962), p. 443.

G 117 "The Truth About Chessman." [Review: *Ninth Life* by Milton Machlin and William Reid Woodfield.] *Punch*, Vol. CCXLII, No. 6354 (June 20, 1962), pp. 954-955.

G 118 "New Light on Old Cases." [Review: *Five Famous Trials* by Maurice Moiseiwitsch with commentaries by Lord Birkett.] *Punch*, Vol. CCXLIII, No. 6360 (August 1, 1962), p. 177.

G 119 "The Detective Story in Britain." *Books and Bookmen*, Vol. 7, No. 11 (September 1962), pp. 22-33

G 120 "Homer Rescored." [Review: *The Odyssey*, translated by Robert Fitzgerald.] *Punch*, Vol. CCXLIII, No. 6376 (November 21, 1962), p. 765.

G 121 "Politics and the Novel." *Twentieth Century*, Vol. 170, No. 1012 (Winter 1962), pp. 147-154.

1963

G 122 "Woofers and Tweeters." *Spectator* (February 22, 1963), p. 232.

G 123 "New Lease of Life for a Light Railway." *Country Life*, Vol. 133 (April 4, 1963), pp. 722-723.

G 124 "Staggering Along." *Spectator* (April 19, 1963), p. 503.

G 125 "Romanticising Interpol." [Review: *Inside Interpol* by Tom Tullett.] Punch, Vol. CCXLIV, No. 6398 (April 24, 1963), p. 611.

G 126 "A Contrary Talent." *Spectator* (May 31, 1963), p. 709.

G 127 "The Days of September." *The Saint*, Vol. 9, No. 4 (British Edition) (June 1963), pp. 88-97.

G 128 "Crime and Punishment." [Review: *The Roots of Evil* by Christopher Hibbert.] *Punch*, Vol. CCXLIV, No. 6407 (June 26, 1963), p. 938.

G 129 "Against Society." [Review: *King of the Lags: The Story of Charles Peace* by David Ward and *The Prince of Thieves: A Biography of George Manolesco* by J.J. Lynx.] *Punch*, Vol. CCXLV, No. 6408 (July 3, 1963), p. 33.

G 130 "Stacked Decks." [Review: *Cheating at Cards* by John Welcome.] *Punch*, Vol. CCXLV, No. 6411 (July 24, 1963), p. 140.

G 131 "Old Lines for New." *Spectator* (August 16, 1963), p. 206.

G 132 "Orwell, A Reminiscence." *London Magazine*, Vol. 3 (September 1963), pp. 35-49.

G 133 "Preventive Detainee." [Review: *The Unknown Citizen* by Tony Parker.] *Punch*, Vol. CCXLV, No. 6418 (September 11, 1963), p. 393.

1964

G 134 "Twentieth Century Verse." *Review*, No. 11-12 (1964), pp. 22-24.

G 135 "An Evening in Maida Vale." On meeting Laura Riding and Robert Graves. *London Magazine*, Vol. 3, No. 10 (January 1964), pp. 34-41.

G 136 "The Death Mongers." [Review: *Things for the Surgeon: A History of the Resurrection Men* by Hubert Cole and *Masterpieces of Murder* by Edmund Pearson.] *Punch*, Vol. CCXLVI, No. 6438 (January 29, 1964), p. 180.

G 137 "Scrutinizing *Scrutiny*." *London Magazine*, Vol. 3 (March 1964), pp. 21-30.

G 138 "Justice 1951." [Review: *The Betrayers* by Jonathan Root.] *Punch*, Vol. CCXLVI, No. 6444 (March 11, 1964), p. 397.

G 139 "Hanging Matters." [Review: *The Homicide Act* by Christopher Hollis.] *Punch*, Vol. CCXLVI, No. 6449 (April 15, 1964), p. 578.

G 140 "Our Servants or Our Masters?" [Review: *The Police* by Ben Whitaker.] *Punch*, Vol. CCXLVI, No. 6451 (April 29, 1964), p. 649.

G 141 "About Frances Newman." *London Magazine*, Vol. 4, No. 3 (June 1964), pp. 36-48.

G 142 "Jo'burg." [Review: *The Outlanders* by Robert Crisp.] *Punch*, Vol. CCXLVII, No. 6468 (August 26, 1964), p. 317.

G 143 "The Little Magazine and 'The Review'." *London Magazine*, Vol. 4, No. 7 (October 1964), pp. 82-86.

G 144 "Miss Edith Sitwell Have and Had and Heard." *London Magazine*, Vol. 4, No. 8 (November 1964), pp. 50-63.

G 145 "Optimistic Assassins." [Review: *The Anarchists* by James Joll.] *Punch*, Vol. CCXLVII, No. 6480 (November 18, 1964), p. 788.

G 146 "Word Factory." [Review: *Edgar Wallace: The Biography of a Phenomenon* by Margaret Lane.] *Punch*, Vol. CCXLVII, No. 6483 (December 9, 1964), p. 900.

1965

G 147 "Putting in the Verbals." [Review: *The Challenor Case* by Mary Grigg.] *Punch*, Vol. CCXLVIII, No. 6493 (February 17, 1965), p. 257.

G 148 "Patriotic Spy?" [Review: *An Instance of Treason: The Story of the Tokyo Spy Ring* by Chalmers Johnson.] *Punch*, Vol CCLXIX, No. 6514 (July 14, 1965), p. 65.

G 149 "For Laughs." [Review: *I Say, Look Herb* by Peter Bull, *Twelve Chairs* by Ilf & Peterov, translated from the Russian by John Richardson), *The Joyous Season* by Patrick Dennis, *A Spaniard in the Woods* by John Lennon, *Amongst the Thistles and Thorns* by Austin C. Clarke, *Maud Noakes, Guerilla* by Alan Neame.] *Punch*, Vol. CCXLIX, No. 6515 (July 21, 1965), p. 102.

G 150 "Black List." [Review: *Unfit to Plead?* by John Rowland, *Crusade Against Crime*, edited by Jerry P. Lewis, *The World's Worst Murderers* by Charles Franklin.] *Punch*, Vol. CCXLIX, No. 6523 (September 15, 1965), p. 406.

G 151 "Cwmdonkin Blues." [Review: *The Life of Dylan Thomas* by Constantine Fitzgibbon.] *Punch*, Vol. CCXLIX, No. 6531 (November 10, 1965), p. 705.

G 152 "Holy Warriors." [Review: *Jackboot: The Story of the German Soldier* by John Laffin.] *Punch*, Vol. CCXLIX, No. 6532 (November 17, 1965), p. 742.

1966

G 153 "How Well Have They Won?: The Good Companions." *The London Times* (January 13, 1966), p. 13.

G 154 "The Suspects." [Review: *The Man Who Disappeared: The Strange History of Noel Field* by Flora Lewis.] *Punch*, Vol. 250, No. 6544 (February 9, 1966), p. 212.

G 155   "Wilson's Way: *The Bit Between My Teeth.*" *London Magazine*, Vol. 6, No. 1 (April 1966), pp. 100-103.

G 156   "Crime and its Causes." [Review: *Dead Men Tell Tales* by Jurgen Thorwald, *Ideology and Crime: A Study of Crime in its Social and Historical Context* by Leon Radzinowicz, *The Mafia and Politics* by Michele Pantaleone, *The Deceivers: Lives of the Great Imposters* by Egon Larsen, *The Meaning of Murder* by John Brophy.] *Punch*, Vol. 250, No. 6557 (May 11, 1966), p. 705.

G 157   "Against the Impis." [Review: *The Washing of the Spears* by Donald R. Morris.] *Punch*, Vol. 250, No. 6559 (May 25, 1966), p. 784.

G 158   "About Frances Newman." *London Magazine*, Vol. 6, No. 3 (June 1966), pp. 36-48.

G 159   "Crusaders." [Review: *T.E. Lawrence: An Arab View* by Suleiman Mousa, *The Letters of T.E. Lawrence* edited by David Garnett, *Gordon: Martyr and Misfit* by Anthony Nutting.] *New Statesman* (July 1, 1966), p. 138.

G 160   "All=Nothing." [Review: *All* by Louis Zukofsky.] *London Magazine*, Vol. 6, No. 5 (August 1966), pp. 82-86.

G 161   "Soldiering On." [Review: *Parades and Politics at Vichy* by Robert O. Paxton, *Two Men Who Saved France* by Major-General Sir Edward Spears, *The Watten S.S.* by George H. Stein, *Inside S.O.E.* by E.H. Cookridge.] *Punch*, Vol. 251, No. 6585 (November 16, 1966), p. 757.

G 162   "Dylan Plain." [Review: *Selected Letters of Dylan Thomas*, edited by Constantine Fitzgibbon.] *Punch*, Vol. 251, No. 6585 (November 23, 1966), p. 787.

G 163   "Birth of a Hero." [Review: *Mafeking: A Victorian Legend* by Brian Gardner.] *Punch*, Vol. 251, No. 6590 (December 28, 1966), p. 970.

1967

G 164   "Concealments." *New Statesman*, Vol. 73 (January 6, 1967), p. 19.

G 165   "Early Auden." *Shenandoah*, Vol. 18, No. 2 (1967), pp. 48-50.

G 166   "The Holmes Case." [Review: *Conan Doyle* by Pierre Nordon.] *London Magazine*, Vol. 6, No. 10 (January 1967), pp. 98-101.

G 167   "T.E. Lawrence." *Sunday Times Magazine* (January 29, 1967), p. 23.

G 168   "Total Accuracy." [Review: *On Translation* edited by Reuben Brower, *The Penguin Book of Modern Verse Translation* edited by George Steiner, *Spleen* by Charles Baudelaire, translated by Laurence Lerner, *The Oxford Book of Scottish Verse* chosen by John MacQueen and Tom Scott, *The*

Force by Peter Redgrove, *Burning Joy* by George Andrews.] *New Statesman,* Vol. 73 (February 3, 1967), p. 154.

G 169 "Gutter and Stamp." *New Statesman,* Vol. 73 (February 10, 1967), p. 196.

G 170 "War Correspondent." [Review: *Russell's Despatches from the Crimea 1854-1856* edited by Nicholas Bently.] *New Statesman,* Vol. 73 (February 17, 1967). pp. 230-231.

G 171 "Gotterdammerung." [Review: *The Secret Surrender* by Allen Dulles.] *Punch,* Vol. 252, No. 6598 (February 22, 1967), p. 281.

G 172 "At Madame Two Swords." *New Statesman,* Vol. 73 (March 10, 1967), p. 337.

G 173 "Other Edens: After the Bomb." *Punch,* Vol. 252, No. 6601 (March 15, 1967), pp. 380-382.

G 174 "Nazi Society." [Review: *Hitler's Social Revolution* by David Schoenbaum.] *Punch,* Vol. 252, No. 6603 (March 29, 1967), p. 469.

G 175 "Singer." [Review: *In My Father's Court* and *Short Friday and Other Stories* by Isaac Bashevis Singer.] *Punch,* Vol. 252, No. 6604 (April 5, 1967), p. 503.

G 176 "The Old Enemies." [Review: *Collected Poems* by Louis MacNeice, edited by E.R. Dodds, *The Colossus* by Sylvia Plath, *Selected Poems* by Miroslave Holub, translated by Ian Milner and George Stener, *The Georgian Revolt: Rise and Fall of a Poetic Idea* by Robert Ross, *Commonwealth Poems of Today* edited by Howard Sergeant, *Australian Poetry 1966* selected by David Campbell, *Rights of Passage* by Edward Brathwaite.] *New Statesman,* Vol. 73 (April 7, 1967), p. 479.

G 177 "Arts and Crafts." [Review: *T.S. Eliot: The Man and His Work*, edited by Allen Tate and *Poetic Craft and Principle* by Robert Graves.] *Punch,* Vol. 252, No. 6608 (May 3, 1967), p. 657.

G 178 "New Poetry." [Review: *On the Way to the Depot* by P.J. Kavanaugh, *Old-Fashioned Pilgrimage* by Austin Clarke, *The Solitaries* by Ted Walker, *The William Carlos Williams Reader* edited by M.L. Rosenthal, *Penguin Modern Poets 9*: Denise Levertov, Kenneth Rexroth, William Carlos Williams, *Buckshee* by Ford Madox Ford.] *New Statesman,* Vol. 73 (May 12, 1967), p. 658.

G 179 "Truths and Consequences." [Review: *The Crystal Spirit: A Study of George Orwell* by George Woodcock.] *Punch,* Vol. 252, No. 6613 (June 7, 1967), p. 849.

G 180   "Moveable Feet." *The New Statesman*, Vol. 73 (June 16, 1967), p. 849.

G 181   "Writing for Periodicals: Reviewing: The Rate and the Job." *Author*, Vol. 78, No. 2 (Summer 1967), pp. 72-75.

G 182   "Cooked and Raw." *New Statesman*, Vol. 74 (July 21, 1967), p. 87.

G 183   "Bonzo." *London Magazine*, Vol. 7, No. 5 (August 1967), pp. 20-30.

G 184   "Stupendous Cairn." [Review: *Collected Poems of Hugh MacDiarmid* edited by John Weston, *A Lap of Honour* by Hugh MacDiarmid, *Poems Addressed to Hugh MacDiarmid* edited by Duncan Glen, *Helsinki* by Pentti Saarikosoki, translated by Anselm Hollow, *A Chosen Light* by John Montague, *Colophon to Lov Respelt* by Robert Graves.] *New Statesman*, Vol. 74 (August 18, 1967), p. 204.

G 185   "Magic and Infamy." [Review: *The Broken Seal* by Ladislas Parago.] *Punch*, Vol. 253, No. 6625 (August 30, 1967), p. 327.

G 186   Comments on: "*Authors Take Sides on Vietnam* edited by Cecil Woolf and John Bagguley." *London Magazine*, Vol. 7, No. 6 (September 1967) pp. 91-94.

G 187   "Ragged Edges." [Review: *The Dark Edge of Europe* by Desmond O'Grady, *The Moving Target* by W.S. Merwin, *With Decorum* by D.M. Black.] *New Statesman*, Vol. 74 (September 15, 1967), pp. 327-328.

G 188   "Looking-Glass War." [Review: *The Handsomest Man in England: Rupert Brooke* by Michael Hastings.] *Punch*, Vol. 253, No. 6630 (October 4, 1967), p. 525.

G 189   "Clean and Clear." [Review: *Collected Poems* by Elizabeth Jennings, *Touch* by Thom Gunn.] *New Statesman*, Vol. 74 (October 13, 1967), p. 476.

G 190   "The Cri." *London Magazine*, Vol. 7, No. 8 (November 1967), pp. 19-23.

G 191   "Parlour Games." [Review: *Concrete Poetry: An International Anthology* edited by Stephen Bann, *TV Baby Poems* by Allen Ginsberg, *We Are Many* by Pablo Neruda, *Selected Poems* by Adrienne Rich.] *New Statesman*, Vol. 74 (November 3, 1967), p. 595.

G 192   "*The Recognition of Edgar Allan Poe*, edited by Eric W. Carlson." *London Magazine*, Vol. 7, No. 9 (December 1967), pp. 96-99.

G 193   "Down with Romance." [Review: *Poems 1942-1967* by Alan Ross, *A Look Round the Estate: Poems 1957-1967* by Kingsley Amis, *An Eye on the World* by Lawrence Ferlinghetti, *To Find the New* by Alan Bold, *The*

Rubaiyyat of Omar Khayaam translated by Robert Graves, *Jets from Orange* by Zulfikar Ghose, *Quiet as Moss* and *Burning as. Light* by Andrew Young, *Seven Modern American Poets* edited by Leonard Unger.] *New Statesman*, Vol. 74 (December 1, 1967), pp. 779-780.

G 194 "Yours in the Ranks of Death." [Review: *Collected Letters of Wilfred Owen*, edited by Harold Owen and John Bell.] *Punch*, Vol. 253, No. 6639 (December 6, 1967), p. 874.

1968

G 195 "How We Lost the War." *London Magazine*, Vol. 7, No. 10 (January 1968), pp. 46-56.

G 196 "Sick Prophet." [Review: *Phoenix II: Uncollected, Unpublished and Other Prose by D.H. Lawrence*, collected and edited by Warren Roberts and Harry T. Moore.] *Punch*, Vol. 254, No. 6647 (January 31, 1968), p. 173.

G 197 "Cardboard Revolution." [Review: *Love, Love, Love: The New Love Poetry* edited by Peter Roche.] *New Statesman*, Vol. 75 (February 2, 1968), p. 146.

G 198 "Versions." [Review: *The Winter Lightning* by Howard Nemervov, *The Second Life* by Edwin Morgan, *Poetry in the Making* by Ted Hughes.] *New Statesman*, Vol. 75 (February 9, 1968), pp. 178-179.

G 199 "Devil's Disciple." [Review: *Ambrose Bierce* by Richard O'Connor and *The Enlarged Devil's Dictionary* by Ambrose Bierce, edited by Professor E.J. Hopkins.] *Punch*, Vol. 254, No. 6651 (February 28, 1968), p. 323.

G 200 "MacSpaunday." [Review: *Selected Poetry* by Roy Campbell, edited by J.M. Lalley, *The Voyage and Other Versions of Poems by Baudelaire* by Robert Lowell, illustrated by Sidney Nolan, *The Golden Chains* by George Barker, *At St. David's a Year* by Brian Earnshaw, *The Storms* by Peter Dale, *Contemporary Poetry and Prose* edited by Roger Roughton.] *New Statesman*, Vol. 75 (March 1, 1968), p. 276.

G 201 "A National Style." [Review: *Modern Canadian Verse*, edited by A.J. Smith.] *Canadian Literature*, No. 36 (Spring 1968), pp. 58-61.

G 202 "The Publishing Scene: A Man from Mars Reports." *Author*, Vol. 79 (Spring 1968), pp. 19-22.

G 203 "*Anna Karenina and Other Essays* by F.R. Leavis." *London Magazine*, Vol. 7, No. 12 (March 1968), pp. 87-90.

G 204 "Last Ditch." [Review: *They Fought Back*, edited and translated by Yuri Suhl.] *Punch*, Vol. 254, No. 6654 (March 20, 1968), p. 437.

G 205   "Dylan." [Review: *Poet in the Making: The Notebooks of Dylan Thomas* edited by Ralph Maud.] *Punch*, Vol. 254, No. 6658 (April 17, 1968), p. 584.

G 206   *"Beyond all this Fiddle: Essays 1955-67* by A. Alvarez." *London Magazine*, Vol. 8, No. 2 (May 1968), pp. 88-90.

G 207   "New Poetry." *Punch*, Vol. 254, No. 6667 (June 19, 1968), p. 902.

G 208   "Man of the Thirties." [Review: *Selected Poems* by George Woodcock.] *Canadian Literature*, No. 37 (Summer 1968), pp. 75-76.

G 209   "Pretourist." [Review: *The Companion Guide to Jugoslavia* by J.A. Cuddon.] *Punch*, Vol. 255, No. 6671 (July 17, 1968), p. 101.

G 210   "New Poetry." *Punch*, Vol. 255, No. 6672 (July 24, 1968), p. 136.

G 211   "Keeping Left." [Review: *Left Review.*] *London Magazine*, Vol. 8, No. 5 (August 1968), pp. 99-102.

G 212   "One Man's America–2." *Author*, Vol. 79, No. 3 (Autumn 1968), pp. 109-113.

G 213   "A Great Social Critic." [Review: *George Orwell. Collected Essays.*] *London Magazine*, Vol. 8, No. 7 (October 1968), pp. 95-100.

G 214   "New Poetry." *Punch*, Vol. 255, No. 6682 (October 2, 1968), p. 485.

G 215   "You're in the Army Now." *London Magazine*, Vol. 8, No. 8 (November 1968), pp. 28-41.

G 216   "New Poetry." *Punch*, Vol. 255, No. 6688 (November 13, 1968), p. 707.

G 217   "An End to Spying: Or, From Pipe Dream to Farce." *Times Literary Supplement* (December 12, 1968), p. 1411.

G 218   "New Poetry." *Punch*, Vol. 255, No. 6694 (December 25, 1968), p. 930.

1969

G 219   "The Detective Story in Britain." *Writers and Their Work*, No. 145 (1969), pp. 1-48.

G 220   "We Have Ways of Finding Out." [Review: *Breach of Security: The German Secret Intelligence File on Events Leading to the Second World War,* edited by David Irving with an introduction by D.C. Watt.] *Punch*, Vol. 256, No. 6696 (January 8, 1969), p. 69.

G 221 "There Was A Young Lady." [Review: *The Line of the Limerick: An Uninhibited History* by William S. Baring-Gould.] *Punch*, Vol. 256, No. 6700 (February 5, 1969), p. 214.

G 222 "New Poetry." *Punch*, Vol. 256, No. 6703 (February 26, 1969), p. 325.

G 223 "*Words That Don't Make Pictures: Selected Poems 1947-1967* by Robin Skelton." *Canadian Literature*, No. 40 (Spring 1969), pp. 64-65.

G 224 "Is There a Poet in the House?" [Review: *The Autobiography of William Carlos Williams.*] *Punch*, Vol. 256, No. 6705 (March 12, 1969), p. 399.

G 225 "Kimberley." [Review: *The Lion's Cage* by Brian Gardner.] New Statesman, Vol. 77 (March 28, 1969), pp. 451-452.

G 226 "A Glimpse of Thirties' Sunlight." *Times Literary Supplement* (April 24, 1969), pp. 433-435.

G 227 "New Poetry." *Punch*, Vol. 256, No. 6709 (April 9, 1969), p. 547.

G 228 "You're in the Army Now—II: Between the Acts." *London Magazine*, Vol. 9, No. 2 (May 1969), pp. 17-26.

G 229 "Patricia Highsmith: Criminals in Society." *London Magazine*, Vol. 9, No. 3 (June 1969), pp. 37-43.

G 230 "New Poetry." *Punch*, Vol. 257, No. 6721 (July 2, 1969), pp. 33-34.

G 231 "A Death." *London Magazine*, Vol. 9, Nos. 4 & 5 (July/August 1969), pp. 61-71.

G 232 "The Thirties Novels." *Agenda*, Vol. 7 Nos. 3 & 4, Wyndham Lewis Special Issue (Summer-Autumn 1969), pp. 37-48.

G 233 "Sensational Journalism." [Review: *New Numbers* by Christopher Logue, *Collected Poems* by Roy Fisher, *In the Year of the Strike* by Remco Campert, *Interior* by Brian Jones, *The Rock Woman* by James K. Baxter.] *London Magazine*, Vol. 9, No. 7 (October 1969), pp. 92-95.

G 234 "New Poetry: From Auden to Ogden Nash." *Punch*, Vol. 257, No. 6734 (October 1, 1969), pp. 556-557.

G 235 "Fixing the Blame." [Review: *Kut: The Death of an Army* by Ronald Millar, *The Siege* by Russell Braddon.] *New Statesman*, Vol. 78 (October 10, 1969), pp. 499-500.

G 236 "An End to Spying: Or, From Pipe Dream to Farce." *Times Literary Supplement*, (December 12, 1969), pp. 1411-1412.

1970

G 237 "Our Friend, Cyril Y. Snaggs." *London Magazine*, Vol. 9, No. 10 (January 1970), pp. 46-56.

G 238 "Criminal Prospects." *Author*, Vol. 81, No. 1 (Spring 70), pp. 19-21.

G 239 "Waiting for the War." *The Sunday Times Books* (April 5, 1970), p. 32.

G 240 "A.P.H." *Author*, Vol. 81, No. 3 (Autumn 1970), pp. 119-120.

G 241 "Irish Whiskey." [Review: *A Pagan Place* by Edna O'Brien, *Trespasses* by Paul Bailey, *Mirrors* by Lucy Warner.] *London Magazine*, Vol. 10, Nos. 4 & 5 (July/August 1970), pp. 184-186.

G 242 "A Passion for Justice." *Folio* (1970), pp. 86-91.

1971

G 243 "Unbuttoned." [Review: *Adventures of the Letter I* by Louis Simpson, *Selected Poems* by Vernon Scannell, *The Lost Country* by Kathleen Raine, *The Frost-God* by Harold Massingham.] *London Magazine*, Vol. 11, No. 5 (December 1971/January 1972), pp. 128-130.

1972

G 244 "In Europe." [Review: *Selected Poems* by Ondra Lysohorsky, by Yehuda Amichai, by Johannes Bobrowski and Horst Bienek, by Giuseppe Ungaretti, by Gunnar Ekelöf, by Abba Kovna and Nelly Sachs.] *London Magazine*, Vol. 11, No. 6 (February/March 1972), pp. 160-164.

G245 "Cowboys and Indians." [Review: *The Tenants* by Bernard Malamud, *Glory* by Vladimir Nobokov, translated from the Russian by Dmitri and Vladimir Nobokov, *The Ordeal* by Vasily Bykov, translated from the Russian by Gordon Clough, *Cold Gradations* by Stanley Middleton.] *The Sunday Times* (March 26, 1972).

G 246 "A Prolonged Adolescence." *London Magazine*, Vol. 12, No. 1 (April/May 1972), pp. 63-71.

G 247 "Action Overshadowed." [Review: *A Happy Man* by P.J. Kavanagh, *Silence* by James Kennaway, *Shadow on the Wall* by Maureen Lawrence, *The Severed Crown* by Jane Lane.] The Sunday Times (August 27, 1972), p. 30.

G 248 "Down to Earth." [Review: *Terminal Moraine* by James Fenton, *Cannibals and Missionaries* by John Fuller, *The Happier Life* by Douglas Dunn, *Air and Chill Earth* by Molly Holden.] *London Magazine*, Vol. 12, No. 3 (August/September 1972), pp. 138-141.

G 249 "Another Suit." [Review: *Epistle to a Godson* by W.H. Auden, *Delusions, Etc.* of John Berryman.] *London Magazine*, Vol. 12, No. 5 (December 1972/January 1973), pp. 129-131.

1973

G 250 "Views on *The Oxford Book of Twentieth Century Verse.*" *Times Literary Supplement* (May 4, 1973), p. 498.

G 251 "Tribute to Kenneth Allott." *Times Literary Supplement* (June 29, 1973), p. 746.

G 252 Views on authors' earnings. *Times Literary Supplement* (June 29, 1973), p. 746.

G 253 "Second Edition." [Review: W.H. Auden. A Bibliography by B.C. Bloomfield and Edward Mendelson.] *London Magazine*, Vol. 13, No. 4 (October/November 1973), pp. 120-122.

G 254 "The Case of Raymond Chandler." *The New York Times Magazine* (December 23, 1973), pp. 13, 22, 25, 27.

1974

G 255 "Criminal Activities." *New Review*, Vol. 1, No. 4 (1974), pp. 60-62.

G 256 "The Promise that Failed." *The Sunday Times* (July 21, 1974), p. 35.

G 257 "Drunk, but Not Disorderly." [Review: *Pentimento* by Lillian Hellman.] *London Magazine*, Vol. 14, No. 3 (August/September 1974), pp. 137-139.

G 258 "*Dictators* by Peter Vansittart." *London Magazine*, Vol. 14, No. 4 (October/November 1974), pp. 141-143.

G 259 "All Aboard with Poirot." *Times Literary Supplement* (December 6, 1974), p. 1367.

1975

G 260 "Sons and Lovers." [Review: *One Hand Clapping* by Colin Middleton Murry, *Another Part of the Wood* by Kenneth Clark, *H.G. Wells and Rebecca West* by Gordon N. Ray.] *London Magazine*, Vol. 15, No. 1 (April/May 1975), pp. 110-113.

G 261 "Freedom of the Press." *Times Literary Supplement* (May 9, 1975), p. 513.

G 262 "Media Matters." [Review: *Radio Power: Propaganda and International Broadcasting* by Julian Hale, *Paper Voices: The Popular Press and Social Change* by A.C.H. Smith with Elizabeth Immerzi and Trevor Blackwell.] *The Sunday Times* (June 1, 1975), p. 35.

G 263 "Ladies' Excuse-me." [Review: *The Life Swap* by Nancy Weber.] *Times Literary Supplement* (July 4, 1975), p. 712.

G 264 "Poisoners: Unsolved Mystery...." [Review: *The Riddle of Birdhurst Rise* by Richard Whittington-Egan.] *The Sunday Times* (August 10, 1975), p. 27.

G 265 "Bar-Room Ballads." [Review: *Closing Times* by Dan Davin.] *London Magazine*, Vol. 15, No. 3 (August/September 1975), pp. 104-107.

1976

G 266 "The Light and the Dark." [Review: *The Letters of Thomas Hood*, edited by Peter F. Morgan.] *Times Literary Supplement* (March 12, 1976), p. 295.

G 267 "New York's Hard Corps." Article on pornographic films. *Times Literary Supplement* (April 9, 1976), p. 428.

G 268 " 'Central Park,' 'Harvard,' 'The Object of an Affair.' " *London Magazine*, Vol. 16, No. 2 (June/July 1976), pp. 64-66.

G 269 "Ishmael and the Inquisitors." [Review: *Scoundrel Time* by Lillian Hellman.] *Times Literary Supplement* (November 12, 1976), p. 1413.

G 270 "Dashiell Hammett." *Times Literary Supplement* (December 17, 1976), p. 1586.

1977

G 271 "Why the Baron Should Now Speak for Himself." [Review: *Frederick Rolfe: Baron Corvo* by Miriam J. Benkovitz.] *The Sunday Times* (January 16, 1977), p. 41.

G 272 "A Year in Academe." *The Times Saturday Review* (January 29, 1977), p. 6.

G 273 "The Education of an American." [Review: *An Autobiographical Novel* by Kenneth Rexroth.] *Times Literary Supplement* (March 25, 1977), p. 332.

G 274 "Surface Polish." [Review: *The Awful Rowing Toward God* by Anne Sexton, *Song of the Battery Hen* and *Here, Now Always* by Edwin Brock, *A State of Justice* by Tom Paulin, *Our Ship* by John Mole, *A Bonus* by Elizabeth Smart.] *The Sunday Times* (April 24, 1977), p. 41.

G 275 "In the Southern Style." [Review: *A Place to Come To* by Robert Penn Warren, *Selected Poems* by Robert Penn Warren.] *Times Literary Supplement* (April 29, 1977), p. 506.

G 276 "Staying in Emily Dickinson's House." *London Magazine*, Vol. 17, No. 1 (April/May 1977), p. 58.

G 277 "Jessica Mitford: The Rebel Who Conformed." [Review: *A Fine Old Conflict* by Jessica Mitford.] *The Sunday Times* (May 15, 1977), p. 40.

G 278 "Echoes of the First Circle." [Review: *No Jail for Thought* by Lev Kopelev, translated and edited by Anthony Austin.] *The Sunday Times* (June 19, 1977), p. 41.

G 279 "More Fiction Than Science." [Review: *The Science Fiction of Edgar Allan Poe*, edited by Harold Beaver.] *Times Literary Supplement* (July 1, 1977), p. 794.

G 280 "Soul Behind Bars." [Review: *Falconer*, by John Cheever.] *Times Literary Supplement* (July 8, 1977), p. 821.

G 281 "The bon times and the bad." [Review: *The Middle Parts of Fortune* by Frederic Manning.] *Times Literary Supplement* (August 19, 1977), p. 997.

G 282 "In a Personal Connection." [Review: *Matters of Fact and of Fiction, Essays 1973-1976* by Gore Vidal.] *Times Literary Supplement* (September 30, 1977), p. 1105.

G 283 "George Woodcock: A Portrait." *London Magazine*, Vol. 17,No. 4 (October 1977), pp. 36-44.

G 284 "Murder Under the Microscope." [Review: *Death of an Expert Witness* by P.D. James.] *Times Literary Supplement* (November 4, 1977), p. 1285.

G 285 "Two Who Dun It." [Review: *An Autobiography* by Agatha Christie, *Rex Stout—A Biography* by John McAleer, *Justice Ends at Home and Other Stories* by Rex Stout.] *The New York Times Book Review* (November 13, 1977), pp. 7 and 78.

G 286 "Saving the Republic." [Review: *Unequivocal Americanism: Right Wing Novels in the Cold War Era* by Macel D. Ezell.] *Times Literary Supplement* (December 9, 1977), p. 1440.

1978

G 287 "The Making of an Unperson." [Review: *Notes of a Non-Conspirator* by Efim Etkind, translated by Peter France.] *The Sunday Times* (February 19, 1978), p. 39.

G 288 "Rescuing a Reputation." *Times Literary Supplement* (February 24, 1978), pp. 222-223.

G 289 "Villains at Work." [Review: *Malice Aforethought* by Francis Iles, *Before the Fact* by Francis Iles.] *Times Literary Supplement* (March 10, 1978), p. 274.

G 290 "Goddess of Reason." [Review: *We Must March My Darlings* by Diana Trilling.] *London Magazine*, Vol. 18, No. 1 (April 1978), pp. 83-87.

G 291 "The Publisher Who Played to Win." [Review: *Gollancz: The Story of a Publishing House 1928-1978* by Sheila Hodges, *Literary Gent* by David Higham.] *The Sunday Times* (April 23, 1978), p. 39.

G 292 "Francis Iles' Reissued Books." *Times Literary Supplement* (April 7, 1978), p. 393.

G 293 "Doubting." [Review: *Caught* by Henry Green, *Concluding* by Henry Green.] *Times Literary Supplement* (June 23, 1978), p. 695.

G 294 "A Master of Disguise." [Review: *Mrs. Dukes' Million* by Wyndham Lewis, edited by Frank Davey, *Wyndham Lewis: A Descriptive Biography* by Omar S. Pound and Phillip Grover.] *Times Literary Supplement* (June 30, 1978), p. 726.

G 295 "The Good Life." *London Magazine*, Vol. 18, No. 4 (July 1978), pp. 51-52.

G 296 "American Americans." [Review: *The American Moment* by Geoffrey Thurley.] *London Magazine*, Vol. 18, Nos. 5 & 6 (August/September 1978), pp. 140-143.

G 297 "From Ritual to Record." *Times Literary Supplement* (September 1, 1978), p. 964.

G 298 "Games and the Numbers-Game." [Review: *From Ritual to Record: The Nature of Modern Sports* by Allen Guttmann.] *Times Literary Supplement* (September 1, 1978), p. 964.

G 299 "The Brush of Madness." [Review: *The Doyle Diary: The Last Great Conan Doyle Mystery*, edited by Michael Baker.] *Times Literary Supplement* (September 22, 1978), p. 1042.

G 300 "Heading for a Fall." [Review: *The Singapore Grip* by J.G. Farrell.] *Times Literary Supplement* (October 6, 1978), p. 1110.

G 301 "Compulsion." [Review: *The Iron Staircase* by Georges Simenon, translated by Eileen Ellenbogen, *The Girl With the Squint* by Georges Simenon, translated by Helen Thomson, *The Family Lie* by Georges Simenon, translated by Isabel Quigly, *Maigret's Pipe* by Georges Simenon, translated by Jean Stewart, *Maigret and the Holy Majestic* by Georges Simenon, translated by Caroline Hillier.] *The New York Review* (October 12, 1978), pp. 34-37.

G 302 "Paperback Writer—3: Stephen Spender." *The Sunday Times* (October 22, 1978), p. 99.

G 303 "The Christie Mystery." *The New York Review of Books* (December 21, 1978), pp. 37-39.

1979

G 304 "Ruthven Todd 1914-1978: Some Details for a Portrait." *London Magazine*, Vol. 19, Nos. 1 & 2 (April/May 1979), pp. 62-80.

G 305 "Edgell Rickword." *PN Review*, Vol. 6, No. 1 (1979), Issue #9 Supplement, p. xxii.

1980

G 306 *"Forays." Times Literary Supplement* (January 4, 1980), p. 6.

G 307 Review: Poetry of Elizabeth Jennings. *Times Literary Supplement* (February 1, 1980), p. 112.

G 308 "A Dark Day." *London Magazine*, Vol. 19, No. 12 (March 1980), pp. 70-71.

G 309 *"Drummond Allison: Poems." Times Literary Supplement* (March 14, 1980), p. 301.

G 310 "Kenneth Allot." *Times Literary Supplement* (March 21, 1980), p. 324.

G 311 "Viewpoint." *Times Literary Supplement* (April 18, 1980), p. 437.

G 312 "Kenneth Allot." *Times Literary Supplement* (April 25, 1980), p. 468.

G 313 "The Great Divide." [Review: *Studies of Dylan Thomas, Allen Ginsberg, Sylvia Plath and Robert Lowell* by Louis Simpson.] *London Magazine*, Vol. 20, Nos. 1 & 2 (April/May 1980), pp. 134-136.

G 314 Review of poetry books. *Times Literary Supplement* (May 23, 1980), p. 586.

G 315 "Out of Time and into Poetry." [Review: *Laura Riding's Pursuit of Truth* by Joyce Piell Wexler.] *Times Literary Supplement* (July 18, 1980), pp. 795-796.

G 316 "Cityscape with Figures." [Review: *The Great Fortune, The Spoilt City, Friends and Heroes* by Olivia Manning.] *London Review of Books*, Vol. 2, No. 16 (August 21-September 3, 1980), p. 16.

G 317 "Alien Invader." [Review: *The Enemy: A Biography of Wyndham Lewis* by Jeffrey Meyers and *Wyndham Lewis: A Revaluation*, edited by Jeffrey Meyers.] London Magazine, Vol. 20, No. 7 (October 1980), pp. 79-83.

G 318 "Hello Darkness." *Times Literary Supplement* (October 24, 1980), p. 1194.

G 319 "Axel and After." [Review: *Edmund Wilson: The Thirties from Notebooks and Diaries of the Period* edited by Leon Edel.] *Times Literary Supplement* (November 7, 1980), p. 1249.

1981

G 320 "Form and Ideology in Crime Fiction." *Times Literary Supplement* (January 9, 1981), p. 30.

G 321 "Beyond Everyday Life." [Review: *The Blaze of Noon* by Rayner Heppenstall.] *London Review of Books*, Vol. 3, No. 4 (March 5-18, 1981), p. 19.

G 322 "Argentine Detective and English Jockey." [Review: *Reflex* by Dick Francis.] *The New York Times Book Review* (March 29, 1981), p. 3.

G 323 "The Tough Guy at the Typewriter." [Review: *Shadow Man: The Life of Dashiell Hammett* by Richard Layman and *Raymond Chandler* by Jerry Speir.] *Times Literary Supplement* (June 5, 1981), p. 619-620.

G 324 "Corsair." *Times Literary Supplement* (June 26, 1981), p. 722.

G 325 "Matthew Josephson, Bourgeois Bohemian." *Times Literary Supplement* (June 26, 1981), p. 722.

G 326 Description of the Crime Writers' International Congress. *Times Literary Supplement* (July 3, 1981), p. 756.

G 327 "*We, the Accused.*" *Times Literary Supplement* (September 12, 1981), p. 993.

G 328 "As I Walked Down New Grub Street." *Times Literary Supplement* (December 18, 1981), p. 1456.

G 329 "My First Books." *Author*, Vol. 92 (Winter 1981), pp. 100-101.

1982

G 330 "The Best of Sherlock Holmes Selected by Top Crime Writer Julian Symons." *Bestseller*, Vol. 3, No. 3 (1982), pp. 2-3.

G 331 "Critical Observations." *Times Literary Supplement* (September 17, 1982), p. 1012.

G 332 "Losing Touch." [Review: *The Faber Book of Modern Verse* by Michael Roberts, revised by Peter Porter.] London Magazine, Vol. 22, No. 7 (October 1982), pp. 65-67.

G 333 "Monsignor Quixote." *Times Literary Supplement* (October 8, 1982), p. 1089.

G 334 "The Case for a Double Standard." *PN Review*, Vol. 9, No. 4 (1982), Issue #30, pp. 23-24.

1983

G 335 "The Strength of Uncertainty: Graham Greene." *Literary Half-Yearly*, Vol. 24, No. 1 (January 1983), pp. 1-12.

G 336 "Buer." *Times Literary Supplement* (January 21, 1983), p. 61.

G 337 "*A Margin of Hope* by Irving Howe." *Times Literary Supplement* (March 4, 1983), p. 203.

G 338 "*Hammett* by William F. Nolan." *The New York Times Book Review* (May 8, 1983), p. 7.

G 339 "*The Life of Katherine Anne Porter* by Joan Givner." *Times Literary Supplement* (June 10, 1983), p. 593.

G 340 "*Cyril Connolly* by David Pryce Jones." *Times Literary Supplement* (July 8, 1983), p. 7210.

G 341 "A Transatlantic Friendship." *London Magazine*, Vol. 23, No. 4 (July 1983), pp. 40-48.

G 342 "Personal Publicist." [Review: *Robert Lowell* by Ian Hamilton.] *London Magazine*, Vol. 23, No. 7 (October 1983), pp. 86-88.

G 343 "*The Mystery of Georges Simenon* by Fenton S. Bresler." *The New York Times Book Review* (October 30, 1983), pp. 12-13.

G 344 "*The Lodger* by Georges Simenon." *The New York Times Book Review* (October 30, 1983), pp. 12-13.

G 345 "*Who Killed Sir Harry Oakes?* by James Leasor. *Times Literary Supplement* (November 25, 1983), p. 1305.

G 346 "*Enthusiasms* by Bernard Levin." *Times Literary Supplement* (December 23, 1983), p. 1440.

G 347 "*Speaking Up* by Bernard Levin." *Times Literary Supplement* (December 23, 1983), p. 1440.

1984

G 348 "*Who Killed Sir Harry Oakes?* by James Leasor." *Times Literary Supplement* (January 6, 1984), p. 13.

G 349 "*Dashiell Hammett* by Diane Johnson." *Times Literary Supplement* (January 27, 1984), p. 78.

G 350   "*The Stabbing of George Harry Storrs* by Jonathan Goodman." *Times Literary Supplement* (March 16, 1984), p. 270.

G 351   "*Belladonna* by Donald Thomas." *Times Literary Supplement* (March 30, 1984), p. 354.

G 352   "Georgie Boy: An Imaginary Memoir." *London Magazine*, Vol. 24, No. 4 (July 1984), pp. 13-24.

G 353   "*Snooty Baronet* by Wyndham Lewis." *Times Literary Supplement* (July 6, 1984), p. 762.

G 354   "*Intimate Memoirs* by Georges Simenon." *The New York Review of Books* (July 19, 1984), pp. 12-14.

G 355   "*Voices in an Empty Room* by Francis King." *Times Literary Supplement* (August 31, 1984), p. 964.

G 356   "*Watson's Apology* by Beryl Bainbridge." *Times Literary Supplement* (October 5, 1984), p. 1118.

G 357   "The Beds that Don't Fit: On Labedz's *Orwell*." *Encounter*, Vol. 63 (November 1984), pp. 74-75.

1985

G 358   "Puffball." [Review: *The Brandon Papers* by Quentin Bell.] *London Magazine*, Vol. 24, No. 11 (February 1985), pp. 98-99.

G 359   "Blast 3." [Review: *Rude Assignment* by Wyndham Lewis.] *The New York Times Book Review* (February 10, 1985), p. 29.

G 360   "*The English Novel in the Twentieth Century* by Martin Burgess Green." *Times Literary Supplement* (February 22, 1985), p. 198.

G 361   "Imaginary Memoirs—II: E.J. Bastable and the Poet of the Era." *London Magazine*, Vol. 24, No. 12 (March 1985), pp. 27-42.

G 362   "*Auden in Love* by Dorothy J. Farnan." *Times Literary Supplement* (March 22, 1985), p. 305.

G 363   "Imaginary Memoirs—III: Ella, A Success Story." *London Magazine*, Vol. 25, No. 4 (July 1985), pp. 18-35.

G 364   "A.J.A. Symons, Brother Speculator." *The Book Collector*, Vol. 34, No. 3 (Autumn 1985), pp. 293-308.

G 365   Comments on works of fiction deserving to be better known. *Times Literary Supplement* (October 18, 1985), p. 1184.

G 366 "Back Numbers." [Review: *The Penguin New Writing 1940-50*, edited by John Lehmann & Roy Fuller, *The New Review Anthology*, edited by Ian Hamilton, *London Reviews: A Selection from the London Review of Books* 1983-85, edited by Nicholas Spice with introduction by Karl Miller.] *London Magazine*, Vol. 25, No. 8 (November 1985), pp. 101-104.

G 367 "*The Vulgar Streak* by Wyndham Lewis." *Times Literary Supplement* (November 8, 1985), pp. 1259.

1986

G 368 "*Orwell: The Road to Airstrip One* by Ian Slater." *Times Literary Supplement* (January 3, 1986), p. 6.

G 369 "*Orwell: The War Commentaries*, edited by W.J. West." *Times Literary Supplement* (January 3, 1986), p. 6.

G 370 "*A Book of One's Own* by Thomas Mallon." *Times Literary Supplement* (January 10, 1986), pp. 41-42.

G 371 "*The Inman Diary* by Arthur Crew Inman." *Times Literary Supplement* (January 10, 1986), pp. 41-42.

G 372 "*Blunt Darts* by Jeremiah Healy." *Times Literary Supplement* (March 14, 1986), p. 266.

G 373 "*The New Black Mask Quarterly*, edited by Matthew J. Bruccoli and Richard Layman." *Times Literary Supplement* (March 14, 1986), p. 266.

G 374 "*Nightlines* by John Lutz." *Times Literary Supplement* (March 14, 1986), p. 266.

G 375 "*Sugartown* by Loren D. Estleman." *Times Literary Supplement* (March 14, 1986), p. 266.

G 376 "Regarding the Master." [Review: *The Young Hemingway* by Michael Reynolds, *Along with Youth* by Peter Griffin, *Hemingway* by Jeffrey Meyers.] *London Magazine*, Vol. 26, No. 3 (June 1986), pp. 85-88.

G 377 "*Lionel Trilling and the Fate of Cultural Criticism* by Mark Krupnick." *Times Literary Supplement* (September 5, 1986), p. 959-960.

G 378 "*Rain or Shine* by Cyra McFadden." *Times Literary Supplement* (September 12, 1986), p. 996.

G 379 "The Queen of Crime: P.D. James." *The New York Times Magazine* (October 5, 1986), pp. 48-50.

G 380 Article on the use of inverted commas. *Times Literary Supplement* (November 28, 1986), p. 1349.

G 381 "*The Fifties* by Edmund Wilson." *Times Literary Supplement* (December 26, 1986), p. 1442.

1987

G 382 "*The Agency* by John Ranelagh." *Times Literary Supplement* (January 30, 1987), p. 101.

G 383 "*The CIA: A Forgotten History* by William Blum." *Times Literary Supplement* (January 30, 1987), p. 101.

G 384 "*One Girl's War* by Joan Miller." *Times Literary Supplement* (January 30, 1987), p. 101.

G 385 "*The Second Oldest Profession* by Philip Knightly." *Times Literary Supplement* (January 30, 1987), p. 101.

G 386 "*Murder in Print* by Melvyn Barnes." *Times Literary Supplement* (February 20, 1987), p. 183.

G 387 "Mansfield Cumming." *Times Literary Supplement* (February 27, 1987), p. 213.

G 388 "*The Paradox of Gissing* by David Grylls." *Times Literary Supplement* (July 24, 1987), p. 803.

G 389 "*A Child of the War* by George MacBeth." *Times Literary Supplement* (August 28, 1987), p. 922.

G 390 "Spellbinder." [Review: *Oscar Wilde* by Richard Ellmann.] *London Magazine*, Vol. 27, No. 7 (October 1987), pp. 91-94.

G 391 "Literary Cartwheels." [Review: *Blackeyes* by Dennis Potter.] *The Listener,* Vol. 118, No. 3031 (October 1, 1987), p. 22.

G 392 "T.S. Eliot." *Times Literary Supplement* (November 18, 1987), p. 1279.

G 393 "*Lucan: Not Guilty* by Sally Moore." *Times Literary Supplement* (December 4, 1987), p. 1346.

G 394 "*Trail of Havoc: In the Steps of Lord Lucan* by Patrick Marnham." *Times Literary Supplement* (December 4, 1987), p. 1346.

1988

G 395 "T.S. Eliot." *Times Literary Supplement* (January 6, 1988), p. 11.

G 396 "Rupert Loxley: Imaginary Biographies: 4." *London Magazine*, Vol. 27, No. 11 (February 1988), pp. 12-26.

G 397   "*Passion and Cunning and Other Essays* by Conor Louise O'Brien."
Times Literary Supplement (March 25, 1988), p. 331.

G 398   "*Orthodox Heresy* by Martin Stoddard." *Times Literary Supplement*
(April 28, 1988), p. 285.

G 399   "*The Secret Lives of Trebitsch Lincoln* by Bernard Wasserstein." *The New
York Times Book Review* (June 26, 1988), pp. 14-15.

G 400   "Ghastly Good Taste." [Review: *Young Betjeman* by Bevis Hillier.] *The
Listener*, Vol. 120, No. 3072 (July 21, 1988), p. 27.

G 401   "*Lewis Percy* by Anita Brookner." *Times Literary Supplement* (August 25,
1988), p. 917.

G 402   "Jackdaw." [Review: *A Serious Character: The Life of Ezra Pound* by
Humphrey Carpenter.] *London Magazine*, Vol. 28, Nos. 5 & 6
(August/September 1988), pp. 124-126.

G 403   "*The Art of Being Ruled* by Wyndham Lewis, edited by Reed Way." *Times
Literary Supplement* (September 22, 1988), p. 1024.

G 404   "*Yours etc.: Letters to the Press 1945-89* by Graham Greene, edited by
Christopher Hawtree." *Times Literary Supplement* (November 10, 1988),
p. 1231.

G 405   "Writers Remembered: Agatha Christie." *Author*, Vol. 99 (Winter 1988),
pp. 108-109.

G 406   "*Trust* by George V. Higgins." *Times Literary Supplement* (December 29,
1988), p. 1447.

1989

G 407   "Snobbery with Violence." [TV adaptation of Margery Allingham's detective novels.] *Listener* (January 26, 1989), pp. 12-13.

G 408   "Crime Stories and Crime Fiction." *The Guardian* (February 22, 1989), p.
47.

G 409   "Any Old Iron." *Times Literary Supplement* (April 7, 1989), p. 363.

G 410   "Woman of Mystery: Ruth Rendell Unveiled." *The Sunday Times Books*
(April 9, 1989), Section G, p. 9.

G 411   "*Orthodox Heresy: The Rise of 'Magic' as Religion and its Relation to Literature* by Martin Stoddard." *Times Literary Supplement* (April 28, 1989)
p. 451.

G 412 "Whose Saint is He, Anyway?" [Review: *The Politics of Literary Reputation: The Making and Claiming of 'St. George' Orwell* by John Rodden.] *The New York Times Book Review* (June 4, 1989), p. 25.

G 413 "Murder Will Out: The Detective in Fiction." *Times Literary Supplement* (July 7, 1989), p. 740.

G 414 "*Lewis Percy* by Anita Brookner." *Times Literary Supplement* (August 25, 1989), p. 917.

G 415 "Will the Real Sir James Please Stand Up?" [Review: *Painting the Darkness* by Robert Goddard.] *Washington Post* (August 27, 1989), p. 8.

G 416 "Victorian Values and Social Change." [Review: *The Haunted Study* by Peter Keating.] *The Sunday Times Books* (September 17, 1989), Section G, p. 10.

G 417 "Darts for Art's Sake." [Review: *London Fields* by Martin Amis.] *London Review of Books*, Vol. 11, No. 18 (September 28, 1989), pp. 7-8.

G 418 "Orwellspeak." [Review: *The Politics of Literary Reputation: The Making and Claiming of 'St. George' Orwell* by John Rodden.] *London Review of Books*, Vol. 11, No. 21 (November 9, 1989), pp. 20-21.

G 419 "*Yours Etc.: Letters to the Press, 1945-89* by Graham Greene." *Times Literary Supplement* (November 10, 1989), p. 1231.

G 420 "*Trust* by George V. Higgins." *Times Literary Supplement* (December 29, 1989), p. 1447.

1990

G 421 "Oms and Huns." [Review: *Ginsberg: A Biography* by Barry Miles.] *London Review of Books*, Vol. 12, No. 6 (March 22, 1990) pp. 16-17.

G 422 "*Futility* by William Gerhardie." *Times Literary Supplement* (April 13, 1990), p. 387.

G 423 "*God's Fifth Column* by William Gerhardie." *Times Literary Supplement* (April 13, 1990), p. 388.

G 424 "*Memoirs of a Polyglot* by William Gerhardie." *Times Literary Supplement* (April 13, 1990), p. 387.

G 425 "*William Gerhardie* by Dido Davies." *Times Literary Supplement* (April 13, 1990), p. 387.

G 426 "What to Do with the Body?" [Review: *The Innocent* by Ian McEwan.] *Times Literary Supplement* (May 11-17, 1990), p. 497.

G 427 "Burlington Bertie." [Review: *The Last Modern: A Life of Herbert Read* by James King.] *London Review of Books*, Vol. 12, No. 11 (June 14, 1990), pp. 13-14.

G 428 "Creatures of Habit and Creatures of Change: Essays on Art, Literature and Society, 1914-1956." [Review: *Tarr* by Wyndham Lewis.] *Times Literary Supplement* (June 15, 1990), p. 628.

G 429 "*A Damned Serious Business* by Graham Ison." *Times Literary Supplement* (June 22, 1990), p. 674.

G 430 "Deep Down." [Review: *The Last Word* by Christoph Raynsmayr, *The End of Lieutenant Boruvka* by Josef Shvorecky, *The Dwarves of Death* by Jonathan Coe, *Last Loves* by Alan Sillitoe.] *London Review of Books*, Vol. 12, No. 12 (June 28, 1990), pp. 20-21.

G 431 "The Challenge of D.H. Lawrence." [Review: *D.H. Lawrence: a Biography* by Jeffrey Meyers.] *Times Literary Supplement* (September 7, 1990), p. 940.

G 432 "Dirty Jokes." [Review: *Brief Lives* by Anita Brookner, *Deception* by Philip Roth, *Homeboy* by Seth Morgan.] *London Review of Books*, Vol. 12, No. 17 (September 13, 1990), pp. 16-17.

G 433 "Paul and Penny." [Review: *Paul Scott: A Life* by Hilary Spurling, *Paul Scott's Raj* by Robin Moore.] *London Review of Books*, Vol. 12, No. 20 (October 25, 1990), p. 26.

G 434 "Who They Think They Are." [Review: *You've Had Your Time* by Anthony Burgess, *An Immaculate Mistake: Scenes from a Childhood and Beyond* by Paul Bailey.] *London Review of Books*, Vol. 12, No. 21 (November 8, 1990), pp. 17-18.

G 435 "Sherlock's Christmas: Part One: 'A Dramatic Departure.'" *Punch*, Vol. 299, No. 7820 (Christmas 1990), p. 46.

G 436 "Sherlock's Christmas: Part Two: 'She Tried it All Ways.'" *Punch*, Vol. 299, No. 7821 (December 12-18, 1990), p. 30.

G 437 "Victor Ludorum." [Review: *The Complete Short Stories* and *Lasting Impressions* by V.S. Pritchett.] *London Review of Books*, Vol. 12, No. 24 (December 20, 1990), pp. 17-18.

G 438 "Sherlock's Christmas: Part Three: 'The Patacake Club.'" *Punch*, Vol. 299, No. 7822 (Almanac 1990), p. 44.

G 439 *Edgell Rickword: Poet at War* by Charles Hobday. *PN Review*, Vol. 16, No. 6 (1990), pp. 53-54.

1991

G 440 "The Clopton Hercules." *Times Literary Supplement* (January 11, 1991), p. 17.

G 441 *"The Journalist and the Murderer* by Janet Malcolm." *Times Literary Supplement* (January 25, 1991), p. 14.

G 442 "What Ho, Giotto!" [Review: *Stanley Spencer* by Kenneth Pople.] *London Review of Books*, Vol. 13, No. 3 (February 7, 1991), p. 20.

G 443 "Talking Heads." [Review: *The Theatre of Embarrassment* by Francis Wyndham.] *The Sunday Times Books* (February 10, 1991), Section 6, p. 3.

G 444 "Urgent." [Review: *By Grand Central Station I Sat Down and Wept and The Assumption of the Rogues and Rascals* by Elizabeth Smart, *Necessary Secrets: The Journals of Elizabeth Smart*, edited by Alice Van Wart.] *London Review of Books*, Vol. 13, No. 4 (February 21, 1991) p. 13.

G 445 "Tribute to a Master." *The Guardian* (April 4, 1991), p. 25.

G 446 "Snobs, Puzzles and Solutions." [Review: *Ngaio Marsh* by Margaret Lewis.] *The Sunday Times Books* (April 14, 1991), Section 6, p. 3.

G 447 "Capacities for Invention." [Review: *Joseph Conrad: A Biography* by Jeffrey Myers.] *The New Criterion*, Vol. 9, No. 9 (May 1991), pp. 68-72.

G 448 *"Critical Crossings: The New York Intellectuals in Postwar America* by Neil Jumonville." *Times Literary Supplement* (May 31, 1991), p. 13.

G 449 "Bourgeois Masterpieces." [Review: *Literature and Liberation: Selected Essays* by Arnold Kettle, edited by Graham Martin and W.R. Owens.] *London Review of Books*, Vol. 13, No. 11 (June 13, 1991), p. 16.

G 450 "City of Dust." [Review: *A Den of Foxes* by Stuart Hood, *Dirty Tricks* by Michael Dibdin, *A Strange and Sublime Address* by Amit Chaudhuri, *Spider* by Patrick McGrath.] *London Review of Books*, Vol. 13, No. 14 (July 25, 1991), pp. 13-14.

G 451 "Making Up." [Review: *Lipstick, Sex and Poetry* by Jeremy Reed, *The Poet Could Not but Be Gay* by James Kirkup, *There Was a Young Man from Cardiff* by Dannie Abse, *String of Beginners* by Michael Hamburger.] *London Review of Books*, Vol. 13, No. 15 (August 15, 1991), p. 16.

G 452 "Conan the Logician." [Review: *The Real World of Sherlock Holmes* by Peter Costello.] *The Sunday Times Books* (September 8, 1991), Section 6, p. 13.

G 453 "The Brief Possibility of a Different Kind of History." [Review: *The Myth of the Blitz* by Angus Calder.] *London Review of Books*, Vol. 13, No. 17 (September 12, 1991), p. 9.

G 454 "*The Last Detective* by Peter Lovesey." *Times Literary Supplement* (September 20, 1991), p. 231.

G 455 "Unlucky Jim." [Review: *The Kindness of Women* by J.G. Ballard.] *London Review of Books,* Vol. 13, No. 19 (October 10, 1991), p. 16.

G 456 "*Orwell: The Authorised Biography* by Michael Shelden." *Times Literary Supplement* (October 18, 1991), p. 12.

G 457 "Lost Felicity." [Review: *Collected Poems* by Henry Reed, edited by Jon Stallworthy.] *Times Literary Supplement* (November 22, 1991), p. 7.

G 458 "Digging up the Past." [Review: *The Mandeville Talent* by George V. Higgins.] *The Sunday Times Books* (November 24, 1991), Section 7, p. 14.

G 459 "Terrible to be Alive." [Review: *Randall Jarrell: A Literary Life* by William Pritchard and *Randall Jarrell: Selected Poems*, edited by William Pritchard.] *London Review of Books*, Vol. 13, No. 23 (December 5, 1991), pp. 21-22.

1992

G 460 "War and Pieces." [Review: *Writers on World War II: An Anthology* edited by Mordecai Richler.] *The New Criterion*, Vol. 10, No. 5 (January 1992), pp. 73-75.

G 461 "Roy Fuller: After the Obituaries." *London Magazine*, Vol. 31, Nos. 11 & 12 (February/March 1992), pp. 34-42.

G 462 "Advice for the New Nineties." [Review: *HMS Glasshouse* by Sean O'Brien, *The Hogweed Lass* by Alan Dixon, *Collected Poems* by Les Murray.] *London Review of Books*, Vol. 14, No. 5 (March 12, 1992), p. 27.

G 463 "Poe's Woes." [Review: *Edgar A. Poe: Mournful and Never-Ending Remembrance* by Kenneth Silverman.] *London Review of Books*, Vol 14, No. 8 (April 23, 1992), pp. 14-15.

G 464 "*Trotsky in Mexico* by Alain Dogrand, translated by Stephen Romer." *Times Literary Supplement* (May 29, 1992), p. 10.

G 465 "The Riddle of Erskine Childers." *Folio* (Summer 1992), pp. 3-7.

G 466   "Friends of the Enemy: Reassessing the Uncomfortable World of Wyndham Lewis." [Review: *Wyndham Lewis* by Paul Edwards.] *Times Literary Supplement* (July 10, 1992), pp. 16-17.

G 467   "Timo of Corinth." [Review: *A Choice of Murder* by Peter Vansittart, *Portrait of the Artist's Wife* by Barbara Anderson, *Turtle Moon* by Alice Hoffman, *Double Down* by Tom Kakonis.] *London Review of Books*, Vol 14, No. 15 (August 6, 1992), p. 19.

G 468   "*Anthony Trollope* by Victoria Glendinning." *Times Literary Supplement* (August 28, 1992), pp. 3-4.

G 469   "Back to the Future." [Review: *The Children of Men* by P.D. James, *A Philosophical Investigation* by Phillip Kerr, *Spoilt* by Georgina Hammick, *The Death of the Author* by Gilbert Adair, *Jerusalem Commands* by Michael Moorcock.] *London Review of Books*, Vol. 14, No. 17 (September 10, 1992), p. 22.

G 470   "Intolerance." [Review: *The God-Fearer* by Dan Jacobson.] *London Review of Books*, Vol. 14, No. 19 (October 8, 1992), p. 10.

G 471   "A Mix-up of Memory and Desire." [Review: *Stephen Spender: A Portrait with Background* by Hugh David.] *The Sunday Times Books* (October 11, 1992), Section 6, p. 4.

G 472   "Life with a Likable Killer." [Review: *Ripley Under Water* by Patricia Highsmith.] *The New York Times Book Review* (October 18, 1992), p. 41.

G 473   "Israel at Vanity Fair" [Review: *Jews and Judaism in the Writings of W.M. Thackeray* by Siegbert Salomon Prawer.] *Times Literary Supplement* (October 30, 1992), p. 6.

G 474   "*Shylock* by John Gross." *Times Literary Supplement* (October 30, 1992), p. 6.

G 475   "Double Life in Crime." [Obituary of John Michael Evelyn.] *The Guardian* (December 8, 1992), p. 10.

1993

G 476   "Hugh Porteus." [Obituary.] *The Guardian* (February 12, 1993), p. 12.

G 477   "Literary Lives, Crimes and Misdemeanours." [Review: *Dorothy L. Sayers: Her Life and Soul* by Barbara Reynolds.] *The Sunday Times Books* (March 14, 1993), Section 7, p. 5.

G 478   "The Monster Rostov." [Review: *Hunting the Devil* by Richard Lourie, *The Killer Department: Detective Viktor Burakov's Eight-Year Hunt for the Most Savage Serial Killer in Russian History* by Robert Cullen, and *Comrade Chikatilo: The Psychopathology of Russia's Notorious Serial Killer* by Mikhail Krivich and Ol'gert Ol'gin, translated by Todd P. Bludeau and edited by Sandi Gelles-Cole.] *The New York Times Book Review* (March 14, 1993), pp. 6-7.

G 479 "Forgotten Man of the Thirties." *Times Literary Supplement* (March 26, 1993), p. 13.

G 480 "*Smash and Grab* by Robert Murphy." *Times Literary Supplement* (April 2, 1993) p. 36.

G 481 "Wartime and Aftermath." [Review: *English Literature and its Background, 1939-1960* by Bernard Bergonzi.] *Times Literary Supplement* (April 30, 1993), p. 13.

G 482 "Puss-in-Cahoots." [Review: *Felidae* by Akif Pirincci, translated by Ralph Noble]. *The Sunday Times Books* (June 6, 1993), Section 6, p. 11.

G 483 "On the Shelf." [Review: *Decline and Fall* by Evelyn Waugh.] *The Sunday Times Books* (June 20, 1993), Section 6, p. 9.

G 484 "Our Man in Zurich." [Review: *The Night Manager* by John le Carré.] *The New York Times Book Review* (June 27, 1993), pp. 1 and 29.

G 485 "Our Jack." [Review: *Imagination of the Heart: The Life of Walter de la Mare* by Theresa Whistler.] *London Review of Books*, Vol. 15, No. 14 (July 22, 1993), pp. 18-19.

G 486 "*Ezra Pound, Wyndham Lewis and Radical Modernism* by Vincent Sherry." *Times Literary Supplement* (July 23, 1993), p. 7.

G 487 "*The Political Aesthetic of Yeats, Eliot and Pound* by Michael North." *Times Literary Supplement* (July 23, 1993), p. 7.

G 488 "*Wyndham Lewis and the Avant Garde: The Politics of the Intellect* by Avard Foshay." *Times Literary Supplement* (July 23, 1993), p. 7.

G 489 "Well-Versed in Deceit." [Review: *The Ern Malley Affair* by Michael Heyward.] *The Sunday Times Books* (August 22, 1993), Section 6, p. 3.

G 490 "Me, Myself and I." [Review: *United States* by Gore Vidal.] *The Sunday Times Books* (October 24, 1993), Section 6, p. 5.

G 491 "Foiled Caresses: A Novelist and His Demons." [Review: *Patrick Hamilton: A Life* by Sean French.] *Times Literary Supplement* (November 12, 1993), pp. 3-4.

G 492 "Ideal Holmes?" [Review: *The Collected Sherlock Holmes* edited by Owen Dudley Edwards.] *The Sunday Times Books* (December 12, 1993), Section 6, p. 11.

1994

G 493 "*Dolphins* by Stephen Spender." *Times Literary Supplement* (February 18, 1994), p. 10.

G 494 "On an Arctic Roll." [Review: *Kolymsky Heights* by Lionel Davidson.] *The Sunday Times Books* (March 13, 1994), Section 7, p. 12.

G 495 "Fears of a Clown." [Review: *John Betjeman Letters Volumn I: 1926-51* edited by Candida Lycett Green.] *The Sunday Times Books* (April 24, 1994), Section 7, pp. 1-2.

G 496 "Lord Peter Wimsey." *The Independent Magazine* (April 30, 1994), p. 46.

G 497 "*The Bank of Fear* by David Ignatius." *The New York Times Book Review* (June 5, 1994), p. 51.

G 498 "*The Well-Mannered Assassin* by Aline Romanones." *The New York Times Book Review* (June 5, 1994), p. 51.

G 499 "A River Runs Through It." [Review: *Coyote* by Richard Thornley.] *The Sunday Times Books* (July 31, 1994), Section 7, p. 9.

G 500 "*Lytton Strachey: New Biography.*" *The Times Literary Supplement* (August 26, 1994), pp. 4-5.

G 501 "Porn Broker." [Review: *The Good Ship Venus: The Erotic Voyage of the Olympia Press* by John de St Jorre.] *The Sunday Times Books* (September 25, 1994), Section 7, p. 4.

G 502 "Dons' Detective Delight." [Obituary: Michael Innes.] *The Guardian* (November 15, 1994), p. 15.

G 503 "The Pick of the Year" [Reviews: *A Stomach for Dissent* by John and Mary Postage; *Journey to the Border* and *Unmentionable Man* by Edward Upward and *The Mormere Stories* by Edward Upward and Christopher Isherwood; *Dead Lagoon* by Michael Dibdin.] *The Sunday Times Books* (November 20, 1994), Section 7, p. 2.

SECTION H

CONTRIBUTIONS TO

ELLERY QUEEN'S

MYSTERY

MAGAZINE

For nearly forty years Julian Symons has been published in the pages of *Ellery Queen's Mystery Magazine*, and for many American readers of mystery books and short stories, this magazine served as their first introduction to Symons's considerable abilities as a short story writer. See also the Appendix that includes a reference to Cooper and Pike's *Detective Fiction* and provides a list of short stories that have appeared in *The Evening Standard* newspaper of London.

H 1   "The Case of XX-2," Vol. 20, No. 105 (August, 1952), pp.108-113.

H 2   "Cat and Mouse," Vol. 20, No. 108 (November, 1952), pp. 74-80.

H 3   "Life and Death in the Scillies," Vol. 23, No. 124 (March, 1954), pp. 76-80.

H 4   "Strolling in the Square One Day," Vol. 39, No. 2 (February, 1962), pp. 52-60.

H 5   "As If By Magic," Vol. 42, No. 3 (September, 1963), pp. 101-104.

H 6   "The Humdrum Murder," Vol. 43, No. 3 (March, 1964), pp. 130-134.

H 7   "The Wimbledon Mystery," Vol. 43, No. 5 (May, 1964), pp. 17-33, 139-150.

H 8   "Credit to Shakespeare," Vol. 44, No. 5 (November, 1964), pp. 93-98.

H 9   "'Twixt the Cup and the Lip," Vol. 45, No. 1 (January, 1965), pp. 6-28.

H 10   "The Tiger's Stripe," Vol. 45, No. 3 (March, 1965), pp. 51-66.

H 11   "Eight Minutes to Kill," Vol. 46, No. 6 (December, 1965), pp. 34-51.

H 12   "The Impossible Theft," Vol. 47, No. 1 (January, 1966), pp. 17-20.

H 13   "Murder on the Race Course," Vol. 48, No. 1 (July, 1966), pp. 46-63.

H 14   "The Santa Claus Club," Vol. 49, No. 1 (January, 1967), pp. 49-58.

H 15   "The Crimson Coach Murders," Vol. 49, No. 4 (April, 1967), pp. 6-30.

H 16   "The Main Chance," Vol. 50, No. 2 (August, 1967), pp. 118-130.

H 17   "A Pearl Among Women," Vol. 51, No. 1 (January, 1968), pp. 117-121.

H 18   "A Theme for Hyacinth," Vol. 52, No. 2 (August, 1968), pp. 41-58.

H 19   "The Hidden Clue," Vol. 52, No. 5 (November, 1968), pp. 99-102.

H 20   "Can you Find the Ace?", Vol. 54, No. 3 (September, 1969), pp. 35-39.

H 21   "Love Affair," Vol. 54, No. 5 (November, 1969), pp. 127-136.

H 22   "Experiment in Personality," Vol. 58, No. 1 (July, 1971), pp. 33-53.

H 23   "Preserving the Evidence," Vol. 58, No. 5 (November, 1971), pp. 45-49.

H 24   "Pickup on the Dover Road," Vol. 60, No. 1 (July, 1972), pp. 6-16.

H 25   "The Sensitive Ears of Mr. Small," Vol. 60, No. 4 (October, 1972), pp. 16-25.

H 26   "How to Trap a Crook," Vol. 61, No. 3 (March, 1973), pp. 113-120.

H 27   "Hot Summer Night," Vol. 66, No. 5 (November, 1975), pp. 45-56.

H 28   "Waiting for Mr. McGregor," Vol. 73, No. 3 (March, 1979), pp. 127-142.

H 29   "The Post Mortem Letters," Vol. 73, No. 5 (May, 1979), pp. 131-141.

H 30   "Flowers That Bloom in the Spring," Vol. 74, No. 1 (July, 1979), pp. 6-21.

H 31   "The Boiler," Vol. 74, No. 5 (November, 1979), pp. 6-16.

H 32   "Value For Money," Vol. 76, No. 6 (December 1, 1980), pp. 140-155.
Author's Note: This issue carries a photograph of Julian Symons on the front cover.

H 33   "The Dupe," Vol. 77, No. 6 (May 20, 1981), pp. 114-127.

H 34   "The Flaw," Vol. 80, No. 1 (July, 1982), pp. 5-21.

H 35   "The Dream Is Better," Vol. 80, No. 3 (August, 1982), pp. 6-18.

H 36   "The Last Time," Vol. 84, No. 1 (July, 1984), pp. 126-134.

H 37   "The Birthmark," Vol. 86, No. 7 (Mid-December, 1985), pp. 3-17.

H 38   "Has Anybody Here Seen Me?", Vol. 90, No. 3 (September, 1987), pp. 19-30.

H 39   "The Borgia Heirloom," Vol. 90, No. 5 (November, 1987), pp. 52-56.

H 40   "Did Sherlock Holmes Meet Hercule—?", Vol. 90, No. 7 (Mid-December, 1987), pp. 67-76.

H 41   "On Our Cover," Vol. 92, No. 5 (November, 1988), p. 95.
Author's Note: This issue carries a photograph of Julian Symons and Peter Lovesey on the cover, along with a story about the Fourth International Congress of Crime Writers that met in New York in May of 1988. The story identifies Julian as "MWA Grand Master...whose credits as writer, poet and critic are too extensive and well celebrated to describe in proper depth here...."

H 42   "I, Too, Lived In Arcadia," Vol. 94, No. 3 (September, 1989), pp. 142-152.

H 43   "The Conjuring Trick," Vol. 95, No.3 (March, 1990), pp. 133-153.
Author's Note: This, the 49th Anniversary Issue, carries a cover photograph of Julian Symons, along with Isaac Asimov, Edward D. Hoch, Antonia Fraser and George Baxt.

H 44   "Holocaust at Mayhem Parva," Vol. 96, No. 4 (October, 1990), pp. 4-16.

H 45   "In the Bluebell Wood," Vol. 103, No. 2 (February, 1994), pp. 4-18.

H 46   "The Man Who Hated Television," Vol. 103, No. 7 (June, 1994), pp. 4-17.

APPENDIX

SELECTED MATERIALS ON JULIAN SYMONS BIOGRAPHICAL AND CRITICAL

1   Bargainnier, Earl F., editor. *Twelve Englishmen of Mystery*. Bowling Green, Ohio: Bowling Green University Popular Press, 1984,, pp. 196-221.
     Larry E. Grimes gives critical comments on each of the crime novels, beginning with *The Immaterial Murder Case* (1958) up to *The Black-heath Poisonings* (1979). "Symons' fiction has about it a sense of cor-pus—of being a solid and singular body of literature... that crime fiction can be serious fiction."

2   Barnes, Melvyn. *Best Detective Fiction: A Guide from Godwin to the Present*. London and Hamden, Conn.: Clive Bingley and Linnet Books, 1975, pp. 93-95.
     Discusses three works: *The Colour of Murder, The Progress of a Crime* and *The End of Solomon Grundy*. "....in his invaluable book, *Bloody Murder*...he traces the development from detective story to crime novel. His own books have followed this pattern."

3   ———. *Murder in Print: A Guide to Two Centuries of Crime Fiction*. London: Barn Owl Books, 1986, pp. 139-141.
     With some slight changes, this is a repeat of the material covered in *Best Detective Fiction* (1975), along with two additional titles: *The Man Who Lost His Wife* and *The Plot Against Roger Rider*.

4   Bourgeau, Art. *The Mystery Lover's Companion*. New York: Crown Publishers, Inc., 1986, p. 178.
     A short plot summary of *Bogue's Fortune, The Belting Inheritance, The Players and the Game, The Plot Against Roger Rider, A Three-Pipe Prob-lem, The Detling Secret* and *The Tigers of Subtopia*. Each title is given a rating, made up of daggers. Five daggers equal a true classic; one dagger is for titles you "only read...when you're drunk." The author gives *The Plot Against Roger Rider* five daggers and the other six titles either three or four daggers.

5   Connolly, Joseph. *Modern First Editions: Their Value to Collectors*. London: MacDonald & Co., Ltd., 1987, pp. 286-287.
     A list of 28 crime fiction titles, giving U.K. and U.S. titles and a scale of val-ues. The first work, *The Immaterial Murder Case*, is valued at "up to £50", while most later works (1964, *The End of Solomon Grundy* to 1983, *The Name of Annabel Lee*) are valued at "up to £10." The author calls Symons "an undisputed master of his genre...not as collected as one might expect. He is collected, but he is rarely eagerly pursued."

6   Cooper, John, and B.A. Pike. *Detective Fiction: The Collector's Guide*. Taunton, Somerset: Barn Owl Books, 1988, pp. 169-171. 211.
     A brief bibliographical summary of the crime novels from 1945 to 1988, with a separate listing of short stories found both in books and in maga-zines or newspapers. At the end of the book is found "A personal choice of books" in which John Cooper recommends *The Man Who Killed Himself*. This book is also useful for it's end sheets, on which are repro-duced the signatures of more than fifty authors, including Julian Symons.

7   Cooper-Clark, Diana. *Designs of Darkness: Interviews with Detective Novelists.*
     Bowling Green, Ohio: Bowling Green State University Popular Press, 1983,
     pp. 172-185.
     Transcribed taped interview in which Symons discusses his philosophy of
     writing and gives some background for his works.

8   Herbert, Rosemary. *The Fatal Art of Entertainment: Interviews with Mystery
     Writers.* Boston: G.K. Hall, 1994, pp. 1-27.
     From the Foreword by Antonia Fraser: "Rosemary Herbert....has chosen
     to act as Boswell to thirteen Dr. Johnsons, ranging from eighty-year-old
     British author Julian Symons, rightly regarded as the dean of crime writers...."

9   Hilfer, Tony. *The Crime Novel: A Deviant Genre.* Austin, Texas: University
     of Texas Press, 1990, pp. 81-82, 96.
     Critical analysis of *The Man Who Killed Himself* and *The Man Whose
     Dreams Came True*, and a shorter reference to *The Color of Murder.*

10   Keating, H.R.F. *Whodunit? A Guide to Crime, Suspense and Spy Fiction.*
     London: Windward, 1982, pp. 55, 58, 234-235.
     Very brief critical remarks, followed by three titles, *The Colour of Mur-
     der, The End of Solomon Grundy* and *The Players and the Game*, each
     of which is given a star ranking for characterization, plot, readability and
     tension. Using this ranking system, *The Players and the Game* scores the
     highest, with nine stars for each area.

11   ———. *Crime & Mystery: The 100 Best Books.* London: Xanadu Publications
     Ltd., 1987, pp. 133-134, 159-160.
     The author states that Julian Symons's crime books come in two modes,
     "the ingenious and the perceptive." For the ingenious mode, he has cho-
     sen *The Man Who Killed Himself*, and for the perceptive mode he has
     chosen *The Players and the Game.*

12   Oleksiw, Susan. *A Reader's Guide to the Classic British Mystery.* Boston:
     G.K. Hall & Co., 1988, pp. 416-423.
     Brief plot outlines for twenty-four Symons crime novels (1945-1986),
     including *the Criminal Comedy of the Contented Couple* (*A Criminal
     Comedy* in the U.S.).

13   Pronzini, Bill, and Marcia Muller. *1001 Midnights: The Aficionado's Guide to
     Mystery and Detective Fiction.* New York: Arbor House, 1986, pp. 766-769.
     Plot summaries of three works: *The Detling Secret, A Three-Pipe Prob-
     lem*, and *The Tigers of Subtopia and Other Stories.* The first and last
     items are given a single star, which denotes "Titles that are especially
     good or interesting, or that represent a particularly notable series or body
     of work."

14   Reilly, John M., editor. *Twentieth-Century Crime and Mystery Writers.* Second
     Edition. New York: St. Martin's Press, 1985, pp. 834-836.

Contains brief biographical comments, a list of crime publications, short stories, plays, verse, non-fiction works, and very brief comment by Julian Symons on his work. All this is followed by a longer piece, written by George Woodcock, giving additional background notes on Symons and his works. This work is useful as a reference for radio and television plays written by Symons.

15   Ross, Alan. "Turning to Crime: An Interview with Julian Symons." *London Magazine*, Vol. 22, Nos. 1 & 2 (April/May 1982), pp. 71-83 86.

16   Salwak, Dale. *Mystery Voices: Interviews with British Crime Writers*. San Bernardino, California: The Borgo Press, 1991.
      Interview, pp. 95-107.
      Julian Symons is interviewed by Dale Salwak, a Professor of English at Citrus College in Southern California.

17   Sinclair, Andrew. *War Like a Wasp: The Lost Decade of the 'Forties*. London: Hamish Hamilton, 1989, pp. 28, 44, 56, 67-8, 74, 94, 98-100, 137-138, 158, 174, 177, 212, 235-236, 269 and 287-288.
      Includes critical comments on Symons, his works, his friends, and his political opinions. Telling of the feeling of Londoners and visitors to London during the blitz, Sinclair comments: "Radicals such as Julian Symons thought he had reached a Utopia, rather like life in Russia in the months after the revolution."

18   Steinbrunner, Chris, and Otto Penzler, editors. *Encyclopedia of Mystery and Detection*. New York: McGraw-Hill Book Company, 1976, pp. 378-379.
      Brief biographical outline followed by a survey of Symons's works. "Symons, long an advocate of the crime novel, has often attempted to blend the literary values of the conventional novel with the excitement of the thriller."

Epilog

With great personal sadness, I received the news that Julian Symons died on Saturday, November 19, 1994, at the age of 82. Obituaries and tributes appeared in the following publications:

The New York Times Obituaries (November 23, 1994), Section C, p. 18.

The Sunday Times Books (November 27, 1994), Section 7, p. 18. Written by H.R.F. Keating.

The Guardian (November 23, 1994), Notes & Queries Section, p. 16. Written by Gavin Ewart.

The Independent (November 23, 1994), p. 16.
Written by Jack Adrain and Reginald Hill (two articles).

The Times (November 22, 1994), p. 23.

London Magazine (April/May, 1995), pp. 48-57.

The American Scholar (Winter, 1996), pp. 107-113. Written by William H. Pritchard.

Julian Symons Remembered: Tributes From Friends. Council Bluffs, Iowa: The Yellow Barn Press, 1996.

Index

PUBLISHERS

PRINTERS

DESIGNERS/ILLUSTRATORS

SHORT FICTION

GENERAL